ROSE'S
BAKING BASICS

ROSE'S
BAKING BASICS

100 ESSENTIAL RECIPES, WITH MORE THAN 600 STEP-BY-STEP PHOTOS

ROSE LEVY BERANBAUM

PHOTOGRAPHY BY MATTHEW SEPTIMUS

HOUGHTON MIFFLIN HARCOURT

BOSTON   NEW YORK   2018

For information about permission to reproduce selections from this book,
write to trade.permissions@hmhco.com or to Permissions,
Houghton Mifflin Harcourt Publishing Company, 3 Park Avenue,
19th Floor, New York, New York 10016.

hmhco.com

Library of Congress Cataloging-in-Publication Data is available.

ISBN 978-0-544-81622-0 (hbk); 978-0-544-81621-3 (ebk)

Book design by Vertigo Design NYC

Printed in China

TOP 10 9 8 7 6 5 4 3 2 1

FOR DAVID SHAMAH, MY STUDENT
WHO BECAME MY TEACHER

CONTENTS

RECIPE LIST

FOREWORD

In the early 1980s, while contemplating career paths, I became obsessed with the culinary world. I read everything I could get my hands on about the subject, and was constantly playing around in the kitchen.

I developed a particular interest in baking, which led to some great discoveries and also some disappointments. Why did my cake fail to rise? Did using the wrong chocolate really change the outcome of a particular recipe? Did the color or finish of a baking pan really matter?

I discovered Rose's first cookbook, *Romantic and Classic Cakes*, and was amazed at how this small volume explained so much of what I wanted to know. I felt compelled to reach out to Rose and was invited to her place to purchase one of her precision thermometers.

As I was greeted at the door, I couldn't help but notice a plaque from the very prestigious Chaîne des Rôtisseurs, which hangs in some of the world's most renowned dining establishments, at the entryway. Who could ignore the large battery of copper pots and pans, the enormous assortment of cordials and spirits, and the first authentic brass duck press I'd ever seen in person?

I was inspired by Rose's passion for the culinary arts and never-ending curiosity about all of its elements. Soon, I began assisting Rose in her cooking classes, testing recipes, and proofreading the recipes and text for the second book that she started working on. It was very intense, but I learned a lot about how Rose did things and why.

We were constantly in pursuit of great presentation, accuracy, and consistent results; yet if I had to distill the most important thing I've learned from Rose, it's the art of intensifying flavors. This principle of taste has followed me wherever I've gone, and totally changed the way I look at a dish.

Unlocking great chocolate flavor is a good example. Rose achieves this in cakes by boiling the water that is added to the cocoa, releasing the flavor and making it possible to use less cocoa, resulting in lighter texture as well as more flavor. When it came to brownies, unlike most brownie recipes that have a cream cheese mixture swirled through them, when Rose uses cream cheese in a brownie, she beats it into the chocolate batter, resulting in a slight tang that elevates the chocolate flavor and enhances the fudgy texture.

Eventually, *The Cake Bible* had a name, and a serious focus and deadline. I knew this book was packed with knowledge and inspiration. Still, I was amazed at the overwhelming success and warm reception Rose and the book received. There were many people like me who were hungry to learn and expand their knowledge. And this book finally addressed that hunger. Coming up in the hospitality business, I found myself applying many of the concepts that I'd learned from Rose to my work.

One book led to another, and lots of personal appearances and an online blog have led to an amazing community of bakers who follow Rose's work. Rose was born to teach, but equally important, she is constantly learning from the challenges and experiences of the baking community.

The book that you are holding represents Rose's desire to reach an even wider audience. All the information that you need is included here. Thanks to over 600 excellent step-by-step photographs, the recipes are pared down, streamlined, and easy to follow, using a minimum of specialized equipment or elaborate techniques.

I hope this book inspires you to get in the kitchen and have fun, and learn, as I have, from Rose's passion that anything is possible.

DAVID SHAMAH
Chef and caterer

INTRODUCTION

A few years ago, after completing *The Baking Bible*, team "RoseWood"—my longtime collaborator, Woody Wolston, and I—was gearing up to embark on a wedding cake book when our visionary editor, Stephanie Fletcher, suggested first doing a book for "beginners." For a few seconds I resisted, saying that beginners work just fine from all of my other books, even young people who win blue ribbons at county fairs. But as the words were halfway out of my mouth I did an immediate about-face as I suddenly, with lightning bolt clarity, realized the potential. So I said: "If we could have step-by-step photos of the recipes and techniques, the book would be invaluable for both the beginner and the advanced baker, and I would have the book of my dreams." And gradually I realized that although all of my books have all the details needed for success, at first glance they may be perceived as challenging—perhaps due to so much detailed information. A photo, however, is indeed worth a thousand words and would not give that perception, especially if we changed the formatting of the text to be as concise as possible. It would also serve to show exactly what the various stages of baking are supposed to look like. Videos are great, but carefully chosen photographs, focused on the specific steps needed, are actually far more useful.

I also realized that the recipes would be more logically written in the way I actually make them, so I put any necessary preparation right at the top where it belongs, and call it "mise en place," just as the setup for ingredients is referred to in professional kitchens.

At the end of most recipes, I have added Baking Pearls that contain special tips for success and good-to-know information. I've also added Make This Recipe Your Own, which will give you tested ideas for suggested substitutions and variations.

One of the changes in this book I'm most pleased about is that ounces are now mostly eliminated and grams come before volume. This is because most kitchen scales now measure both grams and ounces and switching between the two is easy. Weighing is easier and more reliable than measuring by volume. I've preferred it since the publication of my first book more than thirty years ago, and by now many people have embraced it. If you haven't yet, you should. This is an important step to near guarantee a successful outcome.

Another change that turned out to have huge impact on the complete precision of information is that Woody and I decided to do all the preparation and styling for the step-by-step photography on our own, in my dedicated baking kitchen. We knew that this would give us total control of the recipes, including the ability to enter every tweak and improved technique that would ensue from baking the recipes after they were tested and written up in final form. The next step was to find a first rate photographer who embraced the idea of coming to Hope, New Jersey, for many days, over a period of several months, to achieve the more than 600 step-by-step photos. Matthew Septimus was our man. For the "beauty" shots, we were additionally blessed to have our dear friend, the talented food stylist and baking author Erin Jeanne McDowell, join the team.

It is my goal to teach and share with all of you many tried and true favorites, now brought to life with instructional photos, as well as new delicious discoveries and exciting new techniques that make baking more fun than ever before.

Bake with Love,
ROSE

TOP 10 GOLDEN RULES FOR BAKING

MY PERSONAL MANTRA:

"If you are going to achieve excellence in big things, you develop the habit in little matters. Excellence is not an exception, it is a prevailing attitude." —Colin Powell

Studies have shown that baking is excellent for one's disposition. But there is little that is more disillusioning than, after investing time, enthusiasm, and ingredients, to have disappointing results. Here are ten golden rules to ensure that your baking experience will be joyful in spirit, presentation, and flavor:

1. Begin by reading the Solutions for Possible Problems in each chapter introduction.

2. Read the equipment chapter to see the basic tools you will need. Segregate equipment prone to retaining odors to use only for baking, so that it won't retain odors such as garlic or spices from savory cooking. This includes cutting boards, measuring spoons and cups, wooden spoons, and silicone spatulas.

3. Use an accurate oven thermometer or the baking time range specified in the recipe to determine if your oven is calibrated (see page xv for more information). Refer to the recipe instructions for the correct level for the oven rack or racks to ensure proper rising and browning. And always preheat the oven as indicated in the recipe.

4. Read the ingredient chapter to understand the importance of using the correct ingredients, and avoid substitutions until you have tried the recipe for the first time as it is written. (Make This Recipe Your Own, at the end of many of the recipes, will give you tested ideas for suggested substitutions and variations.)

5. Scales make baking easier, faster, and more reliable when weighing ingredient amounts larger than those that can be measured in teaspoons or tablespoons. Most scales switch readily from grams to ounces and back. Grams are more precise.

6. When measuring ingredients like flour by volume, follow the instructions on page xix to avoid inadvertently adding excess flour, which will make cakes dry, cookies and pastry dough crumbly, and bread dense. Use measuring cups with unbroken rims designed for dry ingredients, and measuring cups with pouring spouts for liquids.

7. Read the recipe through before beginning to familiarize yourself with the preliminary preparation (mise en place), temperatures, and timing.

8. When mixing ingredients, the recipes indicate to start on low speed with a gradual increase in speed. This will help keep the ingredients from jumping out of the bowl. It also works well to use the flat beater of a stand mixer to mash ingredients such as the butter so that they

integrate more easily. If the bowl is very full, it is helpful to cover the top with plastic wrap until the dry ingredients are moistened.

The mixer speeds and beating times are for a stand mixer. If you are using a handheld electric mixer instead, use a higher speed than specified and a longer beating time.

With both kinds of mixers, it's important to scrape the sides of the bowl as indicated, to ensure that the batter on the sides gets mixed in evenly. Always stop the mixer when scraping the sides of the bowl. Be sure to reach to the bottom of the bowl, especially when using a stand mixer.

9. High altitude requires adjustments to ingredients and baking temperature depending on elevation. See page xxvi for recommendations of information sources.

10. The Internet is a great source for baking questions and ideas. My blog, realbakingwithrose.com, has a printable errata/corrections section. I update new information and changes if and when they occur.

ESSENTIAL EQUIPMENT FOR BAKING

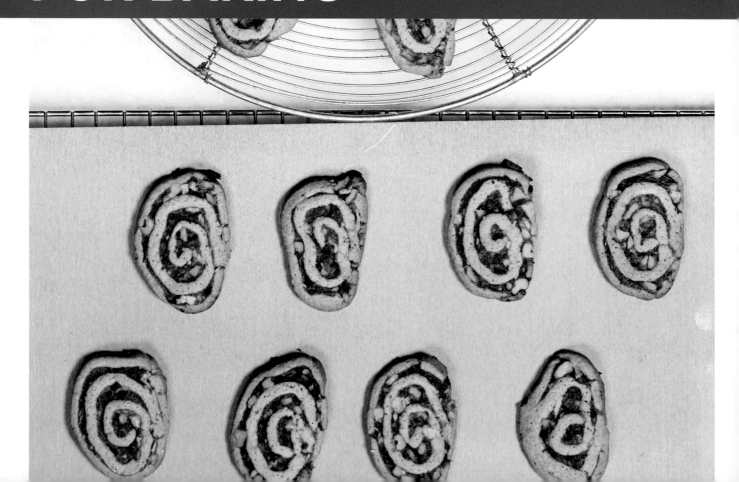

Using the right tools will make things easier and faster, and will ensure success.

As you continue to bake, you will enjoy adding special equipment to your collection.

Equipment is constantly changing and evolving, so rather than give too many specific brand or model recommendations, my advice is to read reviews online. I am, however, listing the brands of equipment that I've designed or that I find essential for accuracy.

Specialty equipment used for just one recipe will be listed in the recipe itself.

It is a good idea to reserve equipment made of anything other than metal, ceramic, or glass for only baking, as other materials such as plastic and wood retain odors from savory cooking and impart them to baked goods.

OVENS

When installing a new oven, make sure that it is level, or your cakes and most other baked goods will not be. Also have the installer calibrate the oven to make sure it heats to the correct temperature and that the temperature display is accurate. (You can also have a manufacturer's representative calibrate the oven at a later date if you discover the temperature is off.) If your oven has a convection setting, follow the manufacturer's directions. They may recommend lowering the temperature by 25°F/15°C when using the convection setting. It's fine to use convection for most cakes, cookies, pies, and pastry; but for bread, only use it toward the end of baking, when it will help crisp the crust. (The beginning of baking requires moisture; convection will have a drying effect.) Note that countertop ovens can be a fine choice but baking temperature, and therefore time, may need to be adjusted. The size of some ovens may not accommodate larger or taller pans.

STAND MIXER

A 5 to 6 quart heavy-duty stand mixer with a flat beater and a whisk beater is ideal for baking recipes. Having two bowls will come in handy, especially when you need to beat egg whites separately before adding them to the batter in another bowl.

HANDHELD MIXER

A handheld electric mixer is useful for small quantities of ingredients such as whipped cream. If it is a powerful model, it can also be used in place of a stand mixer. If it is less powerful, use a higher speed than indicated in the recipe.

FOOD PROCESSOR

A 7 to 12 cup capacity will work for almost all of the recipes in this book. It is also very useful to have a small capacity food processor and/or an immersion blender.

Note that when using a food processor without using the feed tube to add ingredients, it is very helpful to cover the work bowl with a piece of plastic wrap before locking on the cover. This keeps ingredients from leaping into the crevices of the cover. Also, after scraping out the contents of the work bowl, run the processor for a few seconds to spin any residue off the blades.

BAKING PANS

Unless otherwise specified, choose sturdy heavy-gauge, light-colored aluminum or steel pans with a dull finish.

Cake pans other than tube pans should have straight up and down, not sloped, sides. If your pans have sloped sides you will need to add a little less batter.

CAKE PANS

- 9 by 2 inch high round (two)
- 9 by 3 or 2¾ inch high springform (for cheesecake)
- 8 by 2 inch high square
- 13 by 9 by 2 inch high rectangle
- 10 cup fluted cast-aluminum tube pan (preferably Nordic Ware)
- 16 cup two-piece angel food pan (10 inch diameter at the top, 4 inches high)
- Muffin pans (preferably with 6 cavities)
- Rose's Heavenly Cake Strips: I recommend encircling pans with cake strips to ensure even baking when making cakes. These silicone cake strips slow down the baking at the sides of the pan, which otherwise would set sooner than the

center, resulting in doming in the middle and dryness at the edges of the cake. If you don't have these, you can make your own reusable cake strips using a strip of aluminum foil: Cut it long enough to encircle the pan with a little overlap, triple the height of the pan. Wet some paper towels, fold them to the height of the pan, and lay them along the middle of the foil strip. Fold the top, bottom, and ends of the foil over to encase the paper towels. Wrap the strip around the pan and secure it with a metal paper clip or clamp.

TART AND GALETTE PANS

9½ by 1 inch high fluted tart pan (preferably nonstick with a removable bottom, preferably Gobel brand)

PIE PLATES

9 inch standard Pyrex pie plate (4 cup)
Rose's Perfect Pie Plate (4 cup)

FOIL RINGS FOR PIE CRUST RIMS

These prevent overbrowning around the edges. Rather than buying manufactured versions, it is best to make your own from heavy-duty aluminum foil, which will protect the crust without flattening the decorative border. (See page 198 for step-by-step photos.)

LOAF PANS

- 8½ by 4½ inch (6 cups)
- 9 by 5 inch (7 cups)

BAKING SHEETS

These pans have raised rolled edges on all 4 sides. The best quality, heavier weight ones are referred to as sheet pans. The standard size for a "half-sheet pan," used throughout this book, is 17¼ by 12¼ by 1 inch high. They are also available as 13 by 9 inch quarter sheet pans.

COOKIE SHEETS

These pans come either with a rim on one side or without rims. The cookie sheets used throughout this book are 15 by 12 inch.

REUSABLE LINERS

There are two types of nonstick liners used to line baking sheets. Silpat, a combination of silicone and fiberglass, is very durable and ideal as a surface for pouring caramel such as toffee. They are rated safe for temperatures up to 480°F/250°C. Teflon-type liners are less durable because they are thinner. But they are more flexible, and more nonstick, making them ideal for cake rolls. They are rated as safe up to 425°F/220°C.

WIRE RACKS FOR COOLING

These allow for airflow around pans and baked goods for more rapid cooling.

DIGITAL SCALE

I prefer the brand Escali. The range should be from a minimum of 1 gram up to 4 kilograms/8.8 pounds. I give weights for very small amounts of ingredients but it's fine to use measuring spoons for these. Should you want to weigh these ingredients instead, I also recommend the Escali L600 High Precision Digital Scale, which has a weighing range of 0.1 gram to 600 grams.

INSTANT-READ THERMOMETER

(preferably Thermapen by ThermoWorks)

OVEN THERMOMETER

I like the CDN ProAccurate Oven Thermometer or the multifunction ChefAlarm by ThermoWorks, with the optional grate clip.

Baked goods need to bake at the proper temperature. If a cake bakes too quickly because the temperature is too high, for example, it will dome and crack. If it bakes too slowly, the texture will be coarse and the center may dip. If you don't have an oven thermometer, an effective test of oven temperature is baking time. If it takes more or less time to bake than the range of time recommended in the recipe, you may need to have your oven calibrated (see page xv), or adjust the temperature setting to compensate. (Create a chart of adjustments needed that you can refer to each time.)

ROLLING PIN AND DOUGH MAT

If using a wooden rolling pin, be sure to rub it well with flour, as needed, to prevent sticking.

I created Rose's Signature Series Pie Kit, which includes a Magic Rolling Pin and nonstick Magic Dough Pastry Mat that prevent sticking while needing the least amount of flour. The rolling pin is made of SynGlas, a durable nonstick plastic, and the dough mat is also virtually nonstick. Also included are

Silicone Fast Tracks—strips that you set on the mat as a guide to ensure even thickness of the dough. They come in three heights suitable for pies, tarts, and cookies.

To keep the mat from sliding around as you roll, wet the clean counter lightly. Set the mat at the edge of the counter and then slide it forward, which will create a suction that holds it securely in place.

CAST-IRON PIZZA PAN OR BAKING STEEL
(for pies, tarts, and pizza to ensure a browned bottom crust)

BAKING STONE OR UNGLAZED QUARRY TILES
(for bread, pizza, and pie baking)

TIMER

CITRUS JUICE SQUEEZER

FINE-MESH STRAINER
(for straining and sifting)

SET OF GLASS MIXING BOWLS

PYREX CUSTARD CUPS

COOKIE CUTTERS, PLAIN OR SCALLOPED
(for cookies and biscuits)

DISPOSABLE PASTRY BAGS

SMALL STRAIGHT AND OFFSET METAL SPATULAS
(for leveling measuring spoons, unmolding, and applying frosting)

WIRE CAKE TESTERS AND WOODEN SKEWERS
(for testing doneness)

ASSORTED SILICONE SPATULAS
(for high heat stirring and scraping bowls)

PASTRY BRUSH
(preferably silicone)

WOODEN SPOON
(for very stiff mixtures)

PLASTIC BENCH SCRAPER
(for scraping bowls and working with bread dough)

ASSORTED WHISKS
Be sure to include a small piano wire whisk, 10 inches long and 5 inches in circumference, with at least eight loops of fine wire. It will reach into the corners of a saucepan, making it ideal for both preparing a smooth pastry cream and evenly mixing dry ingredients together.

MICROPLANE GRATER
(for grating zest)

MEASURING SPOONS
(preferably POURfect)

DRY CUP MEASURES
If not using a scale, use dry measuring cups with unbroken rims, which can be leveled off (see page xix). I prefer POURfect brand for the most accurate measuring.

LIQUID MEASURING CUPS (WITH A SPOUT)
If measuring liquid by volume instead of weighing, be sure to use a liquid measuring cup, not one for dry ingredients. I prefer POURfect measuring beakers and Anchor Hocking Oven Basics glass measuring cups. Read the measurement at eye level, with the cup set on a flat surface. The measurement should be read below the meniscus (the curved upper surface of the liquid).

PARCHMENT
(preferably flat sheets, for lining pans and blind baking pie crust)

COOKIE SCOOPS
(1¼ or 1½ inch diameter for cookies, 2 inch diameter for cupcakes)

CLEAR PLASTIC RULERS
(18 inches long, with grid marks)

PASTRY JAGGER
This is a small wheel with a zigzag edge used to cut dough, as for a lattice-top pie. You can use a pizza wheel or small knife instead.

PLASTIC WRAP
Stretch-Tite is my favorite plastic wrap because it clings tightly to the bowl or whatever else needs to be wrapped. Plastic wraps are not entirely impermeable and therefore are suitable for freezing baked goods only if used in a couple of layers. Freeze-Tite, however, is significantly thicker and also wider (15 inches).

ESSENTIAL INGREDIENTS FOR BAKING

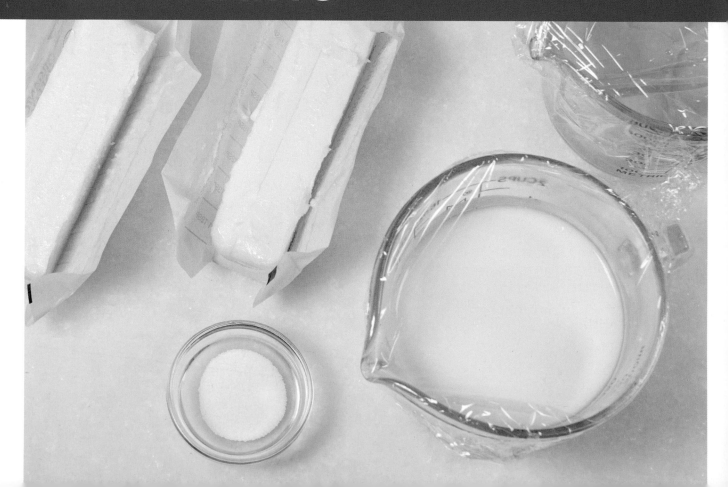

The four most important things to know about ingredients for baking are:

1. The best quality will produce the best results.

2. These recipes are carefully crafted and tested. Substituting may alter the flavor and texture.

3. Weighing is easier, faster, and more accurate than measuring by volume, especially because different brands of measuring cups and spoons vary (see page xvii for recommended brands). I usually use measuring spoons instead of weights for small amounts of ingredients such as salt and spices, but not for yeast because using the most precise amount gives more control over rising times.

4. If measuring by volume, use dry measuring cups for dry ingredients and liquid measuring cups for liquids.

Note: Weight is given first because it is the most accurate. Volume is listed in measuring spoons, cups, and milliliters. In some instances the volume is rounded off so it may be a slightly different weight for the same volume. If using volume rather than weight, you might need to estimate from the nearest marking on the glass. For example, for 120 milliliters, measure to a little bit under the 125 milliliter mark.

WATER
All the recipes in this book were tested with tap water. However, if the water in your region is not suitable, bottled spring water is best. (The high amounts of minerals in mineral water will affect the outcome of baked goods.) When measuring water by volume, set the measuring cup on a flat surface and read the measurement at eye level from the bottom of meniscus (the curved upper surface of the water).

FLOURS
Except when making flourless cakes and meringues, flour is the most important ingredient in baking. The type of flour used, particularly its protein content and whether it is bleached or unbleached, affects both texture and flavor. The types of flour used in this book are:

- Bleached cake flour and bleached all-purpose flour for cakes
- Bleached all-purpose flour and unbleached pastry flour for pie and pastry dough
- Bleached all-purpose flour for cookie dough
- Unbleached all-purpose flour and unbleached bread flour for bread dough
- Wondra flour is optional, but it is ideal for dusting pie, pastry, and cookie dough, as it is precooked and, because of its granularity, will be absorbed less into the dough.

Note: My recommended all-purpose flour is General Mills. (It is important to use a national brand; protein content varies widely with regional ones.) My recommended pastry flours are Bessie and King Arthur. My recommended bread flour is Gold Medal from General Mills, or a mixture of half other bread flour and half unbleached all-purpose flour.

When measuring flour by volume, avoid shaking or tapping the cup as that will increase the amount of flour in the cup and cause the baked good to be heavy, dry, and crumbly.

BAKING SPRAY WITH FLOUR
This is a combination of flour and oil, and is sprayed on baking pans to ensure a clean release. It is faster, neater, and more effective than greasing and flouring. Baker's Joy brand is odor free and releases the best. Alternatively, to grease and flour a pan, coat the inside of the pan with solid vegetable shortening; add flour and rotate the pan so that it coats completely. Then invert the pan and tap out the excess flour.

NONSTICK COOKING SPRAY
This useful product contains oil and lecithin, and is ideal for keeping baked goods from sticking to the wire rack. Pam brand is odor free.

Measuring Dry Ingredients

Whisk flour before measuring it.

Lightly spoon flour into the measuring cup.

Or sift the flour into the cup, as the recipe directs.

Level off the excess flour.

1 cup of cake flour spooned lightly into the cup, weighing 114 grams.

1 cup of sifted cake flour, weighing 100 grams.

SUGAR

Superfine sugar is specified in recipes such as some cookies (for a smoother dough) and meringue (because it dissolves more effectively in the egg white). Fine granulated sugar works well for most recipes. It is coarser than superfine, but can be processed in a food processor to simulate superfine if needed. The two most common brands of granulated and superfine sugar available are C&H and Domino. C&H's superfine is slightly finer.

BROWN SUGAR AND MUSCOVADO SUGAR

Brown sugar is refined sugar to which molasses has been added back after processing. Muscovado sugar contains some of the original molasses that has not been extracted. My preference is India Tree light or dark Muscovado for their delicious complexity of flavor. Light Muscovado is closest in molasses content to a combination of light and dark brown sugars. In recipes where more molasses would overwhelm other flavors, I list light brown

Measuring Small Quantities

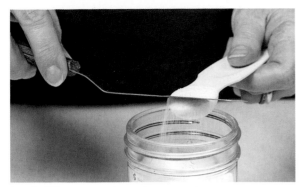

Level off the excess when using measuring spoons.

sugar as a substitute. In recipes where more molasses would enhance the flavor, I list dark brown sugar as a substitute. Store in an airtight container. If it hardens, set a damp piece of paper towel in a shallow cup of foil on top. Cover tightly for several hours.

SALT

Fine sea salt contains no additives and is easiest to measure accurately and consistently. Transfer the salt to a lidded container to make it easier to measure.

BAKING POWDER

Baking powders are mixtures of dry acid or acid salts and baking soda, with starch or flour added to standardize and help stabilize the mixtures. When they react—or liberate carbon dioxide—the carbon dioxide gas causes baked goods to rise. Double-acting baking powders react partially from moisture during mixing and partially when exposed to heat during baking.

Choose a variety that is an all-phosphate product containing calcium acid phosphate, not one containing sodium aluminum sulfate or SAS. I recommend Rumford baking powder. It is found in most supermarkets and health food stores. It lacks the bitter aftertaste associated with SAS baking powders from the aluminum in the sodium aluminum sulfate.

Baking powder should be stored in an airtight container to protect against humidity, which will activate it. Depending on how it is stored, baking

powder can lose a large amount of its power after about a year. Date the top or bottom of the can when you first buy it. To test if it is still active, sprinkle a little over hot water. If it fizzes actively, you can still use it.

The weight of baking powder varies widely depending on storage and humidity. I find that the average weight is 4.5 grams per teaspoon. For consistency when measuring, stir it lightly with a small spatula or spoon before measuring it.

BAKING SODA

Also known as sodium bicarbonate, baking soda causes baked goods to rise when activated. When moistened, it reacts with acidic ingredients in the recipe to produce carbon dioxide. It has an indefinite shelf life if it is not exposed to moisture or humidity. After opening it, transfer it to a canning jar or container with a tight fitting lid. It usually clumps on storage, so if measuring it by volume first use a spoon to mash any large lumps, then dip the measuring spoon into it. Slice through it with the edge of a small metal spatula about three times before sweeping off the excess with the flat part of the blade.

YEAST

I recommend using instant yeast because of its reliability. It is fine to whisk the yeast into the flour before adding the water, but the yeast can also be soaked (hydrated) in warm water from the recipe (at least three times its volume) for 10 minutes. If yeast has been frozen, allow it to come to room temperature before adding water. Instant yeast is nationally available in supermarkets under brand names such as Fleischmann's Bread Machine Yeast or RapidRise Yeast, Red Star Quick-Rise, SAF Instant, and SAF Gourmet Perfect Rise.

If unopened, yeast will last at room temperature for up to 2 years. Once opened, it is best to store it in the freezer. If you buy it in bulk, remove a small amount for regular use and freeze both the larger and smaller amounts to ensure maximum shelf life, which is at least 1 year.

I list weights for yeast because a small amount can make a large difference.

Separating Eggs

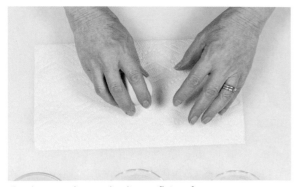

Crack an egg by rapping it on a flat surface.

Use your thumbs to open the egg shell.

Use your hands to separate the white from the yolk.

If a small amount of yolk gets into the white, use the egg shell to remove it.

EGGS

All my recipes use USDA graded large eggs, which means that twelve eggs in the shell should weigh a minimum of 24 ounces/680 grams and a maximum of 30 ounces/850 grams. This does not mean, however, that all large eggs are the same weight. Also, the ratio of white to yolk in an egg can vary to such a degree that a recipe calling for 6 yolks may actually need as many as 9. It is therefore advisable, when making recipes that rely on egg whites for loft or yolks for richness, to weigh or measure the separated whites and yolks and add or reduce if needed. Since cakes are so dependent on eggs for their structure, it is also a good idea to weigh or measure whole eggs, even when using large eggs. The weights given for eggs on the recipe ingredient charts are without the shells.

Eggs, still in the shell, can be brought to room temperature by setting them in a bowl of hot tap water for 5 minutes.

CRACKING AND SEPARATING EGGS

Egg shells break most cleanly when tapped firmly on a flat surface, not on the edge of a bowl.

When whipping egg whites, even a drop of yolk will prevent the whites from whipping to stiff peaks. For that reason, have an extra small bowl for separating one egg at a time before adding the white to a larger bowl.

When separating the yolk from the white, clean hands work better than any separating device. You can also break an egg into a bowl and carefully fish out the yolk with your hand, but if it should break into the white, do not use the white for whipping unless you can remove the yolk completely. If only a drop of yolk gets into the white, the broken shell works like a magnet to remove it.

BEATING EGG WHITES

Make sure the bowl, whisk beater, and egg whites are entirely free of any oil or fat, including egg yolk. Use metal bowls; glass is slippery and the whites won't whip as well. Avoid plastic bowls, which can retain residual oil. If you don't use a dishwasher, as added insurance wet a paper towel and add a little white vinegar. Wipe the inside of the bowl, rinse it thoroughly, and dry it with a clean paper towel.

Start whipping egg whites on medium-low speed. Gradually raise the speed to medium-high and whip until soft peaks form when the beater is raised. In most recipes, sugar, if used, should be added gradually, with the mixer on, to maintain maximum air bubbles. Continue whipping until stiff peaks form when the beater is raised slowly.

CREAM OF TARTAR

Also known as potassium acid tartrate, this by-product of winemaking has an indefinite shelf life if not exposed to moisture or humidity. Use 1 teaspoon cream of tartar per 1 cup/240 grams egg whites (⅛ teaspoon per egg white), *double this amount if using eggs that were pasteurized in the shell*, to stabilize the egg whites and prevent them from drying out by overbeating. When using an electric mixer, it is fine to add the cream of tartar right at the beginning of beating, but if beating by hand using a whisk, add it after the egg white starts foaming. (A teaspoon of cream of tartar, dissolved in the water, also helps to prevent aluminum pans from discoloring when used as a water bath.)

STORING EGGS

Store eggs in a covered container, bottom (larger end) up, for maximum freshness.

Egg whites keep in an airtight container in the refrigerator for up to 10 days.

Unbroken yolks, covered with water or coated with nonstick cooking spray to prevent drying, will keep in an airtight container in the refrigerator for up to 3 days.

Egg whites freeze perfectly and keep for at least 1 year. Store them in small airtight containers, as they should not be refrozen after thawing.

It is also possible to freeze egg yolks. Stir in ½ teaspoon sugar per yolk to keep them from becoming sticky after they are thawed. (Remember to subtract this amount of sugar from any recipe in which you are using them.)

EGG SAFETY FOR RAW OR PARTIALLY COOKED EGGS

Food safety experts agree that the risk of salmonella infection from raw or partially cooked eggs is highest for young children, the elderly, pregnant women, and those whose immune systems are impaired.

To prevent salmonella in preparations calling for uncooked or lightly cooked eggs, the American Egg Board recommends using eggs pasteurized in the shell, such as Safest Choice (available in some markets; "pasteurized" will be marked on the carton), or liquid pasteurized egg whites, which are available in many supermarkets. Cream of tartar can still be added for stability. Pasteurized organic kosher egg whites with no additives can be ordered from Eggology; AllWhites brand is also kosher. They keep refrigerated for up to 4 months and for more than a year if frozen.

Pasteurization makes uncooked eggs safe for buttercreams and prevents contamination of your work area. When beating egg whites without additives or from eggs pasteurized in the shell, use double the cream of tartar specified in the recipe (¼ teaspoon per egg white/2 tablespoons/ 30 grams). Longer beating of the egg whites (a total of about 10 minutes) will be required but will result in the most stable meringue possible.

GELATIN

Gelatin is an animal product that causes liquids to thicken and set. Powdered gelatin is the most common form and the easiest to use. It needs to be bloomed (softened) in cool water for at least 5 minutes before being heated to dissolve it, which enables it to be effective as a thickening agent.

Gelatin requires a minimum of 4 hours to thicken adequately, and will continue to thicken a mixture over a 24 hour period. Once it has reached maximum thickness, it will not thicken more, even on freezing, but freezing will not affect its thickening power. A gelatin mixture can be frozen, thawed, remelted, and refrozen several times before it loses its thickening capability. Kojel produces kosher gelatin, which is made of vegetable gum, tapioca dextrin, and acids.

HEAVY CREAM

Heavy cream, also referred to as "heavy whipping cream," contains 56.6 percent water and 36 to 40 percent butterfat (averaging 36 percent). "Whipping cream" has only 30 percent fat. The higher the butterfat and the colder the cream, the easier it is to whip and the more stable the whipped cream. To determine the fat content, look at the total fat in the nutritional information on the side of the container: 1 tablespoon of 40 percent cream will contain 6 grams total fat. Organic Valley and Stonyfield are two brands that contain 40 percent butterfat.

Heavy cream will not whip when it has been frozen and thawed, but frozen heavy cream can be used for making ganache.

DRY MILK POWDER

Adding dry milk powder when making bread results in a tender texture. My preference is King Arthur Baker's Special Dry Milk because it results in the most tender texture and highest rise. Unlike other dry milk, it is heated to a high enough temperature to deactivate the enzyme protease, which otherwise impairs yeast production and—what is most critical—gluten formation and structure. The high heat produces an exceptionally fine powder that disperses uniformly through the dry ingredients. This fine powder packs down when measuring by volume so if replacing Baker's Special Dry Milk with "instant" dry milk, you will need to double the volume to arrive at the same weight.

BUTTER

It is best to use grade AA or A butter, which contains about 81 percent fat and 15.5 percent water. Lower grades usually contain more water, which will have a detrimental effect in a cake batter; they will not work well at all in mousseline buttercream, will make a less tender pie crust, and will result in a puffier cookie. High fat butter is ideal for buttercreams.

It is best to weigh butter because a 113 gram/4 ounce stick of butter when unwrapped often weighs only 109 grams/3.86 ounces.

I prefer unsalted butter because it makes it easier for the baker to control the total amount of salt in the recipe, and because it has a fresher flavor. I recommend a top-quality butter such as Organic Valley Cultured Butter, Hotel Bar Unsalted Butter, or Land O'Lakes Unsalted Sweet Butter. The flavor of cultured butter is particularly delicious in buttercreams.

Butter freezes well for several months with no perceptible difference in flavor or performance. Because butter absorbs other aromas or odors readily, if freezing it, wrap it well in plastic wrap and place it in a reclosable plastic freezer storage bag.

The temperature of the butter is important to the finished texture of the baked good, so it's included in each recipe. When the recipe calls for softening the butter, if the room is cold and the butter doesn't soften quickly enough, cut it into pieces and it will soften faster.

CREAM CHEESE

Full-fat Philadelphia and Organic Valley cream cheese are the best choices for both flavor and texture for the recipes in this book.

CANOLA AND SAFFLOWER OILS

Flavorless vegetable oils are the best choice for most baked goods made with oil.

CORN SYRUP

I prefer light corn syrup to dark corn syrup for its neutral flavor. A small amount added to sugar when caramelizing helps prevent crystallization. Syrups are sticky, so if measuring by volume rather than weighing, it helps either to coat the cup with nonstick cooking spray or rinse it with water before adding the syrup.

GOLDEN SYRUP

This by-product of sugar refining has a delicious butterscotch flavor. It can be used interchangeably with light corn syrup. If it crystallizes on storage, set it in a pan of simmering water and stir it often until the crystals have dissolved.

VANILLA EXTRACT

Pure vanilla extract imparts a lovely flavor to baked goods and also serves as a flavor enhancer. High-quality brands are available in some supermarkets, in specialty food stores, and online. My favorites are Nielsen-Massey and The Vanilla Company.

VANILLA BEANS

The seeds contained inside the vanilla bean pod add a subtle depth of flavor and unique floral sweetness to baked goods. In most cases, it works best to scrape the seeds into the sugar in the recipe and process them together. The pod can then be dried in the oven at the lowest temperature or near a hot burner. When dry, bury it in sugar. Use the resulting vanilla sugar in recipes, replacing about 8 percent of the sugar in the recipe, or in your coffee or tea if you'd like. When purchasing vanilla beans, choose plump, moist ones. Tahitian vanilla beans are my favorite. They are the most plump, moist, and aromatic. As a rule of thumb, 1 teaspoon of pure vanilla extra is equal to a 2 inch piece of vanilla bean (1 inch if Tahitian). To keep vanilla beans moist, wrap them well and freeze them.

VANILLA BEAN PASTE

This excellent product contains vanilla seeds combined with vanilla extract, natural gum thickeners, and a small amount of sugar, varying by manufacturer. Most can be used in equal volume to replace vanilla extract, but it is best to check the label for suggested amounts.

CHOCOLATE

Dark chocolate is made up of cocoa solids and cocoa butter, referred to as chocolate "liquor" or "cacao." The rest is sugar. The higher the percentage of cacao, the lower the percentage of sugar. Almost all the chocolate recipes in this book were developed using 60% to 62% cacao. A different percentage will affect both the flavor and the texture of the recipe. Milk chocolate has a lower percentage of cacao, and also contains milk solids in addition to sugar.

When purchasing dark or milk chocolate, choose your favorite brand. When purchasing white chocolate, be sure to choose brands that contain only cocoa butter and flavorings, not vegetable oil.

COCOA POWDER

Unsweetened cocoa powder is pulverized pure chocolate liquor (the combined cacao solids and cocoa butter) with three-quarters of its cocoa butter removed. I prefer the flavor of Dutch processed, also known as alkalized cocoa. This refers to the process by which the cocoa powder has been treated with a mild alkali to mellow its flavor and neutralize its acidity; this also makes it easier to dissolve. Three of my favorite cocoas are Green & Black's, Agostoni, and Van Houten. If you are substituting natural cocoa in a recipe that uses baking powder, replace the baking powder with one-quarter to one-third of its volume in baking soda.

NUTS

Always taste nuts before using them because the oils they contain can become rancid. Store nuts in an airtight container in a cool place or the freezer. Frozen they will keep for over a year. Be sure to bring the nuts to room temperature if processing them. Lightly toasting nuts will bring out their flavor and, in the case of walnuts, help to loosen their bitter skins. I give instructions in the recipes when you will want to do this.

APPLES

For baking it is best to choose tart apples with a low water content so that they hold their shape after softening on baking. If a recipe calls for several apples, it is great to use a combination. Some of my favorites are Macoun, Rhode Island Greening, Empire, and Cortland. To get perfect slices for a galette, cut the apple in half and use a melon baller to remove the core.

CITRUS ZEST

Zest is the colored portion of the citrus peel or rind that is grated. The white portion, or pith, beneath should be avoided since it tastes bitter. Fruit should be zested before squeezing (unless the peels are frozen), which is why it is listed in the ingredients charts slightly out of order from where it is added to the recipe. Wash the fruit with liquid dish washing detergent and hot water and rinse it well, or it will add a bitter taste to the recipe. If a recipe calls for finely grated zest, if not using a Microplane type grater, use a chef's knife to chop it to a fine consistency or process it with some of the sugar in the recipe.

APPROXIMATE YIELD OF JUICE AND ZEST FOR AN ORANGE AND LEMON

One Orange
Juice: 63 to 126 grams/¼ to ½ cup/59 to 118 ml
Zest: 12 to 18 grams/2 to 3 tablespoons, loosely packed

One Lemon
Juice: 47 to 63 grams/3 to 4 tablespoons/44 to 59 ml
Zest: 2 to 4 grams/1¼ teaspoons to 2 teaspoons, loosely packed

HIGH ALTITUDE BAKING

If you live at high altitude (above 3,000 feet), I recommend following the USDA guidelines for the appropriate altitude adjustments and the following book: *Pie in the Sky* by baking authority Susan Purdy (who tested recipes at five different altitudes from sea level to 10,000 feet).

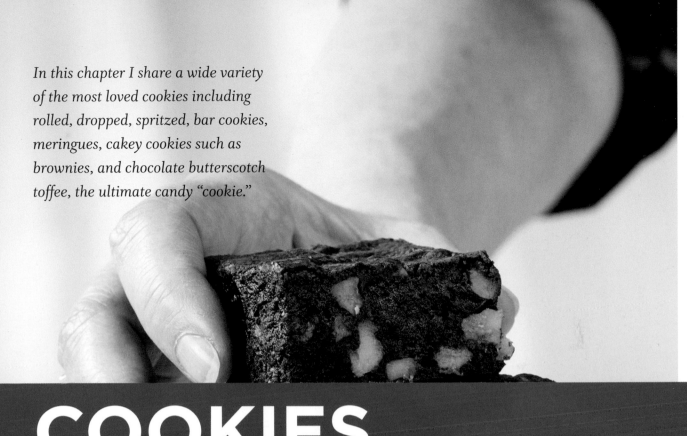

In this chapter I share a wide variety of the most loved cookies including rolled, dropped, spritzed, bar cookies, meringues, cakey cookies such as brownies, and chocolate butterscotch toffee, the ultimate candy "cookie."

COOKIES

SOLUTIONS FOR POSSIBLE PROBLEMS

Rolled cookie dough cracks when rolling.

SOLUTIONS: Try covering the dough with plastic wrap before rolling. If it still doesn't come together smoothly, spritz it with a little water and knead it together until smooth. Or if the dough is too cold, allow it to sit at room temperature until softened.

The cookie dough sticks to your fingers when pressing it down.

SOLUTION: Wrap the bottom of a flat glass tumbler with plastic wrap and use it to press down the cookies.

The cookie dough sticks to the cookie cutter.

SOLUTIONS: If the dough has softened, chill it before cutting. Dip the cutter in flour as needed. For the first cookie, run a small ball of dough along the edges of the cutter before dipping it in flour (see photos, page 52), so that the flour will adhere. For plastic cutters or metal cutters with solid backs, it works well to brush the cut edges and the insides with a little oil and remove any excess before dipping the cutter into flour. Knock off any excess flour. It also helps to roll the dough on an unfloured counter or wax paper and then rub the top of the dough lightly with flour before cutting. This causes the dough to stick slightly to the rolling surface and not to the cutter! Then slide a small offset spatula under the cutout to remove it. If it sticks to the rolling surface, either chill the dough or, if rolling on wax paper, set it close to the edge of the counter and slide it toward you, pulling the wax paper down, allowing the cut shape to fall into your hand.

The cookies spread too much while baking and are too flat.

SOLUTIONS: Use a lower protein flour and/or less sugar. Flour your hands before shaping, to make a more rounded cookie. It also helps to chill the shaped cookie dough before baking. Make sure the cookie sheets come back to room temperature (or colder) in between batches; avoid placing the cookie dough on hot or warm cookie sheets.

The cookies brown too much on the bottoms.

SOLUTIONS: Bake them on a higher rack, or use an insulated sheet or a double layer of two cookie sheets.

Some of the cookies are overbaked while others are still not baked enough.

SOLUTIONS: Make sure the cookies are all the same size. Be sure to rotate the cookie sheet 180 degrees halfway through baking. Unless otherwise indicated, bake only one sheet of cookies at a time.

The cookies are not soft enough.

SOLUTIONS: Remove them from the oven while they are still a little soft. Remove them from the cookie sheet as soon as they are firm enough to lift without bending.

Crisp cookies soften on storage, and soft ones become dry.

SOLUTION: Store different varieties of cookies separately.

Oatmeal Cookies

MAKES EIGHTEEN 3 INCH COOKIES

OVEN TEMPERATURE: 325°F/160°C for the walnuts; 375°F/190°C for the cookies

BAKING TIME: 7 minutes for the walnuts; 8 to 12 minutes for the cookies for each of two batches

BAKING EQUIPMENT: Two 15 by 12 inch cookie sheets, no preparation needed, or lined with parchment

If you like your cookies crisp, crunchy, and chewy, these are the cookies for you. They maintain their texture on storage but become slightly softer in the middle.

Makes 755 grams dough

unsalted butter	113 grams	8 tablespoons (1 stick)
1 large egg	50 grams	3 tablespoons plus ½ teaspoon (47.5 ml)
walnut halves	50 grams	½ cup
bleached all-purpose flour	151 grams	1¼ cups (lightly spooned into the cup and leveled off)
baking powder	2.2 grams	½ teaspoon
baking soda	2.7 grams	½ teaspoon
fine sea salt	3 grams	½ teaspoon
raisins	108 grams	¾ cup
old-fashioned rolled oats	92 grams	1¼ cups
dark chocolate chips, 55% to 63% cacao (see Make This Recipe Your Own, page 4)	85 grams	½ cup (3 ounces)
pure vanilla extract	.	1 teaspoon (5 ml)
light Muscovado or dark brown sugar	108 grams	½ cup, firmly packed

PREHEAT THE OVEN

▪ Twenty minutes or longer before toasting the walnuts, set an oven rack at the middle level. Set the oven at 325°F/160°C.

MISE EN PLACE

▪ About 1 hour ahead, set the butter and egg on the counter at room temperature (65° to 75°F/19° to 24°C).

▪ **TOAST AND CHOP THE WALNUTS:** Spread the walnuts evenly on a cookie sheet and bake for about 7 minutes. Stir once or twice to ensure even toasting and prevent overbrowning. Turn the walnuts onto a dish towel and roll and rub them around to loosen the skins. Discard any loose skin and let the nuts cool completely. Chop into coarse pieces.

▪ In a medium bowl, whisk together the flour, baking powder, baking soda, and salt.

(continued)

The dough must rest for a minimum of 30 minutes after mixing for the oats to soften and the moisture to be distributed evenly. Without this resting period, the oats would be harder and the moisture in the dough would cause it to spread more.

Make This Recipe Your Own

Use your favorite nuts and/or chocolate. Recommendations: Valrhona dark chocolate chips 52% or 60%, Ghirardelli bittersweet chips 60%, Scharffen Berger bittersweet chunks 61%. You can also replace the nuts with an equal volume of extra raisins or chocolate.

■ In another medium bowl, toss together the walnuts, raisins, oats, and chocolate chips.

■ Into a 1 cup measure with a spout, weigh or measure the egg. Add the vanilla and cover with plastic wrap.

MAKE THE DOUGH

1. In the bowl of a stand mixer fitted with the flat beater, beat the sugar and butter on medium speed until smooth and creamy, about 1 minute. Scrape down the sides of the bowl.

2. With the mixer on medium speed, add the egg mixture and beat for 30 seconds, or until incorporated. Scrape down the sides of the bowl.

3. Add the flour mixture and beat on low speed just until all the flour disappears.

4. Add the nut mixture and beat on low speed just until incorporated.

5. Scrape the dough onto a sheet of plastic wrap, wrap tightly, and refrigerate for a minimum of 30 minutes, up to 24 hours.

PREHEAT THE OVEN

■ Thirty minutes or longer before baking, set an oven rack at the middle level. Set the oven at 375°F/190°C.

ROLL THE DOUGH INTO BALLS

6. Divide the dough in half (about 375 grams each). Rewrap one of the pieces in the plastic wrap and refrigerate it while shaping the other piece.

7. Scoop out 9 pieces of dough (2 level tablespoons/41 grams each). Roll each piece between the palms of your hands into a 1¾ inch ball.

8. Set the dough balls a minimum of 2 inches apart on a cookie sheet and press them down to about 2½ inches wide.

BAKE THE COOKIES

9. Bake the cookies for 6 minutes. For even baking, rotate the cookie sheet halfway around. Continue baking for 2 to 6 minutes. The cookies should just begin to brown lightly on the tops, and still feel soft when gently pressed with a fingertip.

COOL THE COOKIES

10. Set the cookie sheet on a wire rack and let the cookies cool for 1 minute. Use a thin pancake turner to lift the cookies onto another wire rack to finish cooling. They will firm up as they cool and are most delicious when eaten slightly warm.

11. Shape, bake, and cool the second batch.

STORE AIRTIGHT: room temperature, 2 weeks; refrigerated 1 month; frozen, 3 months.

Photo opposite, top to bottom: Peanut Butter and Jelly Thumbprints (page 15), Oatmeal Cookies, and Molasses Sugar Butter Cookies (page 6)

Molasses Sugar Butter Cookies

MAKES TWENTY-FOUR 2¾ INCH COOKIES

OVEN TEMPERATURE: 375°F/190°C

BAKING TIME: 8 to 10 minutes for each of two batches

BAKING EQUIPMENT: Two 15 by 12 inch cookie sheets, no preparation needed, or lined with parchment

Optional: a 1½ inch diameter cookie scoop

Clarifying butter (heating it so that any water evaporates) removes the water from the butter and browns the milk solids. This gives these cookies a delicious flavor and extraordinarily chewy texture with crisp crust. Clarifying butter is easy and well worth it.

Makes 562 grams dough

unsalted butter	150 grams	10½ tablespoons (1 stick plus 2½ tablespoons)
¾ large egg	38 grams	2 tablespoons plus 1 teaspoon (35 ml)
bleached all-purpose flour	204 grams	1¾ cups minus 1 tablespoon (lightly spooned into the cup and leveled off)
baking soda	8.2 grams	1½ teaspoons
fine sea salt	.	⅜ teaspoon
ground cinnamon	.	¾ teaspoon
ground cloves	.	⅜ teaspoon
ground ginger	.	⅜ teaspoon
superfine sugar	125 grams	½ cup plus 2 tablespoons
light molasses, preferably Grandma's brand	60 grams	3 tablespoons (45 ml)
superfine sugar, for rolling the dough balls (see Baking Pearls, page 7)	25 grams	2 tablespoons

MISE EN PLACE

■ **CLARIFY AND BROWN THE BUTTER:** Have ready by the cooktop a 1 cup glass measure with a spout.

In a small heavy saucepan, on very low heat, melt the butter, stirring often with a silicone spatula. Raise the heat to low and boil, stirring constantly, until the milk solids on the spatula become a deep brown. Immediately pour the butter into the glass measure, scraping in the browned solids as well. Allow the browned butter to cool to room temperature, or no higher than 80°F/27°C (see Baking Pearls, opposite).

Baking Pearls

If the browned butter is used at a higher temperature than 80°F/27°C, the cookies will not expand to 2¾ inches and will not form cracks. They will also require another 2 minutes of baking.

It is essential to clarify the butter for these cookies, because just melting the butter will result in a thinner cookie that doesn't bake through. Use grade AA butter; lower-quality butter (containing more water) will result in a lesser amount of browned butter. You will need a total of 110 grams/½ cup plus 1 tablespoon/133 ml browned butter.

Superfine sugar will give the finest, most even crunch to the surface of the cookies, but if desired, turbinado sugar can be used instead for more sparkle.

Refrigerating half the dough while you shape the first batch keeps the remaining dough cool, which prevents the baking soda from activating and ensures that the cookies will be uniform in size and shape. The time it takes to roll the remaining twelve dough balls is about the same as it takes to bake the first batch.

The raw dough freezes nicely; however, if the dough is not baked on the same day as mixing, the cookies will be slightly larger, flatter, and darker in color.

- Into another 1 cup measure with a spout or a small bowl, weigh or measure the egg. Cover with plastic wrap.

- In a medium bowl, whisk together the flour, baking soda, salt, cinnamon, cloves, and ginger.

MAKE THE DOUGH

1. In the bowl of a stand mixer fitted with the flat beater, mix the browned butter with its solids, the sugar, molasses, and egg on low speed for 1 minute.

2. Add the flour mixture. Start mixing on the lowest speed to moisten the flour. Raise the speed to low and beat for 30 seconds.

3. Scrape the dough onto a piece of plastic wrap and divide it in half (about 281 grams each). Wrap each piece in plastic wrap and refrigerate for 1 hour, or until firm enough to handle (see Baking Pearls).

PREHEAT THE OVEN

- Thirty minutes or longer before baking, set an oven rack at the middle level. Set the oven at 375°F/190°C.

ROLL THE DOUGH INTO BALLS

4. In a small bowl or large custard cup, place the sugar for rolling the dough balls. Remove one piece of dough from the refrigerator.

5. Measure the dough into the cookie scoop and level it off with a small metal spatula, or scoop out a heaping tablespoon (23 grams). You will get 12 pieces of dough. Roll each piece in the palms of your hands to form a 1¼ inch ball.

6. Roll each dough ball around in the bowl of sugar to coat it well. Set the dough balls a minimum of 1½ inches apart on a cookie sheet.

BAKE THE COOKIES

7. Bake for 4 minutes. For even baking, rotate the cookie sheet halfway around. Continue baking for 4 to 6 minutes. Cracks will appear on the surface, but the inside will look slightly underbaked. When gently pressed with a fingertip, the cookies should still feel soft in the middle. (Baking longer will result in a darker looking and crisper cookie throughout.)

COOL THE COOKIES

8. Set the cookie sheet on a wire rack and let the cookies cool for 3 to 5 minutes, until firm enough to transfer to a wire rack for cooling. Use a thin pancake turner to transfer the cookies to another wire rack. They will firm up as they cool, with a crisp surface and soft chewy interior.

9. Shape, bake, and cool the second batch.

STORE AIRTIGHT: room temperature, 7 days; refrigerated, 2 weeks; frozen, 3 months.

Rose's Chocolate Chip Cookies

**MAKES TWENTY-TWO
2¾ INCH COOKIES**

OVEN TEMPERATURE:
325°F/160°C for the
walnuts; 350°F/175°C
for the cookies

BAKING TIME: 7 minutes
for the walnuts; 8 to 10
minutes for the cookies
for each of two batches

BAKING EQUIPMENT:
Two 15 by 12 inch cookie
sheets, lined with
parchment

I brown the butter for these cookies to add flavor and remove the water (although you can skip this step; see Make This Recipe Your Own, opposite). Adding golden syrup or corn syrup helps to keep them moist and chewy. Golden syrup adds a delicious butterscotch element. Unbleached all-purpose flour gives a slightly chewier texture than bleached flour.

I also like to add walnuts, and lightly toasting them brings out the flavor. Since walnut skins are bitter tasting, removing as much skin as easily possible also removes any bitterness. If you like the slight bitterness, it's okay to skip this step. I like my cookies crisp at the edges and moist and chewy on the inside, so I find it best to bake them just until the centers are still soft and then eat them while still warm from the oven. But I also love the thinner, crisper variation that follows.

Makes 690 grams dough

unsalted butter	113 grams	8 tablespoons (1 stick)
1 large egg	50 grams	3 tablespoons plus ½ teaspoon (47.5 ml)
walnut halves	75 grams	¾ cup
all-purpose flour, preferably unbleached	161 grams	1⅓ cups (lightly spooned into the cup and leveled off)
baking soda	2.7 grams	½ teaspoon
fine sea salt	.	¼ teaspoon
light brown sugar, preferably light Muscovado	81 grams	¼ cup plus 2 tablespoons, firmly packed
granulated sugar	25 grams	2 tablespoons
golden syrup or corn syrup	42 grams	2 tablespoons (30 ml)
pure vanilla extract	.	1 teaspoon (5 ml)
dark chocolate chips, 52% to 63% cacao (see Baking Pearls)	170 grams	1 cup (6 ounces)

PREHEAT THE OVEN

■ Twenty minutes or longer before toasting the walnuts, set an oven rack at the middle level. Set the oven at 325°F/160°C.

MISE EN PLACE

■ About 1 hour ahead, set the butter and egg on the counter at room temperature (65° to 75°F/19° to 24°C).

■ **CLARIFY AND BROWN THE BUTTER:** Have ready by the cooktop a 1 cup glass measure with a spout.

In a small heavy saucepan, on very low heat, melt the butter, stirring often with a silicone spatula. Raise the heat to low and boil, stirring constantly, until the milk solids on the spatula become a deep brown. Immediately pour the butter into the glass measure, scraping in the browned solids as well. Allow the browned butter to cool to room temperature, or no higher than 80°F/27°C.

■ **TOAST AND CHOP THE WALNUTS:** Spread the walnuts evenly on a cookie sheet and bake for about 7 minutes. Stir once or twice to ensure even toasting and prevent overbrowning. Turn the walnuts onto a dish towel and roll and rub them around to loosen the skins. Discard any loose skins (use a skewer for any large stuck-on skins) and let the nuts cool completely. Chop into coarse pieces.

■ In a medium bowl, whisk together the flour, baking soda, and salt.

■ Into the bowl of a stand mixer, weigh or measure the egg.

MAKE THE DOUGH

1. To the bowl of the stand mixer fitted with the flat beater, add the browned butter with its solids, the brown and granulated sugars, golden syrup, and vanilla, and mix on low speed for 1 minute.

2. Add the flour mixture. Starting on the lowest speed, beat just until the flour is moistened. On low speed, continue beating for 30 seconds. Add the chocolate chips and walnuts and continue beating only until evenly incorporated.

3. Divide the dough in half (about 345 grams each). Wrap each piece in plastic wrap. If the dough is very sticky, refrigerate for about 30 minutes.

PREHEAT THE OVEN

■ Twenty minutes or longer before baking, set an oven rack at the middle level. Set the oven at 350°F/175°C.

ROLL THE DOUGH INTO BALLS

4. Divide one piece of the dough into 11 walnut-size pieces (31 grams each). Roll each piece in the palms of your hands to form a 1½ inch ball. Place the balls on a cookie sheet, a minimum of 2 inches apart.

5. Flatten the cookies to about 2 inches wide by ½ inch high. (If desired, freeze the shaped cookie dough to bake at a later time. Baking time will be about 2 minutes longer when baked from the frozen. For the ideal texture, preheat the oven

(continued)

to 325°F/160°C and then raise the temperature to 350°F/175°C once the cookies are in the oven.)

BAKE THE COOKIES

6. Bake for 4 minutes. For even baking, rotate the cookie sheet halfway around. Continue baking for 4 to 6 minutes, or until the cookies are just beginning to brown on the tops. When gently pressed with a fingertip, they should still feel soft in the middle.

COOL THE COOKIES

7. Set the cookie sheet on a wire rack and let the cookies cool for 1 minute, until they are firm enough to transfer to a wire rack for cooling. Use a thin pancake turner to transfer the cookies to another wire rack.

8. Shape, bake, and cool the second batch.

STORE AIRTIGHT: room temperature, 2 weeks; refrigerated, 1 month; frozen, 3 months.

Variations

THIN CRISP AND CHEWY CHOCOLATE CHIP COOKIES

Crisp at the edges and on top but chewy in the middle.

Replace the egg with 30 grams/2 tablespoons/30 ml milk. (This will cause the dough to spread more, so you will be using a little less dough for each cookie and the yield will be greater.)

Replace the chocolate chips with mini chocolate chips and chop the nuts medium fine.

Divide each half of the dough into 14 pieces (25 grams—a rounded 1½ inch cookie scoop, about 2 tablespoons). Roll each piece in the palms of your hands to form a 1⅜ inch ball.

Place the balls on the cookie sheet a minimum of 2 inches apart. Flatten them to about 2 inches wide by ⅜ inch high. (If planning to freeze them or if refrigerating the shaped dough, flatten them to 2¼ inches wide.)

Bake for 8 to 10 minutes, until just beginning to brown and the entire top is still soft. Allow the cookies to cool for 3 minutes before transferring them to a wire rack.

CHOCOLATE CHOCOLATE CHIP COOKIES

Marvelously fudgy on the inside and deeply chocolaty throughout. It's especially pleasing to eat these still warm to experience the little pools of melted chocolate chips contrasting with the fudginess.

Replace the walnuts with 19 grams/¼ cup unsweetened cocoa powder, preferably alkalized (sifted into the cup and leveled off). Add the cocoa to the flour mixture.

Add 30 grams/2 tablespoons/ 30 ml brewed espresso or strong coffee, cooled to room temperature, when adding the vanilla.

Flour your hands lightly when rolling the slightly sticky dough.

Bake for 8 minutes, or just until the edges are set and slightly firmer and the top is still soft. The finished cookies will be about 3 inches in diameter.

Making Rose's Chocolate Chip Cookies

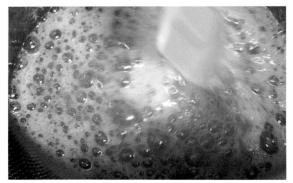

Boil the butter.

Let the browned butter cool.

Remove the skins from the toasted walnuts. Use a skewer for any large stuck-on skins.

The finished dough.

Roll the dough into balls.

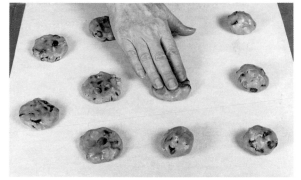

Flatten the dough balls.

Bite-Size Linzer Thumbprints

**MAKES THIRTY-FOUR
1¾ INCH COOKIES**

OVEN TEMPERATURE:
350°F/175°C

BAKING TIME: 10 to
12 minutes for the
hazelnuts; 18 to 20
minutes for the cookies

BAKING EQUIPMENT:
One 15 by 12 inch cookie
sheet, no preparation
needed, or lined with
parchment
Optional: a disposable
pastry bag or quart-size
reclosable freezer bag
with a small semicircle
cut from the tip or one
corner

*This is the cookie version of the famous Linzertorte from Linz,
Austria, which is made with a nut cookie crust filled with raspberry
jam. The combination of toasted hazelnuts, raspberries, butter, and
sugar blended together to make a crunchy, buttery cookie with soft
interior makes this one of my favorites.*

Makes 415 grams dough

unblanched whole hazelnuts	71 grams	½ cup
unsalted butter	113 grams	8 tablespoons (1 stick)
bleached all-purpose flour	145 grams	1 cup (lightly spooned into the cup and leveled off) plus 3 tablespoons, *divided*
granulated sugar	67 grams	⅓ cup
baking powder	2.2 grams	½ teaspoon
fine sea salt	.	⅛ teaspoon
ground cinnamon	.	½ teaspoon
1 large egg yolk	19 grams	1 tablespoon plus ½ teaspoon (17.5 ml)
pure vanilla extract	.	½ teaspoon (2.5 ml)
lemon zest, finely grated	3 grams	1½ teaspoons, loosely packed
seedless raspberry jam	156 grams	½ cup
powdered sugar	18 grams	2 tablespoons

PREHEAT THE OVEN

▪ Twenty minutes or longer before toasting the hazelnuts, set an oven rack at the middle level. Set the oven at 350°F/175°C.

MISE EN PLACE

▪ **TOAST THE HAZELNUTS:** Spread the hazelnuts evenly on a rimmed cookie sheet and bake for 10 to 12 minutes, stirring occasionally, until the skins crack and the exposed nuts are gold. Allow them to cool completely.

▪ Thirty minutes ahead, cut the butter into ½ inch cubes. Wrap and refrigerate.

▪ In a small bowl, whisk together 121 grams/1 cup of the flour, the granulated sugar, baking powder, salt, and cinnamon.

The dark skin of the hazelnuts, which in other recipes is removed to avoid bitterness, here contributes a pleasant flavor.

Do not heat the jam or strain it, or it will become too thin.

Chilling the shaped dough before baking maintains the best shape.

Avoid convection baking because the fan causes the jam to spread onto the borders of the cookies.

- With dish washing liquid, wash the lemons. Rinse, dry, and zest them (see page xxv).

- Into a 1 cup glass measure with a spout, weigh or measure the egg yolk. Add the vanilla and lemon zest. Cover with plastic wrap.

- With a spoon, stir the jam just until smooth.

MAKE THE DOUGH

1. In a food processor, process the nuts with the remaining 24 grams/3 tablespoons flour until fine but not powder fine.

2. Add the flour-sugar mixture and process for a few seconds until evenly mixed.

3. Pulse in the butter until the mixture is in fine crumbs.

4. Add the egg yolk mixture and pulse just until the crumbs are moistened and will hold together when pinched.

5. Empty the dough into a bowl and knead it lightly to form a rough dough.

SHAPE THE COOKIES

6. Measure the dough into a 1 teaspoon measure and level it off with a small metal spatula. For each cookie use 2 level teaspoons (12 grams).

7. Roll each piece of dough between the palms of your hands into a 1 inch ball. Set the dough ball in the cupped palm of your hand and, with your index finger, make an indentation in the middle. (Alternatively, use the rounded ½ inch diameter handle of a wooden spoon.)

8. Set the dough balls 1½ inches apart on the cookie sheet.

9. Using the pastry bag or a ¼ teaspoon measure, fill each indentation with jam. (It will sink down on baking.)

10. Cover the shaped dough with plastic wrap and refrigerate for a minimum of 30 minutes before baking.

BAKE THE COOKIES

11. Bake for 10 minutes. For even baking, rotate the cookie sheet halfway around. Continue baking for 8 to 10 minutes, or until lightly brown.

COOL THE COOKIES

12. Set the cookie sheet on a wire rack. Use a thin pancake turner to lift the cookies onto another wire rack. Cool completely.

13. On the day of serving, dust lightly with powdered sugar. Pipe or spoon a little more raspberry jam into the center to cover the powdered sugar and fill in the indentation. Leave uncovered until serving.

STORE AIRTIGHT: room temperature, 1 week; refrigerated, 2 weeks.

(continued)

Making Bite-Size Linzer Thumbprints

Pulse the dough until moistened.

Lightly knead the dough.

Make an indentation in the center of each cookie.

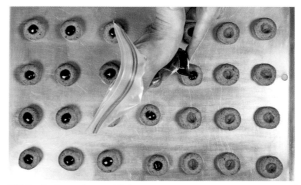

Fill the indentations with jam.

Dust the baked cookies with powdered sugar.

Top with a little more jam.

Peanut Butter and Jelly Thumbprints

MAKES THIRTY 1¾ INCH COOKIES

OVEN TEMPERATURE: 375°F/190°C

BAKING TIME: 10 to 12 minutes for each of two batches

BAKING EQUIPMENT: Two 15 by 12 inch cookie sheets, no preparation needed, or lined with parchment

Optional: a 1¼ inch diameter cookie scoop

A disposable pastry bag with a very small semicircle cut from the tip

For the peanut lover, this really hits the spot.

Makes 360 grams dough

unsalted butter	57 grams	4 tablespoons (½ stick)
bleached all-purpose flour	71 grams	½ cup (lightly spooned into the cup and leveled off) plus 1½ tablespoons
baking soda	2.7 grams	½ teaspoon
fine sea salt	.	¹⁄₁₆ teaspoon
smooth peanut butter, preferably Jif	133 grams	½ cup
½ large egg	25 grams	1½ tablespoons (22.5 ml)
pure vanilla extract	.	¼ teaspoon (1.2 ml)
light brown sugar, preferably light Muscovado	54 grams	¼ cup
granulated sugar	25 grams	2 tablespoons
jelly or jam of your choice	78 grams	¼ cup

MISE EN PLACE

- Thirty minutes to 1 hour ahead, cut the butter into 4 pieces.

- In a small bowl, whisk together the flour, baking soda, and salt.

- Into another small bowl, weigh or measure the peanut butter.

- Into a 1 cup measure with a spout, weigh or measure the egg. Add the vanilla.

MAKE THE DOUGH

1. In a food processor, process the brown and granulated sugars for several minutes, until very fine.

2. With the motor running, add the butter, 1 piece at a time. Process until smooth and creamy, scraping down the sides as needed.

3. Add the peanut butter and process until smooth and creamy.

4. Add the egg mixture and process until incorporated, scraping the sides of the bowl as needed.

(continued)

5. Add the flour mixture and pulse in just until incorporated.

6. Scrape the dough into a bowl. Cover and refrigerate for at least 1 hour, up to overnight, to keep the dough from cracking when shaping.

PREHEAT THE OVEN

■ Thirty minutes or longer before baking, set an oven rack at the middle level. Set the oven at 375°F/190°C.

SHAPE THE COOKIES

7. Measure the dough into the cookie scoop and level it off with a small metal spatula, or use 2 level teaspoons (12 grams each).

8. Roll each piece of dough between the palms of your hands into a 1 inch ball.

9. Set the dough balls 1½ inches apart on a cookie sheet.

10. Make an indentation in the middle of each, using your floured index finger. (Alternatively, use the rounded ½ inch diameter handle of a wooden spoon.)

11. Using a pastry bag or small spoon, fill each indentation with a rounded ¼ teaspoon of the jelly. (It will sink down on baking.)

BAKE THE COOKIES

12. Bake for 5 minutes. For even baking, rotate the cookie sheet halfway around. Continue baking for 5 to 7 minutes, or until lightly brown.

13. While the first batch is baking, shape the dough for the second batch.

COOL THE COOKIES

14. Set the cookie sheet on a wire rack and let the cookies cool for a few minutes to be firm enough to transfer to a wire rack for cooling. Use a thin pancake turner to transfer the cookies to another wire rack.

15. Bake and cool the second batch.

STORE FILLED, AIRTIGHT: room temperature, 1 month.
UNFILLED, AIRTIGHT: room temperature, 3 months.

Walnut Powder Puffs

**MAKES TWENTY-FOUR
2 INCH COOKIES**

OVEN TEMPERATURE:
350°F/175°C

BAKING TIME: 7 minutes
for the walnuts; 15 to 20
minutes for the cookies
for each of two batches

BAKING EQUIPMENT:
One 15 by 12 inch cookie
sheet, no preparation
needed, or lined with
parchment
Optional: a 1¼ inch
diameter cookie scoop

Toasting the walnuts until browned and leaving the skin in place gives a deliciously intense flavor to this crunchy but dissolvingly tender little cookie.

Makes 320 grams dough

unsalted butter	113 grams	8 tablespoons (1 stick)
walnut halves	37 grams	¼ cup plus 2 tablespoons
powdered sugar	57 grams	½ cup (lightly spooned into the cup and leveled off)
fine sea salt	.	a pinch
pure vanilla extract	.	¼ teaspoon (1.2 ml)
bleached all-purpose flour	125 grams	1 cup (lightly spooned into the cup and leveled off) plus ½ tablespoon
powdered sugar, for coating	57 grams	½ cup (lightly spooned into the cup and leveled off)

PREHEAT THE OVEN

▪ Twenty minutes or longer before toasting the walnuts, set an oven rack at the middle level. Set the oven at 350°F/175°C.

MISE EN PLACE

▪ About 1 hour ahead, set the butter on the counter at room temperature (65° to 75°F/19° to 24°C).

▪ **TOAST THE WALNUTS:** Spread the walnuts evenly on a cookie sheet and bake for about 7 minutes. Stir once or twice to ensure even toasting and avoid over-browning. (Do not remove the skins, because they add flavor to this cookie.) Allow them to cool completely.

MAKE THE DOUGH

1. In a food processor, process the nuts with the 57 grams/½ cup powdered sugar and the salt until powder fine.

2. Cut the butter into a few pieces and add it with the motor running. Process until smooth and creamy, scraping down the sides as needed.

3. Pulse in the vanilla.

4. Pulse in the flour just until the dough starts to hold together in clumps, scraping down the sides of the bowl as needed.

5. Scrape the dough onto a large sheet of plastic wrap and use it and your knuckles to knead the dough just until it comes together smoothly.

(continued)

6. Divide the dough in half (about 160 grams each). Wrap each piece in plastic wrap and set them on a flat sheet. Refrigerate for a minimum of 1 hour, up to 3 hours.

SHAPE THE COOKIES

7. Remove one piece of dough. Measure it into the cookie scoop, gently rounded, or use a scant tablespoon (13 grams each).

8. Roll each piece of dough between the palms of your hands into a 1¼ inch ball. Flour your hands if necessary.

9. Set the dough balls 1½ inches apart on the cookie sheet.

BAKE THE COOKIES

10. Bake for 8 minutes. For even baking, rotate the cookie sheet halfway around. Continue baking for 7 to 12 minutes, or until lightly browned.

11. While the first batch is baking, shape the dough for the second batch.

COOL THE COOKIES

12. Set the cookie sheet on a wire rack to cool for 2 to 3 minutes.

COAT THE COOKIES WITH POWDERED SUGAR

13. Lay a sheet of parchment on the counter and place another wire rack on top. Set the powdered sugar in a small bowl. Use a thin pancake turner to lift each cookie from the sheet and roll it in the powdered sugar while still hot. Set the cookie on the rack.

14. Bake the second batch, let cool for 2 to 3 minutes, and then roll in powdered sugar.

15. Spoon the remaining powdered sugar into a sifter or fine-mesh strainer and dust it over the cookies to coat. When the cookies are completely cool, lift away the rack and use any remaining sugar to dust the cookies when storing.

16. Set the cookies in a container, dusting with powdered sugar between each layer of cookies. To keep moisture from softening the sugar and making it sticky, leave the container uncovered for 8 hours before covering it tightly. This will maintain the powdery sugar coating.

STORE AIRTIGHT: room temperature, 1 month; frozen, 6 months (redust with powdered sugar before serving).

Making Walnut Powder Puffs

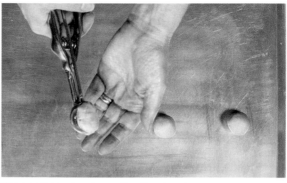

Knead the dough until smooth.

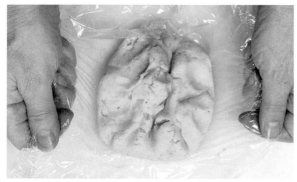

Use a cookie scoop to portion the dough.

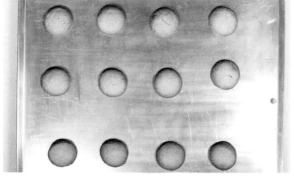

Bake until lightly browned.

Coat the hot cookies with powdered sugar.

Sift more powdered sugar on top.

Clinton Street Brookies

MAKES TWENTY-FOUR 2½ TO 2¾ INCH COOKIES

OVEN TEMPERATURE: 350°F/175°C

BAKING TIME: 10 to 12 minutes for each of two batches

BAKING EQUIPMENT: Two 15 by 12 inch cookie sheets, nonstick, or lined with parchment or nonstick Teflon-type liners

Optional: a 1½ inch diameter cookie scoop

These unusual chocolate cookies, adapted from the Clinton St. Baking Company Cookbook, are the creation of one of their former pastry chefs, Ernie Rich. They derive their name from the inventive cross between a brownie and a cookie. The crackly brownielike top, delightfully chewy and slightly cakey interior, and sweet, deep chocolate flavor make them one of my top favorite chocolate cookies. They are at their very melty best when still warm, but are still soft and chewy when room temperature.

Makes 564 grams dough

dark chocolate, 60% to 62% cacao, coarsely chopped	227 grams	1⅔ cups (8 ounces), *divided* (see Baking Pearl)
canola or safflower oil	13 grams	1 tablespoon (15 ml)
unsalted butter	5 grams	1 teaspoon
2 large eggs	100 grams	⅓ cup plus 1 tablespoon (94 ml)
bleached all-purpose flour	65 grams	½ cup (lightly spooned into the cup and leveled off) plus ½ tablespoon
baking powder	1.1 grams	¼ teaspoon
fine sea salt	.	¼ teaspoon
light Muscovado or dark brown sugar	163 grams	¾ cup, firmly packed
pure vanilla extract	.	¼ teaspoon (1.2 ml)

PREHEAT THE OVEN

▪ Twenty minutes or longer before baking, set an oven rack at the middle level. Set the oven at 350°F/175°C.

MISE EN PLACE

▪ **MELT THE CHOCOLATE:** Thirty minutes to 1 hour ahead, melt half of the chocolate: In the top of a double boiler set over hot, not simmering, water (do not let the bottom of the container touch the water), with a silicone spatula, stir together 113 grams/⅓ cup/4 ounces of the chocolate, the oil, and the butter. Heat the mixture, stirring often, until the chocolate is fully melted. Remove it from the heat and let it cool until room temperature.

▪ Into a medium bowl, weigh or measure the eggs.

Baking Pearl

I sometimes like to use a mix of chocolates for this recipe: 60% to 62% cacao for the half of the chocolate that is melted into the dough, and an 85% cacao for the portion of the chopped chocolate that gets mixed into the dough in Step 3, to temper the sweetness of the cookie. The sweeter chocolate in the cookie dough is necessary to form the cracks in the surface.

MAKE THE DOUGH

1. In a small bowl, whisk together the flour, baking powder, and salt.

2. Add the brown sugar and vanilla to the eggs and whisk until combined. Use the whisk to fold in the melted chocolate mixture.

3. With a silicone spatula or wooden spoon, mix in the flour mixture until evenly combined. Fold in the remaining chopped chocolate.

CHILL THE DOUGH

4. Line a shallow pan, such as a quarter sheet pan or pie plate, with plastic wrap and lightly coat it with nonstick cooking spray. Scrape the dough into the pan; the dough will be very soft. Cover it with another coated sheet of plastic wrap and set it in the freezer for about 15 minutes, or until it is firm enough to scoop.

SHAPE THE DOUGH

5. Scoop out 12 level scoops of dough (23 grams each) and drop them 2 inches apart onto a cookie sheet. You can use a small metal spatula to help the sticky dough release from the scoop. (Alternatively, use 2 teaspoons to drop and mound the dough.) The mounds will be about 1½ inches in diameter. If the kitchen is hot and the dough becomes very soft, return it to the freezer to firm for about 15 minutes.

BAKE THE COOKIES

6. Bake for 5 minutes. For even baking, rotate the cookie sheet halfway around. Continue baking for 5 to 7 minutes, or until the tops are dry and cracked. When pressed lightly on top they should give slightly, and feel firm around the edges but still a little soft all over the top.

7. While the first batch of cookies is baking, shape the dough for the second batch.

COOL THE COOKIES

8. Set the cookie sheet on a wire rack and let the cookies cool for 3 minutes, until firm enough to transfer to a wire rack to finish cooling. Use a thin pancake turner to lift the cookies onto another wire rack.

9. Bake and cool the second batch.

STORE AIRTIGHT: room temperature, 4 days; refrigerated, 1 week; frozen, 2 months.

(continued)

Making Clinton Street Brookies

Fold the melted chocolate into the egg mixture.

Mix in the flour mixture.

Scoop the dough onto the prepared cookie sheet.

Transfer the cookies to a wire rack to cool.

Classic Spritz Cookies

MAKES TWENTY-EIGHT 2 INCH COOKIES

OVEN TEMPERATURE: 375°F/190°C

BAKING TIME: 5 minutes for the almonds; 9 to 12 minutes for the cookies for each of two batches

BAKING EQUIPMENT: Two 15 by 12 inch cookie sheets, no preparation needed, or lined with parchment

A large disposable pastry bag fitted with a ½ inch (#7) star pastry tube, or a cookie press

These rank as many people's favorite Christmas cookies because of their subtle almond flavor and tender texture, as well as for their festive candy centers.

Makes 375 grams dough

sliced almonds, preferably blanched	22 grams	¼ cup minus ½ tablespoon
unsalted butter	113 grams	8 tablespoons (1 stick)
½ large egg	25 grams	1½ tablespoons (22.5 ml)
pure vanilla extract	.	½ teaspoon (2.5 ml)
pure almond extract	.	½ teaspoon (2.5 ml)
bleached all-purpose flour	142 grams	1 cup (lightly spooned into the cup and leveled off) plus 3 tablespoons
fine sea salt	.	a tiny pinch
sugar	75 grams	¼ cup plus 2 tablespoons
14 glacéed cherries, cut in half (optional)	.	.

PREHEAT THE OVEN

▪ Thirty minutes or longer before toasting the almonds, set an oven rack at the middle level. Set the oven at 375°F/190°C.

MISE EN PLACE

▪ TOAST THE ALMONDS: Spread the almonds evenly on a cookie sheet and bake for about 5 minutes, or until pale gold. Stir once or twice to ensure even toasting and prevent overbrowning. Allow them to cool completely.

▪ Thirty minutes to 1 hour ahead, cut the butter into 8 pieces.

▪ Into a 1 cup glass measure with a spout, weigh or measure the egg. Add the vanilla and almond extracts.

▪ In a small bowl, whisk together the flour and salt.

MAKE THE DOUGH

1. In a food processor, process the almonds and sugar until fairly fine. With the motor running, add the butter, 1 piece at a time. Process until smooth and creamy, scraping the sides of the bowl as needed.

2. Add the egg mixture and process until incorporated. Scrape the sides of the bowl.

(continued)

If lining the cookie sheets with parchment, hold it in place with 4 pieces of masking tape while you pipe the dough and then remove the tape before baking.

Don't be afraid of the pastry bag. It's just as easy to use as a cookie press. But do not overfill the bag; otherwise it will be hard to squeeze out the dough.

Use the dough right after mixing it, as chilling makes it too firm to pipe.

If using the cookie press and the dough does not release from the press when piping it onto the parchment or cookie sheet, it is because the dough has become too soft and needs to be chilled slightly.

3. Add the flour mixture and pulse just until blended and the dough begins to form a ball.

SHAPE THE COOKIES

4. Scoop the dough into the pastry bag (or spoon some of the dough into the cookie press and cover the remaining dough). Pipe 14 stars, each about 1¾ inches in diameter (13 grams), onto a cookie sheet, no less than 1 inch apart.

For the best shape, hold the bag in a vertical position (straight up and down) with the toothed edge of the tube just slightly above the cookie sheet. Squeeze the bag firmly without moving it until the shape is as wide as desired, just at the point when the lines in the dough are on the verge of curving. Stop squeezing the tube and push the tube down slightly. Lift the tube straight up and away.

5. Decorate with the glacéed cherries, if desired, gently pressing a half onto the center.

BAKE THE COOKIES

6. Bake for 5 minutes. For even baking, rotate the cookie sheet halfway around. Continue baking for 4 to 7 minutes, or until the cookies are just beginning to brown lightly.

7. While the first batch of cookies is baking, shape the dough for the second batch.

COOL THE COOKIES

8. Set the cookie sheet on a wire rack. Use a thin pancake turner to lift the cookies onto another wire rack. Cool completely.

9. Bake and cool the second batch.

STORE AIRTIGHT: room temperature, 1 month; refrigerated or frozen, 3 months.

Making Classic Spritz Cookies

Use a cookie press to shape the cookies.

Or use a pastry bag to pipe the dough; hold the bag straight up and down.

Stop squeezing before lifting up the pastry tube.

Decorate the cookies with glacéed cherries.

Transfer the cookies to a wire rack to cool.

Chocolate Spangled Meringue Kisses

**MAKES THIRTY-SIX
1¾ INCH COOKIES**

OVEN TEMPERATURE:
200°F/90°C

BAKING TIME: 1 hour
plus 25 to 35 minutes

BAKING EQUIPMENT:
Two 15 by 12 inch
cookies sheets, lined
with parchment

Optional: a disposable
pastry bag fitted with a
½ inch (#7) star pastry
tube

Unsweetened chocolate is a desirable addition to meringue as it tempers the sweetness without changing the texture. These meringues are deliciously crisp, light, and airy with a slight chewiness. If you prefer meringues that are entirely crisp, allow them to sit in the turned-off oven for an hour after baking.

Makes 191 grams meringue batter

2 large egg whites	60 grams	¼ cup (59 ml)
cream of tartar	.	¼ teaspoon
sugar, preferably superfine	56 grams	¼ cup plus ½ tablespoon, *divided*
powdered sugar	57 grams	½ cup (lightly spooned into the cup and leveled off)
fine-quality unsweetened or 99% cacao chocolate, cut into pieces	28 grams	1 ounce

PREHEAT THE OVEN

▪ Twenty minutes or longer before baking, set oven racks in the upper and lower thirds of the oven. Set the oven at 200°F/90°C.

MISE EN PLACE

▪ Thirty minutes to 1 hour ahead, into the bowl of a stand mixer, weigh or measure the egg whites. Add the cream of tartar and cover.

▪ If not using superfine sugar, in a food processor, process the granulated sugar until very fine and empty it into a bowl.

▪ In a food processor, process the powdered sugar with the chocolate until the chocolate is in very fine particles. Cover and refrigerate it.

▪ It is helpful to draw 1¾ inch circles (5 rows of 4 each), evenly spaced, on the underside of the parchment sheets to serve as guides for piping the meringue, then flip the parchment.

MAKE THE MERINGUE

1. In the bowl of a stand mixer with the whisk beater, beat the egg whites and cream of tartar on medium speed until soft peaks form when the beater is raised slowly. Gradually add ½ tablespoon of the superfine sugar. Raise the speed to medium-high and continue beating until stiff peaks form when the beater is

Meringues soften and become sticky in high humidity.

Refrigerating the chocolate and powdered sugar mixture ensures that the chocolate spangles don't melt into the meringue, which provides an attractive contrast.

These meringues need to be shaped soon after mixing.

To prevent cracking, do not use convection and do not open the oven door until after 45 minutes of baking.

If you cover the meringues, but not tightly, they will stay crisp but the insides will become a little chewy.

Make This Recipe Your Own

The meringues can be piped in different shapes, such as rosettes or hearts.

Variation

COCOA MERINGUES
Makes thirty-two 1¾ inch cookies; 176 grams batter

Replace the chocolate with 6 grams/1 tablespoon unsweetened alkalized cocoa powder. For a more attractive color you can add a few drops of red liquid food color to the egg whites before beating. The cocoa meringues require about 10 extra minutes of baking.

raised slowly. Scrape down the sides of the bowl. Gradually add the remaining superfine sugar. Raise the speed to high and beat until the meringue is very stiff and glossy.

2. Disengage the whisk beater and the bowl from the stand and use the whisk beater to fold in the chilled chocolate mixture by hand. You will need to shake it against the sides of the bowl several times as you fold the mixture, just until evenly incorporated. (The meringue initially will ball up in the middle of the whisk, but using the whisk instead of a spatula ensures the lightest possible meringue.)

3. Smudge a dot of the meringue onto each corner of the underside of the parchment to stick it onto the cookie sheet, so that it doesn't lift off when shaping the meringues.

SHAPE THE MERINGUES

4. Spoon about half of the meringue into the pastry bag and pipe 1¾ inch mounds (about 5 grams each) onto each of the cookie sheets. (Hold the pastry bag straight up and down with the pastry tube a little above the surface of the cookie sheet. Stop squeezing and lift off to form a small peak.) Refill the pastry bag as needed. (Alternatively, use two teaspoons to drop mounds of meringue onto the cookie sheet, and use a spoon to swirl the mounds into shape.)

5. Allow the meringues to dry at room temperature for 30 minutes to 1 hour before baking, or until set (when touched lightly with your finger the meringue should barely stick to it).

BAKE THE MERINGUES

6. Bake for 45 minutes. For even baking, rotate the cookie sheets from front to back, exchange their positions from top to bottom, and continue baking for another 35 minutes. The meringues should be completely crisp but not beginning to brown. (Test by breaking one of them or digging out a small amount with the tip of a sharp knife. They should be only slightly sticky.) If longer baking is required, continue baking for about 10 more minutes. To make meringues that are entirely crisp, turn off the oven and leave the meringues in the oven for an hour.

COOL THE MERINGUES

7. Set the cookie sheets on wire racks. Use a thin pancake turner or small metal spatula to lift the meringues onto another wire rack to cool.

STORE AIRTIGHT: room temperature in low humidity, 1 month.

(continued)

Making Chocolate Spangled Meringue Kisses

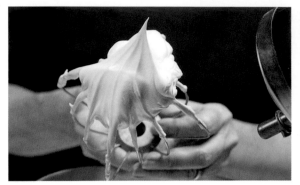

Whip the meringue until stiff and glossy.

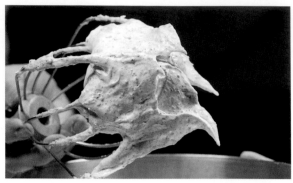

The consistency of the meringue with the ground chocolate.

Fill a pastry bag and use a dough scraper to push the meringue toward the tip.

Twist the top of the pastry bag to seal.

Pipe the meringues, holding the bag straight up.

Stop squeezing and lift up the pastry tube.

Fudgy Praline Pecan Meringue Ice Cream Sandwiches

MAKES TWENTY 2½ INCH COOKIES (10 SANDWICHES)

OVEN TEMPERATURE: 350°F/175°C

BAKING TIME: 5 minutes for the pecans; 10 to 15 minutes for the meringues

BAKING EQUIPMENT: Two 15 by 12 inch cookies sheets, lined with parchment; 2 tablespoons

The original of this treasured recipe was given to me many years ago by chef Vinnie Scotto. This chocolate version features unsweetened chocolate that, in addition to the molasses in the brown sugar, not only further tempers the sweetness of the meringue, but also creates a lusciously fudgy interior with a crisp crust. My favorite ice creams to sandwich in between these meringues are dulce de leche, caramel, coffee, and strawberry.

Makes 400 grams meringue batter

2 large egg whites	60 grams	¼ cup (59 ml)
pecan halves	150 grams	1½ cups, *divided*
light brown sugar, preferably light Muscovado	150 grams	¾ cup minus 1 tablespoon, firmly packed
fine-quality unsweetened or 99% cacao chocolate, grated	56 grams	about ⅓ cup (2 ounces), loosely packed
ice cream of your choice	280 to 360 grams	about 1½ cups

PREHEAT THE OVEN

▪ Twenty minutes or longer before toasting the pecans, set oven racks in the upper and lower thirds of the oven. Set the oven at 350°F/175°C.

MISE EN PLACE

▪ Thirty minutes to 1 hour ahead, into the bowl of a stand mixer, weigh or measure the egg whites. Cover them.

▪ **TOAST AND CHOP THE PECANS:** Spread the pecans evenly on a cookie sheet. Place the pan on the upper rack and bake for 5 minutes, without letting the nuts brown, to enhance the flavor. Stir once or twice to ensure even baking. Cool completely and divide into two equal parts (75 grams/¾ cup each). Chop one part into medium fine pieces.

(continued)

MAKE THE MERINGUES

1. In the bowl of the stand mixer with the whisk beater, beat the egg whites and sugar on medium speed until well mixed, about 1 minute. Scrape down the sides. On medium-high speed, beat for an additional 5 minutes, or until the meringue is very thick and light in color.

2. Remove the bowl from the mixer stand and, using a large silicone spatula, fold in the grated chocolate, then all of the pecans.

SHAPE THE MERINGUES

3. Use two tablespoons to spoon 10 dollops of meringue (20 grams each) onto each of the cookie sheets, a minimum of 1½ inches apart. Use a small offset spatula or the back of a spoon to shape the dollops into 2¼ inch wide by ½ inch high discs. The meringues will spread to about 2½ inches before baking but will not spread any more during baking. Stir the meringue mixture from time to time to ensure that each spoonful includes some of the nuts.

BAKE THE MERINGUES

4. Bake for 10 to 15 minutes. The meringues will crack slightly, which adds to their charm. A wire cake tester inserted in one of the cracks should come out sticky, and the meringues should give slightly to pressure. (An instant-read thermometer should read about 212°F/100°C.) If longer baking is required, rotate the cookie sheets halfway around, exchange their positions from top to bottom, and continue baking for a few more minutes.

COOL THE MERINGUES

5. Set the cookie sheets on wire racks and allow the cookies to cool completely on the sheets. The meringues will firm on sitting, which will make it easy to lift them off the parchment using a thin pancake turner. Sandwich the meringues with ice cream now, or store the cookies airtight for up to 2 months.

SANDWICH THE MERINGUES WITH ICE CREAM

6. Refrigerate the ice cream for 20 minutes to soften it slightly before sandwiching the meringues. Chill a cookie sheet in the freezer.

7. Set 5 of the meringues, flat bottom sides up, on the chilled pan. Spoon about 2 tablespoons (28 to 36 grams) ice cream on top of each cookie. Set a second meringue, flat bottom side down, on top. When the ice cream is soft enough to press down easily, evenly press the top of each meringue bringing the ice cream almost to the edge. If desired, use a small metal spatula to fill the opening at the sides with a little more ice cream and smooth it level with the edge of the meringue. The ice cream should be around ½ inch thick.

8. Repeat with the second batch.

9. Cover the sandwiches with plastic wrap and set them in the freezer until firm. When firm, wrap each sandwich individually in plastic wrap and place them in an airtight container in the freezer.

STORE AIRTIGHT: frozen, 2 months.

Making Fudgy Praline Pecan Meringues

Beat the meringue until stiff.

Fold in the grated chocolate.

Fold in the pecans.

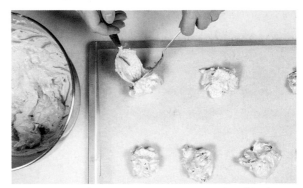

Spoon dollops of meringue onto the prepared cookie sheet.

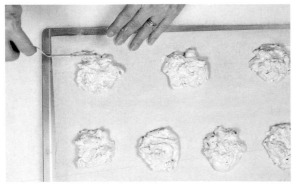

Shape the dollops with a spatula.

A cake tester should come out a little sticky.

Marzipan Cookies

**MAKES TWENTY-FOUR
2 INCH COOKIES**

OVEN TEMPERATURE:
350°F/175°C

BAKING TIME: 12 to 14
minutes

BAKING EQUIPMENT:
One 17¼ by 12¼ by
1 inch half sheet pan or
two 15 by 12 inch cookie
sheets, lined with
parchment

Imagine a cookie with the flavor combination of almond marzipan and apricot, with a tiny accent of salt, and that is soft, chewy, crunchy—and sublimely addictive—with only a few ingredients and no flour. They are called "horns" in Austria and Germany because they are usually shaped to suggest them, but I make mine rounds, which is simpler. I nicknamed them "Bâtards" because I discovered this recipe at Drew Nieporent's wonderful restaurant Bâtard in New York City. These cookies are nothing short of amazing. You will need to use European marzipan for the silkiest texture and best flavor.

Makes 408 grams dough

Lübeck marzipan (see Baking Pearls, page 34)	250 grams	¾ cup plus 1½ tablespoons
sugar, preferably superfine	125 grams	½ cup plus 2 tablespoons
honey	25 grams	1 tablespoon plus ½ teaspoon (17.5 ml)
1 large egg white	30 grams	2 tablespoons (30 ml)
sliced almonds	100 grams	1 cup
apricot preserves, strained (see Baking Pearls, page 34)	62 grams	3 tablespoons
water	.	¾ teaspoon (3.7 ml)
sea salt, preferably Maldon	.	¼ teaspoon

MISE EN PLACE

■ Up to 1 hour ahead, into the bowl of a stand mixer, weigh or measure the marzipan, sugar, honey, and egg white and cover with plastic wrap.

MAKE THE DOUGH

1. In the stand mixer with the flat beater, mix the marzipan mixture on low speed for 1 to 2 minutes, until all the ingredients are smoothly combined. Scrape the mixture into a small bowl, cover tightly with plastic wrap pressed against the surface, and refrigerate for a minimum of 2 hours, up to 24 hours.

PREHEAT THE OVEN

■ Twenty minutes or longer before baking, set an oven rack at the middle level. Set the oven at 350°F/175°C.

(continued)

You will need to start with 87 grams/about 4½ tablespoons preserves to get 62 grams/ 3 tablespoons strained preserves.

Lübeck marzipan contains a higher percentage of almonds than American brands. If you cannot find Lübeck brand, substitute an equal weight of almond paste (¾ cup plus 2 tablespoons by volume). Do not use American marzipan, which would result in flat puddles instead of chewy cookies.

2. Arrange the sliced almonds on a large plate in a single layer. Have a small bowl of water on the counter to moisten your fingers and palms lightly, which will help prevent the marzipan mixture from sticking.

SHAPE THE COOKIES

3. Weigh or measure twenty-four 1 inch balls (17 grams each) of dough.

4. Roll the balls in the almonds to coat, then press them down into the almonds to flatten to 1½ inches in diameter by ½ inch high.

5. Set the cookies a minimum of 1 inch apart on the pan.

BAKE THE COOKIES

6. Bake for 6 minutes. For even baking, rotate the pan halfway around. Continue baking for 6 to 8 minutes, or until lightly browned and they have only a slight give when pressed in the center.

COOL THE COOKIES

7. Set the pan on a wire rack and let the cookies cool for about for 10 minutes before brushing them with apricot glaze.

GLAZE THE COOKIES

8. In a small microwavable bowl or cup, mix together the strained apricot preserves and water and heat until just beginning to bubble. (Alternatively, heat them in a small saucepan over low heat.)

9. Brush a very thin layer of glaze onto each cookie. You will need only about 2 tablespoons of the glaze. Then sprinkle each with just a tiny bit of salt. Use a thin pancake turner to lift the cookies from the pan onto a serving plate. Allow the cookies to cool for 20 minutes before serving.

STORE AIRTIGHT: room temperature or refrigerated, 1 week. (They will stay soft and chewy.)

Making Marzipan Cookies

Press the dough into the almonds.

Arrange the almonds decoratively on top.

Brush the baked cookies with apricot glaze.

Sprinkle with sea salt.

Scottish Shortbread Cookies

**MAKES TWENTY-FOUR
1½ INCH COOKIES**

OVEN TEMPERATURE:
275°F/135°C

BAKING TIME: 55 to 65
minutes

BAKING EQUIPMENT:
Two 15 by 12 inch cookie
sheets, no preparation
needed or lined with
parchment

This versatile dough, consisting of just butter, sugar, and flour, has the purest taste of butter of all cookies. It can be shaped into traditional wedges (see the Variation, opposite), and also serves as the base for Lemon Butter Squares (page 40). Although not traditional, I find that a pinch of salt elevates and counterpoints the buttery flavor. It is traditional, however, to bake at a very low temperature for a long time, which produces the special tender texture and perfectly even browning.

Makes 355 grams dough

unsalted butter	142 grams	10 tablespoons (1 stick plus 2 tablespoons)
powdered sugar	14 grams	2 tablespoons
granulated sugar	25 grams	2 tablespoons
bleached all-purpose flour	181 grams	1½ cups (lightly spooned into the cup and leveled off)
fine sea salt (optional)	.	a small pinch

MISE EN PLACE

- Thirty minutes ahead, cut the butter into ½ inch cubes. Wrap and refrigerate.

PREHEAT THE OVEN

- Twenty minutes or longer before baking, set oven racks in the upper and lower thirds of the oven. Set the oven at 275°F/135°C.

MAKE THE DOUGH

1. In a food processor, process the powdered and granulated sugars for 1 minute, or until the granulated sugar is very fine.

2. Add the butter and pulse until all the sugar disappears.

3. Add the flour and salt and pulse until incorporated. The dough will be crumbly but will hold together when pinched.

4. Scrape the mixture into a plastic bag and, using your knuckles and the heels of your hands, press it together. Transfer the dough to a large sheet of plastic wrap and use the wrap to knead it lightly just until it holds together.

SHAPE THE COOKIES

5. Measure out scant tablespoons of dough (about 14 grams each). Flatten each piece of dough between the palms of your hands, then roll it into a 1 inch round ball. (This keeps the dough from cracking when pressed flat.)

6. Place each ball, right after rolling it, on one of the cookie sheets and flatten it with the flat bottom of a glass tumbler, lightly moistened with water. Use your fingers to press it gently into a 1½ inch round. The cookies should be at least 1 inch apart.

7. Use the tines of a fork to press ⅜ inch lines around the edges and to prick holes in the centers.

BAKE THE COOKIES

8. Bake for 30 minutes. For even baking, rotate the cookie sheets halfway around and exchange their positions from top to bottom. Continue baking for 25 to 35 minutes, or until pale gold.

COOL THE COOKIES

9. Set the cookie sheets on wire racks. Use a thin pancake turner to lift the cookies onto another wire rack. Cool completely.

STORE AIRTIGHT: room temperature or frozen, 3 months.

(continued)

Variation
SHORTBREAD WEDGES
Makes 8 wedges

Shaping the dough into a giant cookie and cutting it into wedges is another traditional design for shortbread. You can roll the dough into an 8 or 9 inch disc between two sheets of plastic wrap, or line an 8 or 9 inch cake pan with plastic wrap and press the dough evenly into it, then transfer the disc to a parchment-lined cookie sheet. For lovely scalloped edges I use a 9½ by 1 inch high fluted tart pan with a removable bottom, set on a cookie sheet; coat the tart pan with baking spray with flour if not using a nonstick pan. I roll the dough into an 8 inch disc and then press it into the pan using the plastic wrap.

For the traditional decoration, use the tines of a fork to press ¾ inch lines, radiating to resemble sun rays, all around the perimeter of the dough. Prick the rest of the dough all over with the fork or a wooden skewer. This keeps the shortbread even. With the tip of a knife, score the dough into 8 wedges, going almost to the bottom of the dough.

Bake in the middle of the oven, preheated to 300°F/150°C for 50 to 60 minutes, or until pale golden, rotating the pan halfway around after the first 30 minutes. While still hot, cut along the score lines again. Cool completely in the pan set on a wire rack. As soon as it is cool, place the tart pan on top of a canister that is smaller than the bottom opening of the tart pan's outer rim. Press down on both sides of the tart ring. The outer rim should slip away easily. To release the shortbread from the bottom of the pan, carefully slide a long metal spatula underneath and slide it onto a cutting board. If it sticks, heat the bottom of the pan briefly with a towel that has been run under hot water and wrung dry. Use a thin-bladed sharp knife to cut the wedges all the way through.

Making Scottish Shortbread Cookies

Pulse the butter and sugar in a food processor.

Pulse in the flour until crumbly.

Use a plastic bag to knead the dough.

Use plastic wrap to finish kneading the dough until it just holds together.

Flatten the dough balls.

Decorate the cookies with the tines of a fork.

Making Shortbread Wedges

Press the dough evenly into the pan.

Decorate the edge with the tines of a fork.

Score the wedges.

Cut the baked shortbread into wedges.

Lemon Butter Squares

MAKES SIXTEEN 2 INCH SQUARES

OVEN TEMPERATURE: 325°F/160°C for the shortbread; 300°F/150°C for the lemon curd

BAKING TIME: 30 to 40 minutes for the shortbread; 10 minutes for the lemon curd

BAKING EQUIPMENT: One 8 by 2 inch square pan, bottom and two sides lined with a 16 by 8 inch strip of heavy-duty aluminum foil, extending a few inches past the edges of the pan

These classic lemon curd–topped shortbread cookies, cut into bars or squares, are one of the most beloved sweets for any time of year.

CRUST

Dough for Scottish Shortbread Cookies (page 36)	335 grams	1 recipe

PREHEAT THE OVEN

- Twenty minutes or longer before baking, set an oven rack at the middle level. Set the oven at 325°F/160°C.

PRESS THE DOUGH INTO THE PAN

1. Use your fingers to press the dough evenly into the prepared pan. Use a fork to prick the dough all over.

BAKE THE SHORTBREAD

2. Bake for 20 minutes. For even baking, rotate the pan halfway around. Continue baking for 10 to 20 minutes, until the surface is pale golden. The edges may begin to brown lightly. Remove it to a wire rack.

3. Reduce the oven temperature to 300°F/150°C.

LEMON CURD Makes 330 grams/1¼ cups

unsalted butter, softened	57 grams	4 tablespoons (½ stick)
lemon zest, finely grated (about 1 lemon)	4 grams	2 teaspoons, loosely packed
lemon juice, freshly squeezed and strained (about 3 lemons)	95 grams	¼ cup plus 2 tablespoons (89 ml)
5 (to 8) large egg yolks (see Baking Pearls, page 41)	93 grams	¼ cup plus 2 tablespoons (89 ml)
granulated sugar	150 grams	¾ cup
fine sea salt	.	a pinch
powdered sugar, for dusting	18 grams	2 tablespoons

MISE EN PLACE

- Thirty minutes to 1 hour ahead, set the butter on the counter.

- With dish washing liquid, wash the lemons. Rinse, dry, and zest them into a medium bowl (see page xxv). Set a medium-mesh strainer suspended over the bowl.

- Into a 1 cup measure with a spout, weigh or measure the lemon juice.

Briefly baking the lemon curd enables the egg yolks to rebond and will make it possible to cut cleanly.

The ratio of white to yolk in an egg can vary to such a degree that you may need as few as 5 or as many as 8 eggs for this recipe. It is therefore advisable to weigh or measure the separated yolks and add or reduce if needed.

Variation

LIME CURD

Replace the lemon juice and zest with equal amounts of lime. Decrease the granulated sugar to 100 grams/½ cup. If desired, for an attractive pale green color, add a few drops of green liquid food coloring.

■ Into a small heavy saucepan, preferably nonstick, weigh or measure the egg yolks.

MAKE THE LEMON CURD

1. Add the butter and granulated sugar to the egg yolks and whisk until blended.

2. Whisk in the lemon juice and salt.

3. Cook over medium-low heat, stirring constantly with a silicone spatula and scraping the sides of the pan as needed, until thickened to a consistency resembling hollandaise sauce. It should thickly coat the spatula but still be liquid enough to pour. The mixture will change from translucent to opaque and begin to take on a yellow color on the back of the spatula. Do not let it boil or it will curdle. If steam appears, remove the pan briefly from the heat, stirring constantly, to keep the mixture from boiling.

4. When the curd has thickened and pools slightly when a little is dropped back on its surface, pour it immediately into the strainer over the bowl with the lemon zest. Press it through into the bowl.

5. Stir gently to mix in the lemon zest.

6. Pour the hot lemon curd on top of the baked shortbread.

BAKE THE LEMON SQUARES

7. Bake for 10 minutes to set the lemon curd.

COOL THE SQUARES

8. Set the pan on a wire rack and cool completely. Refrigerate for 30 minutes to ensure that the lemon curd is firm enough to cut well.

CUT THE SQUARES

9. Run a small metal spatula between the sides of the pan and the pastry on the two sides without the aluminum foil. Lift out the shortbread by grasping the two ends of the foil and set it on a counter. Use a long sharp knife to cut 16 squares.

10. Dust with powdered sugar shortly before serving.

STORE AIRTIGHT: room temperature, 3 days; refrigerated, not dusted with powdered sugar, 3 weeks.

(continued)

Making Lemon Butter Squares

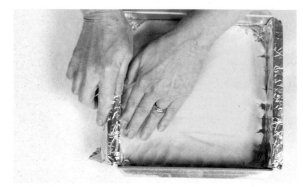

Press the shortbread dough into the pan.

Prick the dough with a fork.

The lemon curd should thickly coat the spatula.

Top the baked shortbread with the lemon curd.

Use the foil to lift out the chilled curd-topped shortbread.

Cut into squares.

Fudgy Pudgy Brownies

MAKES 16 BROWNIES

OVEN TEMPERATURE:
325°F/160°C for the
walnuts; 350°F/175°C
for the brownies

BAKING TIME: 7 minutes
for the walnuts; 30
to 40 minutes for the
brownies

BAKING EQUIPMENT:
One 8 by 2 inch square
baking pan, encircled
with a cake strip (see
Baking Pearl, page 44),
coated with shortening,
lined with two pieces of
crisscrossed parchment
or heavy-duty aluminum
foil (bottom and sides),
extending a few inches
past the edges of the
pan, attached to each
other by a thin coating
of shortening, then
lightly coated with
baking spray with flour

These dense, moist, and fudgy brownies stand up especially well to the slight crunch and assertive flavor of walnuts. The unsweetened chocolate and white chocolate add cocoa butter, which contributes to the brownies' chewy texture and melt-in-the-mouth quality.

unsalted butter	170 grams	12 tablespoons (1½ sticks)
3 large eggs	150 grams	½ cup plus 1½ tablespoons (140 ml)
walnut halves	100 grams	1 cup
fine-quality unsweetened or 99% cacao chocolate	142 grams	5 ounces
white chocolate containing cocoa butter	85 grams	3 ounces
unsweetened alkalized cocoa powder	16 grams	3½ tablespoons (sifted before measuring)
sugar	267 grams	1⅓ cups
pure vanilla extract	.	1½ teaspoons (7.5 ml)
all-purpose flour, either bleached or unbleached	91 grams	¾ cup (lightly spooned into the cup and leveled off)
fine sea salt	.	a pinch

PREHEAT THE OVEN

▪ Twenty minutes or longer before toasting the walnuts, set an oven rack at the middle level. Set the oven at 325°F/160°C.

MISE EN PLACE

▪ About 1 hour ahead, set the butter and eggs on the counter at room temperature (65° to 75°F/19° to 24°C).

▪ Into a 1 cup measure with a spout, weigh or measure the eggs and cover with plastic wrap.

▪ **TOAST AND CHOP THE WALNUTS:** Spread the walnuts evenly on a cookie sheet and bake for about 7 minutes. Stir once or twice to ensure even toasting and prevent overbrowning. Turn the walnuts onto a dish towel and roll and rub them around to loosen the skins. Discard any loose skins and let the nuts cool completely. Chop into coarse pieces.

▪ Chop both chocolates into small pieces.

(continued)

PREHEAT THE OVEN

■ Twenty minutes or longer before baking, set an oven rack at the middle level. Set the oven at 350°F/175°C.

MAKE THE BATTER

1. In the top of a double boiler over hot, not simmering, water (do not let the bottom of the container touch the water), melt the butter and chocolates, stirring often with a silicone spatula. Scrape the melted chocolate mixture into a large bowl.

2. Whisk the cocoa into the melted chocolate mixture, and then the sugar, until incorporated.

3. Whisk in the eggs and vanilla until the mixture becomes thick and glossy.

4. Stir in the flour and salt, just until the flour is moistened.

5. Stir in the walnuts, reaching to the bottom of the bowl, until evenly incorporated.

6. Scrape the batter into the prepared pan and smooth the surface evenly, but mound it slightly in the center, which tends to dip on baking.

BAKE THE BROWNIE

7. Bake for 30 to 40 minutes, or until set to 1 inch from the edges and a toothpick inserted 1 inch from the edge comes out almost clean. (An instant-read thermometer inserted in the center should read about 190°F/88°C.)

COOL AND UNMOLD THE BROWNIE

8. Let the brownie cool in the pan on a wire rack for 10 minutes. Run a small metal spatula between the pan and the foil to ensure that no batter has leaked through and stuck to the sides.

9. Invert the brownie onto a wire rack lined with plastic wrap and lift off the pan. Carefully peel off the foil and reinvert the brownie onto another wire rack. Cool completely.

CUT THE BROWNIE

10. Transfer the brownie to a cutting board. Use a long serrated knife to cut the brownie into 2 inch squares.

STORE AIRTIGHT: room temperature, 1 week; refrigerated, 1 month; frozen, 3 months.

My Best Brownies

MAKES 16 BROWNIES

OVEN TEMPERATURE:
325°F/160°C

BAKING TIME: 7 minutes
for the pecans; 25 to
35 minutes for the
brownies

BAKING EQUIPMENT:
One 8 by 2 inch square
baking pan, encircled
with a cake strip (see
Baking Pearls, page 47),
coated with shortening,
lined with two pieces of
crisscrossed parchment
or aluminum foil
(bottom and sides),
extending a few inches
past the edges of the
pan, attached to each
other by a thin coating
of shortening, then
lightly coated with
baking spray with flour

I have created several recipes for brownies over the years but there are two that I keep returning to as my standard. These are light in texture yet moist and fudgy as they melt in the mouth. If you prefer a cakey brownie, bake it longer, until the brownie springs back when pressed lightly in the center. And if you prefer a much denser and fudgier texture, make the Fudgy Pudgy Brownies (page 43).

unsalted butter	200 grams	14 tablespoons (1¾ sticks)
3 large eggs	150 grams	½ cup plus 1½ tablespoons (140 ml)
full-fat cream cheese, cut into pieces	85 grams	⅓ cup
pecan pieces	113 grams	1 cup
dark chocolate, 60% to 62% cacao	85 grams	3 ounces
unsweetened alkalized cocoa powder	50 grams	⅔ cup (sifted before measuring)
sugar	200 grams	1 cup
pure vanilla extract	.	2 teaspoons (10 ml)
all-purpose flour, either bleached or unbleached	76 grams	½ cup plus 2 tablespoons (lightly spooned into the cup and leveled off)
fine sea salt	.	a pinch

PREHEAT THE OVEN

▪ Twenty minutes or longer before toasting the pecans, set an oven rack at the middle level. Set the oven at 325°F/160°C.

MISE EN PLACE

▪ About 1 hour ahead, set the butter, eggs, and cream cheese on the counter at cool room temperature (65° to 70°F/19° to 21°C).

▪ Into a 1 cup measure with a spout, weigh or measure the eggs and cover them.

▪ **TOAST THE PECANS:** Break the pecans into medium pieces. Spread them evenly on a cookie sheet and bake for about 7 minutes, without letting them brown, to enhance their flavor. Stir once or twice to ensure even toasting. Cool completely.

▪ Chop the chocolate into small pieces.

Baking Pearls

Mixing the batter by hand results in a shinier top crust.

The cake strip keeps the outer edges from getting overbaked and dry.

Make This Recipe Your Own

The pecans can be omitted or replaced with walnuts or other nuts of your choice. They can also be replaced with chocolate chips or chocolate chunks (dark chocolate, milk chocolate, or white chocolate).

To make the brownies more fudgy, serve chilled or frozen.

MAKE THE BATTER

1. In a large bowl over hot, not simmering, water (do not let the bottom of the bowl touch the water), melt the butter and chocolate, stirring often with a silicone spatula. Remove the bowl from the heat source.

2. Whisk the cocoa into the melted chocolate mixture, and then the sugar, until incorporated.

3. Whisk in the eggs and vanilla until the mixture becomes thick and glossy. With a blending fork or wooden spoon, stir and mash in the cream cheese until only small bits remain.

4. Stir in the flour and salt, just until the flour is moistened.

5. Stir in the pecans, reaching to the bottom of the bowl, until evenly incorporated.

6. Scrape the batter into the prepared pan and smooth the surface evenly, but mound it slightly in the center, which tends to dip on baking.

BAKE THE BROWNIE

7. Bake for 25 to 35 minutes, or until the batter has set up to 1 inch from the edge and a toothpick inserted 1 inch from the edge comes out clean. (An instant-read thermometer inserted in the center should read about 190°F/88°C.)

COOL AND UNMOLD THE BROWNIE

8. Let the brownie cool in the pan on a wire rack for 10 minutes. Run a small metal spatula between the pan and the parchment to ensure that no batter has leaked through and stuck to the sides.

9. Invert the brownie onto a wire rack lined with plastic wrap and lift off the pan. Carefully peel off the parchment and reinvert the brownie onto another wire rack. Cool completely.

CUT THE BROWNIE

10. Transfer the brownie to a cutting board. Use a long serrated knife to cut the brownie into 2 inch squares.

STORE AIRTIGHT: room temperature, 1 week; refrigerated, 1 month; frozen, 3 months.

(continued)

Making My Best Brownies

Melt the butter and chocolate together.

Mise en place for the ingredients.

Whisk in the eggs and vanilla.

Mash in the cream cheese.

Mix in the flour and salt until moistened.

Mix in the chopped pecans.

Spread the batter in the pan.

Remove the parchment "sling" from the baked brownie.

Cut the brownies.

Holiday Cookies

**MAKES TWENTY-FOUR
3 INCH COOKIES**

OVEN TEMPERATURE:
350°F/175°C

BAKING TIME: 8 to 12
minutes for each of two
batches

BAKING EQUIPMENT:
Two 15 by 12 inch cookie
sheets, no preparation
needed, or lined with
parchment

Cookie cutters

Optional: a wooden
skewer

This is the ideal dough for rolled decorative cookies for gifting and hanging. It is strong enough to roll thin but also crisp, tender, and flavorful, and keeps well at room temperature.

Makes 340 grams dough

unsalted butter	85 grams	6 tablespoons (¾ stick)
bleached all-purpose flour	160 grams	1⅓ cups (lightly spooned into the cup and leveled off)
fine sea salt	.	⅛ teaspoon
lemon zest, finely grated	3 grams	1½ teaspoons, loosely packed
½ large egg	25 grams	1½ tablespoons (22.5 ml)
pure vanilla extract	.	½ teaspoon (2.5 ml)
sugar	75 grams	¼ cup plus 2 tablespoons

MISE EN PLACE

- Thirty minutes ahead, cut the butter into ½ inch cubes. Wrap and refrigerate.

- In a small bowl, whisk together the flour and salt.

- With dish washing liquid, wash the lemon. Rinse, dry, and zest it into a small bowl (see page xxv).

- Into a 1 cup measure with a spout, weigh or measure the egg. Add the vanilla.

MAKE THE DOUGH

1. In a food processor, process the sugar with the lemon zest until very fine.

2. Add the butter and pulse until all the sugar disappears. Scrape the sides of the bowl as needed.

3. With the motor running, add the egg mixture and process until uniform. Scrape the sides of the bowl as needed.

4. Add the flour mixture and pulse just until the dough begins to clump together. Pinch a little of the dough and if it doesn't hold together, pulse in a few drops of water.

5. Scrape the dough onto a sheet of plastic wrap. Use it to knead the dough together. Wrap the dough in the plastic wrap and flatten it into a thick disc.

6. Refrigerate for at least 2 hours. If refrigerating for longer than 3 hours, you will need to allow it to sit at room temperature for a few minutes to soften enough for rolling.

Baking Pearls

Rolling the dough with plastic wrap on top prevents cracking.

If the dough softens, refrigerate the cut cookies before lifting them off the rolling surface. If using a dough mat, set it first on a cookie sheet. If your refrigerator is too small, roll smaller batches on plastic wrap and slide each onto a cookie sheet of the appropriate size.

Make This Recipe Your Own

TEMPERA FOOD COLORING

This method of painting dates back to ancient Egypt. It works brilliantly for cookies, as the color magically deepens and brightens on baking. You will need about 2 large egg yolks/37 grams/7 teaspoons/ 35 ml for 5 colors. Put about 1 teaspoon/5 ml egg yolk into each of 5 egg shells set in egg cups, or put the egg yolk in small bowls. Mix in the following liquid colors from the color chart below:

Colors using liquid food color
RED: ½ teaspoon (2.5 ml)
GREEN: ¼ teaspoon (1.2 ml)
YELLOW: ½ teaspoon (2.5 ml)
BLUE: ¼ teaspoon (1.2 ml)
BLACK:
    Green: 1½ teaspoons (7.5 ml)
    Red: 1½ teaspoons (7.5 ml)
    Blue: 5 drops

Use a clean small paintbrush to paint the cookies before baking.

PREHEAT THE OVEN

■ Twenty minutes or longer before baking, set an oven rack at the middle level. Set the oven at 350°F/175°C.

ROLL THE DOUGH AND CUT THE COOKIES

7. Set the dough on a lightly floured dough mat or sheet of plastic wrap. Lightly flour the dough and cover it with plastic wrap. Roll the dough ⅛ inch thick.

8. Before cutting the first cookie, run a small ball of dough along the edges of the cutter so that the flour will adhere. Dip the cutter in flour every few cuts to prevent sticking. (See Solutions for Possible Problems, page 2.) Cut out the cookies and use a small metal spatula to transfer them to a cookie sheet, 1 inch apart.

9. To paint the cookies with edible tempera color before baking, see Make This Recipe Your Own, left. Royal Icing decorations (page 355) can be added after baking and cooling (see Gingerbread Folks, page 53). If you are planning to hang the cookies, make small holes with the blunt end of a wooden skewer.

10. Gather up and press together the scraps to reroll. Wrap and refrigerate.

BAKE THE COOKIES

11. Bake the first sheet of cookies for 5 minutes. If you have made holes and they become too small as the dough bakes, set the cookie sheet on a wire rack and reopen them with the end of the wooden skewer. For even baking, rotate the cookie sheet halfway around. Continue baking for 3 to 7 minutes, or until pale gold and the edges deepen slightly in color.

12. While the first batch is baking, roll and cut the scraps to make the second batch.

COOL THE COOKIES

13. Set the cookie sheet on a wire rack and use a thin pancake turner to lift them onto another wire rack to cool completely.

14. Bake and cool the second batch.

STORE AIRTIGHT: room temperature, 3 months.

(continued)

Making Holiday Cookies

Roll the dough ⅛ inch thick.

Prep the cookie cutter with a little bit of dough before cutting the first cookie so the flour will adhere.

Dip the cookie cutter in flour.

Cut out the cookies.

Paint the unbaked cookies.

Adjust the consistency of the royal icing as needed.

Paint baked cookies with royal icing.

Sprinkle the iced cookies with edible glitter.

Gingerbread Folks

**MAKES EIGHTEEN
5 BY 3 INCH COOKIES**

OVEN TEMPERATURE:
350°F/175°C

BAKING TIME: 10 to 12
minutes for each of two
batches

BAKING EQUIPMENT:
Two 15 by 12 inch cookie
sheets, preferably
nonstick, or lightly
coated with nonstick
cooking spray

Gingerbread man and
woman cookie cutters,
5 inches high by about
3 inches wide

A disposable pastry bag
and small round piping
tip

Optional: a wooden
skewer.

Gingerbread men and women cookies hanging from the tree or sitting on the mantel are a charming holiday tradition. Ginger is not only an appealing spicy flavor, it serves as a great preservative. Of course, the dough can be cut into any desired shape and decorated with royal icing and candies.

Makes 490 grams dough

unsalted butter	85 grams	6 tablespoons (¾ stick)
½ large egg	25 grams	1½ tablespoons (22.5 ml)
light molasses, preferably Grandma's	80 grams	¼ cup (59 ml)
bleached all-purpose flour	212 grams	1¾ cups (lightly spooned into the cup and leveled off)
baking soda	2.7 grams	½ teaspoon
fine sea salt	.	⅛ teaspoon
ground ginger	2.2 grams	1 teaspoon
ground cinnamon	.	½ teaspoon
nutmeg, freshly grated	.	¼ teaspoon
ground cloves	.	⅛ teaspoon
dark brown sugar, preferably dark Muscovado	91 grams	⅓ cup plus 1 tablespoon, firmly packed
Royal Icing (page 355), for decoration	530 grams	2¼ cups
décor: raisins, currants, and/or candies	.	.

MISE EN PLACE

- Thirty minutes ahead, cut the butter into ½ inch cubes. Wrap and refrigerate.

- Into a 1 cup measure with a spout, weigh or measure the egg and cover.

- Lightly coat another 1 cup measure with a spout with nonstick cooking spray, weigh or measure the molasses into it, and cover.

- Into a medium bowl, sift together the flour, baking soda, salt, ginger, cinnamon, nutmeg, and cloves. Whisk to mix evenly.

MAKE THE DOUGH

1. In a food processor, process the brown sugar until very fine.

(continued)

Make This Recipe Your Own

If you enjoy thicker, softer cookies, roll the dough ¼ inch thick and bake just until they are set but still slightly soft when gently pressed with a fingertip, about 8 minutes.

2. Add the butter and pulse until the mixture begins to clean the sides of the bowl.

3. Add the molasses and egg and process until smoothly incorporated. Scrape the sides of the bowl as needed.

4. Add the flour mixture and pulse just until the dough begins to clump together.

CHILL THE DOUGH

5. Scrape the dough onto a sheet of plastic wrap and use the wrap to press the dough together to form a ½ inch thick disc. Wrap it with plastic wrap and refrigerate for a minimum of 2 hours, up to overnight.

PREHEAT THE OVEN

■ Twenty minutes or longer before baking, set an oven rack at the middle level. Set the oven at 350°F/175°C.

ROLL THE DOUGH AND CUT THE COOKIES

6. Set the dough on a well-floured dough mat or sheet of plastic wrap. Lightly flour the dough and cover it with plastic wrap. Roll the dough ⅛ inch thick.

7. Use cookie cutters to cut out the shapes. Dip the cutters in flour every few cuts to prevent sticking. Gently brush off any flour on top of the dough. Gather up and press together the scraps to reroll. Wrap and refrigerate the scraps until firm.

8. With a small offset metal spatula or pancake turner, lift the cut dough onto a cookie sheet, placing the cutouts about 1 inch apart. If planning to hang the cookies, use the blunt end of a wooden skewer to make a hole at the top of each cookie.

BAKE THE COOKIES

9. Bake for 5 minutes. If the holes become too small as the dough bakes, set the cookie sheet on a wire rack and reopen them with the end of the wooden skewer. For even baking, rotate the cookie sheet halfway around. Continue baking for 5 to 7 minutes, or until firm to the touch and just beginning to color around the edges.

COOL THE COOKIES

10. Set the cookie sheet on a wire rack and use a thin pancake turner to lift the cookies onto another wire rack to cool completely.

11. Reroll the scraps to make the second batch; cut, bake, and let cool.

DECORATE THE COOKIES

12. Use royal icing to attach decorative elements such as pieces of raisins, currants, or cinnamon red hots or other candy to the dough. The royal icing can be piped onto the cookies for attractive details. If necessary, use a lightly moistened brush to correct imperfections.

STORE AIRTIGHT: room temperature, 3 months; frozen, 6 months.

Making Gingerbread Folks

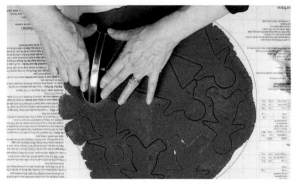

Cut out shapes from the rolled dough.

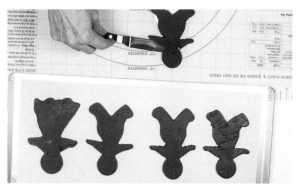

Transfer the cut dough to the prepared cookie sheet.

To hang the cookies, make a hole at the top.

Decorate the baked cookies with royal icing and candies.

Date Nut Roll Cookies

MAKES TWENTY-EIGHT 2¼ BY 2¾ INCH OVAL COOKIES

OVEN TEMPERATURE: 375°F/190°C

BAKING TIME: 12 to 16 minutes for each of two batches

PLAN AHEAD: The filled dough log needs to be frozen for a minimum of 3 hours before cutting and baking.

BAKING EQUIPMENT: Two 15 by 12 inch cookie sheets, nonstick or lightly coated with nonstick cooking spray

My dear friend Sally Longo contributed these special cookies. This treasured family recipe was given to her years ago by her Aunt Evelyn. The cookie dough is rolled around a delicious date nut citrus filling. The cookies are crisp and at the same time moist and chewy, thanks to the dates.

DOUGH Makes 275 grams

unsalted butter	57 grams	4 tablespoons (½ stick)
½ large egg	25 grams	1½ tablespoons (22.5 ml)
bleached all-purpose flour	121 grams	1 cup (lightly spooned into the cup and leveled off)
light brown sugar, preferably light Muscovado	54 grams	¼ cup, firmly packed
baking powder	1.1 grams	¼ teaspoon
baking soda	1.3 grams	¼ teaspoon
fine sea salt	.	a pinch
milk	8 grams	1½ teaspoons (7.5 ml)
pure vanilla extract	.	1½ teaspoons (7.5 ml)

MISE EN PLACE

▪ About 1 hour ahead, set the butter and egg on the counter at room temperature (65° to 75°F/19° to 24°C).

MAKE THE DOUGH

1. In the bowl of a stand mixer fitted with the flat beater, combine the butter, egg, flour, brown sugar, baking powder, baking soda, salt, milk, and vanilla. Beat on medium speed for 1 minute, or until smooth and evenly incorporated.

2. Scrape the dough onto a large piece of plastic wrap. Knead it lightly just until it comes together smoothly and flatten it to form a rectangle. Cover with another large piece of plastic wrap. Roll the dough into a 12 by 9 inch rectangle, about ¹⁄₁₆ inch thick. If the dough softens, slip it onto a cookie sheet and refrigerate it until firm enough to roll. Press along the side edges of the plastic wrap to seal in the dough.

3. Slide a cookie sheet or cutting board under the dough and refrigerate for a minimum of 2 hours, up to overnight. (Alternatively, set it in the freezer until firm, and then refrigerate it until ready spread the filling.)

FILLING

walnut or pecan halves	50 grams	½ cup
pitted dates, about 20	142 grams	1 cup plus 2 tablespoons
granulated sugar	50 grams	¼ cup
orange zest, finely grated (see Baking Pearl, page 58)	2 grams	1 teaspoon, loosely packed
orange juice, freshly squeezed	60 grams	¼ cup (59 ml)

MAKE THE FILLING

4. Chop the nuts medium fine.

5. Cut the dates into halves or thirds and place them in a food processor. Add the granulated sugar and process the dates until finely chopped. (Alternatively, chop the dates using a sharp knife that has been lightly coated with nonstick cooking spray.)

6. Into a small saucepan, place the dates and sugar, and the orange zest and juice. Heat to boiling over medium heat, stirring occasionally. Reduce the heat to a simmer and cook for about 3 minutes, or until most of the liquid has been absorbed.

7. Stir in the chopped nuts and let the filling cool completely. The filling should be a jam-like consistency. If necessary, add a small amount of orange juice to soften it to spreadable consistency.

MAKE THE DOUGH LOG

8. Slip the dough from the cookie sheet onto the counter so that one of the shorter sides faces you. Peel off the top sheet of plastic wrap and set it back onto the dough. Using the bottom sheet of plastic wrap, flip the dough over and peel off the sheet of plastic wrap that is now on top.

9. Use a small offset spatula to spread the filling evenly over the dough, going almost all the way to the edges.

10. Starting at one of the shorter sides and using the plastic wrap to assist in lifting the dough, tightly roll up the dough. The dough log will be about 9½ inches long by 2 inches in diameter.

11. Divide the dough log into two equal lengths. Cover each piece of dough tightly with plastic wrap. Freeze for at least 3 hours, up to 3 months; to maintain the round shape, set the logs so that they stand up on one end.

PREHEAT THE OVEN

■ Thirty minutes or longer before baking, set an oven rack at the middle level. Set the oven at 375°F/190°C.

CUT THE DOUGH INTO COOKIES

12. Remove one frozen dough log from the freezer and place it on a cutting board. Use a sharp knife to cut the roll in half. Because the dough softens very quickly, wrap one of the halves in plastic wrap and return it to the freezer.

(continued)

13. Mark the log into 1 inch long sections. Use the marks as a guide to slice each section into ⅓ inch thick discs; you should end up with 14 slices. While cutting the dough, the log will start to flatten. This creates an attractive oval shape but if you prefer a round shape, simply roll it lightly after making each slice. Repeat with the second log.

14. Set the dough slices 1½ inches apart on a cookie sheet. Smooth any rough edges with a small metal spatula.

BAKE THE COOKIES

15. Bake for 7 minutes. For even baking, rotate the cookie sheet half way around. Continue baking for 5 to 9 minutes, or until lightly browned and puffed.

COOL THE COOKIES

16. Set the cookie sheet on a wire rack and use a thin pancake turner to lift the cookies onto another wire rack. Cool completely.

17. While the first batch of cookies is baking, cut the second dough log and place the cookies on a cookie sheet. Bake after the first batch is removed from the oven.

STORE AIRTIGHT: room temperature, 1 month; frozen, 3 months.

Making Date Nut Roll Cookies

The finished dough.

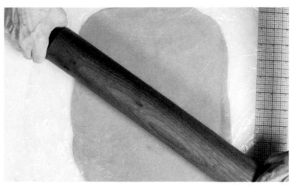

Roll the dough into a 12 by 9 inch rectangle.

Evenly spread the filling over the dough.

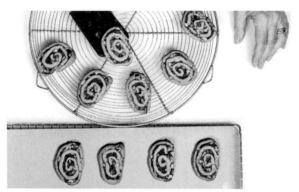

Roll up the dough.

Slice the dough log into discs.

Transfer the baked cookies to a wire rack to cool.

Raspberry Almond Sandwich Cookies

MAKES SIXTEEN 2 INCH ROUND SANDWICH COOKIES

OVEN TEMPERATURE: 375°F/190°C

BAKING TIME: 5 minutes for the almonds; 8 to 10 minutes for the cookies for each of three or four batches

PLAN AHEAD: Fill the cookies the day of serving so that they remain crisp.

BAKING EQUIPMENT: Two 15 by 12 inch cookie sheets, preferably nonstick or lined with parchment
A 2¼ inch scalloped cutter
A ¾ inch plain cookie cutter or (#9) pastry tube

Almond and raspberry have a compelling flavor synergy. These little cookies are delicate and utterly delicious.

Makes 270 grams dough

unblanched sliced almonds	15 grams	2 tablespoons plus 1 teaspoon
unsalted butter	113 grams	8 tablespoons (1 stick)
powdered sugar	29 grams	¼ cup (sifted into the cup and leveled off)
fine sea salt	.	⅛ teaspoon
pure almond extract	.	½ teaspoon (2.5 ml)
pure vanilla extract	.	½ teaspoon (2.5 ml)
bleached all-purpose flour	113 grams	1 cup (lightly spooned into the cup and leveled off) minus 1 tablespoon
raspberry jam, preferably seedless	78 grams	¼ cup

PREHEAT THE OVEN

■ Thirty minutes or longer before toasting the almonds, set an oven rack at the middle level. Set the oven at 375°F/190°C.

MISE EN PLACE

■ **TOAST THE ALMONDS:** Spread the almonds evenly on a cookie sheet and bake for about 5 minutes, or until pale gold. Allow them to cool completely.

■ Thirty minutes to 1 hour ahead, cut the butter into 8 pieces and set it on the counter.

MAKE THE DOUGH

1. In a food processor, process the almonds with the powdered sugar and salt until powder fine.

2. With the motor running, add the butter, 1 piece at a time. Process until smooth and creamy, scraping down the sides as needed.

3. Pulse in the almond and vanilla extracts.

4. Pulse in the flour just until the dough starts to hold together in clumps, scraping down the sides of the bowl as needed.

Baking Pearls

Wondra flour works wonderfully to prevent sticking when rolling out cookie dough. Don't be afraid to add extra flour during rolling, as the cookies will still be very tender.

Wilton makes a seven piece cutter set designed to make windows for sandwich cookies, called "Linzer Cut Outs." It has five different center shapes that can be inserted into the cutter to make perfectly centered cutouts. As it is ¼ inch smaller, you will get a few extra cookies.

If the dough softens after cutting the cookies, cover and refrigerate before lifting them off the rolling surface so that they keep their shape.

5. Scrape the dough into a bowl and refrigerate it, covered, for a minimum of 2 hours, up to overnight.

ROLL THE DOUGH AND CUT THE COOKIES

6. This fragile dough softens quickly, so work with only a small amount at a time, keeping the rest refrigerated. Lightly knead a piece of the dough until it is malleable but still well chilled.

7. Set the dough on a lightly floured dough mat or sheet of plastic wrap. Lightly flour the dough and roll the dough ⅛ inch thick. From time to time, slide the dough to make sure it is not sticking.

8. Cut out the cookies and use a small metal spatula to transfer them to a cookie sheet, 1 inch apart. Dip the cutter in flour every few cuts to prevent sticking.

9. Gather up and press together the scraps to reroll. Wrap and refrigerate.

10. Cut round windows in the centers of half the cookies.

BAKE THE COOKIES

11. Bake for 5 minutes. For even baking, rotate the cookie sheet halfway around. Continue baking for 3 to 5 minutes, or until lightly browned.

COOL THE COOKIES

12. Set the cookie sheet on a wire rack and use a thin pancake turner to lift the cookies onto another wire rack to cool completely.

13. While each batch of cookies is baking, roll and cut the dough for the next batch. After the last batch is cut, knead together all the scraps and reroll, cut, and bake them.

FILL THE COOKIES

14. Use a small offset spatula or butter knife to spread the bottoms of the cookie halves without the cutouts with a thin layer of the jam, and set the second cookies with the cutouts on top, bottom sides down, to create the sandwiches.

STORE FILLED, UNCOVERED: room temperature, 1 day.
UNFILLED, AIRTIGHT: room temperature, 2 months; frozen, 6 months.

(continued)

Making Raspberry Almond Sandwich Cookies

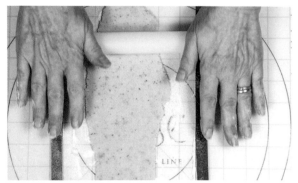

Roll out pieces of the dough.

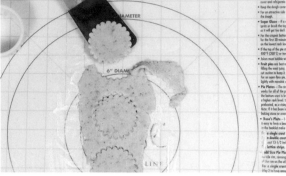

Cut out the cookies and lift them onto the cookie sheet.

Cut out the centers for the tops.

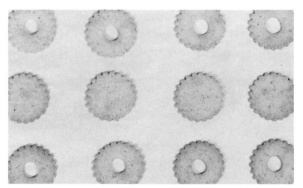

Bake until lightly browned.

Chocolate Wafers

**MAKES TWENTY-SIX
2 INCH SQUARE WAFERS**

OVEN TEMPERATURE:
350°F/175°C

BAKING TIME: 16 to 20 minutes for each of two batches

PLAN AHEAD: Make the dough a minimum of 4 hours before rolling it.

BAKING EQUIPMENT:
Two 15 by 12 inch cookie sheets, lined with parchment

These cookies are wonderful to use for a crumb crust (page 239) or bourbon balls (page 65), but are also crisp, chocolaty, and delicious eaten just as cookies.

Makes 370 grams dough

unsalted butter	43 grams	3 tablespoons
1½ large egg whites	45 grams	3 tablespoons (45 ml)
bleached all-purpose flour	86 grams	⅔ cup (lightly spooned into the cup and leveled off) plus 2 teaspoons
unsweetened alkalized cocoa powder	42 grams	½ cup plus 1 tablespoon (sifted before measuring)
fine sea salt	.	⅛ teaspoon
light brown sugar, preferably light Muscovado	81 grams	¼ cup plus 2 tablespoons, firmly packed
granulated sugar	75 grams	¼ cup plus 2 tablespoons
pure vanilla extract	.	¾ teaspoon (3.7 ml)

MISE EN PLACE

▪ About 1 hour ahead, set the butter on the counter at room temperature (65° to 75°F/19° to 24°C), and into a 1 cup glass measure with a spout, weigh or measure the egg whites.

▪ In a medium bowl, whisk together the flour, cocoa, and salt.

MAKE THE DOUGH

1. In the bowl of a stand mixer fitted with the flat beater, beat the brown and granulated sugars, the butter, and vanilla on medium speed until well mixed and lightened in color, about 5 minutes, scraping the bowl occasionally.

2. Gradually add the egg whites and beat until smoothly incorporated, about 30 seconds. Scrape down the sides of the bowl.

3. Add the flour mixture. Mix on low speed for 30 seconds, until incorporated.

4. Scrape the dough onto a piece of plastic wrap and use the plastic wrap to press it into a rectangle. Divide the dough in half (185 grams each). Wrap each piece of dough in plastic wrap and set them on a small cookie sheet.

5. Refrigerate the dough until it is firm, about 4 hours or overnight. The dough should be firm enough to roll but still pliant.

(continued)

PREHEAT THE OVEN

- Twenty minutes or longer before baking, set an oven rack at the middle level. Set the oven at 350°F/175°C.

ROLL THE DOUGH

6. Set one piece of dough on a lightly floured sheet of plastic wrap. Lightly flour the dough and cover it with a second sheet of plastic wrap. Roll the dough ¼ inch thick, using a bench scraper butted up against the sides to make it into an even 10 by 6 inch rectangle. To make cutting easier, slide the shaped dough on the plastic wrap onto a cookie sheet and set it in the freezer for about 5 minutes.

7. With a pizza wheel or chef's knife, cut the dough into roughly 2 inch squares. Any irregular shapes can be baked alongside the squares.

8. Use a thin pancake turner to set the dough squares a minimum of 1 inch apart on a cookie sheet. With a fork, pierce each one several times to prevent excess puffing.

BAKE THE WAFERS

9. Bake the wafers for 8 minutes. For even baking, rotate the cookie sheet halfway around. Continue baking for 8 to 12 minutes, or until the wafers are firm and slightly puffed, but still a little soft.

10. While the first batch is baking, roll and cut the wafers for the second batch.

COOL THE WAFERS

11. Set the cookie sheet on a wire rack and let the wafers cool completely.

12. Bake and cool the second batch of wafers.

STORE AIRTIGHT: room temperature, 7 days; refrigerated, 2 weeks; frozen, 3 months.

Making Chocolate Wafers

Cut the dough and transfer the squares to the cookie sheet.

The baked wafers.

Bourbon Balls

**MAKES TWENTY-TWO
1¼ INCH BALLS**

PLAN AHEAD: Make a
minimum of 1 day, up to
6 weeks, ahead.

*These no-bake cookies are a holiday favorite of anyone who loves
the flavor of bourbon. I perfected them many years ago for my book
Rose's Christmas Cookies, and the recipe has become a treasured
part of many people's annual tradition. The homemade chocolate
wafers are truly worth the extra effort.*

Makes 450 grams dough

unsalted butter	28 grams	2 tablespoons
chocolate wafers, preferably homemade (page 63)	192 grams	6.7 ounces
pecan halves	75 grams	¾ cup
powdered sugar	72 grams	½ cup plus 2 tablespoons (lightly spooned into the cup and leveled off)
unsweetened alkalized cocoa powder	25 grams	⅓ cup
corn syrup	42 grams	2 tablespoons (30 ml)
bourbon, preferably Maker's Mark	22 to 37 grams	1½ to 2½ tablespoons (22.5 to 37.5 ml)
granulated sugar, for coating the balls	75 grams	¼ cup plus 2 tablespoons

MISE EN PLACE

▪ About 1 hour ahead, set the butter on the counter at room temperature (65°
to 75°F/19° to 24°C).

▪ If using the food processor method, in several batches, pulverize the wafers
into fine crumbs. Empty them into a large bowl.

▪ If using the hand method, finely grate the pecans. Smash the wafers into fine
crumbs by placing them in a reclosable freezer bag and rolling with a rolling pin.
Empty the crumbs into a large bowl.

MAKE THE DOUGH

FOOD PROCESSOR METHOD

1. Process the pecans with the powdered sugar and cocoa until finely ground.

2. Cut the butter into 3 pieces and add it and the corn syrup to the nut mixture.
Process until combined.

(continued)

Make This Recipe Your Own

Bourbon gives the best flavor. However, other whiskeys can be substituted.

A mixture of 30 grams/ 2 tablespoons/30 ml water and 1½ teaspoons /7.5 ml pure vanilla extract can be substituted for the bourbon.

3. Add this mixture to the cookie crumbs and, with your fingers or a wooden spoon, mix until evenly incorporated.

HAND METHOD

1. Sift the powdered sugar and cocoa into the bowl with the cookie crumbs.

2. Add the butter, pecans, and corn syrup.

3. With a wooden spoon, stir until uniform in consistency.

MIX IN THE BOURBON

4. Add 1½ tablespoons/22.5 ml of the bourbon to the cookie crumb mixture. With a wooden spoon, stir the mixture until it is uniform in consistency and begins to clean the bowl. Add a teaspoon at a time of the remaining bourbon if the mixture is too dry to hold together.

5. Let the mixture sit for 30 minutes to absorb evenly. Add more bourbon if needed.

ROLL THE BOURBON BALLS AND COAT WITH SUGAR

6. Scoop out level tablespoons (20 grams each) of the mixture to press and roll between the palms of your hands to shape into 1¼ inch balls.

7. Place the granulated sugar in a small bowl. Add one ball at a time and roll it around in the sugar. The coating is most attractive when dipped three times. Redip after the sugar starts to disappear.

8. Place the balls in a paper towel– or crumpled parchment–lined airtight container.

STORE AIRTIGHT: room temperature, 6 weeks.

Making Bourbon Balls

Mise en place for the ingredients.

Check to see if the mixture holds together.

Press the mixture together to form balls.

Coat the balls in sugar.

Lisa Yockelson's Deeply Chocolate Biscotti

MAKES TWENTY-FOUR
4¼ BY ¾ BY 1¼ INCH
HIGH COOKIES

OVEN TEMPERATURE:
350°F/175°C, then
275°F/135°C

BAKING TIME: 35 to 40
minutes, then about
20 minutes

BAKING EQUIPMENT:
One 15 by 12 inch
cookie sheet, lined with
parchment held in place
with 4 pieces of masking
tape (remove before
baking). (If desired,
draw two 10 inch by
2½ inch rectangles,
about 4 inches apart,
on the underside of the
parchment to serve as
guides.)

Lisa is a very special friend and highly respected colleague who has been included in every one of my recent books, either as the contributor of a special recipe or as the recipient of one that I dedicated to her. These are the best biscotti I've ever tasted. They are marvelously crunchy and are delicious eaten on their own or dipped into coffee or milk. I am thrilled to share this unique recipe.

Makes 1100 grams dough

unsalted butter	113 grams	8 tablespoons (1 stick)
2 large eggs	100 grams	⅓ cup plus 1 tablespoon (94 ml)
1 egg yolk	13 grams	2½ teaspoons (12.5 ml)
strong coffee, freshly brewed	20 grams	4 teaspoons (20 ml)
fine-quality unsweetened or 99% cacao chocolate, chopped	20 grams	0.7 ounce
bleached all-purpose flour	290 grams	2⅓ cups (lightly spooned into the cup and leveled off) plus 1 tablespoon
unsweetened alkalized cocoa powder	56 grams	¾ cup (sifted before measuring)
cornstarch	6 grams	2 teaspoons
baking powder	4.5 grams	1 teaspoon
fine sea salt	4 grams	¾ teaspoon
sugar, preferably superfine	200 grams	1 cup
pure vanilla extract	.	2½ teaspoons (12.5 ml)
dark chocolate chips, 55% to 63% cacao	283 grams	1⅔ cups (10 ounces)
granulated sugar, for topping the dough	37 grams	3 tablespoons

PREHEAT THE OVEN

▪ Twenty minutes or longer before baking, set an oven rack at the middle level. Set the oven at 350°F/175°C.

Baking Pearls

Use your favorite chocolate chips. The chocolate chips add flavor and a contrast of texture to the biscotti. You can vary the contrast in the texture depending on the size of the chocolate chips.

If you have a convection option for your oven, it works especially well to dry the biscotti. Most convection ovens require lowering the temperature by 25°F/15°C.

MISE EN PLACE

■ About 1 hour ahead, set the butter and eggs on the counter at room temperature (65° to 75°F/19° to 24°C).

■ Into a 1 cup measure with a spout, weigh or measure the eggs and egg yolk. Whisk lightly and cover with plastic wrap.

■ Into a small bowl, weigh or measure the hot coffee, cover with plastic wrap, and cool to room temperature.

■ MELT THE CHOCOLATE: About 30 minutes before baking, melt the chopped chocolate: In a small microwavable bowl, stirring with a silicone spatula every 15 seconds, heat the chocolate in the microwave until almost completely melted. (Alternatively, melt the chocolate in the top of a double boiler over hot, not simmering water—do not let the bottom of the container touch the water—stirring often with a silicone spatula.) Remove the chocolate from the heat source and stir until fully melted. Let it cool until it is no longer warm to the touch but still fluid (80° to 85°F/27° to 29°C).

■ In a medium bowl, whisk together the flour, cocoa, cornstarch, baking powder, and salt. Sift the flour mixture onto a sheet of parchment.

MAKE THE DOUGH

1. In the bowl of a stand mixer fitted with the flat beater, beat the butter on medium speed until smooth and creamy, about 2 minutes.

2. With the mixer on, add the sugar in 3 parts, beating for 45 seconds after each addition. Scrape down the sides of the bowl.

3. With the mixer on medium-low speed, gradually add the eggs and egg yolk and beat just until incorporated. Scrape down the sides of the bowl. The mixture will not be smooth.

4. Add the coffee, melted chocolate, and vanilla and beat for about 30 seconds. Scrape down the sides of the bowl.

5. Add half the sifted flour mixture and mix on low speed just until the flour is absorbed. Add the remaining flour mixture together with the chocolate chips and mix just until the flour is absorbed.

6. Scrape the dough into 2 rough strips, 550 grams each, on the lined cookie sheet.

7. Lightly wet your fingers and shape each strip evenly into a 10 by 2½ inch rectangle on the parchment (if you drew rectangles on the parchment, use them as a guide). The dough will be about 1 inch high. (Alternatively, cover each strip with plastic wrap. Use your fingers or a rolling pin to smooth and lengthen the tops, and a bench scraper, butted up against the sides, to shape into even rectangles. Formed in this way the biscotti will be a little lower and wider in shape when baked.) Remove the masking tape.

8. Heavily sprinkle the top of each rectangle with the granulated sugar.

(continued)

BAKE THE RECTANGLES

9. Bake the rectangles for 20 minutes. For even baking, rotate the cookie sheet halfway around. Continue baking for 15 to 20 minutes, or until set, baked through, and a wooden skewer comes out clean.

10. Reduce the oven temperature to 275°F/135°C.

COOL THE RECTANGLES

11. Set the cookie sheet on a wire rack and let the rectangles cool for 10 minutes.

CUT THE BISCOTTI

12. Slip an offset spatula underneath the baked rectangles to loosen them from the parchment. Carefully transfer one rectangle to a cutting board.

13. Using a serrated knife, slice the rectangle on an angle into 12 cookies, slightly under 1 inch wide. Return them, cut side down, to the cookie sheet.

14. Repeat with the second rectangle.

BAKE THE BISCOTTI

15. Bake the cookies for 20 minutes, or until they are firm and dry, turning them over once or twice during the baking time. The cut surfaces of the cookies should appear dry on both sides. (Avoid overbaking so as not to compromise the flavor.)

COOL THE BISCOTTI

16. Let the biscotti sit on the cookie sheet on a wire rack for 5 minutes. Use tongs to transfer the biscotti carefully to a wire rack. Cool completely. Biscotti keep well but have the fullest flavor within the first 3 days after baking.

STORE AIRTIGHT: room temperature, 3 weeks; frozen, 3 months.

Making Deeply Chocolate Biscotti

The consistency of the finished dough.

Form two rectangles of dough.

Heavily coat the dough with sugar.

Bake the dough rectangles.

Cut the rectangles at an angle.

The finished biscotti.

Chocolate Butterscotch Toffee

MAKES 454 GRAMS/ 1 POUND

OVEN TEMPERATURE: 350°F/175°C

BAKING TIME: 7 to 9 minutes for the almonds

BAKING EQUIPMENT: One Silpat sheet set on a 17¼ by 12¼ by 1 inch half-sheet pan, or a nonstick or buttered 15 by 12 inch cookie sheet, set near the cooktop

An instant-read thermometer

This irresistible combination of chocolate, caramel, and almonds is a time-honored crowd pleaser. The molasses in the brown sugar contributes the butterscotch flavor. The baking soda is the secret to this toffee's perfectly crunchy and not sticky texture. You can gauge the depth of the color of the sugar syrup by how it appears on the spatula but here is an instance where an instant-read thermometer really shines and will help to produce the ideal flavor and texture.

sliced almonds, preferably blanched	175 grams	1¾ cups, *divided*
unsalted butter	113 grams	8 tablespoons (1 stick)
dark chocolate, 53% to 70% cacao, chopped	170 grams	6 ounces
light Muscovado or dark brown sugar	270 grams	1¼ cups, firmly packed
corn syrup	82 grams	¼ cup (59 ml)
water	30 grams	2 tablespoons (30 ml)
pure vanilla extract	.	1 teaspoon (5 ml)
baking soda	2.7 grams	½ teaspoon

PREHEAT THE OVEN

▪ Twenty minutes or longer before toasting the almonds, set an oven rack at the middle level. Set the oven at 350°F/175°C.

MISE EN PLACE

▪ About 1 hour ahead, set the butter on the counter at room temperature (65° to 75°F/19° to 24°C).

▪ **TOAST THE ALMONDS:** Spread the almonds evenly on a cookie sheet and bake for 7 to 9 minutes, or until medium gold. Stir a few times to ensure even toasting and prevent overbrowning. Allow them to cool completely.

▪ In a food processor, process the nuts until medium-fine. Remove the blade and sprinkle half of the ground almonds over a roughly 11 by 9 inch area on the prepared sheet pan. Set it near the cooktop.

(continued)

An accurate instant-read thermometer is essential for this recipe.

If the temperature is too low, the toffee will be sticky and chewy.

The higher the temperature of the finished toffee mixture, the crunchier the texture, but too high and it will taste burnt and have a crumbly texture. The purpose of the corn syrup is to help ensure a smooth texture.

■ In the food processor, finely process the chocolate and transfer it to a bowl. (Alternatively, finely chop it on a cutting board with a chef's knife and transfer it to a bowl.)

MAKE THE TOFFEE

1. In a heavy medium saucepan, preferably nonstick, using a wooden spatula or spoon, stir together the brown sugar, corn syrup, butter, and water. (Do not use a silicone spatula unless it has a wooden handle.) Over medium heat, bring the mixture to a boil, stirring constantly. Continue boiling and stirring gently, until an instant-read thermometer reaches 285°F/140°C. Immediately remove the saucepan from the heat. The temperature should continue to rise to 290°F/143°C, which is the ideal temperature.

2. Immediately stir in the vanilla and baking soda. Stir well to distribute the baking soda. The mixture will become lighter in color.

POUR AND COAT THE TOFFEE

3. Pour the toffee over the nuts. If needed, spread it with the back of a silicone spatula to make it even.

4. Immediately scatter the chocolate over the hot toffee.

5. As soon as the chocolate starts to melt, use a long metal spatula, preferably offset, to spread the chocolate in an even layer over the surface of the toffee.

6. Sprinkle the remaining almonds on top of the melted chocolate and use a small offset spatula to move them gently into an even layer.

7. Refrigerate for about 40 minutes to 1 hour, or until cool and the chocolate is set. Break the toffee into irregular pieces.

STORE AIRTIGHT: room temperature, 1 month. (It is still delicious after 1 month, but the sugar may start to crystallize.)

Making Chocolate Butterscotch Toffee

Spread half the almonds in an 11 by 9 inch area.

Boil the caramel until it reaches 285°F/140°C.

Thoroughly stir in the baking soda.

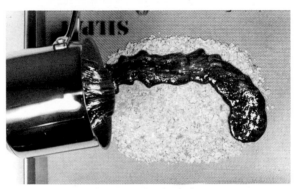

Pour the toffee mixture over the almonds.

Sprinkle the grated chocolate over the hot toffee.

Spread the melted chocolate to coat evenly.

Sprinkle the remaining almonds on top.

Break the cooled toffee into irregular pieces.

Rose's Rugelach

MAKES TWENTY-FOUR 3 BY 1½ INCH COOKIES

OVEN TEMPERATURE: 350°F/175°C

BAKING TIME: 15 to 20 minutes for each of two batches

BAKING EQUIPMENT: Two 15 by 12 inch cookie sheets, lined with parchment, lightly coated with nonstick cooking spray

Two wire racks, one coated with nonstick cooking spray

Traditional rugelach use either a cream cheese or sour cream dough. I prefer the flavor of the cream cheese dough, which is also the same dough as the classic cream cheese pie crust. I chose this dough instead of the sour cream one because it is flakier and easier to roll, which makes the best rugelach.

DOUGH

Perfect Flaky and Tender Cream Cheese Pie Crust (page 188) for a 9 inch standard pie shell (312 grams). Divide the dough into 2 equal pieces (156 grams each) and shape each into a 5 inch disc. Wrap in plastic wrap and refrigerate.

FILLING

granulated sugar	37 grams	3 tablespoons
light brown sugar, preferably light Muscovado	27 grams	2 tablespoons, firmly packed
ground cinnamon	.	¼ teaspoon
golden raisins	54 grams	¼ cup plus 2 tablespoons
walnut halves	50 grams	½ cup
apricot preserves	104 grams	⅓ cup

MISE EN PLACE

■ In a medium bowl, with your fingers, pinch and mix together the granulated and brown sugars and cinnamon until evenly mixed. Divide equally between two small bowls.

■ Cut each raisin in half (or chop them coarsely) and divide them equally between two more small bowls.

■ Coarsely chop the walnuts and add equal amounts to each of the bowls with the raisins.

■ Into two more small bowls, weigh or measure the apricot preserves. Mash them with a fork to break up any large pieces. If necessary, snip them with small scissors.

ROLL THE DOUGH

1. Remove one piece of the dough from the refrigerator and allow it to sit on the counter for 5 to 10 minutes, or until it is malleable enough to roll.

(continued)

Baking Pearl

If the raisins are not soft, before cutting, soak them in 118 grams/½ cup/118 ml boiling water for 30 minutes to 1 hour, and then drain them well.

Make This Recipe Your Own

Raspberry jam and dried cranberries, cut in half, together with the walnuts, also make a great combination.

You can use your choice of preserves, nuts, and/or dried fruits. You can also replace the raisins or nuts with 80 grams/ 6 tablespoons mini chocolate chips.

2. Use a floured rolling pin, on a floured dough mat or lightly floured counter, to roll out the dough into a 10 to 11 inch circle, ³/₃₂ inch (or just under ⅛ inch) thick, rotating it often and adding flour as necessary to ensure that it is not sticking. If the dough becomes too soft or sticky at any time, briefly refrigerate it until it is firm enough to roll.

3. Use a pizza wheel or sharp knife to cut the dough into 12 triangles. (Cut the dough first in quarters and then cut each quarter in thirds.) Use small scissors or a small sharp knife to make a ¼ inch cut in the middle of each triangle's outer edge.

4. Use a small offset spatula or the back of a tablespoon to spread the dough evenly with the apricot preserves, avoiding a 1 inch circle in the center (the preserves will push forward when rolling the dough triangles), and only going up to ¼ inch from the edge.

5. Sprinkle the sugar mixture over the preserves and top with the walnuts and raisins. Press them in gently with your fingers.

6. If necessary, slip a thin knife blade or small offset spatula under the dough to loosen it from the surface. Starting at the wide ends, roll up the triangles and bend the ends around to form a slight crescent shape, turning the ends toward the point.

TOPPING

milk	15 grams	1 tablespoon (15 ml)
sugar	25 grams	2 tablespoons
ground cinnamon	2.2 grams	1 teaspoon

7. Into a small bowl, pour the milk.

8. In another small bowl, whisk or stir together the sugar and cinnamon for the topping and divide the mixture equally into two small bowls.

9. Lift each rugelach with your fingers, and with a pastry brush or feather, brush the entire surface with milk. Holding it over a medium bowl, sprinkle the rugelach evenly with the cinnamon sugar, allowing the excess to fall into the bowl.

10. Place the rugelach, points underneath, about 1½ inches apart on one of the prepared cookie sheets.

11. Cover the rugelach with plastic wrap and refrigerate for a minimum of 30 minutes, up to overnight.

12. Repeat filling and topping with the second batch of dough.

PREHEAT THE OVEN

■ Twenty minutes or longer before baking, set an oven rack at the middle level. Set the oven at 350°F/175°C.

BAKE THE RUGELACH

13. Bake one batch for 10 minutes. For even baking, rotate the cookie sheet halfway around. Continue baking for 5 to 10 minutes, or until lightly browned.

COOL THE RUGELACH

14. Set the cookie sheet on the uncoated wire rack and let the rugelach cool for 2 minutes to firm slightly. During baking, a little of the apricot always melts out onto the parchment. You need to remove the rugelach from the parchment before the apricot hardens completely.

15. Use a thin pancake turner to transfer the rugelach to the coated wire rack to cool completely.

16. Bake and cool the second batch.

STORE AIRTIGHT: room temperature, 5 days; frozen, 3 months.

Making Rugelach

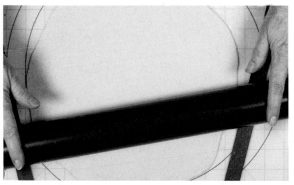

Roll the dough into a 10 to 11 inch disc.

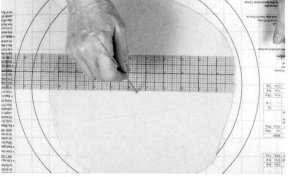

Mark the center of the dough.

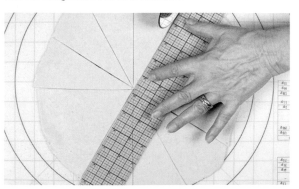

Cut the dough into quarters, and then each quarter into thirds to make 12 triangles.

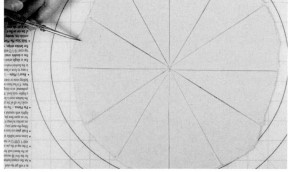

Cut a notch in each triangle.

(continued)

Making Rugelach (cont'd)

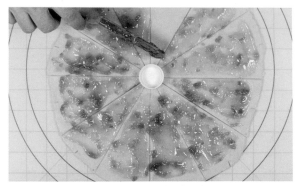

Spread the apricot preserves on the dough.

Press the filling on top of the preserves.

Roll up each triangle.

Curve the ends to make a crescent shape. Brush with milk and dust with cinnamon sugar.

Here are all the basic types of cakes, from layer cakes, cupcakes, pound cakes, quick breads, and muffins to cheesecakes to sponge cakes such as génoise, chiffon, and angel food. You will see the different techniques of mixing the batter used for butter and oil cakes, which depend on chemical leavening (baking powder and/or baking soda), versus sponge cakes, which get their texture from stiffly beaten egg whites or whole egg foam. You will learn about mixing, baking, unmolding, cooling, and storing the cakes, as well as frosting the finished cake.

CAKES

SOLUTIONS FOR POSSIBLE PROBLEMS

Butter and Oil Cakes

The cake has a cracked or peaked surface, or large tunnels.

SOLUTIONS: Try lowering the oven temperature, or decreasing the leavening. Encircling the pan with a cake strip (see page xv) will also prevent this.

The cake has a coarse grain and sunken center.

SOLUTIONS: Try increasing the oven temperature, or mixing the batter until well-combined, or use less leavening.

The cake has poor volume, and a compact structure.

SOLUTIONS: Check the date of your baking powder and replace it if it's old, or try increasing the leavening. Be sure to use butter and eggs that are not cold.

The cake is dry, and the crust is tough.

SOLUTIONS: Use the right size pan; don't use one larger than specified, and do not overbake the cake.

The bottom of the cake is burned and the batter is undercooked.

SOLUTION: Place the cake pans at least 1 inch from the walls of the oven and each other to ensure adequate air circulation in the oven.

The cake is not even.

SOLUTIONS: Make sure your oven rack is level. Rotate the cake halfway around, two-thirds of the way through the baking time. (But do not do this with a génoise or chiffon cake or it will fall.)

There is a denser, darker, clearly demarcated layer of cake at the bottom of a chocolate cake.

SOLUTIONS: Mix the batter until thoroughly combined, using a silicone spatula to lift it up from the bottom of the bowl, and do not use cold butter.

The cake crumb is not even.

SOLUTIONS: There is often a space between the bottom of the beater and the bottom of the mixer bowl. After mixing the batter, be sure to reach down to the bottom of the bowl with a large silicone spatula to mix in any batter that might not have been incorporated thoroughly. For a two-layer cake, when filling the cake pans be sure to go back and forth between the two pans, rather than filling first one and then the other.

Cupcakes

Cupcakes brown too much, are too domed, and are not tender.

SOLUTIONS: Use bleached flour. It is best to make cupcakes in batches of no more than ten at a time because by the time the rest of the batter is placed in the pans, the leavening has started to react, which results in doming.

Cupcakes are too flat.

SOLUTION: Allow the batter to rest for 20 minutes before baking.

Sponge Cakes

The cake does not rise enough.

SOLUTIONS: Beat for the amount of time specified in the recipe and work quickly but gently when incorporating the flour so that the batter does not deflate after aerating. When a meringue is used, be sure to use a grease-free bowl and beater. Do not open the oven door until after the minimum baking time.

The cake is not moist enough and the syrup is not evenly distributed.

SOLUTIONS: Use the amount of syrup indicated in the recipe and brush it on the cake a minimum of 1 day ahead of serving.

The angel food cake tube pan is not large enough for the angel food cake recipe.

SOLUTIONS: My recipe uses 1 egg white per cup capacity of the pan. (To get the volume of your pan, line it with a clean plastic bag and pour in water up to the top.) If your pan is smaller, simply decrease the ingredients proportionately, or bake any extra batter as cupcakes. Be sure to cool cupcakes upside down on a rack to ensure maximum volume. It's useful to know that 16 beaten egg whites will rise to the very top of a 5 quart mixer. Be sure to weigh or measure the whites, as the proportion of whites to yolks can vary.

The chiffon cake or angel food cake fell out of the pan during cooling.

SOLUTIONS: Avoid making these cakes in a humid environment. Underbaking or overbaking will cause the cakes to fall out of the pan when cooling. Also, chiffon cakes and angel food cakes need to be suspended a minimum of 4 inches above the counter in a draft-free area, to allow for effective evaporation of steam. They need to cool completely before unmolding.

The chiffon cake didn't rise enough.

SOLUTIONS: Use the correct amount of cream of tartar as indicated in the recipe, and beat until stiff peaks form when the beater is raised slowly. If not using cream of tartar, use 1 extra egg white (30 grams/2 tablespoons/30 ml) and beat only until curved peaks form. (Without cream of tartar, the beaten egg whites will be far less stable, and will collapse when folded into the rest of the mixture if beaten too stiffly.)

Cheesecakes

The cake splits, forming cracks.

SOLUTION: Coating the sides of the pan with non-stick cooking spray allows the batter to pull away from the sides during baking instead of splitting in the middle.

Frosting

The frosting doesn't go on smoothly.

SOLUTION: Frosting is easiest to apply when it has the consistency of mayonnaise. Let it soften at room temperature, if necessary.

FROSTING THE CAKE

WHEN CHOOSING A FROSTING, the three things to keep in mind are flavor, texture, and quantity. Flavor is a matter of personal preference, but texture and quantity are more a matter of balance. A light sponge cake, such as a chiffon cake, is complemented best by a light accompaniment such as whipped cream, most often served on the side. A génoise works well frosted with whipped cream or buttercream. And a denser layer cake is enhanced by a creamy buttercream or ganache.

My recommended amounts of buttercream are 2 cups for frosting a single 9 inch cake layer and double that, 4 cups, for filling and frosting a two-layer cake. If using ganache, which is more intense, I prefer a thinner layer, using two-thirds those amounts (1⅓ cups for a single 9 inch layer, and 2⅔ cups for a two-layer cake). For cupcakes, my preference is 2 to 3 tablespoons of topping for each.

All toppings in the Toppings and Fillings chapter have both weights and volume for the finished recipe, so you can scale them up or down as desired.

Cakes must be completely cool to the touch before applying the frosting.

Frosting Technique for All Two-Layer Cakes

A cake can be frosted with luscious swirls or smooth, elegant frosting. You can frost a cake directly on the serving plate, but a turntable (heavy duty or inexpensive plastic) makes frosting faster and easier. If you plan to transfer the cake during or after frosting, it's helpful to assemble it on a cardboard round as a base. A 9 inch cardboard round can also serve as a guide to create an even coating of frosting and, if desired, a smooth finish.

IF THE TOPS OF THE CAKE ARE DOMED, you can use a long serrated knife to level them. To avoid crumbs in the frosting, it is always best to invert the layers so that the flat bottoms are facing up because the bottoms have a firm, crumb-free texture. An easy way to transfer cake layers is to invert the layers onto the removable bottom of a tart pan or a cookie sheet, lightly coated with nonstick cooking spray, and then slide them onto the cake base or bottom layer.

BEGIN BY SPREADING A DAB OF FROSTING on a cardboard round or flat serving plate to hold the cake in place. Then slide one of the layers onto it. If frosting the cake on the same serving plate, slip a few pieces of parchment under the cake to keep the edges of the plate clean.

USE AN OFFSET METAL SPATULA to heap a large dollop of frosting onto the top of the cake. Hold the spatula at a 45-degree angle and turn the turntable, or use a side to side motion, without lifting up the spatula (which would lift up crumbs with it), to spread the frosting evenly over the top of the cake. Do not lift up the spatula or it will pull up crumbs with it. If the frosting has softened, refrigerate the cake layer for about 20 minutes, or until firm.

USE THE BOTTOM OF A TART PAN or a cookie sheet to slide the second layer on top. Begin by lining up the edges of each layer then slowly pull away the pan or cookie sheet, keeping it lifted a little above the frosting.

A CRUMB COAT—a thin first coat of frosting—helps to seal in any crumbs from the sides. Use a small angled spatula to spread a thin layer of frosting onto the sides of the cake. Then frost the top of the cake.

TO FROST THE CAKE WITH LARGE LUSCIOUS SWIRLS, apply a thick layer of frosting. Then use a metal spatula to create sideways S-shaped swirls in the frosting.

TO FROST THE CAKE WITH A SMOOTH FINISH or subtle swirls, if the cake is on a cardboard round, set the cake on an inverted cake pan the same diameter as the cake (so the cake is raised above the turntable). Use a long metal spatula to apply more frosting to the sides and then smooth and remove any excess, allowing the frosting to rise about ¼ inch above the top of the cake. If desired, smooth it into the top surface. To make the swirls in the top and sides of the cake, use a small offset spatula and a light touch.

Level the tops of the cake layers, if necessary.

Smooth the filling on top of the inverted layer.

Set the second inverted layer on top.

Apply a crumb coat to the sides.

Frost the top.

Set the cake on an inverted cake pan and use a spatula to smooth the sides.

Smooth the top edge.

Make a decorative design on the sides.

Basic Yellow Layer Cake and Sheet Cake

MAKES TWO 9 INCH
ROUND OR 8 INCH
SQUARE LAYERS, OR
ONE 13 BY 9 INCH SHEET
CAKE

OVEN TEMPERATURE:
350°F/175°C

BAKING TIME: 30 to 40
minutes for layers; 35
to 45 minutes for the
sheet cake

BAKING EQUIPMENT:
Two 9 by 2 inch round
or 8 by 2 inch square
pans, or one 13 by
9 inch by 2 inch high
pan, encircled with cake
strips (see page xv),
bottoms coated with
shortening, topped with
parchment cut to fit,
then coated with baking
spray with flour

This delicious, versatile buttermilk layer cake is one of the lightest and fluffiest of yellow cakes. It also works as a single layer cake (round or square) or an easy to serve sheet cake (see Make This Recipe Your Own). It is also great for cupcakes but, because cupcakes require a slightly different amount of leavening, smaller portions of batter, and a shorter baking time, the slightly different cupcake recipe is on page 90. In these two recipes, minor modifications of baking powder serve to create a slightly domed top for a sheet cake and cupcakes, and a fairly level top for a two-layer cake. You can mix and match any of the frostings in the book for these versatile cakes.

Makes 1573 grams batter

unsalted butter	227 grams	16 tablespoons (2 sticks)
4 large eggs	200 grams	¾ cup plus 2 teaspoons (187 ml)
low-fat buttermilk or whole milk	322 grams	1⅓ cups (316 ml), *divided*
pure vanilla extract	.	1 tablespoon (15 ml)
bleached cake flour OR bleached all-purpose flour	400 grams	4 cups (sifted into the cup and leveled off) OR 3½ cups (sifted into the cup and leveled off)
sugar, preferably superfine	400 grams	2 cups
baking powder (see Make This Recipe Your Own, page 87)	36 grams	2 tablespoons plus 2 teaspoons
fine sea salt	6 grams	1 teaspoon

PREHEAT THE OVEN
■ Twenty minutes or longer before baking, set an oven rack in the lower third of the oven. Set the oven at 350°F/175°C.

MISE EN PLACE
■ About 1 hour ahead, set the butter and eggs on the counter at room temperature (65° to 75°F/19° to 24°C).

Baking Pearl

When unmolding the two layers, leave them upside down to help flatten the slightly rounded top. When composing the cake, set the first layer bottom side up on the cardboard round or plate. Frost the top. Slide the second layer, bottom side up, on top.

Make This Recipe Your Own

For a single layer, divide the recipe in half, including the leavening.

For a 13 by 9 inch sheet cake, use only 33.7 grams/2½ tablespoons baking powder. Bake for 35 to 45 minutes and let cool in the pan for 15 minutes before unmolding.

MAKE THE BATTER

1. Into a 2 cup measure with a spout, weigh or measure the eggs. Add 81 grams/⅓ cup/79 ml of the buttermilk and the vanilla and whisk just until lightly combined.

2. In the bowl of a stand mixer fitted with the flat beater, mix the flour, sugar, baking powder, and salt on low speed for 30 seconds.

3. Add the butter and the remaining buttermilk. Holding the beater with your hand, mash the butter and buttermilk into the flour mixture a little so that it doesn't jump out of the bowl when beating. Then reattach the beater and mix on low speed until the flour mixture is moistened. Raise the speed to medium and beat for 1½ minutes. Scrape down the sides of the bowl.

4. Starting on medium-low speed, gradually add the egg mixture to the batter in three parts, beating on medium speed for 20 seconds after each addition to incorporate the ingredients and strengthen the structure. Scrape down the sides of the bowl.

5. Scrape the batter into the prepared pans (786 grams each) and smooth the surfaces.

BAKE THE CAKES

6. Bake for 30 to 40 minutes, or until a wire cake tester inserted into the centers comes out clean.

COOL THE CAKES

7. Let the cakes cool in the pans on wire racks for 10 minutes. Run a metal spatula between the sides of the pans and the cakes, pressing firmly against the pans, and invert the cakes onto wire racks that have been lightly coated with nonstick cooking spray. Peel off the parchment and reinvert onto clean wire racks. Cool completely.

COMPOSE THE CAKE

8. Fill and frost the cake with the frosting of your choice following the instructions on page 84.

STORE AIRTIGHT: room temperature, 3 days; refrigerated, 1 week; frozen, 3 months.

(continued)

Making a Basic Yellow Layer Cake

Mise en place for the ingredients.

Add 81 grams/⅓ cup/79 ml of the buttermilk to the eggs.

Mash the butter into the flour mixture.

Scrape down the sides of the bowl before adding the eggs.

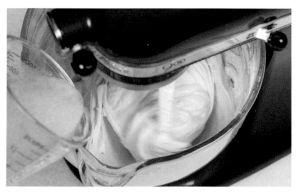

Add the egg mixture.

The consistency of the finished batter.

Level the batter in the pans.

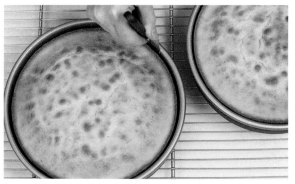

Loosen the sides of the baked cake from the pans.

Invert the cake onto a wire rack.

Peel off the parchment.

Buttermilk Cupcakes

MAKES 10 CUPCAKES

OVEN TEMPERATURE:
350°F/175°C

BAKING TIME: 20 to 25 minutes

BAKING EQUIPMENT:
10 cupcake liners, no coating needed, set in muffin pans or custard cups

This is the baby version of the Basic Yellow Layer Cake on page 86. Because a smaller cake can support more butter without becoming too fragile, the cupcake has just slightly more butter proportionally, as well as a smaller yield. This gives extra flavor and softer texture.

Makes 400 grams batter

unsalted butter	71 grams	5 tablespoons (½ stick plus 1 tablespoon)
1 large egg	50 grams	3 tablespoons plus ½ teaspoon (47.5 ml)
low-fat buttermilk	81 grams	⅓ cup (79 ml), *divided*
pure vanilla extract	.	¾ teaspoon (3.7 ml)
bleached cake flour OR bleached all-purpose flour	100 grams	1 cup (sifted into the cup and leveled off) OR ¾ cup (sifted into the cup and leveled off) plus 2 tablespoons
sugar, preferably superfine	100 grams	½ cup
baking powder	6.7 grams	1½ teaspoons
fine sea salt	.	¼ teaspoon

PREHEAT THE OVEN

■ Twenty minutes or longer before baking, set an oven rack in the lower third of the oven. Set the oven at 350°F/175°C.

MISE EN PLACE

■ About 1 hour ahead, set the butter and egg on the counter at room temperature (65° to 75°F/19° to 24°C).

MAKE THE BATTER

1. Into a 1 cup measure with a spout, weigh or measure the egg. Add 45 grams/ 3 tablespoons/45 ml of the buttermilk and the vanilla and whisk just until lightly combined.

2. In the bowl of a stand mixer fitted with the flat beater, mix the flour, sugar, baking powder, and salt on low speed for 30 seconds.

3. Add the butter and the remaining buttermilk. Mix on low speed until the flour mixture is moistened. Raise the speed to medium and beat for 1½ minutes. Scrape down the sides of the bowl.

4. Starting on medium-low speed, gradually add the egg mixture to the batter in two parts, beating on medium speed for 30 seconds after each addition to incorporate the ingredients and strengthen the structure. Scrape down the sides of the bowl.

FILL THE CUPCAKE LINERS

5. Spoon the batter into the cupcake liners, two-thirds full (40 grams each). Smooth the tops.

BAKE THE CUPCAKES

6. Bake for 20 to 25 minutes, or until a wire cake tester inserted into the centers comes out clean and the cupcakes spring back when pressed lightly in the centers.

COOL THE CUPCAKES

7. Set the pans on wire racks and cool the cupcakes for 10 minutes. Remove the cupcakes from the pans and set them on another wire rack. Cool completely.

STORE AIRTIGHT: room temperature, 2 days; refrigerated, 5 days; frozen, 2 months.

Making Buttermilk Cupcakes

Setting the pan on a scale lets you weigh the batter for each cupcake so they are the same size.

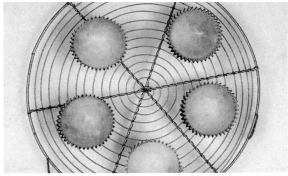

Finished cupcakes.

Basic White Layer Cake and Sheet Cake

MAKES TWO 9 INCH ROUND OR 8 INCH SQUARE LAYERS, OR ONE 13 BY 9 INCH SHEET CAKE

OVEN TEMPERATURE: 350°F/175°C

BAKING TIME: 30 to 40 minutes (35 to 45 minutes for the sheet cake)

BAKING EQUIPMENT: Two 9 by 2 inch round or 8 by 2 inch square pans, or one 13 by 9 inch by 2 inch high pan, encircled with cake strips (see page xv), bottoms coated with shortening, topped with parchment rounds, then coated with baking spray with flour

A layer cake made with all egg whites is the softest and most delicate in flavor and texture of all layer cakes. The sheet cake and cupcakes (page 95) will have slightly domed tops, but the two-layer cake will have a level top. This cake marries well with any nonchocolate buttercream. Chocolate tends to overwhelm the delicate flavor of the cake.

Makes 1560 grams batter

unsalted butter	227 grams	16 tablespoons (2 sticks)
6 large egg whites	180 grams	¾ cup (177 ml)
milk	322 grams	1⅓ cups (316 ml), *divided*
pure vanilla extract	.	1 tablespoon (15 ml)
bleached cake flour OR bleached all-purpose flour	400 grams	4 cups (sifted into the cup and leveled off) OR 3½ cups (sifted into the cup and leveled off)
sugar, preferably superfine	400 grams	2 cups
baking powder (see Make This Recipe Your Own, page 93)	24 grams	1 tablespoon plus 2⅓ teaspoons
fine sea salt	6 grams	1 teaspoon

PREHEAT THE OVEN

▪ Twenty minutes or longer before baking, set an oven rack in the lower third of the oven. Set the oven at 350°F/175°C.

MISE EN PLACE

▪ About 1 hour ahead, set the butter on the counter at room temperature (65° to 75°F/19° to 24°C). Into a 2 cup glass measure with a spout, weigh or measure the egg whites.

MAKE THE BATTER

1. To the egg whites, add 81 grams/⅓ cup/79 ml of the milk and the vanilla and whisk just until lightly combined.

2. In the bowl of a stand mixer fitted with the flat beater, mix the flour, sugar, baking powder, and salt on low speed for 30 seconds.

3. Add the butter and the remaining milk. Holding the beater with your hand,

Baking Pearl

When composing the cake, set the first layer bottom side up on the cardboard round or plate. Frost the top and slide the second layer, bottom side up, on top.

Make This Recipe Your Own

For a single layer, divide the recipe in half but use 2½ plus ⅛ teaspoons/11.8 grams baking powder.

For a 13 by 9 inch sheet cake, use only 22.5 grams/ 1 tablespoon plus 2 teaspoons baking powder. Bake for 35 to 45 minutes and let cool for 15 minutes before unmolding.

You can add about ½ teaspoon finely grated citrus zest for each cup of flour in the recipe.

mash the butter and milk into the flour mixture so that it doesn't jump out of the bowl when beating. Then reattach the beater and mix on low speed until the flour mixture is moistened. Raise the speed to medium and beat for 1½ minutes. Scrape down the sides of the bowl.

4. Starting on medium-low speed, gradually add the egg white mixture to the batter in three parts, beating on medium speed for 20 seconds after each addition to incorporate the ingredients and strengthen the structure. Scrape down the sides of the bowl.

5. Scrape the batter into the prepared pans (780 grams each) and smooth the surfaces.

BAKE THE CAKES

6. Bake for 30 to 40 minutes, or until a wire cake tester inserted into the centers comes out clean.

COOL THE CAKES

7. Let the cakes cool in the pans on a wire rack for 10 minutes. Run a metal spatula between the sides of the pans and the cakes, pressing firmly against the pans, and invert the cakes onto wire racks that have been lightly coated with nonstick cooking spray. Peel off the parchment and reinvert onto wire racks. Cool completely.

COMPOSE THE CAKE

8. Fill and frost the cake with the frosting of your choice following the instructions on page 84.

STORE AIRTIGHT: room temperature, 3 days; refrigerated, 1 week; frozen, 3 months.

White Cupcakes and Chocolate Cupcakes (page 100)
frosted with Mousseline (page 342), Classic Ganache (page 345),
and Chocolate Meringue Buttercream (page 336)

Basic White Cupcakes

This is the baby version of the Basic White Layer Cake on page 92. It requires less leavening to have a nicely domed top.

Makes 380 grams batter

unsalted butter	57 grams	4 tablespoons (½ stick)
1½ large egg whites	45 grams	3 tablespoons (45 ml)
milk	81 grams	⅓ cup (79 ml), *divided*
pure vanilla extract	.	¾ teaspoon (3.7 ml)
bleached cake flour OR bleached all-purpose flour	100 grams	1 cup (sifted into the cup and leveled off) OR ¾ cup (sifted into the cup and leveled off) plus 2 tablespoons
sugar, preferably superfine	100 grams	½ cup
baking powder	5.3 grams	1⅛ plus ¹⁄₁₆ teaspoons
fine sea salt	.	¼ teaspoon

PREHEAT THE OVEN

■ Twenty minutes or longer before baking, set an oven rack in the lower third of the oven. Set the oven at 350°F/175°C.

MISE EN PLACE

■ About 1 hour ahead, set the butter on the counter at room temperature (65° to 75°F/19° to 24°C).

■ Into a 1 cup glass measure with a spout, weigh or measure the egg whites.

MAKE THE BATTER

1. To the egg whites, add 20 grams/4 teaspoons/20 ml of the milk and the vanilla and whisk just until lightly combined.

2. In the bowl of a stand mixer fitted with the flat beater, mix the flour, sugar, baking powder, and salt on low speed for 30 seconds.

3. Add the butter and the remaining milk. Mix on low speed until the flour mixture is moistened. Raise the speed to medium and beat for 1½ minutes. Scrape down the sides of the bowl.

4. Starting on medium-low speed, gradually add the egg mixture to the batter in two parts, beating on medium speed for 30 seconds after each addition to incorporate the ingredients and strengthen the structure. Scrape down the sides of the bowl.

(continued)

FILL THE CUPCAKE LINERS

5. Spoon the batter into the cupcake liners, almost three-quarters full (47 grams each). No need to smooth the tops.

BAKE THE CUPCAKES

6. Bake for 20 to 25 minutes, or until a wire cake tester inserted into the centers comes out clean and the cupcakes spring back when pressed lightly in the centers.

COOL THE CUPCAKES

7. Set the pans on wire racks and cool the cupcakes for 10 minutes. Remove the cupcakes from the pans and set them on another wire rack. Cool completely.

STORE AIRTIGHT: room temperature, 2 days; refrigerated, 5 days; frozen, 2 months.

Basic Chocolate Layer Cake and Sheet Cake

MAKES TWO 9 INCH ROUND OR 8 INCH SQUARE LAYERS, OR ONE 13 BY 9 INCH SHEET CAKE

OVEN TEMPERATURE: 350°F/175°C

BAKING TIME: 30 to 40 minutes (35 to 45 minutes for a sheet cake)

BAKING EQUIPMENT: Two 9 by 2 inch round or 8 by 2 inch square pans, or one 13 by 9 inch by 2 inch high pan, encircled with cake strips (see page xv), bottoms coated with shortening, topped with parchment rounds, then coated with baking spray with flour

Cocoa dissolved in boiling water offers an extraordinarily full and intense chocolate flavor. This cake also has a soft and tender texture. My mother once commented that it tastes just like a chocolate bar but softer. This cake is great for any special occasion. Chocolate lovers will adore a ganache frosting but just about any frosting will work with this cake. The single layer and cupcakes will have slightly domed tops, but the two-layer cake will have a level top.

Makes 1600 grams batter

unsweetened alkalized cocoa powder	84 grams	1 cup plus 2 tablespoons (sifted before measuring)
boiling water	237 grams	1 cup (237 ml)
canola or safflower oil	54 grams	¼ cup (59 ml)
unsalted butter	227 grams	16 tablespoons (2 sticks)
4 large eggs	200 grams	¾ cup plus 2 teaspoons (187 ml)
water	45 grams	3 tablespoons (45 ml)
pure vanilla extract	.	1 tablespoon (15 ml)
bleached cake flour OR bleached all-purpose flour	333 grams	3⅓ cups (sifted into the cup and leveled off) OR 3 cups (sifted into the cup and leveled off) minus 1½ tablespoons
sugar, preferably superfine	400 grams	2 cups
baking powder	22.5 grams	5 teaspoons
fine sea salt	6 grams	1 teaspoon

PREHEAT THE OVEN

■ Twenty minutes or longer before baking, set an oven rack in the lower third of the oven. Set the oven at 350°F/175°C.

MISE EN PLACE

■ One hour or longer ahead, in a 4 cup glass measure with a spout, whisk the cocoa and boiling water until smooth. Add the oil, cover with plastic wrap, and cool to room temperature.

(continued)

Baking Pearls

Alkalized cocoa makes the neutralizing effect of baking soda unnecessary, eliminating the slightly bitter edge often associated with baking soda chocolate cakes.

It is important to cover the cocoa mixture to prevent evaporation, which would cause the cake to be dry. Adding the oil, which floats to the top, helps as well.

When composing the cake, set the first layer bottom side up on the cardboard round or plate. Frost the top and slide the second layer, bottom side up, on top.

Make This Recipe Your Own

For a single layer, divide all the ingredients in half, including the leavening.

For a 13 by 9 inch sheet cake, prepare the pan as above; do not change the leavening.

■ About 1 hour ahead, set the butter and eggs on the counter at room temperature (65° to 75°F/19° to 24°C).

MAKE THE BATTER

1. Into a 2 cup measure with a spout, weigh or measure the eggs. Add the water and vanilla, and whisk just until lightly combined.

2. In the bowl of a stand mixer fitted with the flat beater, mix the flour, sugar, baking powder, and salt on low speed for 30 seconds.

3. Add the butter and the cocoa mixture. Holding the beater with your hand, mash the butter and cocoa into the flour mixture so that it doesn't jump out of the bowl when beating. Then reattach the beater and mix on low speed until the flour mixture is moistened. Cover the top of the bowl with plastic wrap or use the splash shield. Raise the speed to medium and beat for 1½ minutes. Scrape down the sides of the bowl.

4. Starting on medium-low speed, gradually add the egg mixture in three parts, beating on medium speed for 20 seconds after each addition to incorporate the ingredients and strengthen the structure. Scrape down the sides of the bowl.

5. Scrape the batter into the prepared pan(s) about half full (800 grams each for 9 inch round or 8 inch square pans) and smooth the surfaces.

BAKE THE CAKES

6. Bake for 30 to 40 minutes (35 to 45 for a sheet cake), or until a wire cake tester inserted into the centers comes out clean.

COOL THE CAKES

7. Let the cakes cool in the pans on wire racks for 10 minutes (15 minutes for a sheet cake). Run a metal spatula between the sides of the pans and the cakes, pressing firmly against the pans, and invert the cakes onto wire racks that have been lightly coated with nonstick cooking spray. Peel off the parchment and reinvert onto wire racks. Cool completely.

COMPOSE THE CAKE

8. Fill and frost the cake with the frosting of your choice following the instructions on page 84.

STORE AIRTIGHT: room temperature, 3 days; refrigerated, 1 week; frozen, 3 months.

Making a Basic Chocolate Sheet Cake

Top the chocolate mixture with oil to prevent evaporation as it cools.

Mash the butter and cocoa mixture into the flour mixture.

The consistency of the finished batter.

Spread the batter evenly in the pan.

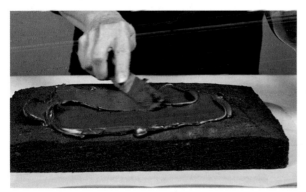

Spread the frosting on the cake.

Pull out the parchment strips.

Basic Chocolate Cupcakes

This is the baby version of the Basic Chocolate Layer Cake on page 97, but extra moist as it can support a little extra water.

MAKES 8 CUPCAKES

OVEN TEMPERATURE:
350°F/175°C

BAKING TIME: 20 to 25 minutes

BAKING EQUIPMENT:
8 cupcake liners, coated with baking spray with flour, set in muffin pans or custard cups

Makes 400 grams batter

unsweetened alkalized cocoa powder	21 grams	¼ cup plus ½ tablespoon (sifted before measuring)
boiling water	59 grams	¼ cup (59 ml)
canola or safflower oil	13 grams	1 tablespoon (15 ml)
unsalted butter	57 grams	4 tablespoons (½ stick)
1 large egg	50 grams	3 tablespoons plus ½ teaspoon (47.5 ml)
water	22 grams	1½ tablespoons (22.5 ml)
pure vanilla extract	.	¾ teaspoon (3.7 ml)
bleached cake flour OR bleached all-purpose flour	83 grams	¾ cup (lightly spooned into the cup and leveled off) OR ⅔ cup (lightly spooned into the cup and leveled off)
sugar, preferably superfine	100 grams	½ cup
baking powder	4.5 grams	1 teaspoon
baking soda	0.3 gram	¹⁄₁₆ teaspoon
fine sea salt	.	¼ teaspoon

PREHEAT THE OVEN

- Twenty minutes or longer before baking, set an oven rack in the lower third of the oven. Set the oven at 350°F/175°C.

MISE EN PLACE

- One hour or longer ahead, in a 1 cup glass measure with a spout, whisk the cocoa and boiling water until smooth. Add the oil and cover with plastic wrap. Cool to room temperature.

- About 1 hour ahead, set the butter and egg on the counter at room temperature (65° to 75°F/19° to 24°C).

MAKE THE BATTER

1. Into another 1 cup or larger measure with a spout, weigh or measure the egg. Add the water and vanilla and whisk just until lightly combined.

2. In the bowl of a stand mixer fitted with the flat beater, mix the flour, sugar, baking powder, baking soda, and salt on low speed for 30 seconds.

It is important to cover the cocoa mixture to prevent evaporation, which would cause the cupcakes to be dry. Adding the oil, which floats to the top, helps as well.

Baking soda is added only for the cupcakes and not the larger cakes as it is needed to prevent them from dipping.

3. Add the butter and cocoa mixture and mix on low speed until the flour mixture is moistened. Raise the speed to medium and beat for 1½ minutes. Scrape down the sides of the bowl.

4. Starting on medium-low speed, gradually add the egg mixture in two parts, beating on medium speed for 30 seconds after each addition to incorporate the ingredients and strengthen the structure. Scrape down the sides of the bowl.

FILL THE CUPCAKE LINERS

5. Spoon the batter into the cupcake liners, three-quarters full (50 grams each). Smooth the tops.

BAKE THE CUPCAKES

6. Bake for 20 to 25 minutes, or until a wire cake tester inserted into the centers comes out clean and the cupcakes spring back when pressed lightly in the centers.

COOL THE CUPCAKES

7. Set the pans on wire racks and cool the cupcakes for 10 minutes. Remove the cupcakes from the pans and set them on another wire rack. Cool completely.

STORE AIRTIGHT: room temperature, 2 days; refrigerated, 5 days; frozen, 2 months.

Marble Cake

SERVES 12 TO 14

OVEN TEMPERATURE:
350°F/175°C

BAKING TIME: 50 to 60
minutes

BAKING EQUIPMENT:
One 10 cup metal fluted
tube pan, coated with
baking spray with flour

The sour cream base of this cake gives it an exceptionally fine texture and fabulous flavor.

unsalted butter	255 grams	18 tablespoons (2 sticks plus 2 tablespoons)
6 (to 9) large egg yolks (see Baking Pearl, page 103)	112 grams	¼ cup plus 3 tablespoons (103 ml)
dark chocolate, 60% to 62% cacao, chopped	85 grams	3 ounces
full-fat sour cream	242 grams	1 cup, *divided*
pure vanilla extract	.	2 teaspoons (10 ml)
bleached cake flour OR bleached all-purpose flour)	300 grams	3 cups (sifted into the cup and leveled off) OR 2⅔ cups (sifted into the cup and leveled off)
sugar, preferably superfine	300 grams	1½ cups
baking powder	4.5 grams	1 teaspoon
baking soda	4.1 grams	¾ teaspoon
fine sea salt	6 grams	1 teaspoon

PREHEAT THE OVEN

▪ Twenty minutes or longer before baking, set an oven rack in the lower third of the oven. Set the oven at 350°F/175°C.

MISE EN PLACE

▪ Thirty minutes to 1 hour ahead, set the butter and eggs on the counter at room temperature (65° to 75°F/19° to 24°C).

▪ **MELT THE CHOCOLATE:** About 30 minutes ahead, melt the chocolate: In a small microwavable bowl, stirring with a silicone spatula every 15 seconds, heat the chocolate until almost completely melted. (Alternatively, melt the chocolate in the top of a double boiler over hot, not simmering water—do not let the bottom of the container touch the water—stirring often with a silicone spatula.) Remove the chocolate from the heat source and stir until fully melted. Let it cool until it is no longer warm to the touch but is still fluid (80° to 85°F/27° to 29°C).

MAKE THE BATTER

1. Into a 2 cup measure with a spout, weigh or measure the egg yolks. Add 60 grams/¼ cup of the sour cream and the vanilla and whisk just until lightly combined.

The ratio of white to yolk in an egg can vary to such a degree that you may need as few as 6 or as many as 9 eggs for this recipe. It is therefore advisable to weigh or measure the separated yolks and add or reduce if needed.

Make This Recipe Your Own

If desired, glaze the cake with 184 grams/⅔ cup of Ganache Drizzle Glaze (page 348).

2. In the bowl of a stand mixer fitted with the flat beater, mix the flour, sugar, baking powder, baking soda, and salt on low speed for 30 seconds.

3. Add the butter and the remaining sour cream. Holding the beater with your hand, mash the butter and sour cream into the flour mixture so that it doesn't jump out of the bowl when beating. Then reattach the beater and mix on low speed until the flour mixture is moistened. Raise the speed to medium and beat for 1½ minutes. Scrape down the sides of the bowl.

4. Starting on medium-low speed, gradually add the egg mixture to the batter in three parts, beating on medium speed for 20 seconds after each addition to incorporate the ingredients and strengthen the structure. Scrape down the sides of the bowl.

5. Remove almost one-third of the batter (354 grams/1½ cups) to a bowl and stir in the melted chocolate until uniform in color.

6. Spoon one-third of the remaining batter into the prepared pan. Top with dollops of half the chocolate batter. Spread it gently but evenly. Top with half the remaining plain batter and then with dollops of the remaining chocolate batter. Spread it evenly. Top with the remaining plain batter, spreading it evenly over the top.

7. Use a regular tablespoon to marbleize the batter lightly: Dip in the tablespoon, without touching the bottom or sides of the pan, and lift up the batter in a folding motion like the roll of a wave. Repeat this motion 6 to 8 times, all around the pan. Smooth the surface.

BAKE THE CAKE

8. Bake for 50 to 60 minutes, or until a cake tester inserted between the tube and the side comes out clean and the cake springs back when pressed lightly in the center. During baking the cake will rise above the center tube, but on cooling it will be almost level with the sides of the pan. The cake should start to shrink from the sides of the pan only after removal from the oven.

COOL AND UNMOLD THE CAKE

9. Let the cake cool in the pan on a rack for 10 minutes. Use a small sharp knife to dislodge the cake inside the rim of the pan. Loosen the cake by jiggling it up and down until it moves slightly. Invert it onto a wire rack coated with cooking spray. Cool completely before wrapping airtight or glazing (see Make This Recipe Your Own, left).

STORE AIRTIGHT: room temperature, 3 days; refrigerated, 1 week; frozen, 3 months.

(continued)

Making Marble Cake

Add one-third of the white batter.

Dollop on half of the chocolate batter.

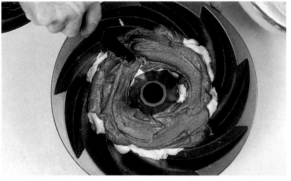

Smooth the chocolate dollops. Repeat with the remaining batter.

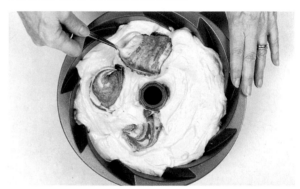

Marble the two batters with a folding motion.

Cream Cheese Crunch Pound Cake

SERVES 8 TO 10

SIZE: 8½ by 4½ by 2¾ inches high with crunch coating, 8 by 4 by 3 inches high without

OVEN TEMPERATURE: 350°F/175°C

BAKING TIME: 55 to 65 minutes

BAKING EQUIPMENT: One 9 by 5 by 2¾ inch (8 cup) loaf pan, coated with shortening, lined with two pieces of crisscrossed parchment extending a few inches past the edges of the pan and attached to each other by a thin coating of shortening. Lightly coat any exposed corner areas of the pan with baking spray with flour.

This is an exceptionally moist, velvety, and tender cake, but the texture depends on the use of bleached cake flour, the acidity of which emulsifies the ingredients—no substitutes! It also makes a terrific party cake when baked in a large rectangle (see Variations, page 106). A pecan crunch coating on the bottom and sides provides little jewels of delicious crunchiness.

LOUISIANA PECAN CRUNCH COATING Makes 236 grams/1⅔ cups

unsalted butter	43 grams	3 tablespoons
graham crackers	47 grams	3 double rectangles (5 by 2¼ inches)
pecan halves	75 grams	¾ cup
granulated sugar	75 grams	¼ cup plus 2 tablespoons

CAKE BATTER

unsalted butter	85 grams	6 tablespoons (¾ stick)
full-fat cream cheese	42 grams	2 tablespoons plus 2 teaspoons
3 to 4 large egg yolks	56 grams	3½ tablespoons (52.5 ml)
full-fat sour cream	121 grams	½ cup, *divided*
pure vanilla extract	.	1 teaspoon (5 ml)
bleached cake flour	150 grams	1½ cups (sifted into the cup and leveled off)
superfine sugar	150 grams	¾ cup
baking powder	1.1 grams	¼ teaspoon
baking soda	2 grams	⅜ teaspoon
fine sea salt	.	¼ teaspoon

PREHEAT THE OVEN

- Twenty minutes or longer before baking, set an oven rack in the lower third of the oven. Set the oven at 350°F/175°C.

MISE EN PLACE FOR BATTER INGREDIENTS

- About 1 hour ahead, set the butter, cream cheese, and eggs on the counter at room temperature (65° to 75°F/19° to 24°C).

(continued)

Make This Recipe Your Own

Add the seeds from two vanilla beans (one if Tahitian) to the batter of the main recipe or the first variation.

Variations

For a plain pound cake without the crunch coating, use an 8½ by 4½ inch loaf pan (6 cups), bottom coated with shortening, topped with parchment, then coated with baking spray with flour. Bake 45 to 55 minutes. Cool 10 minutes. Run a small metal spatula between the sides of the pan and the cake, pressing firmly against the pan, and invert the cake onto a wire rack that has been lightly coated with nonstick cooking spray. Lift off the pan and peel off the parchment. Reinvert onto another wire rack to cool completely, top side up.

For a large party cake without the crunch, use a 13 by 9 inch by 2 inch high baking pan, bottom coated with shortening, topped with parchment, then coated with baking spray with flour, and encircled with cake strips (see page xv). Double the batter recipe but increase the baking soda to 4.1 grams/ ¾ teaspoon. Bake for 35 to 45 minutes. Cool for 15 minutes before unmolding onto a wire rack. Reinvert and cool completely top side up.

MAKE THE CRUNCH COATING

1. In a 1 cup glass measure with a spout in the microwave, or in a small saucepan over medium-low heat, melt the butter.

2. Into a food processor, break the crackers into a few pieces. Add the nuts and granulated sugar. Process until fine crumbs.

3. Add the melted butter and pulse it in until evenly incorporated.

4. Spoon about one-half of the crunch mixture (118 grams) into the prepared pan and press it evenly across the bottom. Press the remaining mixture against the sides, up to about 1 inch from the top of the pan. Begin by tilting the pan to one side and use a bench scraper to lift, spread, and press the coating against the side of the pan. Without tilting the pan, repeat with the remaining three sides. Use the back of a small spoon to press and even the coating on the sides and against the corners of the pan. Cover with plastic wrap and refrigerate for a minimum of 30 minutes, up to 3 days.

MAKE THE BATTER

1. Into a 1 cup measure with a spout, weigh or measure the egg yolks and whisk them together with 30 grams/2 tablespoons of the sour cream and the vanilla, just until lightly combined.

2. In the bowl of a stand mixer fitted with the flat beater, mix the flour, sugar, baking powder, baking soda, and salt on low speed for 30 seconds.

3. Add the butter, cream cheese, and the remaining 91 grams/6 tablespoons sour cream. Mix on low speed until the flour mixture is moistened. Raise the speed to medium and beat for 1½ minutes. Scrape down the sides of the bowl.

4. Starting on medium-low speed, gradually add the egg mixture to the batter in two parts, beating on medium speed for 30 seconds after each addition to incorporate ingredients and strengthen the structure. Scrape down the sides of the bowl after each addition.

5. Carefully spoon the batter into the crunch coating–lined pan and smooth the surface evenly with a small offset spatula. If you would like to have a crack that forms during baking, make a long mark down the center of the batter.

BAKE THE CAKE

6. Bake for 55 to 65 minutes, or until a wooden skewer inserted into the center comes out clean.

COOL THE CAKE

7. Let the cake cool on a wire rack for 20 minutes. Use a small metal spatula to dislodge the crunch coating at the corners.

UNMOLD THE CAKE

8. Invert the cake onto a wire rack that has been lightly coated with nonstick cooking spray. Carefully lift off the pan, then very carefully peel off the parchment. To prevent the crunch coating from splitting, prop up each end of the cake with a folded paper towel. When completely cool, reinvert the cake onto a serving plate or cutting board. With a serrated knife, cut into ½ inch thick slices to serve.

STORE AIRTIGHT: room temperature 3 days; refrigerated, 5 days; frozen, 3 months.

Making Cream Cheese Crunch Pound Cake

Press half the crunch mixture into the bottom of the pan.

Use a dough scraper to press the remaining crunch mixture up the sides.

Spoon in the cake batter.

Slip folded paper towels under the ends while the cake cools to keep it from breaking.

Triple Lemon Velvet Bundt Cake

OVEN TEMPERATURE:
350°F/175°C

BAKING TIME: 45 to 55 minutes

PLAN AHEAD: For best flavor and texture, bake and syrup the cake 1 day ahead.

BAKING EQUIPMENT: The pan must be a minimum of 14 cup capacity such as a Nordic Ware Anniversary Bundt Pan with 10 to 15 cup capacity (or use a 12 cup Bundt pan and bake the extra batter as 4 cupcakes). Coat the pan with baking spray with flour. Do not use an angel food pan, because the cake will break apart when unmolding it.

The combination of butter, lemon, and vanilla is one of the most glorious ones in cake realm. This soft, velvety, tender, and lofty cake is contrasted by a crunchy crust and crisp, classic lemon sugar glaze. This is my favorite of all lemon cakes. Baked in two smaller pans (see Make This Recipe Your Own, page 110), it makes terrific holiday gifts.

unsalted butter	270 grams	19 tablespoons (2 sticks plus 3 tablespoons)
7 (to 11) egg yolks (see Baking Pearls, page 110)	130 grams	½ cup (118 ml)
lemon zest, finely grated (5 to 6 lemons)	18 grams	3 tablespoons, loosely packed
full-fat sour cream	242 grams	1 cup, *divided*
pure vanilla extract	.	2½ teaspoons (12.5 ml)
bleached cake flour OR bleached all-purpose flour	312 grams	3 cups plus 2 tablespoons (sifted into the cup and leveled off) OR 2¾ cups (sifted into the cup and leveled off)
sugar, preferably superfine	312 grams	1½ cups plus 1 tablespoon
baking powder	10.1 grams	2¼ teaspoons
baking soda	2.7 grams	½ teaspoon
fine sea salt	3.7 grams	½ plus ⅛ teaspoon

PREHEAT THE OVEN

- Twenty minutes or longer before baking, set an oven rack in the lower third of the oven. Set the oven at 350°F/175°C.

MISE EN PLACE

- Thirty minutes to 1 hour ahead, set the butter and eggs on the counter at room temperature (65° to 75°F/19° to 24°C).

- With dish washing liquid, wash the lemons. Rinse, dry, and zest them (see page xxv).

(continued)

The ratio of white to yolk in an egg can vary to such a degree that you may need as few as 7 or as many as 11 eggs for this recipe. It is therefore advisable to weigh or measure the separated yolks and add or reduce if needed.

The butter smooths the texture of the lemon glaze.

½ teaspoon (2.5 ml) high-quality lemon oil such as Boyajian, added with the vanilla to the cake, can be substituted for the lemon zest.

Make This Recipe Your Own

To bake as two baby cakes, you will need two 6 cup Bundt pans or two 8½ by 4½ inch loaf pans, lightly coated with baking spray with flour. Divide the batter between the two pans, filling them about 1 inch from the top (640 grams each). Bake for 40 to 45 minutes. The batter will rise about ¼ inch above the rims but will be level on cooling. Cool for 10 minutes before unmolding.

Add 50 grams/⅓ cup poppy seeds to the flour mixture. Be sure to use fresh poppy seeds. (They keep for months in the freezer.)

MAKE THE BATTER

1. Into a 2 cup measure with a spout, weigh or measure the egg yolks. Add 60 grams/¼ cup of the sour cream and the vanilla, and whisk lightly until combined.

2. In the bowl of a stand mixer fitted with the flat beater, add the flour, sugar, baking powder, baking soda, salt, and lemon zest and mix on low speed for 30 seconds.

3. Add the butter and the remaining 182 grams/¾ cup sour cream. Mix on low speed until the flour mixture is moistened. Raise the speed to medium and beat for 1½ minutes to aerate and develop the cake's structure. The mixture will lighten in color and texture. Scrape down the sides.

4. Starting on low speed, gradually add the egg mixture in two parts, beating on medium speed for 30 seconds after each addition to incorporate the ingredients smoothly.

5. Scrape the batter into the prepared pan and smooth the surface evenly. (If using a 12 cup Bundt pan, first fill four cupcake liners two-thirds full (50 grams each) and then scrape the remaining batter into the pan.)

BAKE THE CAKE

6. Bake for 45 to 55 minutes (15 to 20 minutes for the cupcakes), or until a wire cake tester inserted near the center comes out clean and the cake springs back when pressed. The cake should start to shrink from the sides of the pan only after removal from the oven.

- Shortly before the cake is finished baking, make the lemon syrup.

LEMON SYRUP Makes 200 grams/2⅔ cup/158 ml

lemon juice, freshly squeezed and strained (about 2 lemons)	95 grams	6 tablespoons (89 ml)
sugar	113 grams	½ cup plus 1 tablespoon

MAKE THE LEMON SYRUP

1. In a small pan over medium heat, stir the lemon juice and sugar until dissolved. Cover it and set it aside.

APPLY THE SYRUP AND COOL THE CAKE

2. As soon as the cake comes out of the oven, place the pan on a rack, poke the cake all over with a wire cake tester, and brush it with about one-third (66 grams/50 ml) of the syrup. Cool the cake in the pan for 15 minutes. Invert the cake onto a serving plate.

3. Brush the top and sides of the cake with the remaining syrup. Cool completely and then cover with plastic wrap. At least 1 hour before serving, apply the lemon glaze.

LEMON GLAZE Makes 141 grams/7 tablespoons/100 ml

powdered sugar	115 grams	1 cup (lightly spooned into the cup and leveled off)
lemon juice, freshly squeezed and strained (1 lemon)	21 grams	4 teaspoons (20 ml)
unsalted butter, melted and cooled	5 grams	1 teaspoon

MAKE THE GLAZE

1. Into a small bowl, sift the powdered sugar.

2. Add the lemon juice and stir until all the sugar is moistened. Stir in the butter.

3. Whisk the glaze until completely smooth. When you lift the whisk, the mixture should drop thickly and pool for a few seconds before disappearing smoothly into the surface. If necessary, add more lemon juice by the drop to thin the glaze. If the glaze is too thin, whisk in more powdered sugar. Cover if not using at once.

APPLY THE GLAZE

4. Use a teaspoon to drizzle the glaze onto the cake. You can also pipe the glaze, or even pour it over the top, allowing it to cascade down the sides.

STORE AIRTIGHT: room temperature, 3 days; refrigerated, 5 days; frozen, 2 months.

(continued)

Making Triple Lemon Velvet Bundt Cake

Mix the lemon zest and dry ingredients.

The consistency of the finished batter.

Smooth the batter in the cake pan.

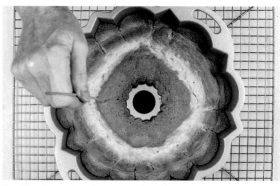

Test for doneness; the tester should come out clean.

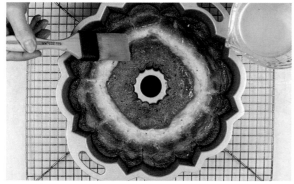

Brush the top of the hot cake with one-third of the syrup.

Brush the cake with the remaining syrup.

Apple Walnut Bundt Cake

SERVES 12 TO 14

OVEN TEMPERATURE:
350°F/175°C

BAKING TIME: 50 to 60
minutes

BAKING EQUIPMENT:
The pan must be
a minimum 12 cup
capacity, such as
a Nordic Ware
Anniversary Bundt
Pan with 10 to 15 cup
capacity, or a 12 cup
Bundt pan, coated with
baking spray with flour;
or a 16 cup two-piece
angel food pan, bottom
lined with parchment,
then coated with baking
spray with flour

This is the perfect apple cake for the fall season, but it can be enjoyed any time of the year. It is great to have this Bundt cake in your repertoire as it is easy to make and stays moist and flavorful for 5 days at room temperature, up to 10 days refrigerated. Because it is made with oil, it can be enjoyed at room temperature or cold. The caramel glaze is an optional but fabulous accompaniment.

3 large eggs	150 grams	½ cup plus 1½ tablespoons (140 ml)
walnut halves	100 grams	1 cup
bleached all-purpose flour	300 grams	2½ cups (lightly spooned into the cup and leveled off)
baking soda	5.5 grams	1 teaspoon
fine sea salt	6 grams	1 teaspoon
ground cinnamon	4.4 grams	2 teaspoons
4 large tart apples (see page xxv), 657 grams/1½ pounds	525 grams (diced)	4 cups (diced)
canola or safflower oil	269 grams	1¼ cups (296 ml)
granulated sugar	200 grams	1 cup
light brown sugar	163 grams	¾ cup
pure vanilla extract	.	2 teaspoons (10 ml)

PREHEAT THE OVEN

- Twenty minutes or longer before toasting the walnuts, set an oven rack in the lower third of the oven. Set the oven at 350°F/175°C.

MISE EN PLACE

- Thirty minutes to 1 hour ahead, set the eggs on the counter at room temperature (65° to 75°F/19° to 24°C).

- **TOAST AND CHOP THE WALNUTS:** Spread the walnuts evenly on a cookie sheet and bake for 5 minutes. Turn the walnuts onto a clean dish town and roll and rub them around to loosen the skins. Discard any loose skins and let the nuts cool completely. Chop medium coarse.

- In a medium bowl, whisk together the flour, baking soda, salt, and cinnamon.

- Peel, core, and cut the apples into ⅛ to ¼ inch dice.

(continued)

Make This Recipe Your Own

Drizzle Caramel Sauce and Glaze (page 353) over the cake after unmolding.

MAKE THE BATTER

1. Into the bowl of a stand mixer, weigh or measure the eggs. Add the oil, granulated and brown sugars, and the vanilla. Attach the flat beater and beat on medium speed for 1 minute, until blended.

2. Add the flour mixture and beat on low speed for 20 seconds, just until incorporated. Scrape down the sides of the bowl.

3. Detach the bowl from the stand and with a large spoon stir in the apples and walnuts. Spoon the batter into the prepared pan.

BAKE THE CAKE

4. Bake for 50 to 60 minutes, or until a wire cake tester inserted near the center comes out clean and the cake springs back when pressed lightly in the center.

COOL THE CAKE

5. Let the cake cool in the pan on a wire rack for 30 minutes. If using a straight sided pan, run a metal spatula between the sides of the pan and the cake. Invert the cake onto a wire rack that has been lightly coated with nonstick cooking spray and cool completely for about 1½ hours.

STORE AIRTIGHT: room temperature, 5 days; refrigerated, 10 days; frozen, 2 months.

Making Apple Walnut Bundt Cake

Scrape down the sides of the bowl before stirring in the apples and walnuts.

Spoon the batter into the pan.

Unmold the baked cake.

Pour the glaze over the cake.

Whoopie Pies

MAKES SIX 3½ INCH
WHOOPIES

OVEN TEMPERATURE:
400°F/200°C

BAKING TIME: 8 to 10
minutes

BAKING EQUIPMENT:
Two 15 by 12 inch cookie
sheets, coated with
nonstick cooking spray
or with shortening
Optional: 2 inch
diameter cookie scoop

This recipe is said to have originated in the Pennsylvania Dutch country. Although it is called "pie," it is actually a cake. The batter is stiff enough to scoop and bake free form on a cookie sheet, but the results are light and moist. Whoopie pies are usually filled with an airy vanilla buttercream such as Mousseline (page 342) but Neoclassic Buttercream (page 332), Chocolate Mousse Ganache (page 351), or any Whipped Cream (page 329) would also be great choices.

Makes 510 grams batter

unsalted butter	28 grams	2 tablespoons
1 large egg	50 grams	3 tablespoons plus ½ teaspoon (47.5 ml)
dark chocolate, 60% to 62% cacao, chopped	42 grams	1.5 ounces
bleached all-purpose flour	125 grams	1 cup (lightly spooned into the cup and leveled off) plus ½ tablespoon
unsweetened alkalized cocoa powder	19 grams	¼ cup (sifted before measuring)
baking powder	2.2 grams	½ teaspoon
baking soda	2.7 grams	½ teaspoon
fine sea salt	3 grams	½ teaspoon
low-fat buttermilk	121 grams	½ cup (118 ml)
canola or safflower oil	27 grams	2 tablespoons (30 ml)
dark brown sugar, preferably dark Muscovado	120 grams	½ cup, firmly packed
filling of your choice (see headnote)	.	1⅓ cups

PREHEAT THE OVEN

■ Thirty minutes or longer before baking, set an oven rack at the middle level. Set the oven at 400°F/200°C.

MISE EN PLACE

■ About 1 hour ahead, set the butter and egg on the counter at room temperature (65° to 75°F/19° to 24°C).

■ **MELT THE CHOCOLATE:** About 30 minute ahead, melt the chocolate: In a small microwavable bowl, stirring with a silicone spatula every 15 seconds, heat the chocolate until almost completely melted. (Alternatively, melt the chocolate in the top of a double boiler over hot, not simmering water—do not let the bottom of the container touch the water—stirring often with a silicone spatula.) Remove the chocolate from the heat source and stir until fully melted. Let it cool until it is no longer warm to the touch but is still fluid (80° to 85°F/27° to 29°C).

- In a medium bowl, whisk together the flour, cocoa, baking powder, baking soda, and salt. Then sift the mixture if necessary to remove any lumps from the cocoa and baking soda.

- Into a 1 cup measure with a spout, weigh or measure the egg.

- Into a 2 cup measure with a spout, weigh or measure the buttermilk.

MAKE THE BATTER

1. In the bowl of a stand mixer fitted with the flat beater, beat the butter, oil, sugar, and egg on medium speed for about 5 minutes. Scrape down the sides of the bowl as needed. The mixture will be smooth and paler in color.

2. Add the cooled melted chocolate and beat on low speed until incorporated.

3. Add one-third of the flour mixture with one-third of the buttermilk, and beat on low speed just until incorporated. Scrape down the sides of the bowl. Repeat with another third of the flour mixture and buttermilk, and then the final third. Raise the speed to medium and beat for about 15 seconds, until smooth.

SHAPE THE WHOOPIES

4. Measure the batter into a 2 inch cookie scoop, gently rounded, or use 2 spoons to drop 6 rounded mounds (42 grams each) of batter, evenly spaced, onto one of the prepared cookie sheets. They should be about 2 inches wide by 1 inch high.

BAKE THE WHOOPIES

5. Bake for 6 minutes. For even baking, rotate the pan halfway around. Continue baking for 2 to 4 minutes, or just until the cakes spring back when pressed lightly with a fingertip.

6. While the first batch is baking, mound the remaining batter on the second cookie sheet. Bake as soon as the first batch is removed from the oven.

COOL THE WHOOPIES

7. Set the pans on wire racks for 5 to 10 minutes. Using a thin pancake turner, lift the whoopies from the pans and set them on wire racks. Cool completely.

SANDWICH THE WHOOPIE PIES

8. Place a mound (about 3 gently rounded tablespoons) filling between two whoopies to make a sandwich. Press down lightly until the filling reaches the edges.

STORE UNFILLED, AIRTIGHT: room temperature, 3 days; refrigerated, 1 week; frozen, 3 months.
FILLED, AIRTIGHT: cool room temperature, 1 day.

(continued)

Making Whoopie Pies

Sift together the dry ingredients.

Beat the egg mixture until smoother and paler in color.

The consistency of the finished batter.

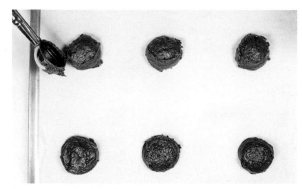

Scoop mounds of the batter.

Bake the cakes until springy.

Spread the filling on the cakes.

Apple Cinnamon Coffee Cake

SERVES 12 TO 16

OVEN TEMPERATURE:
350°F/175°C

BAKING TIME: 55 to 65 minutes

BAKING EQUIPMENT:
One 13 by 9 by 2 inch high pan, encircled with cake strips (see Baking Pearls, page 120), bottom coated with shortening, topped with parchment, then coated with baking spray with flour. (If the sides of the pan are sloped, coat them with shortening and line them with parchment extending about 1 inch above the top to compensate for the smaller volume.)

Apple coffee cake is a real favorite, and as a sheet cake it is perfect for a party or picnic. This soft, buttery layered cake is filled with tart apples and a layer of cinnamon streusel, and then topped with a crunchy streusel topping.

CRUMB FILLING AND TOPPING Makes 465 grams/3¼ cups

unsalted butter	71 grams	5 tablespoons (½ stick plus 1 tablespoon)
walnut halves	150 grams	1½ cups
granulated sugar	37 grams	3 tablespoons
light Muscovado or dark brown sugar	108 grams	½ cup, firmly packed
ground cinnamon	4.4 grams	2 teaspoons
bleached all-purpose flour	100 grams	¾ cup (lightly spooned into the cup and leveled off) plus 1 tablespoon
pure vanilla extract	.	¾ teaspoon (3.7 ml)

MAKE THE CRUMB FILLING AND TOPPING

1. In the microwave in a 1 cup glass measure with a spout, or in a small saucepan over medium-low heat, melt the butter.

2. In a food processor, pulse the walnuts, granulated and brown sugars, and cinnamon until the walnuts are coarsely chopped.

3. Into a small bowl, spoon out 178 grams/1¼ cups to use for the filling.

4. To the nut mixture remaining in the food processor, add the flour, melted butter, and vanilla and pulse briefly to form a coarse, crumbly mixture for the topping.

5. Scrape the crumb topping into a medium bowl and refrigerate for about 20 minutes to firm up the butter, which will make it easier to crumble.

(continued)

Baking Pearls

Cake strips (see page xv) help to keep the crust from browning too deeply during the long baking period.

If you prefer, it's fine to add the crumb topping before baking, but be sure to tent the cake loosely with foil after the first 40 minutes of baking to prevent overbrowning.

BATTER Makes 1040 grams

unsalted butter	255 grams	18 tablespoons (2¼ sticks)
3 large eggs	150 grams	½ cup plus 1½ tablespoons (140 ml)
2 medium tart apples (see page xxv), 288 grams/⅓ pound	230 grams (sliced)	2 cups (sliced)
lemon juice, freshly squeezed and strained (1 lemon)	16 grams	1 tablespoon (15 ml)
full-fat sour cream	242 grams	1 cup, *divided*
pure vanilla extract	.	2 teaspoons (10 ml)
bleached all-purpose flour	300 grams	2½ cups (lightly spooned into the cup and leveled off)
sugar, preferably superfine	300 grams	1½ cups
baking powder	2.2 grams	½ teaspoon
baking soda	4.1 grams	¾ teaspoon
fine sea salt	.	¼ teaspoon

PREHEAT THE OVEN

▪ Twenty minutes or longer before baking, set an oven rack in the lower third of the oven. Set the oven at 350°F/175°C.

MISE EN PLACE

▪ About 1 hour ahead, set the butter and eggs on the counter at room temperature (65° to 75°F/19° to 24°C).

▪ Shortly before mixing the batter, peel, core, and cut the apples into ¼ inch thick slices. Place them into a small bowl and sprinkle them with the lemon juice.

MAKE THE BATTER

1. Into a medium bowl, weigh or measure the eggs. Add 60 grams/¼ cup of the sour cream and the vanilla and whisk lightly until combined.

2. In the bowl of a stand mixer fitted with the flat beater, mix the flour, sugar, baking powder, baking soda, and salt on low speed for 30 seconds. Add the butter and the remaining 182 grams/¾ cup sour cream and mix on low speed until the flour mixture is moistened. Raise the speed to medium and beat for 1½ minutes. Scrape down the sides of the bowl.

3. Starting on medium-low speed, gradually add the egg mixture in two parts, beating on medium speed for 30 seconds after each addition to incorporate the ingredients and strengthen the structure. Scrape down the sides of the bowl.

4. Scrape about two-thirds of the batter (700 grams) into the prepared pan and smooth the surface evenly. With your fingers, sprinkle lightly with the reserved crumb filling (do not press it into the batter).

5. Quickly top with four rows of apple slices.

6. Drop the remaining batter in large blobs over the apples and carefully spread it evenly. (See Baking Pearls for a way to add the crumb topping at this point.)

BAKE THE CAKE

7. Bake for 40 minutes.

8. While the cake is baking, use your fingertips to pinch together the crumb topping, breaking up the larger pieces so that about one-third of the mixture is in ¼ inch balls or clumps. (Do not make the balls larger because they will be hard to cut when serving.) Let them fall onto a large piece of parchment and add the rest of the lightly pinched crumbs.

9. Remove the pan from the oven and gently place it on a wire rack. Use the parchment as a funnel to strew the crumb topping quickly and evenly over the surface.

10. Continue baking for 15 to 25 minutes, or until an instant-read thermometer inserted into the center of the cake, without touching the pan, reads about 208°F/98°C. (A cake tester may come out clean well before it is fully baked, so if not using a thermometer, bake for a minimum of 20 minutes after adding the topping.)

COOL AND SERVE THE CAKE

11. Let the cake cool completely in the pan on a wire rack for about 1½ hours. To serve, run a metal spatula between the sides of the pan and the cake, pressing firmly against the pan. Cut the cake into squares and lift them out onto serving plates with a small pancake turner.

STORE AIRTIGHT: room temperature, 3 days; refrigerated, 1 week; frozen, 3 months.

(continued)

Making Apple Cinnamon Coffee Cake

Smooth two-thirds of the batter in the pan.

Sprinkle with the crumb filling.

Arrange the apple slices.

Dollop on the remaining batter.

Evenly spread the batter.

Strew on the crumb topping after baking for 40 minutes.

Apple Cider Cake Doughnuts

MAKES SIX 3 INCH
DOUGHNUTS

OVEN TEMPERATURE:
350°F/175°C

BAKING TIME: 14 to 16
minutes

BAKING EQUIPMENT:
One 6 cavity doughnut
pan, well coated with
baking spray with flour

Optional: a disposable
pastry bag or quart-size
reclosable freezer bag

These apple doughnuts are so superior to most commercial dough-nuts as they are less sweet, more appley, and firmer and more mel-low the day after baking. They are most delicious when made with fresh autumn apple cider, but are still great made with pasteurized apple cider. The secret to the special flavor is reducing the apple cider by one-third to intensify its flavor.

BATTER Makes 345 grams

unsalted butter	57 grams	4 tablespoons (½ stick)
2 to 3 large yolks	37 grams	2 tablespoons plus 1 teaspoon (35 ml)
unsweetened apple cider	244 grams	1 cup (232 ml)
pure vanilla extract	.	1 teaspoon (5 ml)
all-purpose flour, preferably unbleached	108 grams	¾ cup (lightly spooned into the cup and leveled off) plus 2 tablespoons
sugar	67 grams	⅓ cup
baking powder	1.1 grams	¼ teaspoon
baking soda	1.3 grams	¼ teaspoon
fine sea salt	.	¼ teaspoon

PREHEAT THE OVEN

▪ Twenty minutes or longer before baking, set an oven rack at the middle level. Set the oven at 350°F/175°C.

MISE EN PLACE

▪ About 1 hour ahead, set the butter and eggs on the counter at room temperature (65° to 75°F/19° to 24°C).

▪ **REDUCE THE APPLE CIDER:** In a small saucepan, preferably nonstick, over medium-high heat, boil down the apple cider until reduced to 86 grams/ ⅓ cup/79 ml. Cover tightly to prevent further evaporation and allow it to cool to room temperature.

(continued)

Baking Pearls

For perfectly smooth exteriors and open centers to the doughnuts, fill the cavities only three-quarters full instead of nearly to the top so that they don't rise above the center post, and bake the excess as a cupcake.

If you do not have a doughnut pan, you can bake these as 7 cupcakes: Coat cupcake liners with baking spray with flour. Set in muffin pans or custard cups, and fill each about two-thirds full (about 50 grams). Bake for 20 to 25 minutes, until they test done as above. After unmolding, brush the tops with the melted butter and dust with the cinnamon sugar.

MAKE THE BATTER

1. Into a 1 cup or larger measure with a spout, weigh or measure the egg yolks. Add the cooled reduced apple cider and vanilla and whisk just until lightly combined.

2. In the bowl of a stand mixer fitted with the flat beater, mix the flour, sugar, baking powder, baking soda, and salt on low speed for 30 seconds.

3. Add the butter and about one-quarter of the egg mixture. Holding the beater with your hand, mash the butter and egg mixture into the flour mixture so that it doesn't jump out of the bowl when beating. Then reattach the beater and mix on low speed until the flour mixture is moistened. Raise the speed to medium and beat for 1½ minutes. Scrape down the sides of the bowl.

4. Starting on medium-low speed, gradually add the remaining egg mixture to the batter in two parts, beating on medium speed for 30 seconds after each addition, and scraping the sides of the bowl as needed, to incorporate the ingredients and strengthen the structure.

5. Scrape the batter into a disposable pastry bag or reclosable freezer bag. Cut a 1 inch diameter semicircle from the tip. Pipe (or spoon) the batter into the prepared pan, filling each cavity almost to the top (56 grams into each) and leaving the center post uncovered.

6. Bake for 14 to 16 minutes, or until golden brown and a wire cake tester inserted between the center post and sides comes out clean. An instant-read thermometer should read about 203°F/95°C.

COOL AND UNMOLD THE DOUGHNUTS

7. Set the pan on a wire rack and cool the doughnuts for 5 minutes. Invert the doughnuts onto a second wire rack for a few minutes until cool enough to handle. If desired, cut out the centers to make smooth holes: Set the doughnuts on a cutting board and use a 1 inch cookie cutter or the wide end of a pastry tube to cut out the centers.

CINNAMON SUGAR TOPPING

unsalted butter	35 grams	2½ tablespoons
sugar, preferably superfine	50 grams	¼ cup
ground cinnamon	2.2 grams	1 teaspoon

MAKE THE TOPPING

8. In a small saucepan on low heat or in a small bowl in the microwave, melt the butter.

9. In a medium bowl, whisk together the sugar and cinnamon. If there are any lumps pass it through a fine-mesh strainer.

10. Brush a doughnut on all sides with the melted butter and set it, flat bottom side down, on top of the cinnamon sugar. Spin it around to coat it and then, holding it bottom side down in your hand over the bowl containing the cinnamon sugar, sprinkle the entire top and sides with the topping. Set it on a plate and repeat with the remaining doughnuts. When all are coated, use the remaining topping to give a second coat to the tops. To keep the coating crunchy, allow the doughnuts to cool completely before storing.

STORE AIRTIGHT: room temperature, 3 days; refrigerated, 5 days; frozen, 2 months.

Making Apple Cider Cake Doughnuts

Pipe the batter into the pan.

Invert the pan with the baked doughnuts.

Unmold the doughnuts.

Cut out the centers.

Brush with melted butter.

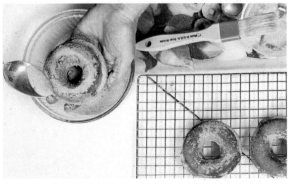

Coat with cinnamon sugar.

Carrot Cake

SERVES 16 TO 20

OVEN TEMPERATURE:
350°F/175°C

BAKING TIME: 45 to 55 minutes

BAKING EQUIPMENT:
Two 9 by 2 inch round or 8 by 2 inch square pans, encircled with cake strips (see page xv), bottoms coated with shortening, topped with parchment cut to fit, then coated with baking spray with flour

One of the most beloved American layer cakes, this cake uses oil instead of butter, which means it maintains its excellent texture even when chilled. This makes it possible to pair the layers with a cream cheese based frosting, which requires refrigeration.

Makes 1580 grams batter

4 large eggs	200 grams	¾ cup plus 2 teaspoons (187 ml)
carrots (568 grams/1¼ pounds)	454 grams, coarsely shredded	3 cups coarsely shredded, firmly packed
unbleached all-purpose flour	300 grams	2½ cups (lightly spooned into the cup and leveled off)
baking powder	6.7 grams	1½ teaspoons
baking soda	5.5 grams	1 teaspoon
fine sea salt	6 grams	1 teaspoon
unsweetened cocoa powder, preferably alkalized	5 grams	1 tablespoon
ground cinnamon	4.4 grams	2 teaspoons
granulated sugar	300 grams	1½ cups
light brown sugar, preferably light Muscovado	100 grams	½ cup minus ½ tablespoon, firmly packed
canola or safflower oil	269 grams	1¼ cups (296 ml)
pure vanilla extract	.	2 teaspoons (10 ml)

PREHEAT THE OVEN

- Twenty minutes or longer before baking, set an oven rack in the lower third of the oven. Set the oven at 350°F/175°C.

MISE EN PLACE

- Thirty minutes to 1 hour ahead, set the eggs on the counter at room temperature (65° to 75°F/19° to 24°C).

- Shred the carrots.

- In a medium bowl, whisk together the flour, baking powder, baking soda, salt, cocoa, and cinnamon.

(continued)

Make This Recipe Your Own

If you enjoy raisins in a carrot cake, you can add 142 grams/ 1 cup golden or dark raisins. (Alternatively, you can add 100 grams/1 cup coarsely chopped, lightly toasted walnuts.) To keep them from settling at the bottom, add half of them together with the carrots and scatter the remaining raisins or nuts evenly on top of the batter in each pan. Use the back of a fork to push them gently into the batter.

For a single layer, divide the recipe in half.

MAKE THE BATTER

1. Into the bowl of a stand mixer, weigh or measure the eggs. Add the granulated and brown sugars, oil, and vanilla. Attach the flat beater and beat on low speed for 1 minute, until blended.

2. Add the flour mixture and beat on low speed for 20 seconds, just until incorporated. Scrape down the sides of the bowl.

3. Add the carrots and beat for another 12 seconds.

4. Scrape the batter into the prepared pans (790 grams each) and smooth the surfaces.

BAKE THE CAKES

5. Bake for 45 to 55 minutes, or until a wire cake tester inserted near the centers comes out clean and the cakes spring back when pressed lightly in the centers. The cakes should just start to shrink from the sides of the pans.

COOL AND UNMOLD THE CAKES

6. Let the cakes cool in the pans on wire racks for 10 minutes. Run a small metal spatula between the sides of the pans and the cakes, pressing firmly against the pan, and invert the cakes onto wire racks that have been lightly coated with nonstick cooking spray. Peel off the parchment and reinvert onto wire racks. Cool completely.

COMPOSE THE CAKE

7. Make one recipe of White Chocolate Cream Cheese Frosting (page 338) or Peanut Butter Cream Cheese Frosting (page 339). Fill and frost the cake following the instructions on page 84.

STORE UNFROSTED, AIRTIGHT: room temperature, 3 days; refrigerated, 1 week; frozen, 3 months.
FROSTED, AIRTIGHT: room temperature, 1 day; refrigerated, 1 week; frozen, 3 months.

Making Carrot Cake

The batter before adding the carrots.

Add the carrots.

Fill the cake pans.

Loosen the sides of the cakes from the pans.

Spread the frosting over the first layer.

Set the second inverted layer on top.

Frost the sides of the cake.

Frost the top and make decorative swirls.

Banana Walnut Loaf

MAKES ONE 8¼ BY 4½ BY 3¼ INCH HIGH LOAF

OVEN TEMPERATURE: 350°F/175°C

BAKING TIME: 5 minutes for the walnuts; 55 to 65 minutes for the bread

PLAN AHEAD: Allow the bananas to ripen for several days in a warm area until they are covered with black spots.

BAKING EQUIPMENT: One 9 by 5 inch by 2¾ inch (8 cup) loaf pan, coated with baking spray with flour

This combination of bananas and walnuts, accented by lemon zest and mellowed by buttermilk, is my favorite banana bread. Be sure to use very ripe bananas for maximum sweetness and flavor. Using a food processor makes this a very quick quick bread but mixing by hand in a bowl with a fork to mash the bananas and a wooden spoon to mix the rest of the ingredients also works well.

unsalted butter	28 grams	2 tablespoons
2 large eggs	100 grams	⅓ cup plus 1 tablespoon (94 ml)
walnut halves	75 grams	¾ cup
lemon zest, finely grated	3 grams	1½ teaspoons, loosely packed
bleached all-purpose flour	225 grams	1¾ cups (lightly spooned into the cup and leveled off) plus 2 tablespoons
sugar	150 grams	¾ cup
baking soda	5.5 grams	1 teaspoon
fine sea salt	3 grams	½ teaspoon
pure vanilla extract	.	1 teaspoon (5 ml)
2 very ripe large bananas, about 340 grams/12 ounces before peeling	227 grams	1 cup mashed
low-fat buttermilk	60 grams	¼ cup (59 ml)

PREHEAT THE OVEN

▪ Twenty minutes or longer before toasting the walnuts, set an oven rack in the lower third of the oven. Set the oven at 350°F/175°C.

MISE EN PLACE

▪ About 1 hour ahead, set the eggs on the counter at room temperature (65° to 75°F/19° to 24°C). Cut the butter into 4 pieces.

▪ **TOAST AND CHOP THE WALNUTS:** Spread the walnuts evenly on a cookie sheet and bake for 5 minutes. Turn the walnuts onto a clean dish towel and roll and rub them around to loosen the skins. Discard any loose skins and let the nuts cool completely. Chop medium coarse.

Baking Pearls

The peel of a banana represents about one-third of its weight.

Baby bananas have the sweetest and most intense flavor. You will need about four 5 inch long bananas.

Toasting walnuts keeps them from discoloring during baking, helps to remove the bitter skin, and intensifies their flavor.

You can replace the buttermilk with an equal amount of whole milk plus 1 teaspoon lemon juice but the batter will be thinner and not distribute the nuts as evenly.

Make This Recipe Your Own

The nuts can be replaced with an equal amount of mini chocolate chips or chopped chocolate of your choice.

■ With dish washing liquid, wash the lemons. Rinse, dry, and zest them (see page xxv).

■ In a medium bowl, whisk together the flour, sugar, baking soda, and salt.

■ Into a 1 cup measure with a spout, weigh or measure the eggs. Add the vanilla and lemon zest.

MAKE THE BATTER

1. In a food processor, process the bananas and butter until a coarse consistency. Add the buttermilk and pulse until incorporated. Then process until smooth, scraping the sides of the bowl as needed.

2. Add the egg mixture and pulse just until smoothly incorporated.

3. Add the flour mixture and pulse several times, just until no dry particles remain. Scrape the sides of the bowl.

4. Add the nuts and pulse about 5 times, just until mixed through.

5. Scrape the batter into the prepared pan. Smooth the surface with a spatula. It will fill the pan to about 1½ inches from the top.

BAKE THE BANANA BREAD

6. Bake for 55 to 65 minutes, or until a wooden skewer inserted into the center comes out clean. (The bread may shrink from the sides of the pan before this point, so judge by the skewer test.)

COOL THE BANANA BREAD

7. Let the bread cool in the pan on a wire rack for 10 minutes. Run a small metal spatula between the sides of the pan and the bread, pressing firmly against the pan, and tilt the pan to slide out the bread onto the wire rack. Cool completely top side up.

STORE AIRTIGHT: room temperature, 3 days; refrigerated, 1 week; frozen, 3 months.

(continued)

Making a Banana Walnut Loaf

Mise en place for the ingredients.

Process the banana and butter.

Process the remaining ingredients and scrape the sides of the bowl.

Scrape the batter into the pan.

Zucchini Bread

The zucchini does not contribute any noticeable flavor to this quick bread—the flavor comes from the spices, brown sugar, and toasted walnuts—but the zucchini lends moistness and structure.

2 large eggs	100 grams	⅓ cup plus 1 tablespoon (94 ml)
walnut halves	50 grams	½ cup
bleached all-purpose flour	181 grams	1½ cups (lightly spooned into the cup and leveled off)
baking powder	3.3 grams	¾ teaspoon
baking soda	4.1 grams	¾ teaspoon
fine sea salt	.	¼ teaspoon
ground cinnamon	2.2 grams	1 teaspoon
ground ginger	.	½ teaspoon
340 grams/12 ounces green zucchini	227 grams, shredded	2 cups shredded, firmly packed
light brown sugar	163 grams	¾ cup, firmly packed
canola or safflower oil	108 grams	½ cup (118 ml)
pure vanilla extract	.	1 teaspoon (5 ml)

PREHEAT THE OVEN

▪ Twenty minutes or longer before toasting the walnuts, set an oven rack in the lower third of the oven. Set the oven at 350°F/175°C.

MISE EN PLACE

▪ Thirty minutes to 1 hour ahead, set the eggs on the counter at room temperature (65° to 75°F/19° to 24°C).

▪ **TOAST AND CHOP THE WALNUTS:** Spread the walnuts evenly on a cookie sheet and bake for 5 minutes. Turn the walnuts onto a clean dish towel and roll and rub them around to loosen the skins. Discard any loose skins and let the nuts cool completely. Chop medium fine.

▪ In a medium bowl, whisk together the flour, baking powder, baking soda, salt, cinnamon, ginger, and walnuts.

▪ Shred the zucchini on the medium shredding holes of a food processor or grater (not the finest holes).

(continued)

This is a great recipe to use up leftover egg whites, as the flavors of this quick bread come primarily from the spices so the extra flavor from egg yolks would not be missed. Three large egg whites (90 grams/¼ cup plus 2 tablespoon/89 ml) can be substituted for the 2 whole eggs.

MAKE THE BATTER

1. Into the bowl of a stand mixer, weigh or measure the eggs. Add the brown sugar, oil, and vanilla. Attach the flat beater and beat on low speed for 1 minute, until blended.

2. Add the flour mixture and beat on the lowest speed just until incorporated, about 20 seconds.

3. Add the zucchini and beat for another 12 seconds, just until incorporated.

4. Scrape the batter into the prepared pan. It will be about 1¼ inches from the top.

BAKE THE ZUCCHINI BREAD

5. Bake for 55 to 65 minutes, or until dark brown and a wooden skewer inserted into the center comes out clean.

COOL THE ZUCCHINI BREAD

6. Let the bread cool in the pan on a wire rack for 10 minutes. Run a small spatula between the sides of the pan and the bread pressing firmly against the pan, and tilt the pan to slide out the bread onto the wire rack. Cool completely top side up.

- If desired, serve with softened butter or cream cheese.

STORE AIRTIGHT: room temperature, 3 days; refrigerated, 1 week; frozen, 3 months.

Making Zucchini Bread

Shred the zucchini.

Mise en place for the ingredients.

Add the flour mixture.

Add the zucchini.

Blueberry Muffins

MAKES 6 MUFFINS

OVEN TEMPERATURE:
375°F/190°C

BAKING TIME: 20 to 30 minutes

BAKING EQUIPMENT: 6 cupcake liners, lightly coated with baking spray with flour, set in a muffin pan or custard cups

These muffins are quick to mix and can be made in a bowl with a wooden spoon instead of a mixer. Sour cream gives a mellow flavor. The optional sugar topping creates a delightful crunch.

Makes 534 grams batter

unsalted butter	57 grams	4 tablespoons (½ stick)
1 large egg	50 grams	3 tablespoons plus ½ teaspoon (47.5 ml)
blueberries, preferably small	100 grams	¾ cup
lemon zest, finely grated	6 grams	1 tablespoon, loosely packed
bleached all-purpose flour	150 grams	1¼ cups (lightly spooned into the cup and leveled off)
baking powder	2.2 grams	½ teaspoon
baking soda	1.3 grams	¼ teaspoon
fine sea salt	.	¼ plus ⅛ teaspoon
full-fat sour cream	81 grams	⅓ cup
pure vanilla extract	.	1 teaspoon (5 ml)
sugar	100 grams	½ cup
sugar, for topping (optional)	.	¾ teaspoon
nutmeg, freshly grated (optional)	.	a dusting

PREHEAT THE OVEN

■ Thirty minutes or longer before baking, set an oven rack in the lower third of the oven. Set the oven at 375°F/190°C.

MISE EN PLACE

■ About 1 hour ahead, set the butter and egg on the counter at room temperature (65° to 75°F/19° to 24°C).

■ Rinse the blueberries and allow them to dry on paper towels.

■ With dish washing liquid, wash the lemons. Rinse, dry, and zest them (see page xxv).

■ In a medium bowl, whisk together the flour, baking powder, baking soda, and salt.

■ Into another medium bowl, weigh or measure the sour cream and cover it with plastic wrap.

Baking Pearl

A 6 cup silicone muffin pan makes the best shaped muffins. Coat the cavities with baking spray with flour and set it on a cookie sheet. Allow the cupcakes to cool completely in the pans before unmolding.

Make This Recipe Your Own

You can make smaller muffins by filling 8 cupcake liners only three-quarters full (66 grams each) but the larger muffins have crunchier edges as they spread slightly over the top of the liners.

If you like extra blueberries, you can add up to another 35 grams/¼ cup and divide the batter between 8 cupcake liners, about three-quarters full (71 grams each).

■ Into a 1 cup measure with a spout, weigh or measure the egg. Add the vanilla and lightly whisk it in.

MAKE THE BATTER

1. In the bowl of a stand mixer fitted with the flat beater, beat the butter, sugar, and lemon zest on medium speed for 1 to 2 minutes, until light and fluffy. Beat in the egg mixture until incorporated.

2. Add one-half of the flour mixture together with one-half of the sour cream and beat on low speed just until it is fully incorporated. Repeat with the remaining flour mixture and sour cream.

3. With a silicone spatula, gently fold in the blueberries.

FILL THE CUPCAKE LINERS

4. Spoon the batter into the cupcake liners, mounding it slightly above the top (89 grams each). No need to smooth the tops. Sprinkle with sugar and grate nutmeg lightly on top, if desired.

BAKE THE MUFFINS

5. Bake for 20 to 30 minutes, or until the muffins spring back when pressed lightly in the centers and a wooden skewer inserted in the centers comes out clean.

COOL AND UNMOLD THE MUFFINS

6. Set the pan on a wire rack and cool the muffins for 10 minutes. Remove the muffins from the pan and set them on another wire rack to cool until warm or room temperature.

STORE AIRTIGHT: room temperature, 2 days; refrigerated, 5 days; frozen, 2 months.

(continued)

Making Blueberry Muffins

Fold the blueberries into the batter.

Sprinkle sugar on top.

Grate fresh nutmeg over the top.

The baked muffins with crunchy tops.

Apple Walnut Muffins

OVEN TEMPERATURE:
375°F/190°C

BAKING TIME: 25 to 35
minutes

BAKING EQUIPMENT:
12 cupcake liners, lightly
coated with baking
spray with flour or
nonstick cooking spray,
set in muffin pans or
custard cups

Optional: a 2 inch
cookie scoop

These muffins are best when served soon after you make them or reheated for about 5 minutes (15 minutes if frozen) in a preheated 350°F/175°C oven, so that the tops become crisp. (The large amount of apples can make the muffins become too moist on storage, especially if they are put in a closed container.)

Using butter instead of oil adds a lovely flavor. The butter is clarified to avoid adding extra moisture to the batter, since the apples already provide just the right amount. If you prefer to use oil, see Make This Recipe Your Own on page 140.

Makes 864 grams batter

unsalted butter	92 grams	6½ tablespoons (¾ stick plus ½ tablespoon)
unbleached or bleached all-purpose flour	200 grams	1⅓ cups (lightly spooned into the cup and leveled off)
baking soda	2.7 grams	½ teaspoon
fine sea salt	.	⅜ teaspoon
ground cinnamon	3.3 grams	1½ teaspoons
nutmeg, preferably freshly grated	.	⅜ teaspoon
walnut halves	75 grams	¾ cup
3 medium tart apples (see page xxv), 454 grams/1 pound	350 grams (diced)	about 2⅓ cups (diced)
1 large egg	50 grams	3 tablespoons plus ½ teaspoon (47.5 ml)
1 large egg yolk	19 grams	1 tablespoon plus ½ teaspoon (17.5 ml)
sugar, preferably superfine	133 grams	⅔ cup
pure vanilla extract	.	½ teaspoon (2.5 ml)

PREHEAT THE OVEN

■ Twenty minutes or longer before baking, set an oven rack in the lower third of the oven. Set the oven at 375°F/190°C.

(continued)

MISE EN PLACE

- About 1 hour ahead, set the butter and eggs on the counter at room temperature (65° to 75°F/19 to 24°C).

- **CLARIFY AND BROWN THE BUTTER:** Have ready by the cooktop a 1 cup glass measure with a spout.

- In a small heavy saucepan, on very low heat, melt the butter, stirring often with a silicone spatula. Raise the heat to low and boil, stirring constantly, until the milk solids on the spatula become a deep brown. Immediately pour the butter into the glass measure, scraping in the browned solids as well. Allow the browned butter to cool to room temperature, or no higher than 80°F/27°C.

- In a medium bowl, whisk together the flour, baking soda, salt, cinnamon, and nutmeg.

- Chop or break the walnuts into medium coarse pieces and add them to the flour mixture. Whisk to combine.

- Peel, core, and cut the apples into ⅛ to ¼ inch dice. Set them in a large bowl.

- Into another 1 cup measure with a spout, weigh or measure the egg and egg yolk.

MAKE THE BATTER

1. Add the egg and yolk to the apples. With a silicone spatula, stir and fold to coat the apples.

2. Add the sugar, browned butter with the solids, and vanilla, and stir them in. Allow the mixture to sit for 10 minutes so that the apples start to exude a little liquid.

3. Stir in the flour mixture until well combined. Scrape down the sides of the bowl. The batter will be thick and slightly dry.

FILL THE CUPCAKE LINERS

4. Use a cookie scoop or a large spoon to place the batter into each of the prepared muffin cups (72 grams each), almost to the top.

BAKE THE MUFFINS

5. Bake 25 to 35 minutes, or until the tops of the muffins are crisp and brown and a wooden skewer inserted in the centers comes out clean.

COOL THE MUFFINS

6. Set the pans on wire racks and cool the muffins for 10 minutes. Invert the muffins onto a wire rack and remove the pans. Gently dislodge any muffins that may have stuck. Reinvert the muffins. Cool completely.

STORE AIRTIGHT: room temperature, 1 day; refrigerated, 3 days.

Making Apple Walnut Muffins

Mise en place for the ingredients.

Stir in the egg and yolk to coat the apples.

Stir in the remaining ingredients.

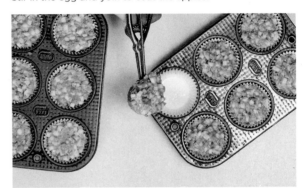

Fill the muffin cups with a cookie scoop.

Banana Walnut Muffins

MAKES 9 MUFFINS

OVEN TEMPERATURE:
350°F/175°C

BAKING TIME: 5 minutes
for the walnuts; 15 to 25
minutes for the muffins

PLAN AHEAD: Allow
the bananas to ripen
for several days in a
warm area until they
are covered with black
spots.

BAKING EQUIPMENT:
9 cupcake liners, no
preparation needed,
set in muffin pans or
custard cups

This soft, full flavored muffin can also support various additions such as nuts and/or chocolate, because the fiber in the banana gives it extra structure and the muffins won't spread as much at the top.

Makes 515 grams batter

unsalted butter	71 grams	5 tablespoons (½ stick plus 1 tablespoon)
1 large egg	50 grams	3 tablespoons plus ½ teaspoon (47.5 ml)
walnut halves	50 grams	½ cup
lemon zest, finely grated	2 grams	1 teaspoon, loosely packed
2 baby bananas (5 inches) or 1 large banana, very ripe, about 170 grams/6 ounces before peeling	113 grams	½ cup, lightly mashed
full-fat sour cream	60 grams	¼ cup
pure vanilla extract	.	¾ teaspoon (3.7 ml)
bleached cake flour OR bleached all-purpose flour	100 grams	1 cup (sifted into the cup and leveled off) OR ¾ cup plus 2 tablespoons (sifted into the cup and leveled off)
sugar, preferably turbinado	75 grams	¼ cup plus 2 tablespoons
baking powder	2.2 grams	½ teaspoon
baking soda	2.7 grams	½ teaspoon
fine sea salt	.	¼ teaspoon

PREHEAT THE OVEN

▪ Twenty minutes or longer before toasting the walnuts, set an oven rack in the lower third of the oven. Set the oven at 350°F/175°C.

MISE EN PLACE

▪ About 1 hour ahead, set the butter and egg on the counter at room temperature (65° to 75°F/19° to 24°C).

▪ **TOAST AND CHOP THE WALNUTS:** Spread the walnuts evenly on a cookie sheet and bake for 5 minutes. Turn the walnuts onto a clean dish towel and roll and rub them around to loosen the skins. Discard any loose skins and let the nuts cool completely. Chop medium fine.

▪ With dish washing liquid, wash the lemons. Rinse, dry, and zest them (page xxv).

▪ Into a 1 cup measure with a spout, weigh or measure the egg.

Fold into the finished batter 42 grams/1.5 ounces/¼ cup mini chocolate chips or your favorite chocolate, chopped medium fine. The walnuts can be eliminated or replaced with up to a total of 82 grams/½ cup of the chocolate.

MAKE THE BATTER

1. In a food processor, process the bananas and sour cream, scraping the sides of the bowl as needed. Add the egg, lemon zest, and vanilla and process just until smooth.

2. In the bowl of a stand mixer fitted with the flat beater, mix the flour, sugar, baking powder, baking soda, and salt on low speed for 30 seconds.

3. Add the butter and half of the banana mixture. Mix on low speed until the flour mixture is moistened. Raise the speed to medium and beat for 1½ minutes. Scrape down the sides of the bowl.

4. Starting on medium-low speed, gradually add the remaining banana mixture to the batter in two parts, beating on medium speed for 30 seconds after each addition to incorporate ingredients and strengthen the structure. Scrape down the sides of the bowl.

5. On low speed, mix in the walnuts.

FILL THE CUPCAKE LINERS

6. Spoon the batter into the cupcake liners, three-quarters full (57 grams each). Smooth the tops.

BAKE THE MUFFINS

7. Bake for 15 to 25 minutes, or until the muffins spring back when pressed lightly in the centers and a wooden skewer inserted in the centers comes out clean.

COOL AND UNMOLD THE MUFFINS

8. Set the pans on wire racks and cool the muffins for 10 minutes. Remove the muffins from the pans and set them on another wire rack to cool until warm or room temperature.

STORE AIRTIGHT: room temperature, 2 days; refrigerated, 5 days; frozen, 2 months.

Carrot Muffins

OVEN TEMPERATURE:
350°F/175°C

BAKING TIME: 20 to 25 minutes

BAKING EQUIPMENT:
8 cupcake liners, no preparation needed, set in muffin pans or custard cups

These muffins or cupcakes are moist, velvety, and delicious by themselves or topped with cream cheese frosting. They have a lovely tall shape thanks to the fiber in the carrot and double the egg compared with the carrot layer cake on page 127, both of which provide extra structure.

Makes 450 grams batter

2 large eggs	100 grams	⅓ cup plus 1 tablespoon (94 ml)
142 grams/5 ounces carrots	114 grams, coarsely shredded	¾ cup coarsely shredded, firmly packed
bleached all-purpose flour	75 grams	½ cup (lightly spooned into the cup and leveled off) plus 2 tablespoons
baking powder	1.7 grams	⅜ teaspoon
baking soda	1.3 grams	¼ teaspoon
fine sea salt	.	¼ teaspoon
unsweetened cocoa powder, preferably alkalized	.	¾ teaspoon
ground cinnamon	.	½ teaspoon
granulated sugar	75 grams	¼ cup plus 2 tablespoons
light brown sugar, preferably light Muscovado	25 grams	1½ tablespoons plus ½ teaspoon, firmly packed
canola or safflower oil	67 grams	¼ cup plus 1 tablespoons (74 ml)
pure vanilla extract	.	½ teaspoon (2.5 ml)

PREHEAT THE OVEN

▪ Twenty minutes or longer before baking, set an oven rack in the lower third of the oven. Set the oven at 350°F/175°C.

MISE EN PLACE

▪ Thirty minutes to 1 hour ahead, set the eggs on the counter at room temperature (65° to 75°F/19° to 24°C).

▪ Peel and coarsely shred the carrots.

▪ In a small bowl, whisk together the flour, baking powder, baking soda, salt, cocoa, and cinnamon.

▪ Into a 1 cup measure with a spout, weigh or measure the eggs.

The carrot layer cake works well with unbleached flour, but due to the extra egg in these muffins, they require bleached flour to avoid a rubbery texture.

To make more muffins, it is best to make multiple batches, one batch at a time, because as the batter stands, the baking powder activates prematurely, causing the resulting muffins to dome more.

MAKE THE BATTER

1. In the bowl of a stand mixer fitted with the flat beater, beat the granulated and brown sugars, oil, eggs, and vanilla on low speed for 1 minute, until blended.

2. Add the flour mixture and beat on low speed for 20 seconds, just until incorporated. Scrape down the sides of the bowl.

3. Add the carrots and beat for another 12 seconds.

4. Scrape the very liquid batter into a 4 cup measure with a spout.

FILL THE CUPCAKE LINERS

5. Pour the batter into the cupcake liners a little more than three-quarters full (56 grams each). Smooth the tops.

BAKE THE MUFFINS

6. Bake for 20 to 25 minutes, or until the muffins spring back when pressed lightly in the centers and a wooden skewer inserted in the centers comes out clean.

COOL AND UNMOLD THE MUFFINS

7. Set the pans on wire racks and cool the muffins for 10 minutes. Remove the muffins from the pans and set them on another wire rack to cool until warm or room temperature.

STORE AIRTIGHT: room temperature, 2 days; refrigerated, 5 days; frozen, 2 months.

Corn Muffins

OVEN TEMPERATURE:
400°F/200°C

BAKING TIME: 15 to 18 minutes

BAKING EQUIPMENT:
6 cupcake liners, coated with baking spray with flour, set in a muffin pan or custard cups

These muffins are best enjoyed still warm out of the oven. They are quick to make and have a delightfully crunchy top and tender crumb.

Makes 405 grams batter

unsalted butter	28 grams	2 tablespoons
1 large egg	50 grams	3 tablespoons plus ½ teaspoon (47.5 ml)
full-fat sour cream	161 grams	⅔ cup
bleached all-purpose flour	75 grams	½ cup (lightly spooned into the cup and leveled off) plus 2 tablespoons
fine cornmeal, preferably stone ground	64 grams	½ cup
sugar	33 grams	2 tablespoons plus 2 teaspoons
baking powder	4.5 grams	1 teaspoon
baking soda	1.3 grams	¼ teaspoon
fine sea salt	3 grams	½ teaspoon
cornmeal, for dusting	.	½ teaspoon

PREHEAT THE OVEN

- Thirty minutes or longer before baking, set an oven rack in the lower third of the oven. Set the oven at 400°F/200°C.

MISE EN PLACE

- In a small microwavable custard cup, in the microwave, or saucepan on medium-low heat, melt the butter. Set it in a warm place to cool to room temperature but still be fluid.

- Into a 2 cup measure with a spout or bowl, weigh or measure the egg and sour cream. Lightly whisk them together.

MAKE THE BATTER

1. In a medium bowl, whisk together the flour, fine cornmeal, sugar, baking powder, baking soda, and salt.

2. Stir the egg mixture into the flour mixture just until moistened. There should still be a few lumps. Fold in the melted butter just until incorporated.

(continued)

Baking Pearls

Stone ground cornmeal has more flavor because it contains the germ and husk. Since the germ is high in oil, it needs to be stored in the freezer.

Coarse cornmeal will result in a coarser, more crumbly texture.

FILL THE MUFFIN CUPS

3. Spoon the batter into the muffin cups, almost to the top (68 grams each). With a small metal spatula, smooth the batter. Place the cornmeal for dusting in a small strainer and hold it over the muffins. Stir the cornmeal so that it sprinkles evenly over the tops.

BAKE THE MUFFINS

4. Bake for 15 to 18 minutes, or until the muffin tops are golden brown and a wooden skewer inserted in the centers comes out clean.

COOL AND UNMOLD THE MUFFINS

5. Set the pan on a wire rack and cool the muffins for 10 minutes. Invert the muffins onto a wire rack and remove the pan. Gently dislodge any muffins that may have stuck. Reinvert the muffins to cool until warm or room temperature.

STORE AIRTIGHT: room temperature, 2 days; refrigerated, 5 days; frozen, 2 months.

Chocolate Spangled Angel Food Cake

SERVES 8 TO 10

OVEN TEMPERATURE:
350°F/175°C

BAKING TIME: 30 to 40 minutes

PLAN AHEAD: For best flavor and texture, complete the cake 1 day ahead.

BAKING EQUIPMENT:
One uncoated 10 inch (16 cup) two-piece angel food pan

If your pan has feet, you'll need a wire rack, elevated about 4 inches or higher above the work surface by setting it on top of three or four cans, coffee mugs, or glasses of equal height.

If your pan does not have feet, you will need a long-neck glass bottle, small enough to fit into the opening of the tube and weighted with sugar or marbles to keep it from tipping.

An angel food cake is a valuable asset to have in your repertoire. Not only is it a favorite party cake, it is also an excellent vehicle for any leftover egg whites you might have in the freezer. Adding finely grated unsweetened chocolate is a great way to temper the intrinsic sweetness. If you prefer a pure white cake, simply omit the chocolate.

fine-quality 85% or 99% cacao or unsweetened chocolate, chilled	56 grams	2 ounces
16 large egg whites	480 grams	2 cups (473 ml)
superfine sugar	300 grams	1½ cups
cream of tartar	.	2 teaspoons
fine sea salt	.	¼ teaspoon
Wondra flour OR bleached cake flour	100 grams	¾ cup (lightly spooned into the cup and leveled off) OR 1 cup (sifted into the cup and leveled off)
pure vanilla extract	.	4 teaspoons (20 ml)

PREHEAT THE OVEN

■ Twenty minutes or longer before baking, set an oven rack in the lower third of the oven. Set the oven at 350°F/175°C.

MISE EN PLACE

■ Break or chop the chocolate into pieces. Cover and refrigerate it for a minimum of 30 minutes. Then process in a food processor until finely grated. Refrigerate until ready to add to the batter.

■ Into the bowl of the stand mixer, weigh or measure the egg whites. Lightly whisk in the sugar, cream of tartar, and salt. Cover and allow to sit at room temperature for a minimum of 30 minutes, up to 4 hours.

■ In a medium bowl, weigh or measure the flour.

MAKE THE BATTER

1. Attach the whisk beater to the stand mixer. Beat the egg white mixture on medium-low speed until foamy. Gradually raise the speed to high and beat for 10 minutes, or until very stiff peaks form when the beater is raised slowly.

(continued)

Baking Pearls

Cakes whose leavening is based primarily on stiffly beaten egg whites, like this one, are best made in low humidity.

The mixer bowl and whisk must be free of any grease to enable the whites to beat to stiff peaks.

The very lightest and most tender texture comes from using Wondra flour, as it blends easily into the batter without deflating it significantly.

Refrigerating the chocolate ensures that the chocolate spangles stay separate from the batter, providing an attractive contrast.

Make This Recipe Your Own

Fresh berries and whipped cream are a lovely accompaniment, but do not serve this cake with a sauce; it is too delicate and will fall apart.

2. Beat in the vanilla just until combined.

3. Remove the bowl from the stand and dust the flour mixture, ¼ cup at a time, onto the egg white mixture, folding it in quickly but gently with a large wire whisk, slotted skimmer, or large silicone spatula. For the last addition, use a large silicone spatula to make sure that all the flour mixture is incorporated, reaching down to the bottom of the bowl.

4. Add the cold grated chocolate and fold it in just until evenly incorporated.

5. To ensure smooth sides, spread a thin layer of batter onto the sides of the pan. Gently spoon the rest of the batter evenly into the pan. It will be ½ inch from the top.

6. Run a small metal spatula or knife through the batter to prevent air pockets and smooth the surface.

BAKE THE CAKE

7. Bake for 30 to 40 minutes, until golden brown with no moist spots in the cracks, and a wooden skewer inserted between the tube and the sides comes out clean. An instant-read thermometer should read 206°F/97°C. During baking, the center will rise about 1 inch above the pan, but will sink to almost level with the pan when done. The surface will have attractive cracks. While the cake is baking, set up the bottle in a draft free area for unmolding the cake, if needed.

COOL THE CAKE

8. Invert the pan immediately onto the prepared wire rack or over the neck of the bottle. Cool completely in the pan, about 2 hours.

UNMOLD THE CAKE

9. Use a small sharp knife to dislodge the cake inside the rim of the pan. To loosen the sides of the cake from the pan, use a rigid metal spatula, at least 4 inches long and preferably with a squared off end, scraping firmly against the pan's sides and slowly and carefully circling the pan. In order to ensure that you are scraping well against the sides of the pan, and not removing the crust from the sides of the cake, begin by angling the spatula about 20 degrees away from the cake and toward the pan, pushing the cake inward a bit. It works best to advance the spatula about 1 inch, lift it out, and reinsert it just behind where you pulled it out. Continue in this way around the entire cake.

10. Place the cake pan on top of a canister or can that is smaller than the bottom opening of the pan's outer rim. Press down on both sides of the pan to release the outer pan. Alternatively, grasp the center core and lift out the cake. Run a wire cake tester or wooden skewer around the center core. Dislodge the cake from the bottom with a metal spatula or thin sharp knife. Invert the cake onto a wire rack that has been lightly coated with nonstick cooking spray. Reinvert onto a serving plate.

11. Allow the cake to sit for 1 hour or until the top is no longer sticky. Then cover it with a cake dome or wrap it airtight.

STORE AIRTIGHT: room temperature, 3 days; refrigerated, 7 days; do not freeze, as freezing toughens the texture.

Making Chocolate Spangled Angel Food Cake

Beat the meringue to very stiff peaks.

Fold in the grated chocolate.

Spread batter onto the sides of the pan before adding the rest of the batter.

Run a spatula through the batter.

Cool the cake upside down.

Release the sides of the cake from the pan.

Glazed Mocha Chiffon

Incredibly light, soft, moist, and tender, imbued with coffee and glazed with chocolate, this is a stellar dessert.

BATTER

canola or safflower oil	108 grams	½ cup (118 ml)
9 (to 11) large eggs, separated: 7 (to 11) yolks (see Baking Pearls, page 154)	130 grams	½ cup (118 ml)
9 whites	270 grams	1 cup plus 2 tablespoons (266 ml)
instant espresso powder, preferably Medaglio d'Oro (see Baking Pearls, page 154)	8 grams	2 tablespoons
water	158 grams	⅔ cup (158 ml)
pure vanilla extract	.	1 teaspoon (5 ml)
bleached cake flour (see Baking Pearls, page 160)	225 grams	2¼ cups (sifted into the cup and leveled off)
superfine sugar	300 grams	1½ cups, *divided*
baking soda	2.7 grams	½ teaspoon
fine sea salt	3 grams	½ teaspoon
cream of tartar	.	1⅛ teaspoons
Kahlúa, for brushing	267 grams	1 cup (237 ml), *divided*

PREHEAT THE OVEN

▪ Twenty minutes or longer before baking, set an oven rack in the lower third of the oven. Set the oven at 325°F/160°C.

MISE EN PLACE

▪ Thirty minutes to 1 hour ahead, set the oil and eggs on the counter at room temperature (65° to 75°F/19° to 24°C).

▪ Into separate bowls, weigh or measure the egg yolks and egg whites.

▪ Into a 2 cup measure with a spout, transfer the egg yolks. Add the oil.

▪ Into a 1 cup measure with a spout, stir together the espresso powder, water, and vanilla until the coffee granules are dissolved. Cover tightly with plastic wrap.

MAKE THE BATTER

1. In the bowl of a stand mixer fitted with the whisk beater, mix the flour, all but 25 grams/2 tablespoons of the sugar, the baking soda, and salt on low speed for 30 seconds. Make a well in the center.

(continued)

Baking Pearls

The ratio of white to yolk in an egg can vary to such a degree that you may need as few as 7 or as many as 11 eggs for this recipe. It is therefore advisable to weigh or measure the separated yolks and add or reduce if needed.

If you want to use bleached all-purpose flour, you will need the same weight, but by volume only 2 cups minus 2 tablespoons (lightly spooned into the cup and leveled off). You will also need to use only 6 egg whites (180 grams/¾ cup/ 177 ml) and only ¾ teaspoon cream of tartar. The batter will fill the pan about 2 inches from the top.

You can replace the espresso powder and water in the cake with 2 shots of brewed espresso or 158 grams/⅔ cup/ 158 ml strong coffee; if using espresso, add water to equal the same weight or volume.

If the sides of the cake are not smooth, it's fine to apply a crumb coat first: Use a long metal spatula to spread a thin layer of the glaze on the sides before pouring on the rest of it.

2. Add the espresso mixture and the egg yolks and oil to the well in the flour mixture, and beat on low speed until the flour mixture is moistened, scraping down the sides of the bowl as necessary. Raise the speed to medium-high and beat for 1½ minutes, until thicker and lighter in color.

▪ Wash, rinse, and dry the whisk beater to remove any trace of oil. If you do not have a second mixer bowl, scrape this mixture into a large bowl and thoroughly wash, rinse, and dry the mixer bowl to remove any trace of oil.

BEAT THE EGG WHITES INTO A STIFF MERINGUE

3. In the bowl of the stand mixer fitted with the whisk beater, beat the egg whites and cream of tartar on medium-low speed until foamy. Gradually raise the speed to medium-high and beat until soft peaks form when the beater is raised. Beat in the remaining 25 grams/2 tablespoons sugar and continue beating until stiff peaks form when the beater is raised slowly.

ADD THE MERINGUE TO THE BATTER

4. Using a large slotted skimmer or large silicone spatula, gently fold the meringue into the batter just until blended. Use a silicone spatula to reach to the bottom of the bowl to ensure that all the meringue is incorporated.

5. Pour and scrape the batter into the pan. Run a small metal spatula in circles through the batter to prevent air pockets. There is no need to smooth the surface. The batter will come to about 1 inch from the top of the rim.

BAKE THE CAKE

6. Bake for 50 to 60 minutes, or until a wooden skewer inserted between the tube and the sides comes out clean, the cake springs back when pressed lightly, and the cracks on top are no longer moist. (During baking, the cake will dome above the top of the pan and cracks will form.) Avoid opening the oven door before the minimum baking time, or the fragile cake could fall. While the cake is baking, set up the unmolding bottle in a draft free area.

COOL THE CAKE

7. Immediately invert the pan onto the prepared bottle. Cool completely in the pan, about 2 hours.

UNMOLD AND SYRUP THE CAKE

8. Use a small sharp knife to dislodge the cake inside the rim of the pan. To loosen the sides of the cake from the pan, use a rigid metal spatula, at least 4 inches long and preferably with a squared off end, scraping firmly against the pan's sides and slowly and carefully circling the pan. In order to ensure that you are scraping well against the sides of the pan, and not removing the crust from the sides of the cake, begin by angling the spatula about 20 degrees away from the cake and toward the pan, pushing the cake inward a bit. It works best to advance the spatula about 1 inch, lift it out, and reinsert it just behind where you pulled it out. Continue in this way around the entire cake.

9. Place the cake pan on top of a canister that is smaller than the bottom opening of the pan's outer rim. Press down on both sides of the pan to release the outer pan. Alternatively, grasp the center core and lift out the cake. Run a wire cake

Make This Recipe Your Own

If desired, before the glaze has set, garnish with chocolate-covered coffee beans. Alternatively, you can drizzle it with quick tempered white chocolate (see below).

Variation

WHITE CHOCOLATE DRIZZLE GLAZE

Quick temper 56 grams/ 2 ounces of white chocolate by melting it but removing it from the heat source before fully melted and then stirring until fully melted. Stir in 1 tablespoon/15 ml of flavorless oil or 4 teaspoons/20 ml of Cognac. Fill a disposable pastry bag or plastic squeeze bottle with the mixture and pipe onto the top of the cake or plate.

tester or wooden skewer around the center core. Dislodge the cake from the bottom with a metal spatula or thin sharp knife. Invert the cake onto a wire rack that has been covered with plastic wrap, then lightly coated with nonstick cooking spray.

10. Brush the bottom and sides of the cake with all but 33 grams/2 tablespoons/30 ml of the Kahlúa. Reinvert the cake onto the 9 inch cake round and set it on another wire rack. Set the rack on a sheet of foil or a cookie sheet.

11. Brush the top of the cake with the remaining Kahlúa.

MOCHA GLAZE Makes 340 grams/1⅔ cups/393 ml

dark chocolate, 60% to 62% cacao, chopped	170 grams	6 ounces
instant espresso powder, preferably Medaglio d'Oro	.	2 teaspoons
heavy cream	174 grams	¾ cup (177 ml)
Kahlúa	33 grams	2 tablespoons (30 ml)

MAKE THE GLAZE

▪ Have ready a fine-mesh strainer suspended over a small glass bowl.

1. In a food processor, process the chocolate and espresso powder until very fine. Scrape the mixture into a medium heat-proof bowl.

2. In a 1 cup glass measure with a spout, in the microwave, scald the cream: Heat it to the boiling point; small bubbles will form around the periphery. (Alternatively, scald it in a small saucepan over medium heat, stirring often.) Pour three-quarters of the hot cream (130 grams/a little more than ½ cup/133 ml) over the chocolate. Cover and allow it to sit for 5 minutes to melt the chocolate. Stir gently until smooth so as not to create air bubbles.

3. Pass the glaze through the fine-mesh strainer. Stir in the Kahlúa and allow the mixture to cool until tepid. A small amount of glaze should mound a bit when dropped from a spoon before smoothly disappearing. If the glaze is too thick, add some of the remaining warm cream by the teaspoonful. When the consistency is correct, use it at once, or store and reheat it.

GLAZE THE CAKE

4. Set the cake, still on the rack, over a clean pan or piece of foil to catch the dripping chocolate. Pour the glaze evenly over the top of the cake, spreading and smoothing the top with a metal spatula and allowing it to drip down over the sides. With a small metal spatula, lift the glaze from the bottom surface and apply it to cover the sides of the cake.

5. Allow the cake to sit at room temperature for at least 2 hours, until the glaze has set. Avoid refrigerating the glazed cake as it will dull slightly.

6. Use two pancake turners to transfer the cake to a flat serving plate.

STORE AIRTIGHT: room temperature, 3 days; refrigerated, 10 days; frozen, 2 months.

(continued)

Making Glazed Mocha Chiffon

Mise en place for the ingredients for the cake.

The batter before the meringue is added.

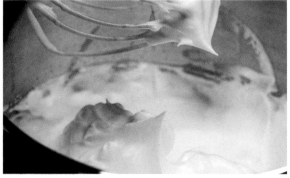

Beat the meringue until stiff.

Fold the meringue into the batter.

Pour the batter into the pan.

Run a spatula through the batter.

Suspend the cake over a long-neck bottle to cool.

Angle the spatula to release the sides of the cake cleanly.

Remove the sides of the pan.

Dislodge the cake from the bottom of the pan.

Lift out the center tube.

Brush with Kahlua.

Strain the glaze into a bowl.

The glaze should mound on the surface.

Pour the glaze over the cake.

Spread the glaze over the sides.

Orange Chiffon

SERVES 12 TO 14

OVEN TEMPERATURE:
325°F/160°C

BAKING TIME: 45 to 55 minutes

BAKING EQUIPMENT:
One uncoated 10 inch (16 cup) two-piece angel food pan

A long-neck glass bottle (weighted with sugar or marbles to keep it from tipping) or a large funnel that will fit into the opening at the top of the pan

This is one of the great truly American cakes, created by Harry Baker in the 1920s. It has the richness of a butter cake with the soft, moist airiness of a sponge cake.

9 (to 11) large eggs, separated: 7 (to 11) yolks (see Baking Pearls, page 160)	130 grams	½ cup (118 ml)
9 whites	270 grams	1 cup plus 2 tablespoons (266 ml)
orange zest, finely grated	12 grams	2 tablespoons, loosely packed
orange juice, freshly squeezed and strained (about 3 to 4 oranges)	181 grams	¾ cup (177 ml)
canola or safflower oil	108 grams	½ cup (118 ml)
pure vanilla extract	.	1 teaspoon (5 ml)
bleached cake flour (see Baking Pearls, page 160)	225 grams	2¼ cups (sifted into the cup and leveled off)
superfine sugar	300 grams	1½ cups, *divided*
baking powder	9 grams	2 teaspoons
fine sea salt	3 grams	½ teaspoon
cream of tartar	.	1⅛ teaspoons

PREHEAT THE OVEN

■ Twenty minutes or longer before baking, set an oven rack in the lower third of the oven. Set the oven at 325°F/160°C.

MISE EN PLACE

■ Thirty minutes to 1 hour ahead, set the eggs on the counter at room temperature (65° to 75°F/19° to 24°C).

■ With dish washing liquid, wash the oranges. Rinse, dry, zest, and juice them (see page xxv).

■ Into separate bowls, weigh or measure the egg yolks and egg whites.

■ Into a 4 cup measure with a spout, transfer the egg yolks. Add the orange zest, orange juice, oil, and vanilla.

MAKE THE BATTER

1. In the bowl of a stand mixer fitted with the whisk beater, add the flour, all but 25 grams/2 tablespoons of the sugar, the baking powder, and salt and mix on low speed for 30 seconds. Remove the bowl from the stand and make a well in the center.

2. Tilt the bowl and add the egg yolk mixture to the well in the flour mixture. Beat on low speed until the flour mixture is moistened, scraping down the sides of the bowl as necessary. Raise the speed to medium-high and beat for 1½ minutes, until thicker and lighter in color.

(continued)

The ratio of white to yolk in an egg can vary to such a degree that you may need as few as 7 or as many as 11 eggs for this recipe. It is therefore advisable to weigh or measure the separated yolks and add or reduce if needed.

I prefer the flavor of chiffon cake made with bleached cake flour. If you want to use bleached all-purpose flour, you will need the same weight but by volume only 2 cups minus 2 tablespoons (lightly spooned into the cup and leveled off).

Variation

LEMON CHIFFON

Replace the orange zest with 18 grams/3 tablespoons lemon zest, and the orange juice with 30 grams/2 tablespoons/30 ml freshly squeezed and strained lemon juice plus 158 grams/ ⅔ cup/158 ml water.

Replace the baking powder with 2.7 grams/½ teaspoon baking soda.

If desired, make the lemon sugar glaze from the Triple Lemon Velvet Bundt Cake (page 111) or replace the lemon juice in that glaze with orange juice.

- Wash, rinse, and dry the whisk beater to remove any trace of oil. If you do not have a second mixer bowl, scrape this mixture into a large bowl and thoroughly wash, rinse, and dry the mixer bowl to remove any trace of oil.

BEAT THE EGG WHITES INTO A STIFF MERINGUE

3. In the bowl of a stand mixer fitted with the whisk beater, beat the egg whites and cream of tartar on medium-low speed until foamy. Gradually raise the speed to medium-high and beat until soft peaks form when the beater is raised. Beat in the remaining 25 grams/2 tablespoons sugar and continue beating until stiff peaks form when the beater is raised slowly.

ADD THE MERINGUE TO THE BATTER

4. Using the whisk beater, a large slotted skimmer, or a large silicone spatula, gently fold the meringue into the batter just until blended. If using the whisk, you will need to shake out the meringue that gathers in the center as you fold.

5. Scrape the batter into the pan. Run a small spatula in circles through the batter to prevent air pockets. There is no need to smooth the surface. The batter will come to about 1 inch from the top of the rim.

BAKE THE CAKE

6. Bake for 45 to 55 minutes, or until a wooden skewer inserted between the tube and the sides comes out clean and the cake springs back when pressed lightly. During baking, a few cracks will form. Avoid opening the oven door before the minimum baking time, or the fragile cake could fall. While the cake is baking, set up the unmolding bottle in a draft free area. If using a funnel, lightly coat the upper inch below the stem with nonstick cooking spray.

COOL THE CAKE

7. Immediately invert the pan onto the glass bottle or funnel. Cool completely in the pan, about 2 hours.

UNMOLD THE CAKE

8. Use a small sharp knife to dislodge the cake inside the rim of the pan. To loosen the sides of the cake from the pan, use a rigid metal spatula, at least 4 inches long and preferably with a squared off end, scraping firmly against the pan's sides and slowly and carefully circling the pan. In order to ensure that you are scraping well against the sides of the pan, and not removing the crust from the sides of the cake, begin by angling the spatula about 20 degrees away from the cake and toward the pan, pushing the cake inward a bit. It works best to advance the spatula about 1 inch, lift it out, and reinsert it just behind where you pulled it out. Continue in this way around the entire cake.

9. Place the cake pan on top of a canister or can that is smaller than the bottom opening of the pan's outer rim. Press down on both sides of the pan to release the outer pan. Alternatively, grasp the center core and lift out the cake. Run a wire cake tester or wooden skewer around the center core. Dislodge the cake from the bottom with a metal spatula or thin sharp knife. Invert the cake onto a wire rack that has been lightly coated with nonstick cooking spray. Reinvert onto a serving plate.

STORE AIRTIGHT: room temperature, 3 days; refrigerated, 10 days; frozen, 2 months.

Making Orange Chiffon

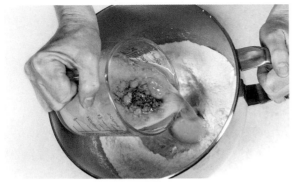

Add the egg mixture to the flour mixture.

Beat the meringue until stiff.

Use a slotted skimmer to fold in the meringue.

Pour the batter into the pan.

Run a spatula through the batter.

Suspend the cake over a long-neck bottle to cool.

Remove the sides of the pan.

Invert the cake onto a wire rack and then remove the center tube.

Classic Génoise

SERVES 8 TO 10

OVEN TEMPERATURE:
350°F/175°C

BAKING TIME: 20 to 30 minutes

PLAN AHEAD: For best flavor, compose the cake 1 day ahead.

BAKING EQUIPMENT:
One 9 by 2 inch round cake pan, coated with baking spray with flour, then lined with a parchment round (do not coat the parchment with baking spray)

Optional: a 9 inch cardboard round

This clarified butter sponge cake is the most renowned and elegant cake in the French repertoire. The flavorful syrup, applied after baking, gives the cake the perfect moistness and sweetness. Whipped Cream (page 329) or Chocolate Mousse Ganache (page 351) are lovely frostings for this light and airy cake. You will need 2 cups of the frosting of your choice.

BATTER

unsalted butter	57 grams	4 tablespoons (½ stick)
pure vanilla extract	.	1 teaspoon (5 ml)
4 large eggs	200 grams	¾ cup plus 2 teaspoons (187 ml)
1 large egg yolk	19 grams	1 tablespoon plus ½ teaspoon (17.5 ml)
bleached cake flour OR bleached all-purpose flour	50 grams	½ cup (sifted into the cup and leveled off) OR ½ cup minus 1 tablespoon (sifted into the cup and leveled off)
cornstarch, preferably Rumford	50 grams	½ cup (lightly spooned into the cup and leveled off) minus 1 tablespoon
superfine sugar	100 grams	½ cup

PREHEAT THE OVEN

- Twenty minutes or longer before baking, set an oven rack in the lower third of the oven. Set the oven at 350°F/175°C.

MISE EN PLACE

- About 1 hour ahead, set the butter on the counter at room temperature (65° to 75°F/19° to 24°C).

- **CLARIFY AND BROWN THE BUTTER:** Have ready by the cooktop a 2 cup glass measure with a spout, with a fine-mesh strainer suspended over it.

In a small heavy saucepan, on very low heat, melt the butter, stirring often with a silicone spatula. Raise the heat to low and boil, stirring constantly, until the milk solids on the spatula become a deep brown. Immediately pour the butter into the strainer. Add the vanilla to the clarified butter, cover, and set in a warm place.

- Into the bowl of a stand mixer, weigh or measure the eggs and egg yolk.

- Onto a piece of parchment, sift together the flour and cornstarch.

MAKE THE BATTER

1. Add the sugar to the eggs and set the bowl over a pan of simmering water. Stir constantly with a long-handled wire whisk only until warm to the touch. An instant-read thermometer should read about 110°F/43°C.

2. Set the bowl in the stand and attach the whisk beater. Beat on high speed for a full 5 minutes but no longer. The egg foam will more than quadruple in volume and become very thick and airy. (If using a handheld electric mixer, beat for at least 10 minutes.)

3. If necessary, reheat the browned clarified butter until almost hot (110° to 120°F/40° to 50°C). Remove about 60 grams/1 cup of the egg foam and whisk it thoroughly into the butter.

4. Return the flour mixture to the sifter and sift half of it onto the remaining egg foam. Fold it in gently but quickly with a large slotted skimmer or silicone spatula, until almost all traces of flour have disappeared. Repeat with the remaining flour mixture until all traces of the flour have disappeared.

5. Fold in the butter mixture just until incorporated. Use a silicone spatula to reach to the bottom of the bowl to ensure that no flour particles remain (see Baking Pearls, left).

6. Scrape the batter into the prepared pan and smooth the surface evenly. The pan will be about two-thirds full.

BAKE THE CAKE

7. Bake for 20 to 30 minutes, until golden brown and the cake starts to shrink slightly from the sides of the pan. When pressed lightly in the center with your finger, it will spring back.

UNMOLD AND COOL THE CAKE

8. To prevent collapse of the delicate foam structure, the génoise must be unmolded as soon as it is baked, while still hot. Have ready a small metal spatula and two wire racks coated with cooking spray.

9. Set the cake pan on an uncoated wire rack. Run the metal spatula between the sides of the pan and the cake, pressing firmly against the pan, and invert the cake onto a prepared wire rack. Leaving the parchment in place, immediately reinvert it onto the second prepared rack so that the firm upper crust keeps it from sinking. Cool completely.

SYRUP Makes 200 grams/¾ cup/177 ml

sugar	56 grams	¼ cup plus ½ tablespoon
water	118 grams	½ cup (118 ml)
liqueur of your choice OR pure vanilla extract	28 grams OR .	2 tablespoon (30 ml) OR 2 teaspoons (10 ml)

(continued)

MAKE THE SYRUP

1. In a small saucepan, stir together the sugar and water. Stirring constantly, bring it to a rolling boil. Cover and remove it from the heat. When cool, transfer the syrup to a 1 cup measure with a spout. Stir in the liqueur. If necessary, add water to equal ¾ cup/177 ml. Cover tightly until ready to use.

APPLY THE SYRUP

2. Use a long serrated knife and your fingertips to remove the top crust from the cake. Invert the cake onto another wire rack, remove the parchment, and scrape off any remaining bottom crust. If there are any white pellets of undissolved flour on the edge of the cake, remove them with tweezers reserved for baking or with a wood skewer.

3. Brush the bottom of the cake with half the syrup. Carefully invert it onto a cardboard round or serving plate and brush the top with the remaining syrup.

FROST THE CAKE

1. Frost the cake (see page 84).

STORE UNFROSTED, AIRTIGHT: génoise with or without syrup: room temperature, 2 days; refrigerated, 5 days; frozen, 2 months.
FROSTED: room temperature, 1 day; refrigerated, 5 days; frozen, 2 months.

Making Classic Génoise

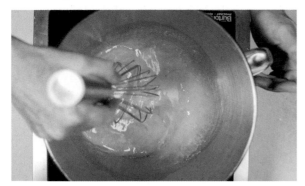

Heat the eggs.

Remove about 60 grams/1 cup of the egg foam to add to the clarified butter.

Sift the flour onto the egg foam.

Use a slotted skimmer to fold in the flour.

Scrape the batter into the pan.

Invert and then reinvert the cake to cool.

Remove the top crust.

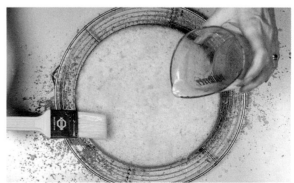

Brush the cake with syrup.

Thin Golden Sponge Cake Roll or Base

MAKES ONE 16¾ BY 11¾ BY ½ INCH HIGH RECTANGLE

OVEN TEMPERATURE: 450°F/230°C

BAKING TIME: 7 to 10 minutes

BAKING EQUIPMENT:
One 17¼ by 12¼ by 1 inch half sheet pan, bottom coated with shortening, then lined with parchment (have the parchment extend 1 inch past one of the long sides of the pan) and coated with baking spray with flour

A large wire rack

An extra inverted half sheet pan, lightly coated with nonstick cooking spray

Light yet velvety, this sponge cake is exceptionally useful. It is a splendid dessert on its own or rolled around a filling of your choice such as Whipped Cream (page 329) or Chocolate Mousse Ganache (page 351). The cake is absorbent but holds its texture well even when moistened, which makes it an ideal base for cheesecakes (see Variations, page 168).

5 to 8 large eggs, separated:		
5 (to 8) yolks (see Baking Pearls, page 167)	93 grams	¼ cup plus 2 tablespoons (89 ml)
about 4 whites	120 grams	½ cup (118 ml), *divided*
bleached cake flour OR bleached all-purpose flour	33 grams	⅓ cup (sifted into the cup and leveled off) OR ¼ cup plus 2 teaspoons (sifted into the cup and leveled off)
cornstarch, preferably Rumford	23 grams	2½ tablespoons
superfine sugar	113 grams	½ cup plus 1 tablespoon, *divided*
pure vanilla extract	.	¾ teaspoon (3.7 ml)
cream of tartar	.	¼ teaspoon

PREHEAT THE OVEN

- Thirty minutes or longer before baking, set an oven rack at the middle level. Set the oven at 450°F/230°C.

MISE EN PLACE

- Thirty minutes to 1 hour ahead, set the eggs on the counter at room temperature (65° to 75°F/19° to 24°C).

- In a small bowl, whisk together the flour and cornstarch.

- Into separate bowls, weigh or measure the egg yolks and egg whites.

MAKE THE BATTER

1. In the bowl of a stand mixer fitted with the whisk beater, place the egg yolks, half the egg whites (60 grams/¼ cup/59 ml), and 100 grams/½ cup of the sugar. Beat on high speed until thick, fluffy, and tripled in volume, about 5 minutes.

Baking Pearls

The ratio of white to yolk in an egg can vary to such a degree that you may need as few as 5 or as many as 8 eggs for this recipe. It is therefore advisable to weigh or measure the separated yolks and whites and add or reduce if needed.

Rumford brand cornstarch will give the cake the finest texture.

Make This Recipe Your Own

If using lemon curd, which is not as moist a filling as whipped cream, make 100 grams/⅓ cup/79 ml syrup to brush on the cake before adding the filling.

To make the syrup: In a small saucepan, stir together 25 grams/2 tablespoons sugar and 59 grams/¼ cup/59 ml water. Stirring constantly, bring it to a rolling boil. Cover and remove it from the heat. When cool, transfer the syrup to a 1 cup measure with a spout. Stir in 1 tablespoon/15 ml liqueur or 1 teaspoon/5 ml pure vanilla extract. If necessary, add water to equal 100 grams/⅓ cup/79 ml. Cover tightly until ready to use.

2. Lower the speed to medium and beat in the vanilla.

■ Wash, rinse, and dry the whisk beater to remove any trace of oil. If you do not have a second mixer bowl, scrape this mixture into a large bowl and thoroughly wash, rinse, and dry the mixer bowl to remove any trace of oil.

3. Sift half the flour mixture over the egg mixture and, using a large slotted skimmer or silicone spatula, fold it in quickly but gently until almost all of the flour has disappeared. Repeat with the remaining flour mixture until all traces of the flour have disappeared.

BEAT THE EGG WHITES INTO A STIFF MERINGUE

4. In the bowl of a stand mixer fitted with the whisk beater, beat the remaining half of the egg whites and the cream of tartar on medium-low speed until foamy. Gradually raise the speed to medium-high and beat until soft peaks form when the beater is raised. Beat in the remaining 13 grams/1 tablespoon sugar and continue beating until stiff peaks form when the beater is raised slowly.

ADD THE MERINGUE TO THE BATTER

5. Using a large slotted skimmer or large silicone spatula, gently fold the meringue into the batter. Scrape the batter into the prepared pan and use a small offset spatula to smooth the surface as evenly as possible.

BAKE THE CAKE

6. Bake for 7 to 10 minutes, or until golden brown and the cake springs back when pressed lightly in the center.

UNMOLD THE CAKE

7. Loosen the sides with the tip of a sharp knife. Immediately slip a small offset spatula under the edges of the parchment to loosen it. Grasp the parchment and gently slide the cake onto the large wire rack.

ASSEMBLE THE CAKE ROLL (OPTIONAL)

8. After sliding the cake onto the wire rack, sprinkle it lightly with powdered sugar, or cocoa if making a chocolate version. While the cake is still hot, place a clean dish towel on top of it, set the coated inverted half sheet pan on top, and invert it. Carefully remove the parchment. Then with a long side facing you, tightly roll up the cake, towel and all. Set it on a wire rack and allow it to cool until no longer warm to the touch.

9. When ready to fill, unroll the cake and spread it with about 2 cups of filling of your choice. Reroll the cake. If desired, dust with powdered sugar or cocoa before serving.

STORE UNFILLED, AIRTIGHT: room temperature, 3 days; refrigerated, 5 days; frozen, 2 months.
FILLED, AIRTIGHT: refrigerated, 3 days.

(continued)

Variations

CAKE BASE FOR A CHEESECAKE

Let the cake cool completely, flat, about 20 minutes. Invert the cake onto an inverted half sheet pan that's been coated with nonstick cooking spray and peel off the parchment. Allow it to air dry until no longer sticky and then use scissors and a template to cut to size. Set the cake base, crust side down, into the springform pan. Cover with plastic wrap and refrigerate until ready to add the filling.

THIN CHOCOLATE SPONGE CAKE

Replace the cornstarch with unsweetened alkalized cocoa powder (25 grams/⅓ cup, sifted before measuring).

In a small bowl, with a silicone spatula, stir together the cocoa and 59 grams/¼ cup/59 ml boiling water until smooth. Stir in the vanilla, cover tightly with plastic wrap to prevent evaporation, and cool to room temperature, about 20 minutes.

In step 1, increase the sugar to 133 grams/⅔ cup. Add the dissolved cocoa mixture in step 2.

Proceed as for the golden version, including adding the 13 grams/1 tablespoon of sugar in step 4.

Making a Thin Golden Sponge Cake

Beat the eggs until tripled in volume.

Use a slotted skimmer to fold in the flour.

Fold in the meringue.

The finished batter.

Evenly spread the batter in the pan.

Slide the baked cake out of the pan.

Chocolate Roll

SERVES 8

OVEN TEMPERATURE:
350°F/175°C

BAKING TIME: 16 to 18 minutes

BAKING EQUIPMENT:
One 17¼ by 12¼ by 1 inch half-sheet pan, coated with shortening and lined with a nonstick Teflon-type liner or parchment, leaving a 2 inch overhang on the long sides, coated with baking spray with flour (see Baking Pearl, page 172)

This ethereal chocolate roll is a no-compromise dessert for the gluten intolerant and also one of my favorite cakes in my entire repertoire. I like to fill it with 2 cups Lightly Sweetened Whipped Cream.

6 (to 9) large eggs, separated:		
6 (to 9) yolks (see Baking Pearls, page 172)	112 grams	¼ cup plus 3 tablespoons (104 ml)
6 whites	180 grams	¾ cup (177 ml)
unsweetened alkalized cocoa powder	37 grams	½ cup (sifted before measuring), *divided*
boiling water	59 grams	¼ cup (59 ml)
pure vanilla extract	.	1 teaspoon (5 ml)
unsalted butter	28 grams	2 tablespoons
sugar, preferably superfine	133 grams	⅔ cup, *divided*
cream of tartar	.	¾ teaspoon
Lightly Sweetened Whipped Cream (page 329), for filling	244 grams	2 cups

PREHEAT THE OVEN

▪ Twenty minutes or longer before baking, set an oven rack at the middle level. Set the oven at 350°F/175°C.

MISE EN PLACE

▪ Thirty minutes to 1 hour ahead, set the eggs on the counter at room temperature (65° to 75°F/19° to 24°C).

▪ Cut the butter into cubes.

▪ In a small glass bowl, whisk 32 grams/7 tablespoons of the cocoa and the boiling water until smooth. Whisk in the butter and vanilla. Cover with plastic wrap and cool to room temperature.

▪ Into separate bowls, weigh or measure the egg yolks and whites.

MAKE THE BATTER

1. In the bowl of a stand mixer fitted with the whisk beater, beat 100 grams/ ½ cup of the sugar with the egg yolks on high speed for 5 minutes, or until very thick and fluffy (tripled in volume), and when the beater is raised the mixture falls in ribbons.

(continued)

If you need this cake to be 100 percent flourless or gluten-free, spray the pan liner with non-stick cooking spray without flour. The cake will be harder to remove from the liner but doable with a little care.

The ratio of white to yolk in an egg can vary to such a degree that you may need as few as 6 or as many as 9 eggs for this recipe. It is therefore advisable to weigh or measure the separated yolks and add or reduce if needed.

Egg yolks will become dry and crusty if they sit with the sugar for more than a few minutes before beating. Therefore, do not add the sugar until just before starting to beat them.

If you would like to store the cake roll for up to 2 days, use the Cornstarch-Stabilized Whipped Cream on page 330.

Make This Recipe Your Own

Replace the whipped cream with Chocolate Mousse Ganache (page 351).

2. With a silicone spatula, scrape in the cocoa mixture and beat on medium speed, scraping the sides of the bowl as needed, until evenly incorporated. Be sure to reach into the bottom of the bowl to incorporate any cocoa mixture that may have settled on the bottom.

■ Wash, rinse, and dry the whisk beater to remove any trace of oil. If you do not have a second mixer bowl, scrape the mixture into a large bowl and thoroughly wash, rinse, and dry the mixer bowl to remove any trace of oil.

3. In the bowl of the stand mixer fitted with the whisk beater, beat the egg whites and cream of tartar on medium-low speed until foamy. Gradually raise the speed to medium-high and beat until soft peaks form when the beater is raised. Gradually beat in the remaining sugar and continue beating until stiff peaks form when the beater is raised slowly.

4. Detach the beater and use it to fold one-quarter of the meringue into the chocolate mixture to lighten it. Gently fold in the remaining meringue. Finish folding with a large silicone spatula.

5. Scrape the mixture into the prepared pan, spreading it evenly with an offset spatula.

BAKE THE CAKE

6. Bake for 16 to 18 minutes. The cake will have puffed and lost its shine, and will spring back when pressed lightly in the center. Meanwhile, wet a clean dish towel and wring it out well.

COOL THE CAKE

7. Set the pan on a wire rack. Sift the remaining cocoa evenly over the top of the cake. Cover it immediately with the damp towel and allow it to cool completely.

ASSEMBLE THE CAKE ROLL

8. Remove the towel and, lifting by a long edge of the liner, gently slide the cake from the pan onto the counter. Spread at once with the whipped cream and roll up from the long side, using the liner for support and gently peeling it away as you go. If desired, dust lightly with more cocoa or with powdered sugar.

STORE UNCOVERED: room temperature, 1 hour.
COVERED: refrigerated, 2 days.

Making a Chocolate Roll

Beat the egg yolk mixture until tripled in volume.

Fold in the dissolved cocoa.

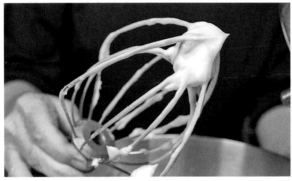

Beat the egg whites to stiff peaks.

Fold in the egg whites.

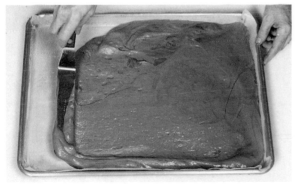

Spread the batter evenly in the pan.

Dust the baked cake with cocoa.

Top with whipped cream and roll up the cake.

Finish rolling the cake.

Flourless Chocolate Almond Cake

SERVES 10 TO 12

OVEN TEMPERATURE:
350°F/175°C

BAKING TIME: 5 minutes
for the almonds; 75 to
80 minutes for the cake

BAKING EQUIPMENT:
One 9 by 3 or 2¾ inch
high springform pan,
bottom lined with
parchment, encircled
with cake strips (see
page xv)

A flourless chocolate cake requires more support than a cake roll. Nut flour (finely ground nuts) adds structure, texture, and flavor to this moist and chocolaty cake. This is a great cake for Passover (see Baking Pearls) or for anyone who is gluten intolerant. The cake will be about 2⅛ inches high at the sides and will have a ¼ inch depression—perfect for filling with softly whipped, lightly sweetened cream.

unsalted butter	300 grams	21 tablespoons (2½ sticks plus 1 tablespoon)
8 (to 12) large eggs, separated:		
8 (to 12) yolks (see Baking Pearls, page 175)	149 grams	½ cup plus 4 teaspoons (138 ml)
8 whites	240 grams	1 cup (237 ml)
unsweetened alkalized cocoa powder	66 grams	¾ cup plus 2 tablespoons (sifted before measuring)
boiling water	133 grams	½ cup plus 1 tablespoon (133 ml)
pure vanilla extract	.	1½ teaspoons (7.5 ml)
unblanched sliced almonds	225 grams	2¼ cups
sugar, preferably superfine	300 grams	1½ cups, *divided*
fine sea salt	.	⅛ teaspoon
cream of tartar	.	1 teaspoon

PREHEAT THE OVEN

▪ Twenty minutes or longer before toasting the almonds, set an oven rack in the lower third of the oven. Set the oven at 350°F/175°C.

MISE EN PLACE

▪ About 1 hour ahead, set the butter and eggs on the counter at room temperature (65° to 75°F/19° to 24°C).

▪ Thirty minutes to 1 hour ahead, in a 2 cup glass measure with a spout, whisk the cocoa and the boiling water until smooth. Whisk in the vanilla. Cover with plastic wrap and cool to room temperature.

▪ **TOAST THE ALMONDS:** Spread the almonds evenly on a cookie sheet and bake for about 5 minutes, or until pale gold. Stir once or twice to ensure even toasting and prevent overbrowning. Allow them to cool completely.

The ratio of white to yolk in an egg can vary to such a degree that you may need as few as 8 or as many as 12 eggs for this recipe. It is therefore advisable to weigh or measure the separated yolks and add or reduce if needed.

If making this cake for Passover, omit the cream of tartar but take care to beat the egg whites only until almost stiff peaks form, to avoid breaking them down. (The peaks should curve slightly when you raise the beater.)

■ In a food processor, process the almonds with 66 grams/⅓ cup of the sugar until finely ground.

■ Into separate bowls, weigh or measure the egg yolks and whites.

MAKE THE BATTER

1. In the bowl of a stand mixer fitted with the flat beater, on medium speed, beat the butter with 200 grams/1 cup of the remaining sugar for 3 minutes, or until light and fluffy.

2. Add the egg yolks and continue beating until incorporated, scraping down the sides of the bowl as needed.

3. With a silicone spatula, scrape in the cocoa mixture and almond mixture. Beat on medium speed, scraping the sides of the bowl as needed, until evenly incorporated. Be sure to reach into the bottom of the bowl to incorporate any cocoa mixture that may have settled on the bottom.

■ If you do not have a second mixer bowl, scrape the mixture into a large bowl and thoroughly wash, rinse, and dry the mixer bowl to remove any trace of oil.

4. In the bowl of the stand mixer fitted with the whisk beater, beat the egg whites, salt, and cream of tartar on medium-low speed until foamy. Gradually raise the speed to medium-high and beat until soft peaks form when the beater is raised. Gradually beat in the remaining sugar and continue beating until stiff peaks form when the beater is raised slowly.

5. Detach the whisk beater and use it to fold one-quarter of the meringue into the batter by hand to lighten it. Gently fold in the remaining meringue in two parts. Finish folding with a large silicone spatula.

6. Scrape the batter into the prepared pan, spreading it evenly with an offset spatula. It will fill a 3 inch high pan by about two-thirds.

BAKE THE CAKE

7. Bake for 30 minutes. Tent it loosely with aluminum foil and continue baking for 45 to 50 minutes, or until the center springs back when very lightly pressed with your finger. An instant-read thermometer inserted into the center should read 202°F/94°C.

COOL THE CAKE

8. Set the pan on a wire rack and allow it to cool for 50 minutes. As it cools, it will form a ¼ inch depression.

UNMOLD THE CAKE

9. Run a small metal spatula between the sides of the cake and the pan, pressing firmly against the pan. Invert the cake onto a wire rack that has been lightly coated with nonstick cooking spray. Peel off the parchment and reinvert it onto another wire rack or serving plate to cool completely.

10. If desired, shortly before serving, dust lightly with cocoa or powdered sugar, or fill the center with softly whipped, lightly sweetened cream (page 329).

STORE AIRTIGHT: room temperature, 3 days; refrigerated, 5 days; frozen, 2 months.

Pure Chocolate Flourless Cake

SERVES 6 TO 8

OVEN TEMPERATURE:
350°F/175°C

BAKING TIME: 30 to 40 minutes

BAKING EQUIPMENT:
One 8 by 2¾ inch or higher springform pan (see Baking Pearls, page 178), encircled with cake strips (see page xv), bottom coated with shortening, topped with a parchment round, then coated with baking spray with flour

If you like your chocolate uninterrupted by flour or nuts, this cake is for you. It is based on one of the most beloved chocolate cakes in The Cake Bible, The Chocolate Oblivion Truffle Torte, *so called because its dense, creamy texture is similar to a chocolate truffle. This new version, which is not baked in a water bath, is more reminiscent of a baked chocolate mousse. The egg whites are beaten separately into a meringue with extra sugar, which creates a lighter, moist interior and crackly crisp exterior.*

The cake will be a little over 1½ inches high at the sides and will have a ½ inch depression. Like the Flourless Chocolate Almond Cake (page 174), it is also deliciously enhanced by a topping of softly whipped, lightly sweetened cream.

unsalted butter	113 grams	8 tablespoons (1 stick)

4 (to 5) large eggs, separated:
    4 (to 5) yolks (see Baking Pearls, page 178)
    4 whites
	
	74 grams
	
	120 grams
		
		¼ cup plus 2 teaspoons (69 ml)
		½ cup (118 ml)

pure vanilla extract	.	1 teaspoon (5 ml)
dark chocolate, 60% to 62% cacao, chopped	227 grams	8 ounces
cream of tartar	.	½ teaspoon
sugar, preferably superfine	100 grams	½ cup

PREHEAT THE OVEN

■ Twenty minutes or longer before baking, set an oven rack in the lower third of the oven. Set the oven at 350°F/175°C.

MISE EN PLACE

■ About 1 hour ahead, set the butter and eggs on the counter at room temperature (65° to 75°F/19° to 24°C).

(continued)

The ratio of white to yolk in an egg can vary to such a degree that you may need 4 or 5 eggs for this recipe. It is therefore advisable to weigh or measure the separated yolks and add or reduce if needed.

If making this cake for Passover, omit the cream of tartar but take care to beat the egg whites only until almost stiff peaks form to keep them from breaking down. (The peaks should curve slightly when you lift the beater.) Also, use only nonstick cooking spray (without flour).

If your springform pan is higher than 2¾ inches, the surface of the cake will not crack until the cake is cooling.

Make This Recipe Your Own

This cake has the most appealing shape baked in an 8 inch springform. If using a 9 inch springform, multiply all the ingredients by 1.25.

- Thirty minutes ahead, weigh or measure the egg yolks into a medium bowl and the whites into the bowl of a stand mixer.

- Add the vanilla to the egg yolks, whisk them together, and cover tightly with plastic wrap.

MAKE THE BATTER

1. In a large bowl set over hot, not simmering, water (do not let the bottom of the bowl touch the water), melt the chocolate and butter, stirring often with a silicone spatula. Remove the bowl from the heat source.

2. In the bowl of the stand mixer, fitted with the whisk beater, beat the egg whites and cream of tartar on medium-low speed until foamy. Gradually raise the speed to medium-high and beat until soft peaks form when the beater is raised. Gradually beat in the sugar and continue beating until stiff peaks form when the beater is raised slowly.

3. Detach the whisk and use it to fold one-quarter of the meringue into the egg yolk mixture to lighten it.

4. Scrape the egg yolk mixture into the chocolate mixture and gently fold it in until almost fully incorporated.

5. Gently fold in the remaining meringue in two parts. Finish folding with a large silicone spatula.

6. Scrape the mixture into the prepared pan, spreading it evenly with an offset spatula. It will fill the pan by about half.

BAKE THE CAKE

7. Bake for 30 to 40 minutes, until the cake is set but still looks moist inside any cracks that form on the surface. An instant-read thermometer inserted into the center should read 180°F/82°C.

COOL THE CAKE

8. Set the pan on a wire rack and allow it to cool completely. As it cools it will form a ½ inch depression.

UNMOLD THE CAKE

9. Run a small metal spatula between the sides of the cake and the pan, pressing firmly against the pan. Release the sides of the springform pan but leave the cake on the pan bottom because it is too fragile to invert.

10. If desired, shortly before serving, dust lightly with cocoa or powdered sugar, or fill the center with softly whipped, lightly sweetened cream (page 329).

STORE AIRTIGHT: room temperature, 3 days; refrigerated, 5 days.

Making Pure Chocolate Flourless Cake

Beat the meringue to stiff peaks.

Use the whisk beater to fold in one-quarter of the meringue.

Fold in the remaining meringue.

Finish folding using a large silicone spatula.

Smooth the batter in the pan.

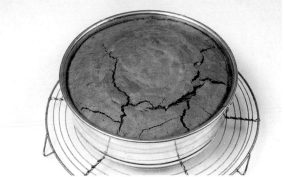

Let cool on a wire rack.

Creamy Cheesecake

SERVES 10 TO 12

OVEN TEMPERATURE:
350°F/175°C

BAKING TIME: 50
minutes (55 minutes
if using a silicone pan
instead of aluminum foil
for the water bath), plus
1 hour with the oven off

PLAN AHEAD: Make
the cheesecake at least
1 day before serving.

BAKING EQUIPMENT:
One 9 by 3 or 2¾ inch
high springform pan,
lightly coated with
nonstick cooking spray,
set in a slightly larger
silicone pan or wrapped
with a *double* layer of
heavy-duty aluminum
foil to prevent seepage

A 12 inch cake pan or
roasting pan to serve as
a water bath

Optional: a 9 inch
cardboard cake round

Lusciously creamy and tangy on its own, a cheesecake is deliciously complemented by topping with fresh berries or sour cherries (see Make This Recipe Your Own, page 182) or lemon curd (page 40). A base of thin sponge cake, purchased lady fingers, or cookie crumbs are also pleasing enhancements.

BATTER

full-fat cream cheese	454 grams	1 pound
sugar	200 grams	1 cup
cornstarch	9 grams	1 tablespoon
3 large eggs	150 grams	½ cup plus 1½ tablespoons (140 ml)
lemon juice, freshly squeezed and strained (1 to 2 lemons)	47 grams	3 tablespoons (45 ml)
pure vanilla extract	.	1½ teaspoons (7.5 ml)
fine sea salt	.	¼ teaspoon
full-fat sour cream	726 grams	3 cups

PREHEAT THE OVEN

■ Twenty minutes or longer before baking, set an oven rack in the lower third of the oven. Set the oven at 350°F/175°C.

MISE EN PLACE

■ One hour ahead, into the bowl of a stand mixer, place the cream cheese, sugar, and cornstarch at cool room temperature (65° to 70°F/19° to 21°C).

■ Into a 1 cup measure with a spout, weigh or measure the eggs and whisk just until lightly combined. Cover with plastic wrap.

■ Into another 1 cup measure with a spout, weigh or measure the lemon juice. Cover with plastic wrap.

■ If using a cake base (see Make This Recipe Your Own, page 182), trim it to size and set it on the bottom of the pan. If using lady fingers, cut off the rounded edges and arrange them on the bottom of the pan, placing them flat sides down and cutting or tearing smaller pieces to fit into any gaps. Cover the pan with plastic wrap while making the filling.

This is an incredibly light and creamy cheesecake. If you prefer a denser version, simply reduce the sour cream to 484 grams/2 cups.

As ovens may vary, this method of finishing the baking by the residual heat in the oven virtually ensures that the batter will cook completely. If your oven temperature is off and the batter is not set and jiggles more than slightly when removed from the oven, remove the cake from the water bath, set it on a cookie sheet, and continue baking the cake for a few minutes, just until done.

Unflavored dental floss, held taut, works better than a knife to cut a cheesecake without the cherry or berry topping. With a topping, a thin sharp knife works best.

MAKE THE BATTER

1. Attach the whisk beater and beat the cream cheese mixture on medium-high speed until very smooth, scraping down the sides of the bowl once or twice, about 3 minutes.

2. Gradually beat in the eggs and continue beating until smooth, scraping down the sides of the bowl as needed.

3. On medium-low speed, add the lemon juice, vanilla, and salt and beat until incorporated.

4. Add the sour cream and continue beating just until fully blended, 20 to 30 seconds. Detach the whisk beater and use it to reach down and whisk in any mixture that has settled to the bottom of the bowl.

5. Scrape the batter into the prepared pan and smooth the surface evenly.

BAKE THE CHEESECAKE

6. Set the pan into the larger pan and surround it with 1 inch of very hot water. Add about 1 teaspoon of cream of tartar to the water and stir to dissolve it. (This will prevent discoloration of the aluminum pan.) Bake for 25 minutes. For even baking, rotate the pan halfway around. Continue baking for 25 minutes (30 minutes if using the silicone pan). Turn off the oven without opening the door and let the cake cool for 1 hour. When moved, the center will jiggle slightly.

COOL AND CHILL THE CHEESECAKE

7. Remove the pan from the water bath but leave the silicone pan or foil in place to contain any liquid that may seep from the cake. Set it on a wire rack to cool to room temperature or just warm, 1 to 2 hours. To absorb condensation, place a paper towel, curved side up, over the pan with the ends overhanging. Place an inverted plate, larger than the springform pan, on top of the paper towel.

8. Refrigerate the cheesecake for 8 hours or overnight, still covered with the paper towel and plate. (The filling needs to be very firm before unmolding and pouring on a topping.)

UNMOLD THE CHEESECAKE

9. Remove the plate and paper towel. Use a small propane torch or wipe the sides of the pan several times with a towel that has been run under hot water and wrung out. Release the sides of the springform pan. If the sides of the cheesecake are uneven, run a small metal spatula under hot water and use it to smooth them.

10. Place a piece of plastic wrap, lightly coated with nonstick cooking spray, on top of the cheesecake. Set a 9 inch cake pan or cookie sheet, bottom side down, on top of the cake. Invert the cake together with the cookie sheet or cake pan and set it on a counter. Remove the springform pan bottom and parchment and blot any moisture with a paper towel if necessary.

(continued)

11. If using just a cake or lady finger base, it's fine to reinvert the cheesecake directly onto a serving plate, or to leave it on the pan bottom if using a springform with a glass bottom.

▪ If adding a cookie crumb base, you will need about 75 grams/¾ cup for the bottom and sides of the cake. Pat a layer of crumbs gently onto the surface. Reinvert the cake onto a cardboard round. Hold the cheesecake over the bowl with the remaining crumbs, tilting it slightly, and with your other cupped hand lift the crumbs onto the sides of the cake, pressing them in lightly. Place the cheesecake, still on the cake round, on a serving plate.

STORE AIRTIGHT: refrigerated, 5 days; do not freeze, as the texture will become less smooth.

Make This Recipe Your Own

BASES

Cake Base: Use the Thin Golden Sponge Cake Base (page 166).

Cookie Crumbs: You will need about ¾ cup/75 grams of cookie crumbs of your choice.

TOPPINGS

For a fresh raspberry or strawberry topping, you will need about 454 grams/2 pints raspberries or hulled small strawberries. Up to 6 hours ahead, arrange the berries on the top of the cake, pointed ends up. Brush the berries with 77 grams/¼ cup melted currant jelly.

For a sour cherry topping, prepare half the recipe of the cherry pie filling on page 218, but use 100 grams/½ cup sugar and 1½ tablespoons/14 grams cornstarch. Up to 8 hours before serving, spoon the hot filling onto the chilled cake. Return it to the refrigerator for 1 hour to set.

For a lemon curd topping, remove the chilled but unmolded cake from the refrigerator. Remove the plate and paper towel. Make the lemon curd on page 40, but without the zest (you will need 200 grams/¾ cup). As soon as it has thickened, pour the lemon curd into the strainer and press it through. Avoid scraping the saucepan as the residue is thicker and will mar the surface of the cheesecake. For the smoothest topping, immediately pour the hot lemon curd quickly onto the chilled cheesecake. Tilt the cake pan as necessary to even the topping. If needed, smooth the topping with a small offset spatula. Let it sit for 15 minutes to allow the steam to escape from the topping. Then cover with a paper towel (curved side up) and an inverted plate and refrigerate the cheesecake for at least 2 hours before unmolding.

Making Creamy Cheesecake

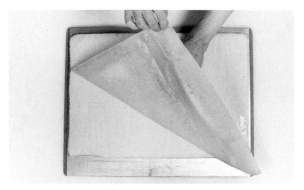
Peel the parchment off the sponge cake.

Cut out a circle to fit the base of the pan.

Set the cake circle in the pan.

Wrap the pan in a double layer of heavy-duty foil.

Alternatively, set it inside a silicone pan.

Scrape the batter into the cake-lined pan.

Set in a water bath and add cream of tartar to the water.

Heat the sides of the pan to unmold the baked cheesecake.

(continued)

Making Creamy Cheesecake (cont'd)

Remove the pan's sides.

Press crumbs onto the sides of the cheesecake.

Here are all the essential pie crusts, including flaky pie crust, sweet cookie tart crust (pâte sucrée), and crumb crusts, and all my favorite pies and tarts. You will also learn how to bake other similar pastries including scones, galettes, crisps, cobblers, and meringue pastry (the Pavlova).

PIES AND TARTS

SOLUTIONS FOR POSSIBLE PROBLEMS

Flaky Pie Crust

The dough sticks when rolling and the baked pie crust is not flaky.

SOLUTION: The dough is too warm and needs to be chilled until firm.

The pie crust shrinks during baking.

SOLUTIONS: While rolling, lift it and allow it to shrink in. When placing it in the pie plate, ease it in place and avoid stretching it. Let it rest, refrigerated, for a minimum of 1 hour before baking.

The pie crust is too tender and falls apart.

SOLUTIONS: Avoid mixing the cream cheese and/or butter too finely into the flour. Knead the dough until slightly stretchy when tugged so that it will hold together.

The pie crust is tough.

SOLUTIONS: Use a lower protein flour such as pastry flour or, if making your own pastry flour (see Baking Pearls, page 190), increase the proportion of cake flour to bleached all-purpose flour. Alternatively, sugar works well to tenderize the dough. See the Baking Pearls for Perfect Flaky and Tender Cream Cheese Pie Crust (page 190).

When setting parchment in the dough-lined pan for blind baking, it pleats and doesn't conform to the shape of the pan.

SOLUTION: Crumple the parchment lightly before setting it in the pan.

The unfilled pie crust develops holes during baking.

SOLUTION: Seal the hole or holes with a little melted white or dark chocolate and chill or let it set at room temperature before adding the filling.

The border becomes too dark during baking.

SOLUTION: Protect the border with a foil ring (see page 198) right from the beginning of baking.

The bottom of the pie is soggy.

SOLUTIONS: Preheat a cast-iron pizza pan or baking stone for a minimum of 45 minutes and place the pie or tart pan directly on the hot surface when baking. Alternatively, if using a metal or ceramic pan (not a Pyrex pan), set it on the floor of the oven for the first 20 minutes of baking. Then raise it to a rack to finish baking. For very juicy pies such as the Apple Pie (page 210), baking from frozen gives the bottom crust a chance to start baking before the filling thaws.

The pie crust has a bitter flavor.

SOLUTIONS: Use only calcium-based baking powder such as Rumford. Sodium aluminum sulfate (SAS) based baking powder will result in a bitter taste. Be sure to brush off any excess flour on top of the dough after shaping it, as it will taste bitter after baking.

The fruit filling does not set.

SOLUTIONS: Bake until the filling is bubbling or the cornstarch will not be activated fully. Let it cool completely before slicing.

Sweet Cookie Tart Crust (Pâte Sucrée)

The dough cracks when rolling it.

SOLUTIONS: Gather it up and knead it until smooth. If absolutely necessary, spritz with a little water. Rolling with plastic wrap on top helps to prevent cracking.

The dough becomes too soft to transfer after rolling.

SOLUTION: Cover it with plastic wrap and refrigerate for 5 to 7 minutes until it becomes firmer but is still flexible.

The dough, when pressed into the pan, is too thick where the bottom meets the sides.

SOLUTION: Use the bottom of a glass tumbler or your fingers to press it well to thin it in this area before chilling and baking.

During blind baking in a tart pan, the dough slips down the sides.

SOLUTIONS: The dough will always slip down 1/8 to 1/4 inch, but to prevent it from slipping farther, make sure to freeze the dough-lined tart pan for a minimum of 8 hours before baking, and push the rice or beans well up against the sides of the pan.

The bottom crust sticks to the tart pan when unmolding.

SOLUTIONS: Heat the bottom of a 9 inch cake pan by filling it with very hot water. Empty the water and invert it onto the counter. Set the tart on top and let it sit for about 1 minute, or until the bottom no longer feels cold. Repeat if necessary. (You can also use a blow dryer to heat the inverted cake pan.) If necessary, slide a thin-bladed knife or long metal spatula under the crust to release it.

Perfect Flaky and Tender Cream Cheese Pie Crust

MAKES DOUGH FOR A 9 INCH PIE OR TART SHELL; A DEEP DISH 9 INCH PIE SHELL OR A 9 TO 12 INCH GALETTE; A 10 STRIP LATTICE 9 INCH PIE; OR A DOUBLE CRUST OR 12 TO 14 STRIP LATTICE 9 INCH PIE

OVEN TEMPERATURE: 425°F/220°C for a blind-baked pie or tart shell

BAKING TIME: 23 to 27 minutes for a blind-baked pie or tart shell

BAKING EQUIPMENT:

One standard or deep dish 9 inch pie plate

An expandable flan ring or cardboard template

A large coffee filter, several smaller cup-style coffee filters, or crumpled parchment

Dried beans or rice as weights for blind baking

A foil ring to protect the edges of the crust

This is my favorite pie crust for many reasons. It is the most flavorful and the most tender, but sturdy enough to transfer to a pie plate or tart pan, or to make lattice strips that don't break. It is also wonderfully flaky. It is ideal for a pie that will be served at room temperature. When making a tart that needs to be refrigerated, however, it is best to choose the Sweet Cookie Tart or Pie Crust (page 200), as that crust's texture stays the most crisp and tender when cold. Here I give the ingredient quantities for several sizes, so you can adjust the recipe depending on which pie you are making.

Baking powder contributes added tenderness and helps lift the dough into a flaky, puffy crust during baking without compromising the strength of the raw dough when shaping it.

Pastry flour results in the perfect ratio of tenderness to flakiness. Bleached all-purpose flour, which has a higher protein content, will not make as tender a pastry, and unbleached all-purpose flour will be even less tender. There are two solutions if you are unable to find pastry flour: Either cut the all-purpose flour with cake flour (see Baking Pearls, page 190), or add a tablespoon or two of sugar to the flour mixture, which helps tenderize the dough.

Weighing is far preferable to measuring by volume, as no matter how you measure flour by volume, the results are not consistent. If you choose to measure by volume, be sure to stir up the flour before measuring it, spoon it lightly into the cup without shaking or tapping the cup, and level it off with a metal spatula or knife blade.

The food processor method is the easiest way to mix the dough because it is faster, the dough gets handled less, and it stays more chilled, but if you work quickly, the hand method will produce a crust that will be slightly flakier. With both methods, be sure to keep the ingredients very cold to maintain flakiness. It helps to work in an air-conditioned room.

DOUGH FOR A 9 INCH PIE OR TART SHELL Makes 312 grams

unsalted butter, cold	85 grams	6 tablespoons (¾ stick)
pastry flour OR bleached all-purpose flour (see Baking Pearls, page 188)	145 grams	1¼ cups (lightly spooned into the cup and leveled off) OR 1 cup plus 3 tablespoons (lightly spooned into the cup and leveled off)
fine sea salt	.	¼ teaspoon
baking powder, only an aluminum-free variety (see Solutions for Possible Problems, page 186)	0.6 gram	⅛ teaspoon
full-fat cream cheese, cold	64 grams	¼ cup
heavy cream, cold	22 grams	1½ tablespoons (22.5 ml)
cider vinegar, cold	.	1½ teaspoons (7.5 ml)

DOUGH FOR A DEEP DISH 9 INCH PIE SHELL, OR A 9 TO 12 INCH GALETTE (FREE FORM TART) WITH A SMALL BORDER OR FULL TOP CRUST Makes 414 grams

unsalted butter, cold	113 grams	8 tablespoons (1 stick)
pastry flour OR bleached all-purpose flour	184 grams	1½ cups plus 2 tablespoons (lightly spooned into the cup and leveled off) OR 1½ cups (lightly spooned into the cup and leveled off)
fine sea salt	.	¼ plus ¹⁄₁₆ teaspoon
baking powder, only an aluminum free variety (see Solutions for Possible Problems, page 186)	0.7 gram	⅛ plus ¹⁄₃₂ teaspoon
full-fat cream cheese, cold	85 grams	⅓ cup
heavy cream, cold	29 grams	2 tablespoons (30 ml)
cider vinegar, cold	.	2 teaspoons (10 ml)

(continued)

Baking Pearls

To simulate pastry flour, use a mixture of (by weight) two-thirds all-purpose flour to one-third cake flour. You can mix up a big batch of simulated pastry flour for your pie and pastry baking using this basic formula: for 456 grams/4 cups sifted pastry flour use 304 grams/2⅔ cups sifted bleached all-purpose flour plus 152 grams/1½ cups sifted bleached cake flour. Be sure to whisk the flours together to mix them evenly. Note: If measuring by volume rather than weighing, sift the flour into the cup, without tapping or shaking the cup, and level it off with a flat blade.

If using bleached all-purpose flour alone, to make the dough more tender you can add about 4.5 percent sugar:

For 312 grams of dough: 13 grams/1 tablespoon sugar

For 414 grams of dough: 19 grams/1½ tablespoons sugar

For 480 grams of dough: 21 grams/1 tablespoon plus 2 teaspoons sugar

For 624 grams of dough: 25 grams/2 tablespoons sugar

DOUGH FOR A 10 STRIP LATTICE 9 INCH PIE Makes 480 grams

unsalted butter, cold	128 grams	9 tablespoons (1 stick plus 1 tablespoon)
pastry flour OR bleached all-purpose flour	213 grams	1¾ cups plus 2 tablespoons (lightly spooned into the cup and leveled off) OR 1¾ cups (lightly spooned into the cup and leveled off)
fine sea salt	.	¼ plus ⅛ teaspoon
baking powder, only an aluminum free variety (see Solutions for Possible Problems, page 186)	0.8 gram	⅛ plus 1/16 teaspoon
full-fat cream cheese, cold	101 grams	⅓ cup plus 1 tablespoon
heavy cream, cold	34 grams	2 tablespoons plus 1 teaspoon (35 ml)
cider vinegar, cold	.	2⅓ teaspoons (11.5 ml)

DOUGH FOR A DOUBLE CRUST, OR 12 TO 14 STRIP LATTICE 9 INCH PIE
Makes 624 grams

unsalted butter, cold	170 grams	12 tablespoons (1½ sticks)
pastry flour OR bleached all-purpose flour	290 grams	2½ cups (lightly spooned into the cup and leveled off) OR 2⅓ cups (lightly spooned into the cup and leveled off) plus 1 tablespoon
fine sea salt	3 grams	½ teaspoon
baking powder, only an aluminum free variety (see Solutions for Possible Problems, page 186)	1.1 grams	¼ teaspoon
full-fat cream cheese, cold	128 grams	½ cup
heavy cream, cold	43 grams	3 tablespoons (45 ml)
cider vinegar, cold	.	1 tablespoon (15 ml)

MISE EN PLACE

- **FOR THE FOOD PROCESSOR METHOD:** Cut the butter into ½ inch cubes. Wrap it in plastic wrap and freeze for at least 30 minutes, until frozen solid.

- Into a gallon-size reclosable freezer bag, place the flour, salt, and baking powder. Freeze for at least 30 minutes.

- **FOR THE HAND METHOD:** Refrigerate the butter cubes for at least 30 minutes. Place a medium bowl in the freezer.

MAKE THE DOUGH

FOOD PROCESSOR METHOD

1. Empty the flour mixture into the food processor. Set the bag aside.

2. Cut the cream cheese into 3 or 4 pieces and add it to the flour. Process for about 20 seconds, or until the mixture resembles coarse meal.

3. Add the frozen butter cubes and pulse until none of the butter is larger than the size of a pea. Toss with a fork to see it better.

(continued)

Making Perfect Flaky and Tender Cream Cheese Pie Crust in a Food Processor

Add the cream cheese to the flour mixture.

Process the mixture to a coarse meal.

Add the frozen butter cubes.

Most of the butter should be the size of small peas.

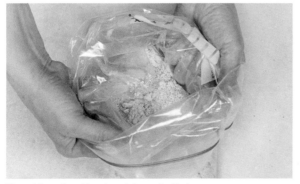
Knead together the dough in a plastic bag.

Smooth the edges of the dough disc.

Baking Pearls

If using the hand method of making a pie crust, if you have warm hands it helps to dip your fingers in a bowl of ice water from time to time to cool them. Be sure to dry them.

Here is an alternate way to shape the dough discs for both methods: In place of the plastic bag and plastic wrap, latex gloves also work well to press together the dough directly on a lightly floured countertop, and also to shape the dough into a disc. (This will also work for the Sweet Cookie Crust, page 200.)

For an extra-flaky pie crust approaching puff pastry, but more tender, roll the dough into a rectangle and give it a business letter fold (fold it in thirds). Roll it again to flatten it and make it a fairly even square. Use the plastic wrap to push in the corners to round the dough. Wrap and refrigerate as in step 8.

4. Remove the cover and evenly pour on the cream and vinegar. Pulse until most of the butter is the size of small peas. The mixture will be in particles and will not hold together unless pinched.

5. Spoon the mixture into the freezer bag. (For a double crust pie or 12 to 14 strip lattice pie, use two plastic bags and divide the mixture in half.)

HAND METHOD

1. Into the chilled bowl, place the flour, salt, and baking powder. Whisk to combine.

2. Add the cream cheese and rub the mixture between your fingers to blend the cream cheese into the flour until it resembles coarse meal.

3. Spoon the mixture, together with the cold butter, into a gallon-size reclosable freezer bag. Express any air from the bag and close it. Refrigerate the bowl or return it to the freezer.

4. With a rolling pin, flatten the butter into thin flakes. Place the bag in the freezer for at least 10 minutes, until the butter is very firm. Transfer the mixture back into the chilled bowl, scraping the sides of the bag. Set the bag aside.

5. Sprinkle the mixture with the cream and vinegar, tossing lightly with a silicone spatula. Spoon the mixture back into the plastic bag. (For a double crust pie, or 12 to 14 strip lattice pie, use two plastic bags and divide the mixture in half.)

BOTH METHODS

6. Hold either side of the bag opening and use the heel of your hand and your knuckles to knead and press the mixture from the outside of the bag, alternating sides, until most of it holds together in one piece.

7. Cut open the bag and empty the dough onto a large sheet of plastic wrap. Use the plastic wrap to finish kneading the dough just until it feels slightly stretchy when pulled. Use your hands and the plastic wrap to shape the dough into a rough disc or discs. Use a rolling pin to flatten it and your hands to press in the edges, which tend to crack, to make the smooth. There should be thin flakes of butter throughout the dough. If there are any large pieces of butter, spread them using the heel of your hand.

SHAPE THE DOUGH

- **FOR A SINGLE CRUST 9 INCH PIE OR TART:** Flatten the dough into one 6 to 7 inch disc.

- **FOR A DEEP DISH 9 INCH PIE OR 9 TO 12 INCH GALETTE:** Flatten the dough into an 8 inch disc.

- **FOR A DOUBLE CRUST PIE:** Divide the dough equally in half and flatten each into a 6 to 7 inch disc.

- **FOR A 12 TO 14 LATTICE STRIP PIE:** Divide the dough equally in half and flatten one piece into a 6 to 7 inch disc and the other into a rectangle.

■ **FOR A 10 STRIP LATTICE PIE:** Divide the dough into two unequal-size pieces, two-thirds and one-third. Use about 316 grams for the shell and the rest for the lattice, flattening the smaller part into a rectangle.

8. Wrap the dough with plastic wrap and refrigerate for a minimum of 45 minutes, up to 2 days.

STORE REFRIGERATED up to 2 days, frozen 3 months.

Making Perfect Flaky and Tender Cream Cheese Pie Crust by Hand

Flake the cream cheese into the flour mixture.

Roll the butter into thin flakes.

Transfer the mixture to a chilled bowl.

Add the cream and vinegar.

Toss with a spatula.

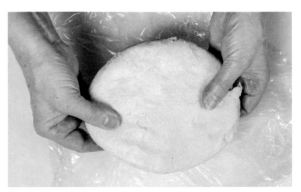
The finished dough disc.

ROLLING THE DOUGH AND FITTING IT INTO THE PAN

Rolling the Dough

THE IDEAL TEMPERATURE FOR ROLLING DOUGH IS 60°F/15°C, which is the temperature of a very cold air-conditioned room. At this temperature, the dough is malleable enough to roll without cracking but cool enough to keep the butter from softening.

IF WORKING IN A WARM ROOM, it helps to ice down and dry the countertop. If the dough softens while rolling and becomes sticky, slip a cookie sheet under the dough mat, cover the dough with plastic wrap, and refrigerate it for about 10 minutes before continuing to roll it.

MY FAVORITE SURFACE for rolling dough is my Magic Dough Pastry Mat (see page xvi). Alternatively, use two large sheets of plastic wrap, preferably Freeze-Tite (see page xvii), or a pastry cloth rubbed with flour. If using plastic wrap, two or three times during rolling, flip the dough over, lift off the plastic wrap to prevent it from creasing into the dough, and dust the dough lightly with flour if needed. I like to use Wondra flour for dusting, as its particles work like tiny ball bearings.

My Rose's signature nonstick Magic Rolling Pin is the most nonstick rolling pin I've ever used, and requires very little—if any—extra flour to keep it from sticking. Alternatively, if you have a wooden rolling pin, a knitted pastry sleeve slipped onto the rolling pin and rubbed with flour works well, or rub the wooden rolling pin with flour as needed. Or you can roll the dough between sheets of lightly floured plastic wrap, flipping it over to reposition the plastic wrap and reflouring as needed.

SILICONE FAST TRACKS serve as spacers between the counter and the rolling pin to ensure an evenly rolled crust and to prevent overrolling the edges. My general preference is to roll the dough ³⁄₃₂ inch (slightly under ⅛ inch) thick.

Roll the dough from the center outward using firm, steady pressure. Lift the dough from time to time as you are rolling and add flour as necessary to keep it from sticking. Before measuring the dough, make sure to lift it from the surface to allow it to shrink in so that it doesn't retract when set in the pie plate.

FOR ROLLING THE DOUGH VERY THIN, such as for a galette, it is best to work in a cool room and work quickly. With practice you will be able to roll the dough ¹⁄₁₆ inch—thin enough to read the writing on the dough mat! It is especially helpful to have thinner dough because when folding the edges of the dough over the entire galette filling, the dough as it pleats will not be too thick. If the dough is thicker it will require longer baking and will be less evenly baked.

Cutting the Dough

It is easier to cut the dough to the right size before transferring it to the pie plate or tart pan, rather than transferring a larger piece and then trimming the edges. I use an expandable flan ring (used in professional kitchens as a cake or pastry mold) like a giant cookie cutter to cut neat circles of dough. You can also use a cardboard template or platter and a pizza wheel or small sharp knife to cut the rolled out dough.

For cutting the dough for a tart pan, see Cutting the Dough, page 204.

To determine the ideal size for a pie plate, measure your pie plate. Use a flexible tape measure and start at one inside edge, not including the rim. Go down the side, across the bottom, and up the other side. Then measure the width of the rim. You need enough dough around the edge to make a decorative crimped border, but if it is too thick, it will droop and/or not bake through. Use these guidelines:

FOR SPECIALTY PIE PLATES: For a single crust pie, a double thickness border is desirable, so multiply the size of the rim by 4. For a lattice pie, multiple the size of the rim by 3. For a double crust pie, multiple the size of the rim by 2.

FOR A STANDARD 9 INCH PIE PLATE WITH A ½ INCH RIM: Cut a 12½ inch diameter disc of dough for the bottom crust. Cut a 12 to 12½ inch disc of dough for the top crust, depending on how much the filling will be mounded.

FOR ROSE'S PERFECT PIE PLATE: For a single crust or lattice crust bottom, cut a 14 inch disc of dough. For a double crust pie, cut the bottom crust 12½ inches and the top crust 13½ to 14 inches, depending on how much the filling will be mounded.

FOR MAKING A LATTICE: After cutting the dough for the bottom crust, add any scraps to the dough for the lattice by layering the strips on top of it. Lay a sheet of plastic wrap on top and roll the scraps into the dough. Flip it over so that it is smooth side up and roll the dough into a 12 by 11 inch wide oval. Cut ¾ inch wide strips, either with a straight or zigzag edge, using a pastry jagger, pizza cutter, or small sharp knife.

The lattice strips should extend ½ inch over the edge of the pie plate so that they can be tucked under the bottom crust, which should have a thinner border than a single crust pie to accommodate the extra layers of dough from the lattice strips.

Transferring the Dough to the Pie Plate or Tart Pan

The easiest way to transfer the dough is to fold it first in quarters. Set the point of the dough at the center of the pie plate and unfold and ease it into the plate. Avoid stretching the dough, or it will shrink back on baking.

FOR A DOUBLE CRUST PIE: When lining the pie plate, the bottom crust should come to the outer edge of the pie plate. Then, when draping the top crust over the filling, the top crust will extend far enough so that it can be tucked under the bottom crust, pressed down, and fluted decoratively if

desired. To make it easier to transfer, you can slide it onto a cookie sheet, cover it with plastic wrap, and refrigerate or freeze it until firm. Moisten the border of the bottom crust by brushing it lightly with water. Slip your hands under the crust to lift it, and place it over the filling. If chilled, allow it to soften for a few minutes to be flexible. Tuck the overhang under the edge of the bottom crust and press down well all along the top, extending slightly past the edge to allow for shrinkage.

Making a Border

FOR A RUSTIC STYLE, simply press the dough down with your fingers. Or crimp the dough with your fingers, pressing the dough between your thumb and index finger of one hand into the tip of the index finger of your other hand to create a fluted edge. If the dough softens, either refrigerate it until firm or dip your fingers in flour. Alternatively, instead of tucking the top crust under the bottom, press the two together with the tines of a fork and use scissors to cut the excess.

FOR A TART, fold down the excess dough on the sides as described on page 204. For a thinner side crust without a decorative border, see the Baking Pearl on page 197.

Baking the Crust

FOR A SINGLE CRUST PIE OR TART: After lining the pie plate or tart pan and creating the border, it is best to freeze it for at least 8 hours before blind baking it to ensure that it keeps its shape. It is necessary to do this for a tart to keep the sides from slipping down excessively. You can refrigerate it for up to 24 hours, or freeze it for up to 6 months if it is not in a Pyrex pie plate. Be sure to wrap it well to avoid loss of moisture. If refrigerating, use two layers of plastic wrap; if freezing, use a gallon-size reclosable freezer bag.

Baking Pearl

Dough scraps can be layered and rerolled, chilled, or frozen. When you have enough, make Rose's Rugelach, page 77.

Rolling, Cutting, and Blind Baking a Pie Crust

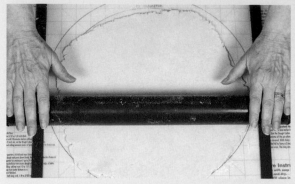

Roll the dough from the center outward.

Use a flan ring or a knife to cut the dough.

Place the folded dough in the pie plate.

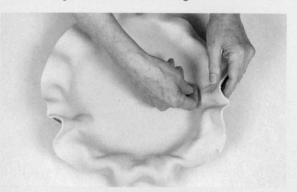

Ease the dough into the plate without stretching it.

Press the border into the rim of the pie plate.

Fill the parchment or coffee filter with weights and blind bake the crust.

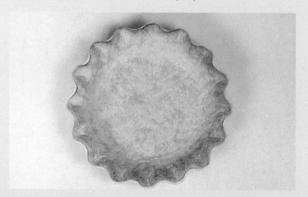

Lining a Tart Pan with Perfect Flaky and Tender Cream Cheese Dough

Fold the dough in half and then in quarters.

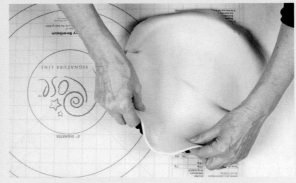

Ease the dough into the pan without stretching it.

Press the dough against the sides of the pan.

Press the dough against the top edge.

Roll over the top of the dough.

Push the dough up ⅛ inch above the edge to allow for shrinkage.

Baking Pearls

If you prefer a thinner side crust without a decorative border: Roll the dough ⅛ inch thick. When lining the tart pan, after easing the dough into the bottom and against the sides, fold over the excess dough so that it drapes over the edge of the pan. Run a rolling pin over the top of the pan to cut off the excess dough. Then use your fingertip to press the dough gently against the side of the pan so that it rises about ⅛ inch above the rim.

Set the dough-lined tart pan, lightly covered with plastic wrap, in the freezer for a minimum of 8 hours before blind baking. By not turning in the excess dough against the sides of the pan it does not slip down more than just a little.

To unmold filled tarts that have been chilled, see Solutions for Possible Problems (page 187).

Making a Foil Ring to Protect the Edge

Cut off a piece of heavy-duty aluminum foil a few inches larger than the diameter of the pie plate or tart pan. Use a pencil to mark a circle in the center that is about 1 inch smaller than the diameter of the pie plate (about 8 inches) so that only the decorative edge will be covered. With sharp scissors, cut out the ring (the ring will be about 3 inches wide). Shape it so that it will curve over the rim of the pie crust. The ring can be washed carefully and reused.

Making a Foil Ring

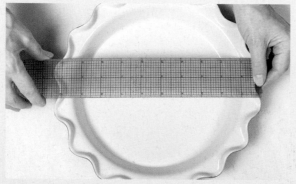

Measure the pie plate.

Trace the outlines of the foil ring.

Cut out the foil ring.

Cut out the center of the ring.

Fit the foil ring to the pie plate.

Shape the foil ring.

Blind Baking (Prebaking) a Single Crust Pie or Tart Shell

When making an open face pie (without a top crust) or a tart such as the Pecan Tart on page 259, baking the bottom crust completely before baking it with the filling will ensure a crisper crust.

THIRTY MINUTES OR LONGER BEFORE BAKING, set an oven rack at the lowest level. Set the oven at 425°F/220°C.

If using a tart pan, set it on a foil-lined cookie sheet to catch the small amount of butter that will leak out the bottom.

USING NONSTICK COOKING SPRAY, lightly coat the bottom of a large coffee filter or several smaller ones, or a sheet of parchment, crumpled so that it conforms to the shape of the pie plate. Set it in the pie shell and fill it with dried rice or beans.

BAKE FOR 20 MINUTES. Carefully lift out the coffee filter with the rice by first easing away the sides from the pastry.

Place a foil ring on top to protect the border from overbrowning and bake for 3 to 7 more minutes, just until the crust is golden. Watch carefully. If the dough puffs in places, use the back of a spoon to press it down gently. It is best to use a fork only if you will not be using a sticky filling such as for the pecan tart, as there is a risk that the fork might pierce all the way through to the bottom and the filling would leak through during baking and stick to the bottom of the pie plate or tart pan.

REMOVE THE PIE PLATE OR TART PAN, still on the cookie sheet, to a wire rack. For an extra crisp crust, while the crust is still hot, brush the bottom and sides with about 1 tablespoon/15 ml lightly beaten egg white.

If any small holes should form in the bottom crust, use melted white or dark chocolate to fill them. It is an ideal filler because, when hardened, it forms a barrier between the crust and the pie or tart filling, but the bottom of the pie or tart pan can be heated to melt the chocolate, making unmolding easy. Allow the pie or tart shell to cool completely before filling.

Baking a Double Crust Pie from Frozen

Baking a double crust pie from the frozen state will result in a crisper bottom crust. This is because in addition to the regular baking time, the crust begins to bake for extra time while the filling is still thawing.

A frozen pie needs to bake at a lower temperature of 400°F/200°C and needs an extra 30 to 45 minutes of baking time, depending on the filling.

If you only have one pie plate and want to freeze more than one pie, line the plate with plastic wrap before composing the pie, then freeze the pie. Once the pie is frozen solid, you can lift it out, place it in a gallon-size reclosable freezer bag, and use the pie plate to shape the next pie. (Unwrap the pie and place it in a pan before baking.)

Baking Pearls

If a crunchy and sparkling effect on the top crust is desired, just before baking spritz or brush the top crust or lattice with a little water or milk (avoid the border as it will get too dark on baking). Dust with granulated sugar.

For the crispest bottom crust, if possible, and only if using a metal or ceramic pie plate (not Pyrex), bake directly on the floor of the oven for the first 30 minutes. Alternatively, again only if using a metal or ceramic pie plate, bake on a preheated baking stone set on the lowest rack level. But when baking that low in the oven, avoid making too large a border, or it will droop.

If the top of the pie starts to get too brown, either reduce the oven temperature to 400°F/200°C or tent the pie loosely with foil with a steam vent cut into it.

I prefer cornstarch as the thickener for fruit pies as it has the best flavor. It is important to bake the pie until the juices bubble within the center vents in order for the filling to thicken upon cooling. (Cornstarch does not thicken completely until it reaches a full boil.)

Fruit pies are best eaten the day of baking, when the crust is the most crisp and the filling the most juicy, with just enough flow. If storing a cut pie, cover only the cut section to keep it from drying without making the crust soggy. For an open face pie, cover the fruit with plastic wrap that has been lightly coated with nonstick cooking spray.

Sweet Cookie Tart or Pie Crust (Pâte Sucrée)

MAKES ONE 9½ INCH TART SHELL OR ONE 9 INCH SINGLE PIE CRUST

OVEN TEMPERATURE: 425°F/220°C, then 375°F/190°C

BAKING TIME: 25 to 35 minutes

BAKING EQUIPMENT:
For a tart: One 9½ by 1 inch high fluted tart pan with removable bottom, coated with baking spray with flour if not nonstick

An expandable flan ring or 12 inch round cardboard template

An 8 by 2 inch round cake pan

A cookie sheet lined with nonstick aluminum foil or with regular aluminum foil lightly coated with nonstick spray

For a pie: One standard 9 inch pie plate

Optional: a second 9 inch pie plate, to aid in shaping

For both: A large coffee filter, several smaller cup-style coffee filters, or crumpled parchment

Dried beans or rice as weights for blind baking

A foil ring to protect the edges of the crust

A cookie crust is firmer but more tender than a flaky pie crust. It maintains its crisp and tender texture even when chilled, which makes it more suitable for tarts that require refrigeration.

Makes 321 grams

unsalted butter	85 grams	6 tablespoons (¾ stick)
1 large egg yolk (reserve the egg white; see Baking Pearls, page 209)	19 grams	1 tablespoon plus ½ teaspoon (17.5 ml)
heavy cream	29 grams	2 tablespoons (30 ml)
bleached all-purpose flour (see Baking Pearl, opposite)	150 grams	1¼ cups (lightly spooned into the cup and leveled off)
fine sea salt	.	⅛ teaspoon
superfine sugar	37 grams	3 tablespoons
lemon zest, finely grated (optional)	3 grams	1½ teaspoons, loosely packed

MISE EN PLACE

- Cut the butter into ½ inch cubes and refrigerate.

- Into a 1 cup measure with a spout, weigh or measure the egg yolk and cream. Cover and refrigerate.

MAKE THE DOUGH
FOOD PROCESSOR METHOD

1. In a medium bowl, whisk together the flour and salt.

2. In a food processor, pulse together the sugar and lemon zest, if using, until the zest is very finely grated.

3. Add the cold butter cubes and pulse until the sugar coats the butter.

4. Add the flour mixture and pulse until the butter is no larger than small peas.

5. Add the egg yolk and cream and pulse just until incorporated. The dough will be in crumbly pieces unless pinched.

6. Scrape the dough into a plastic bag and press it from the outside of the bag just until it holds together. Remove the dough from the plastic bag and place it on a very large sheet of plastic wrap. Use the plastic wrap to knead the dough a few times until it becomes one smooth piece. There should be no visible pieces of butter. (Visible pieces of butter in the dough will melt and form holes during

Baking Pearl

Unbleached all-purpose flour will result in as tender a crust, but due to its higher protein content, you will need to use slightly more cream: Use a total of 38 grams/2 tablespoons plus 2 teaspoons (40 ml) cream. The higher protein content in the flour will cause the crust to brown more quickly, so watch carefully when baking.

baking.) If there are visible pieces of butter, use the heel of your hand in a forward motion to smear them into the dough.

HAND METHOD

1. Very finely chop the lemon zest, if using. In a medium bowl, stir together the lemon zest, flour, sugar, and salt.

2. With a pastry cutter or two knives, cut in the cold butter until the mixture resembles coarse meal.

3. Mix the egg yolk and cream into the flour mixture until the dough comes together and can be formed into a large ball.

BOTH METHODS

CHILL THE DOUGH

7. Flatten the dough into a 6 inch disc. Wrap it with plastic wrap and refrigerate for 30 minutes, or until firm enough to roll or press into the pan. (If pressing the dough, see page 206). It can be refrigerated for up to 3 days or frozen for up to 6 months. If chilled for more than 30 minutes, depending on the room temperature it can take as long as 40 minutes to become malleable for rolling.

(continued)

Variations

SAME DAY SWEET TART COOKIE CRUST

For when you don't have time to freeze the dough-lined tart pan for a minimum of 8 hours before baking, or if you prefer a tart shell with thinner sides and without a decorative border.

Roll the dough ⅛ inch thick and transfer it to the tart pan. After easing the dough into the bottom and against the sides of the pan, fold over the excess dough so that it drapes over the edge of the pan. Run a rolling pin over the top of the pan to cut off the excess dough. Then use your fingertip to press the dough gently against the side of the pan so that it rises about ⅛ inch above the rim. (There is no need to remove dough from the outside of the pan because this method prevents any dough from getting stuck.)

Freeze the dough-lined tart pan, lightly covered with plastic wrap, for an hour before blind baking. The thinner dough on the sides will not slip down more than just a little, even without extended chilling. The sides, however, are more fragile, so take care when removing the filter.

SWEET ALMOND COOKIE CRUST (ALMOND PÂTE SUCRÉE)

For the French Chocolate Tart on page 267.

Omit the lemon zest and use only 106 grams/ ¾ cup flour. Add 50 grams/½ cup sliced, preferably unblanched almonds, and process them with the sugar until finely ground. (If making the dough by hand, grate the almonds with a rotary grater or use store-bought almond flour instead.)

SWEET CHOCOLATE COOKIE TART CRUST (CHOCOLATE PÂTE SUCRÉE)

Makes 455 grams/about 1½ cups

Another choice for the French Chocolate Tart or the Pecan Tart (page 259). Cocoa powder replaces some of the flour, powdered sugar gives a fine texture, and a whole egg replaces the egg yolk and cream for a little more structure. If pairing with a very sweet filling such as in the pecan tart, it's fine to decrease the powdered sugar to 57 grams/½ cup, lightly spooned into the cup and leveled off.

unsalted butter	113 grams	8 tablespoons (1 stick)
bleached all-purpose flour	185 grams	1½ cups (lightly spooned into the cup and leveled off), plus ½ tablespoon
unsweetened alkalized cocoa powder	23 grams	¼ cup plus 1 tablespoon (sifted before measuring)
fine sea salt	.	a pinch
powdered sugar	86 grams	¾ cup (lightly spooned into the cup and leveled off)
1 large egg, lightly beaten	50 grams	3 tablespoons plus ½ teaspoon (47.5 ml)

1. Cut the butter into ½ inch cubes and refrigerate.

2. Process or sift together the cocoa, flour, and salt to remove any lumps. Empty it into a bowl and proceed with either the food processor or hand method as for the plain sweet cookie crust.

3. After baking and removing the weights, fill the tart shell without continuing to blind bake first; longer baking will make the crust less tender if it continues to bake with the filling.

Making Sweet Cookie Tart or Pie Dough in a Food Processor

Combine the butter cubes and sugar in a food processor.

Process until the sugar disappears.

Add the flour and process until the butter is the size of small peas.

Add the egg yolk and cream.

The dough should be crumbly, but hold together when pinched.

Knead the dough together in a plastic bag.

Finish kneading lightly with plastic wrap.

Shape into a disc.

ROLLING THE DOUGH

SET THE DOUGH BETWEEN lightly floured large sheets of plastic wrap. Roll it into an even disc ³⁄₃₂ inch (slightly under ⅛ inch) thick. For a tart pan, it should be slightly larger than 12 inches in diameter; for a standard pie plate, slightly larger than 11½ inches. (If using a different pie plate, measure the pie plate using a flexible tape measure, running it from the top of one inside edge, down the side, across the bottom, and up the other side. Then add 1½ inches to allow for a small border.)

While rolling the dough, sprinkle it with a little more flour on each side as needed. If it softens significantly, slip it onto a cookie sheet (still on the plastic wrap) and refrigerate it for about 10 minutes until firm but still flexible. From time to time, flip the dough with the plastic wrap and lift off and flatten out the plastic wrap as necessary to make sure it does not wrinkle into the dough.

Cutting the Dough

REMOVE THE TOP SHEET OF PLASTIC WRAP. Use an expandable flan ring, or a pizza wheel or small sharp knife with a cardboard template as a guide, to cut a 12 inch disc for a tart pan, or 11½ inches or larger for a pie plate, depending on the size of the plate. Take care not to cut through the bottom plastic wrap. If the dough softens after cutting the disc, refrigerate it until firm. It will not drape over the pan unless it is flexible, so if it becomes too rigid in the refrigerator, let it sit and soften for a few minutes.

Lining a Tart Pan

USE THE PLASTIC WRAP TO LIFT THE DOUGH and set it, plastic wrap side down, over an inverted 8 inch cake pan. Smooth down the sides so they will fit into the tart pan, and place the removable bottom of the tart pan on top. Carefully place the fluted ring upside-down on top.

Place a flat plate or cardboard round over the tart pan to keep it from separating, and invert the pans. Slide and butt the cake pan against the sides and then remove it.

Carefully peel off the plastic wrap and gently ease the dough down to reach the bottom and sides of the pan. If the dough breaks at any point, simply patch and press it into the pan with your fingers.

Making a Border

FOLD DOWN THE EXCESS DOUGH about halfway to create a thicker layer for the sides of the tart, and press the dough against the sides of the tart pan so that it is even in thickness all around and extends above the top. Where pleats form in the dough, you can cut off the little excess triangles. If necessary, trim the dough to ⅛ to ¼ inch above the rim of the pan.

For an attractive border, if desired, use the back of a knife to make diagonal marks all around. On the outside of the pan, use your finger to remove any dough that may have stuck over the edge, because during baking, when the dough shrinks slightly, it will pull down and make holes in the sides of the crust.

Rolling the Dough and Lining a Tart Pan

Roll out the dough to ³⁄₃₂ inch (slightly under ⅛ inch) thick.

Use a knife and a cardboard template to cut the disc.

Drape the dough over an inverted 8 inch cake pan.

Set the tart pan on top of the dough. Set a round base on top to keep the tart pan from separating.

Use the cake pan to press the dough against the sides of the tart pan.

Fold down the excess dough halfway.

Cut out excess pleats of dough.

Press the dough against the sides to about ¼ inch above the rim.

(continued)

Make a decorative border with the back of a knife.

Detach any dough from the outside of the pan.

Pressing the Dough into the Tart Pan by Hand

Begin by pinching off pieces of dough. Roll them into logs a little under ½ inch in diameter. Press them against the sides of the pan to reach about ⅛ inch above the top. (If making a decorative border, roll the logs ½ inch in diameter and press the dough to reach about ¼ inch above the sides.) Press the rest of the dough evenly into the bottom of the pan. For a ⅛ inch thick bottom crust, hold out 35 to 53 grams/2 to 3 tablespoons of the dough (so that the dough will be thinner). If the dough softens, cover it with a piece of plastic wrap before continuing to press it. Be sure to press along the juncture where the bottom of the dough meets the sides, to prevent it from being thicker.

Lining a Pie Plate

Cut out a 12 inch disc of dough as on page 204. It is helpful to have a second pie plate to help transfer the dough evenly into the pie plate. Invert one of the pie plates and use the bottom sheet of plastic wrap to lift the dough and drape it evenly, plastic wrap side down, over the pie plate. Set the second pie plate on top of the dough and invert the pie plates. (You can also invert an 8 inch cake pan and drape the dough over it, as on page 205, or you can press the dough into the pie plate by hand.)

Lift off the top pie plate and carefully peel off the plastic wrap. Turn under the edge of the dough and, if desired, use your fingers to make a slightly raised ridge to form a border on top of the rim. Do not allow it to extend past the edge of the pie plate, or it will droop during baking.

Chilling the Tart Shell or Pie Crust

Cover the tart shell or pie crust with plastic wrap and refrigerate it, or if not in a Pyrex pie plate, freeze it, for a minimum of 8 hours. For a tart shell where the dough is folded down to form a thicker layer for the sides, it is best to freeze it.

Pressing Dough into a Tart Pan

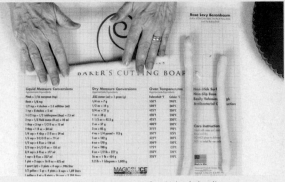

Roll the dough into logs just under ½ inch in diameter.

Connect the logs together around the bottom of the pan.

Press the dough a little above the rim.

Press the rest of the dough into the bottom of the pan, right to the edge.

Press it evenly over the bottom.

Make the rim even.

(continued)

Blind Baking the Tart Shell or Pie Crust

PREHEAT THE OVEN thirty minutes or longer before baking, set an oven rack at the lowest level. Set the oven at 425°F/220°C.

Run a finger along the outside fluted edge of the pan a second time to make absolutely sure that no dough is attached.

COAT THE BOTTOM OF A LARGE COFFEE FILTER or crumpled parchment with nonstick cooking spray. Set it in the tart pan or pie plate and fill it three-quarters full with dried beans or rice, pushing them up against the sides. If using a tart pan, set it on the foil-lined cookie sheet and then set it on the oven rack. To prevent breakage if using a Pyrex pie plate, do not bake it on a solid surface; set it directly on the oven rack.

BAKE AT 425°F/220°C FOR 5 MINUTES; lower the heat to 375°F/190°C and bake for 15 to 20 minutes, or until set. If not set, the dough will stick to the coffee filter. Test for doneness by carefully lifting away a little of the filter from the side; if it sticks to the dough, bake for a little longer.

LIFT OUT THE COFFEE FILTER WITH THE BEANS, first easing it gently away from the sides. Set the foil ring on top of the edges, and continue baking for 3 to 10 more minutes. If the dough starts to puff in places, press it down quickly with the back of a spoon. Bake until the crust is pale gold and feels set but still soft to the touch. It will continue to firm while cooling, just the way cookies do.

Cooling the Tart Shell or Pie Crust

Remove the tart pan or pie plate, still on the cookie sheet, to a wire rack. If any holes have formed, seal them with a little melted chocolate, as described on page 186.

STORE UNBAKED, AIRTIGHT: refrigerated, 1 week; frozen, about 6 months. Baked, not brushed with egg white, airtight: room temperature, 2 days.

THE UNBAKED TART OR PIE SHELL can be refrigerated for 1 week or frozen for about 6 months. The baked tart shell (without any brushed egg white; see Baking Pearls, right) will keep at room temperature in an airtight container for 2 days.

Baking Pearls

Always keep the dough covered when letting it rest to keep it from drying or crusting.

Scraps can be kneaded together, flattened into a disc, and chilled or frozen. The disc can be rerolled and used to make small tarts or cookies.

If filling the pie with a moist filling, such as for the Lemon Meringue Pie, after cooling the baked crust for 3 minutes, brush it with about 1 tablespoon of the reserved lightly beaten egg white; this will help moisture proof it.

It is best to press down the dough as it puffs, rather than pierce it with a fork, because if it is pierced all the way through to the bottom, the filling will leak through on further baking and stick to the bottom of the pan.

To unmold filled tarts that have been chilled, see Solutions for Possible Problems (page 187).

Apple Pie

SERVES 8

OVEN TEMPERATURE:
425°F/220°C

BAKING TIME: 45 to 55 minutes

BAKING EQUIPMENT:
One 9 inch standard pie plate

A baking stone or cookie sheet, lined with aluminum foil

A foil ring to protect the edges of the crust

The secret to this pie's pure apple flavor, with just a slight touch of caramel, is boiling down and concentrating the apples' juices. You can omit this step (see Baking Pearls, opposite), but if you do so, you will need to add an additional 2 grams/½ teaspoon cornstarch to thicken the juices.

PERFECT FLAKY AND TENDER CREAM CHEESE PIE CRUST

Dough for a double crust pie (page 190)	624 grams	1 recipe

APPLE FILLING

about 6 large tart apples (see page xxv), 1135 grams/2½ pounds	907 grams (sliced)	8 cups (peeled, cored, and sliced ¼ inch thick)
lemon juice, freshly squeezed and strained (1 lemon)	16 grams	1 tablespoon (15 ml)
light brown sugar, preferably light Muscovado	54 grams	¼ cup, firmly packed
granulated sugar	50 grams	¼ cup
ground cinnamon	2.2 grams	1 teaspoon
nutmeg, preferably freshly grated	.	¼ teaspoon
fine sea salt	.	¼ teaspoon
unsalted butter	28 grams	2 tablespoons
cornstarch	12 grams	1 tablespoon plus 1 teaspoon

MISE EN PLACE

■ **ROLL OUT THE BOTTOM CRUST:** Following the instructions on page 204, roll the dough 12 inches in diameter or large enough to line the pie plate and extend slightly past the edge. Fit the dough into the pie plate. Trim the dough almost even with the edge. Cover it with plastic wrap and refrigerate.

■ **MACERATE THE APPLES:** In a large bowl, combine the apples, lemon juice, brown and granulated sugars, cinnamon, nutmeg, and salt and toss to mix. Allow them to macerate for a minimum of 30 minutes, or up to 3 hours, at room temperature. Transfer the apples to a colander suspended over a bowl to capture the juices. The mixture will release at least ½ cup/118 ml juice.

MAKE THE APPLE FILLING

1. In a small saucepan, preferably nonstick, over medium-high heat, boil down the juices with the butter until syrupy and lightly caramelized, about ⅓ cup/

Baking Pearls

Some of my favorite pie apples are Northern Spy, Macoun, Stayman-Winesap, Cortland, and Jonathan. In the winter, I use Granny Smith or Golden Delicious apples from the supermarket, which also make an excellent pie. Avoid apples with high water content, such as McIntosh, which are ideal for applesauce but not for pie.

If not concentrating the apples' juices, use a total of 14 grams/1½ tablespoons cornstarch.

Depending on their moisture content, the apples will settle down a little on baking, leaving a space between the upper crust and the filling. It will disappear on serving. Arranging the apples in concentric circles helps minimize any extra space between the apples and the crust. Not chilling the pie before baking will also minimize this space, but the border will not be as well-defined.

79 ml. Swirl but do not stir. (Or coat a 4 cup glass measure with a spout with nonstick cooking spray, add the juices and butter, and boil in the microwave for a few minutes, stirring every 30 seconds, until reduced. Watch carefully, as it goes really quickly toward the end.)

2. Meanwhile, transfer the apples to a bowl and toss them with the cornstarch until all traces of it have disappeared. Pour the hot syrup over the apples, tossing gently. Don't be concerned if the syrup hardens on the apples; it will dissolve during baking.

3. Transfer the apple filling to the pie shell. The apples will mound well above the top of the pie plate, but will settle down considerably during baking. To help prevent a gap between the apples and top crust, see Baking Pearls (left).

ROLL OUT AND PLACE THE TOP CRUST

4. Roll and cut the top crust to 12½ inches in diameter. To make it easier to transfer, slide it onto a cookie sheet, cover it with plastic wrap, and refrigerate or freeze it until firm. Moisten the border of the bottom crust by brushing it lightly with water. Slip your hands under the top crust to lift it and place it over the apples. If chilled, allow it to soften for a few minutes to be flexible. Tuck the overhang under the bottom crust border and press down well all along the top, extending the border slightly past the edge to allow for shrinkage. If desired, make a decorative border.

MAKE STEAM VENTS AND CHILL THE PIE

5. Cut about five 2 inch slashes, evenly spaced, starting about 1 inch from the center and radiating toward the edge. Cover the pie loosely with plastic wrap and refrigerate for 1 hour before baking to chill and relax the pastry. This will maintain flakiness and minimize shrinking.

PREHEAT THE OVEN

■ Forty-five minutes or longer before baking, set an oven rack at the lowest level and place the baking stone or cookie sheet on it. Set the oven at 425°F/220°C.

BAKE THE PIE

6. Place the foil ring on top of the pie to protect the edges from overbrowning and set the pie on the baking stone. Bake for 20 minutes. For even baking, rotate the pie halfway around. Continue baking for 25 to 35 minutes, or until the juices bubble through the slashes and the apples feel tender but not mushy when a wire cake tester or small sharp knife is inserted through a slash. They will continue softening slightly on cooling.

COOL THE PIE

7. Set the pie on a wire rack and cool for at least 4 hours before cutting. Serve warm or room temperature.

STORE UNCOVERED: room temperature, 2 days; refrigerated, 4 days.

(continued)

Making Apple Pie

Collect the apple juices.

Add the butter to the juices.

Reduce the apple juice to a syrup.

Pour the hot syrup over the apples.

Trim the edge of the pie crust.

Brush the border with water.

Arrange the top crust over the apples.

Form a border.

Cut steam vents.

Cover the edges with a foil ring.

Apple Galette

SERVES 6 TO 8

OVEN TEMPERATURE:
400°F/200°C

BAKING TIME: 40 to 45
minutes

BAKING EQUIPMENT:
One 12 to 14 inch pizza
pan, preferably dark
metal, or a 17¼ by 12¼
by 1 inch half sheet pan

A baking stone or
cookie sheet

Another cookie sheet,
for holding the apples

A galette is a free form tart that can be made with many fruits or berries. It is easy to make, but by arranging the apple slices in concentric circles, the finished tart looks extraordinarily beautiful. This apple version is crisp, buttery, tart, and elegant. For the crispest bottom crust, be sure to use a preheated baking stone.

PERFECT FLAKY AND TENDER CREAM CHEESE PIE CRUST

Dough for a galette (page 189)	414 grams	1 recipe

APPLE FILLING

about 4 large tart apples (see Baking Pearls, page 216), 753 grams/1⅔ pounds	604 grams (sliced)	5⅓ cups (peeled, cored, and sliced into wedges no more than ¼ inch thick)
lemon juice, freshly squeezed and strained	.	2 teaspoons (10 ml)
sugar	50 grams	¼ cup
unsalted butter	28 grams	2 tablespoons
apricot preserves	170 grams	½ cup
apricot brandy or water (optional)	15 grams	1 tablespoon (15 ml)

PREHEAT THE OVEN

▪ Forty-five minutes or longer before baking, set an oven rack at the lowest level and place the baking stone or cookie sheet on it. Set the oven at 400°F/200°C.

MISE EN PLACE

▪ Twenty minutes to 1 hour, ahead, slice the apples. Set them in a medium bowl and toss them with the lemon juice and sugar until evenly coated. (This will soften the apple slices, making them easier to arrange.)

▪ Cut the butter into small pieces and refrigerate.

▪ Have ready a fine-mesh strainer set over a small bowl.

MAKE THE GALETTE

1. Follow the instructions on page 204 for rolling the crust. Roll the dough as thin as possible—under ⅛ inch; 1⁄16 inch is ideal—and at least large enough to cut a 16 inch diameter disc. If at any point the dough softens, slip it, still on the dough mat, onto a cookie sheet. Cover and refrigerate for about 30 minutes, until firmer.

(continued)

The same varieties of apples as listed for Apple Pie (see Baking Pearls, page 211) are a good choice for a galette.

The dough under the thin layer of apples will puff up during baking. Either poke it in a few places with a wooden skewer after the first 20 minutes of baking, which will cause it to settle down, or omit the baking powder in the pie crust and double the salt. The baking powder, however, gives the side border the puffiest texture.

In order to roll the dough thinly, it is best to work in a cool room.

If your oven allows, instead of using a baking stone, it works very well to set the pizza pan directly onto the floor of the oven. Be sure to check after the first 20 minutes of baking and if the bottom crust is nicely browned, move it to a higher shelf.

Make This Recipe Your Own

You can use 3 to 3½ cups of other favorite fruit pie fillings, such as peaches (Peaches and Cream Kuchen, page 247), for other excellent galettes. Spread them in a single layer in the center of the dough, about 9 inches in diameter, and fold over the edge of the dough to cover the fruit almost completely, leaving a small opening in the center. Be sure to set a sheet of aluminum foil on top of the cookie sheet underneath to catch any possible drips from the bottom edges of the galette.

2. Brush any flour from the dough. Gently fold the dough in quarters and transfer it to the pizza pan or half sheet pan. Carefully unfold it, leaving the overhang draped on the counter.

3. Empty the apple slices onto a cookie sheet so that you can separate the smaller from the larger ones. Arrange the apple slices, overlapping, in concentric circles within a 12 to 14 inch diameter (to the edge of the pizza pan, if using), starting toward the outer edge of the circle with the larger pieces, cored sides facing toward the center. If necessary, push a few slices of the fruit closer together and insert more slices evenly in between. Save the smaller pieces for the center. (A few seconds in the microwave will help to make the slices for the center more flexible.) Brush the apples with any liquid that remains in the bowl.

4. Dot the apples with the pieces of butter.

5. Fold the overhanging border of dough over the outer edge of the apples, allowing it to pleat softly at even intervals.

6. For a crunchy border, spritz or brush the dough rim lightly with water and sprinkle with a little sugar. If necessary, brush away any sugar on the surface of the pan.

BAKE THE GALETTE

7. Set the galette, on the pan, on the baking stone. Bake for 20 minutes. For even baking, rotate it halfway around. Continue baking for 20 to 25 minutes, or until the apples feel tender when pierced with a wire cake tester. If the edges of the apples start to brown, tent loosely with aluminum foil. Toward the end of baking, with a metal spatula, carefully lift up the crust to make sure it is not overbrowning. If necessary, lower the heat to 375°F/190°C, or lift the pan from the stone and move it to a higher shelf.

COOL THE GALETTE

8. Set the galette on a wire rack and cool until warm before glazing.

GLAZE THE GALETTE

9. In a small saucepan over medium-low heat, heat the apricot preserves until boiling. Press them through the strainer. If necessary, stir in the brandy to thin slightly. Brush the glaze onto the apples.

10. Serve warm or room temperature.

STORE APPLE PORTION COVERED WITH LIGHTLY COATED PLASTIC WRAP: room temperature, 2 days; refrigerated, 4 days.

Making Apple Galette

Roll the dough at least 16 inches in diameter.

Cut out a 16 inch round.

Fold the dough in quarters and transfer to the pan.

Arrange the dough in the pan.

Arrange the apples in overlapping circles.

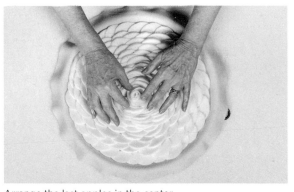

Arrange the last apples in the center.

Fold over and pleat the border, and dot the galette with butter.

Brush the baked galette with apricot glaze.

Cherry Pie

Tart sour cherries, generally available at farmers' markets in early summer, have a color and vibrancy unlike any other fruit. They can be frozen for many months so you can enjoy this pie any time of the year. A woven lattice crust is the most spectacular, but alternatively, five strips can be placed evenly on top of the filling and then the remaining five placed perpendicularly on top, without weaving.

PERFECT FLAKY AND TENDER CREAM CHEESE PIE CRUST

Dough for a 10 strip lattice pie (page 190)	480 grams	1 recipe

CHERRY FILLING

sour cherries (680 grams/ 1½ pounds)	567 grams pitted	about 3¾ cups (3½ cups pitted)
sugar (see Baking Pearls, opposite)	175 grams	¾ cup plus 2 tablespoons
cornstarch	23 grams	2½ tablespoons
fine sea salt	.	a pinch
pure almond extract	.	¼ teaspoon (1.2 ml)

MISE EN PLACE

▪ **ROLL OUT THE BOTTOM CRUST:** Following the instructions on page 194, roll and cut the crust 12½ inches in diameter, or large enough to line the pie plate and extend enough to turn about halfway under the border just past the edge; see Baking Pearls, opposite. Fit the dough into the pie plate. If necessary, trim the edge and then turn it under so that it is even with the pie plate. Cover the dough-lined pie plate with plastic wrap and refrigerate.

▪ Pit the cherries, placing them in a medium bowl along with any juices they exude. There should be 567 grams/3½ cups.

MAKE THE PIE FILLING

1. In a medium saucepan, stir together the sugar, cornstarch, and salt. Gently stir in the cherries along with any juices. Allow the mixture to sit for at least 10 minutes to liquefy the sugar mixture.

2. Over medium heat, stirring constantly, bring the cherry mixture to a boil and simmer for about 1 minute, until thickened. Scrape the mixture into a wide bowl and allow it to cool completely.

3. Stir in the almond extract and transfer the cherry filling into the dough-lined pie plate. Leave the pie unrefrigerated so that the crust border softens in order to be able to attach the strips.

Baking Pearls

A large heavy hairpin makes the best cherry pitter for sour cherries. Insert the looped end into the stem end of the cherry, hook it around the pit, and pull it out.

To freeze pitted cherries, add 50 grams/¼ cup of the sugar from the recipe. Store the cherry mixture in a quart-size canning jar or plastic container and label the cap with the amount of sugar added. When making the pie, be sure to subtract it from the total amount of sugar. Thaw either overnight in the refrigerator or for a few hours at room temperature before adding the rest of the ingredients.

Some years' harvests and some varieties of sour cherries are more tart; it's fine to use as much as 200 grams/1 cup sugar.

If using a pie plate with a larger rim, such as Rose's Perfect Pie Plate, which requires rolling the bottom crust 14 inches in diameter, add any scraps to the dough for the lattice by layering the strips on top of it. Lay a sheet of plastic wrap on top and roll the scraps into the dough. Flip it over so that it is smooth side up and roll the dough into a 12 by 11 inch wide oval. Cut ¾ inch wide strips.

ROLL THE DOUGH FOR THE LATTICE AND CUT STRIPS

4. Roll the second piece of dough into a 12 by 11 inch wide oval (the same thickness as the bottom crust, under ⅛ inch) and cut ten long, ¾ inch wide strips using a ruler and pastry jagger, pizza wheel, or sharp knife. (If you are right-handed, start from the left side.) Set aside any remaining dough to make the cherry cutout, if desired.

WEAVE THE LATTICE

5. Arrange five of the strips spaced evenly over the filling, starting at the center. Carefully curve back the second and fourth strips, a little past the center, so that the next strip can be placed perpendicular to the first strips, at the center of the pie. Uncurve the strips so that they lie flat on top of the perpendicular strip. Working in the same direction, curve back the strips that were not curved back the first time. Lay a second perpendicular strip on top and uncurve the strips. Repeat with the third strip.

6. Apply the remaining two strips to the other side of the pie. Start toward the center and work in the opposite direction toward the edge. Always alternate the strips that are curved back so that the strips weave in and out.

FORM THE BORDER

7. Use sharp scissors to trim the strips to ½ inch longer than the edge of the pie plate. Use water to moisten under the ends of each strip, and tuck the overhang under the bottom crust border, pressing down to attach it and to keep the border from becoming too thick. If desired, use a cookie cutter to cut out a cherry shape from the extra dough for decoration, set it toward the middle of the lattice, and press it gently into place.

CHILL THE PIE

8. Cover the pie loosely with plastic wrap and refrigerate it for 1 hour before baking to chill and relax the pastry. This will maintain flakiness and minimize shrinking.

PREHEAT THE OVEN

▪ Forty-five minutes or longer before baking, set an oven rack at the lowest level and place the baking stone or cookie sheet on it. Set the oven at 425°F/220°C.

BAKE THE PIE

9. Place the foil ring on top of the pie to protect the edges from overbrowning, and set the pie on the baking stone. Bake for 20 minutes. For even baking, rotate the pie halfway around. Continue baking for 15 to 25 minutes, or until the juices bubble thickly near the edges and the center is slightly puffed.

COOL THE PIE

10. Set the pie on a wire rack and cool for at least 3 hours before cutting. Serve warm or room temperature.

STORE UNCOVERED: room temperature, 2 days; refrigerated, 4 days.

(continued)

Making Lattice-Topped Cherry Pie

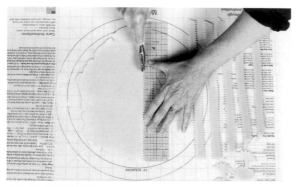

Cut the strips with a pastry jagger.

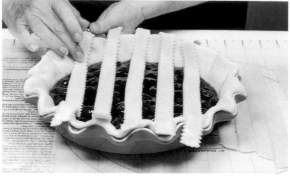

Set the first five strips on top of the pie.

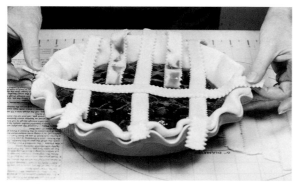

Curve back every other strip and set the next strip at a right angle in the center.

Replace the strips, curve back every strip that was not previously curved back, and set another strip in place.

Continue folding back and adding new strips to finish weaving the top.

Trim the overhanging strips.

Moisten the ends of the strips, tuck them under the bottom crust, and press into the rim of the pie plate.

Set a decorative cutout in place.

Pumpkin Pie

SERVES 6 TO 8

OVEN TEMPERATURE:
375°F/190°C

BAKING TIME: 50 to 60 minutes

BAKING EQUIPMENT:
One 9 inch standard pie plate

A baking stone or cookie sheet

A foil ring to protect the edges of the crust

This pie has an unusually silky texture and mellow flavor. The crisp bottom crust results from pressing in a fine layer of gingersnaps and ground pecans, which absorbs any excess liquid from the filling, and from baking the pie on a baking stone.

PERFECT FLAKY AND TENDER CREAM CHEESE PIE CRUST

Dough for a 9 inch pie shell (page 189)	312 grams	1 recipe
2 inch gingersnaps	29 grams	4 each
pecan halves	25 grams	¼ cup

PUMPKIN FILLING

3 large eggs	150 grams	½ cup plus 1½ tablespoons (140 ml)
pure vanilla extract	.	½ teaspoon (2.5 ml)
milk	161 grams	⅔ cup (158 ml)
heavy cream	155 grams	⅔ cup (158 ml)
one 14 ounce can unsweetened pumpkin, preferably Libby's	425 grams	1¾ cups
light brown sugar, preferably light Muscovado	163 grams	¾ cup, firmly packed
ground ginger	4.4 grams	2 teaspoons
ground cinnamon	3.3 grams	1½ teaspoons
fine sea salt	3 grams	½ teaspoon

MISE EN PLACE

■ **ROLL OUT THE CRUST:** Following the instructions on page 194, roll and cut the dough 13 inches in diameter, or large enough to line the bottom of the pie plate and extend ¾ inch past the edge of the rim. Fit the dough into the pie plate. If necessary, trim the edge of the dough. Fold the dough under so that it is flush with the outer edge of the pie plate. Make a small decorative border (see photos, page 223). Cover the dough-lined pie plate with plastic wrap and leave at room temperature so that the dough is soft enough to be able to press in the cookie and nut crumbs.

■ **PROCESS THE GINGERSNAPS AND PECANS:** Into a food processor, break the cookies into a few pieces. Add the pecans and process until finely ground. Sprinkle them over the bottom of the pie crust and, using your fingers and the back of a

(continued)

Baking Pearls

Avoid making a high raised border for the crust, since baking the pie low in the oven (for a crisp bottom crust) will cause the border to droop.

I like to make a checkerboard design for the border. Use a small sharp knife to make ¾ inch slashes evenly around the border. Then gently turn in every other dough flap. The flaps will pop up a little to form a ruffled effect. Alternatively, for a more distinct checkerboard effect, press in every other dough flap so that they touch the surface of the pie.

If your oven allows, and if you are using a metal or ceramic pie plate, for the crispest bottom crust, bake directly on the floor of oven for the first 30 minutes, with an oven rack above. Then finish baking the pie on the rack.

Small cracks will form around the edges and in the center. Characteristic star-burst cracking, however, is the result of overbaking. If desired, cover any cracks, should they develop, with baked pastry cut-outs made from the dough scraps. When rolling the pie crust, after cutting the disc, layer the scraps and roll between sheets of lightly floured plastic wrap to the same thickness as the pie crust. Chill the dough until firm and use a decorative cutter such as a maple leaf. Veins can be drawn in with the tip of a sharp knife. Bake the cutouts on a parchment-lined cookie sheet in the preheated 375°F/190°C oven for about 10 minutes or until lightly brown. Transfer the cutouts to a wire rack and cool completely before placing on the pie.

spoon, press them into the dough to coat the entire bottom, going about ½ inch up the sides. Refrigerate, lightly covered with plastic wrap, while you make the filling.

■ Into a 1 cup measure with a spout, weigh or measure the eggs. Lightly whisk in the vanilla and cover with plastic wrap.

■ Into a 2 cup measure with a spout, weigh or measure the milk and cream. Cover with plastic wrap and refrigerate.

PREHEAT THE OVEN

■ Forty-five minutes or longer before baking, set an oven rack at the lowest level and place the baking stone or cookie sheet on it. Set the oven at 375°F/190°C.

MAKE THE PIE

1. In a small heavy saucepan, stir together the pumpkin, sugar, spices, and salt. Over medium heat, bring the mixture to a sputtering simmer, stirring constantly. Reduce the heat to low and cook, stirring constantly, for 3 to 5 minutes, until thick and shiny.

2. Scrape the mixture into a food processor and process for 1 minute. With the motor on, add the milk and cream, processing until incorporated. Scrape the sides of the work bowl. With the motor on, add the egg mixture in 3 parts, processing just to incorporate for about 5 seconds after each addition.

3. Pour the mixture into the pie shell. With a small offset spatula, smooth the surface to make it even. Refrigerate for 30 minutes to set the border.

BAKE THE PIE

4. Set the pie on the baking stone and bake for 30 minutes. For even baking, rotate the pie halfway around and cover with a foil ring to protect the edges. Continue baking for 20 to 30 minutes, or just until a knife inserted between the sides and center comes out almost clean. The filling will have puffed and the surface dulled except for the center. It will shake like jelly when moved. (This will happen before it has finished baking, so it cannot be used as a firm indication of doneness; but if it is too loose in consistency, you can be sure that it is not baked adequately.)

COOL THE PIE

5. Set the pie on a wire rack and cool for at least 1 hour before cutting. Serve at room temperature.

STORE UNCOVERED: refrigerated, 4 days. Remove to room temperature 30 minutes to 1 hour before serving.

Making Pumpkin Pie

Make a checkerboard border on the crust.

Press the gingersnap mixture onto the crust.

Combine the filling ingredients.

Cook the filling until thick and shiny.

Pour the filling into the pie shell.

Smooth the surface.

Glazed Strawberry Pie

SERVES 6 TO 8

REFRIGERATION TIME:
about 4 hours

BAKING EQUIPMENT:
One 9 inch standard pie plate

Fresh juicy strawberries, held together by a flavorful cran-raspberry glaze and set in a flaky buttery crust, are a seasonal favorite.

PERFECT FLAKY AND TENDER CREAM CHEESE PIE CRUST

Dough for a 9 inch pie shell (page 189), prebaked and brushed with egg white (see page 209)	312 grams	1 recipe

STRAWBERRY FILLING

strawberries	454 grams	4 cups
cran-raspberry juice or sweetened cranberry juice	704 grams	3 cups (710 ml)
sugar	100 grams	½ cup
cornstarch	27 grams	3 tablespoons

MISE EN PLACE

- Rinse, hull, and dry the strawberries.

MAKE THE GLAZE

1. Into a 2 quart saucepan, weigh or measure the cran/raspberry juice. On medium heat, bring the juice to a boil and continue cooking until reduced by half, to 352 grams/1½ cups/355 ml.

2. Remove the saucepan from the heat and whisk the sugar into the hot juice until dissolved. Cover and allow to cool until no longer warm to the touch (85°F/29°C). To speed cooling, set the covered saucepan in an ice water bath.

3. Whisk the cornstarch into the reduced juice until dissolved. Over medium heat, bring the mixture to a boil, stirring constantly with the whisk. Reduce the heat to low and simmer for 1 minute, stirring gently, until well thickened. When dropped from the whisk, it will pool slightly. You will have about 434 grams/1¾ cups/414 ml glaze.

4. Scrape the glaze into a medium bowl and allow it to cool, covered to prevent evaporation, until no longer warm to the touch. To speed cooling, you can set the bowl into an ice water bath and gently fold the mixture with a silicone spatula every few minutes. Use as soon as it is no hotter than warm to the touch.

MAKE THE PIE

5. While the glaze is cooling, cut the berries in half, or quarters if they are very large, and set them in a medium bowl.

(continued)

Baking Pearl

If you want to serve the pie sooner, use 32 grams/ 3½ tablespoons cornstarch; it will take only 1 hour to set.

6. Pour the glaze over the berries and gently fold them into the glaze.

7. Scrape the mixture into the prepared pie shell and refrigerate for about 4 hours or until set. Remove it from the refrigerator 30 minutes to an hour before serving.

STORE UNCOVERED: refrigerated, 2 days.

Making Glazed Strawberry Pie

Stir the cornstarch mixture until thickened.

Scrape the berry mixture into the baked pie shell.

Fresh Blueberry Pie

SERVES 6 TO 8

BAKING EQUIPMENT:
One 9 inch standard pie plate

This pie is my favorite way to eat blueberries. The extraordinary burst of blueberry comes from keeping most of the berries raw while cooking just enough of them to hold the mixture together. This filling is very quick and easy to make, and delicious served even without the pie crust, for example as a compote with ice cream.

PERFECT FLAKY AND TENDER CREAM CHEESE PIE CRUST

Dough for a 9 inch pie shell (page 189), prebaked and brushed with egg white (see page 209)	312 grams	1 recipe

BLUEBERRY FILLING

blueberries, rinsed and dried	567 grams	4 cups, *divided*
water	148 grams	½ cup plus 2 tablespoons (148 ml), *divided*
cornstarch	18 grams	2 tablespoons
sugar (see Baking Pearl, page 228)	100 grams	½ cup
lemon juice, freshly squeezed and strained	.	1 teaspoon (5 ml)
fine sea salt	.	a pinch

MISE EN PLACE

■ Sort through the blueberries, measuring out 150 grams/1 cup of the softest ones. Place these in a medium saucepan together with 118 grams/½ cup/118 ml of the water.

■ In a small bowl or custard cup, whisk together the cornstarch and the remaining 130 grams/2 tablespoons/30 ml water.

MAKE THE PIE

1. Bring the blueberries and water to a boil, covered. When it comes to a boil, turn the heat to low and simmer, stirring constantly, for about 3 minutes, or until the blueberries begin to burst and the juices thicken.

2. While stirring constantly, add the cornstarch mixture, sugar, lemon juice, and salt. Simmer for about 1 minute until the mixture becomes translucent.

3. Immediately remove the mixture from the heat and quickly fold in the rest of the blueberries.

(continued)

4. Spoon the blueberry filling into the baked pie shell and allow it to sit at room temperature for at least 2 hours to set before serving. The berries will remain very juicy but will not flow.

STORE UNCOVERED: room temperature, 2 days; refrigerated, 4 days.

Making Fresh Blueberry Pie

Combine the berries and cornstarch mixture.

Simmer until the mixture becomes translucent.

Pour the berries into the baked pie shell.

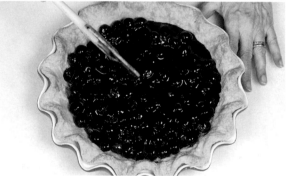
Spread the berries evenly.

Lemon Meringue Pie

SERVES 6 TO 8

OVEN TEMPERATURE:
350°F/175°C for the
filled pie; broiler for the
meringue

BAKING TIME: 25 to
35 minutes for the
pie shell; 5 minutes,
plus about 1 minute
for broiling for the
meringue.

PLAN AHEAD: The
pie benefits from a
minimum of 4 hours
refrigeration after
baking and cooling to
room temperature, so
it's best to make the
crust a day ahead and
the pie the morning
before serving it.

BAKING EQUIPMENT:
One 9 inch standard pie
plate
A cookie sheet

The combination of tart, creamy lemon filling topped with billowy sweet-but-not-too-sweet meringue is the making of a dream pie. Beating hot sugar syrup into the meringue makes it more stable and prevents moisture from seeping out, but for the best results, avoid making the pie on humid or rainy days. The textures of lemon meringue pie are at their best the day it is made. If serving the pie chilled, the Sweet Cookie Pie Crust is a better choice than a flaky crust because it stays tender even when cold. It can also be shaped into a decorative border, but when unmolding the border will break off; it can be served on the side.

SWEET COOKIE TART OR PIE CRUST (PÂTE SUCRÉE)

Sweet Cookie Tart or Pie Crust (page 200), prebaked in a 9 inch pie plate and brushed with egg white (see page 209)	321 grams	1 recipe

LEMON FILLING

unsalted butter	43 grams	3 tablespoons
lemon zest, finely grated	9 grams	1½ tablespoons, loosely packed
lemon juice, freshly squeezed and strained (about 3 lemons)	126 grams	½ cup (118 ml)
8 to 12 large egg yolks (reserve 4 whites/120 grams/½ cup/118 ml for the meringue)	149 grams	½ cup plus 4 teaspoons (138 ml)
sugar	300 grams	1½ cups
cornstarch	85 grams	½ cup (lightly spooned into the cup and leveled off) plus 3 tablespoons
water	590 grams	2½ cups (590 ml)
fine sea salt	.	a pinch

PREHEAT THE OVEN

■ Twenty minutes or longer before baking, set an oven rack at the middle level. Set the oven at 350°F/175°C.

MISE EN PLACE

■ Thirty minutes to 1 hour ahead, cut the butter into 4 pieces and set it on the counter at room temperature (65° to 75°F/19° to 24°C).

(continued)

- With dish washing liquid, wash the lemons. Rinse, dry, and zest them (see page xxv).

- Into a 1 cup measure with a spout, weigh or measure the lemon juice.

- Into a 2 cup measure with a spout, weigh or measure the egg yolks.

- Into the bowl of a stand mixer, weigh or measure the 4 egg whites for the meringue.

- Place the pie plate on the cookie sheet.

MAKE THE LEMON FILLING

1. Lightly whisk the egg yolks.

2. In a heavy medium saucepan, whisk together the sugar and cornstarch. Gradually whisk in the water until smooth. Cook on medium heat, stirring constantly with the whisk, until very thick, smooth, and translucent, about 5 minutes. An instant-read thermometer should read 190°F/88°C. Lower the heat to low.

3. Whisk a few spoonfuls of this mixture into the egg yolks. Then add the yolks to the saucepan, whisking constantly, until big bubbles begin to form around the outside edge. An instant-read thermometer should read 180°F/82°C. (See Baking Pearl, page 232.)

4. Remove the pan from the heat and gently whisk in the butter until melted, then the lemon zest, lemon juice, and salt. Whisk until the mixture is uniform and thickened.

5. Scrape the filling into the prepared pie shell. To keep the filling from forming a slight skin, set a piece of plastic wrap that has been lightly coated with nonstick cooking spray on top, pressed directly against the surface.

LIGHT ITALIAN MERINGUE Makes 225 grams/6½ cups

4 large egg whites	120 grams	½ cup (118 ml)
cream of tartar	.	½ teaspoon
sugar, preferably superfine	100 grams	½ cup
water	30 grams	2 tablespoons (30 ml)
pure vanilla extract	.	¼ teaspoon (1.2 ml)

MISE EN PLACE

- Have ready a 1 cup glass measure with a spout (not coated with nonstick cooking spray) near the cooktop.

- Into the bowl of a stand mixer, weigh or measure the egg whites and add the cream of tartar.

MAKE THE MERINGUE

1. In a small heavy saucepan, preferably nonstick and with a spout, stir together the sugar and the water until the sugar is completely moistened. Cook on medium heat, stirring constantly, until the sugar dissolves and the syrup is bubbling. Stop

(continued)

If you prefer a flaky pie crust and want to serve the pie at room temperature, it is best to add ½ teaspoon gelatin to the sugar and cornstarch mixture so that the filling will set up firmer even at room temperature.

It is necessary for the filling to be heated to 180°F/82°C in Step 3 to deactivate an enzyme in the egg yolks called amylase, which would otherwise cause the filling to thin on sitting.

If desired, instead of covering the filling with plastic wrap, sprinkle it with about ½ cup fine cake crumbs. This will more securely attach the meringue and keep it from sliding.

Variation

INDIVIDUAL BOTTOMLESS LEMON MERINGUES

Omit the crust. Divide the lemon filling between eight 8 ounce ramekins. Spread the meringue on top of the filling, making sure it touches the edges of the ramekin all around. Use a small metal spatula to make attractive swirls and peaks. If desired, for extra crunch, dust the meringue with powdered sugar. Bake, brown and cool as for the large pie and refrigerate for a minimum of 2½ to 3 hours.

---

stirring and turn down the heat to the lowest setting. (If using an electric cooktop, remove from the heat.)

2. Attach the whisk beater and beat the egg whites and cream of tartar on medium-high speed until stiff peaks form when the beater is raised slowly.

3. Increase the heat on the cooktop and boil the syrup until an instant-read thermometer registers 236°F/113°C. Immediately pour the syrup into the glass measure to stop the cooking.

4. With the mixer off, pour a small amount of syrup over the whites. Immediately beat on high speed for 5 seconds. Stop the mixer and add one-third of the syrup. Beat on high speed for 5 seconds. Add the remaining syrup in two parts, with the mixer off between additions. For the last addition, use a silicone scraper to remove the syrup clinging to the glass measure and scrape it against the beater.

5. Continue beating on medium speed for 2 minutes. Beat in the vanilla.

APPLY THE MERINGUE TO THE PIE

6. Use a small metal spatula to spread the meringue on top of the hot filling, covering the filling entirely and making sure the meringue is touching the border of the crust all the way around. This will keep the meringue from shrinking. It works best to start from the crust border and work your way to the center. Mound it so that it is higher in the center. Use the back of a spoon to make decorative swirls.

BAKE AND BROWN THE MERINGUE

7. Bake the pie for 5 minutes.

8. Turn the oven to broil and brown the meringue for 20 seconds to 1 minute, watching to prevent burning, until the meringue is golden. Alternatively, use a kitchen butane torch to brown the meringue. To avoid burning, move it in a back and forth motion until the meringue just begins to brown.

COOL THE PIE

9. Set the pie, still on the cookie sheet, on a wire rack in a draft free area to cool to room temperature, about 1 hour. Then refrigerate uncovered, preferably for at least 4 hours.

SERVE THE PIE

10. Just before serving, wet a large dish towel with very hot water. Set it in the sink and shape it into a nest. Set the pie plate into the hot towel so that it surrounds the entire pie plate up to the rim, and allow it to sit for a minute before slicing and serving. When adequately heated, the crust will detach easily from the pie plate.

11. Cut the pie with a wet knife. After removing the first piece, it helps to run a small offset spatula under the bottom crust to be sure it releases. If necessary, return the pie plate to the hot towel. If you have one, an onion holder, which looks like an oversized fork with long tines, dipped in water first, helps to make cleaner slices through the meringue before cutting through the rest of the slice with a knife.

STORE: Best eaten the day it is made. To keep for a second day, refrigerate, tented lightly with foil to keep the meringue from drying. If the meringue weeps, it is due to overheating which squeezes out moisture.

Making Lemon Meringue Pie

Cook the cornstarch mixture until it reaches 190°F/88°C.

Temper the egg yolks by adding a little of the cornstarch mixture.

Whisk in the tempered egg yolks.

Whisk in the lemon juice.

Scrape the filling into the baked pie shell.

The hot filling ready to cover with plastic wrap.

Swirl on the meringue.

Brown the meringue.

"Key Lime" Pie

SERVES 6 TO 8

OVEN TEMPERATURE:
350°F/175°C

BAKING TIME: 15 to 20
minutes

BAKING EQUIPMENT:
One 9 inch standard pie
plate, preferably Pyrex

This is my favorite key lime pie—but my secret is that I don't use key limes! I discovered that I much prefer the flavor of ordinary limes to key limes, and a whipped cream topping to meringue. Cornstarch-Stabilized Whipped Cream (page 236) has a fabulously luxurious texture and does not become watery as it sits, but it's fine to use a meringue topping here instead (page 340). I always, however, add one stiffly beaten egg white to the filling to lighten it slightly. This pie is extra delicious if served semi freddo *(semifrozen) as they do at Joe's Stone Crab in Miami.*

GRAHAM CRACKER CRUMB CRUST FOR A 9 INCH PIE
Makes about 255 grams/1½ cups

unsalted butter	71 grams	5 tablespoons (½ stick plus 1 tablespoon)
about 10 double graham crackers (5 by 2¼ inch)	151 to 170 grams (depending on the size of the crackers)	1⅓ to 1½ cups crumbs, lightly packed
sugar	25 grams	2 tablespoons
fine sea salt	.	a pinch
pure vanilla extract	.	½ teaspoon (2.5 ml)

MAKE THE CRUST

1. In a 1 cup glass measure with a spout, in the microwave, or in a small saucepan over medium-low heat, melt the butter

FOOD PROCESSOR METHOD

2. Break the crackers into the food processor and process together with the sugar and salt into fine crumbs. Add the melted butter and vanilla and pulse a few times just until incorporated.

HAND METHOD

2. Place the crackers in a reclosable freezer bag and use a rolling pin to crush them into fine crumbs. Transfer the crumbs to a medium bowl and, with a fork, mix in the sugar and salt. Stir in the melted butter and vanilla and toss to incorporate.

BOTH METHODS

3. Use your fingers or the back of a spoon to press the crumb mixture into the pie plate and part way up the sides. If the crumbs stick to your fingers, place plastic wrap on top of the crumbs.

4. After the crumbs have been spread out, use a flat-bottomed, straight-sided measuring cup or glass tumbler to smooth the crumbs evenly over the bottom and all the way up the sides. Press the crumbs at the juncture where the bottom meets the sides, which always tends to be thicker.

5. As you press the crumbs against the sides they will rise above the rim. To create an attractive border, use your opposing thumb to press against them from the other direction, which will form a little ridge. Chilling the crust for a few minutes will firm the butter and make this easier. Refrigerate the pie shell while making the filling.

LIME FILLING

lime zest, finely grated PLUS extra lime zest to use for the crystal lime zest décor (page 237; optional) OR lime zest in long strips	3 grams PLUS (12 grams)	1½ teaspoons, loosely packed PLUS (2 tablespoons) OR a few strips
lime juice, freshly squeezed and strained (4 to 6 medium limes)	189 grams	¾ cup (177 ml)

4 (to 6) large eggs, separated:
    4 (to 6) yolks (see Baking Pearls, page 236)
    1 white
	
	74 grams
	
	30 grams
		
		¼ cup plus 2 teaspoons (69 ml)
		
		2 tablespoons (30 ml)

cream of tartar	.	⅛ teaspoon
one 14 ounce can sweetened condensed milk	400 grams	1¼ cups (296 ml)

PREHEAT THE OVEN

■ Twenty minutes or longer before baking, set an oven rack at the middle level. Set the oven at 350°F/175°C.

MISE EN PLACE

■ With dish washing liquid, wash the limes. Rinse, dry, and zest them (page xxv).

■ Into a 1 cup measure with a spout, weigh or measure the lime juice.

■ Into a small metal bowl, weigh or measure 1 egg white (30 grams/2 tablespoons/30 ml). Whisk in the cream of tartar.

■ In a large glass bowl, weigh or measure the egg yolks. Add the sweetened condensed milk.

MAKE THE LIME FILLING

1. Whisk together the egg yolks and the sweetened condensed milk. Gradually whisk in the lime juice. Whisk in the zest.

(continued)

I prefer not to prebake the graham cracker crust, as it is more tender.

If you make crumb crusts often, it pays to get a 6 inch round cake pan. It is the ideal flat-bottomed tool for pressing the crumbs evenly into the bottom of the pie plate.

The ratio of white to yolk in an egg can vary to such a degree that you may need as few as 4 or as many as 6 eggs for this recipe. It is therefore advisable to weigh or measure the separated yolks and add or reduce if needed.

Make This Recipe Your Own

Sweet Cookie Tart or Pie Crust (page 200), blind baked, can be used instead of a graham cracker crust. Do not use a flaky pie crust, as it becomes too firm when the pie is chilled.

2. With a handheld mixer, beat the egg white on medium speed, gradually increasing to high speed, until stiff peaks form when the beater is raised. Fold this meringue into the lime mixture.

3. Scrape the mixture into the pie shell.

BAKE THE PIE

4. Bake for 15 to 20 minutes, or until set. When the pie is gently moved, the filling will shimmy only very slightly.

COOL THE PIE

5. Set the pie on a wire rack and cool completely. Refrigerate for a minimum of 4 hours before serving. The whipped cream topping can be added after 1 hour of refrigeration.

CORNSTARCH-STABILIZED WHIPPED CREAM Makes 244 grams/2 cups/474 ml

heavy cream	232 grams	1 cup (237 ml), *divided*
pure vanilla extract	.	1 teaspoon (5 ml)
powdered sugar	14 grams	2 tablespoons
cornstarch	.	1 teaspoon

MAKE THE WHIPPED CREAM

1. At least 15 minutes before whipping, into a medium metal bowl, pour 174 grams/¾ cup/177 ml of the cream and the vanilla. Cover and refrigerate, with the handheld mixer beaters alongside.

2. In a small saucepan, mix together the powdered sugar and cornstarch. Gradually whisk in the remaining cream.

3. Bring the mixture to a boil, stirring constantly with the whisk, just until thickened.

4. Immediately scrape the mixture into a small bowl or custard cup and allow it to cool just to room temperature. Cover until ready to whip the cream.

5. Using a handheld mixer, whip the reserved refrigerated cream, starting on low speed and gradually raising the speed to medium-high as it thickens, just until traces of the beater marks begin to appear.

6. Continuing by hand with a whisk, add the cooled cream-cornstarch mixture in four or five additions, whisking lightly after each one. Whisk just until stiff peaks form when the whisk is lifted.

APPLY THE WHIPPED CREAM

7. Spread the whipped cream onto the pie, leaving about a ¼ inch border. If desired, sprinkle the border with the crystal lime zest décor or garnish with a few long strips of lime zest (this identifies the pie as lime).

CRYSTAL LIME ZEST DÉCOR (OPTIONAL) Makes 8 grams/2 tablespoons

lime zest, finely grated (reserved from Lime Filling, above)	12 grams	2 tablespoons, loosely packed
superfine sugar	.	1 teaspoon

- In a small bowl, rub the sugar into the lime zest. Spread the sugared zest in a thin layer on a plate. Place the plate in the oven and turn on the oven light, which will provide just the right amount of heat. Let the zest dry to the touch for about 4 hours, scraping the plate every hour to dislodge any zest stuck to the plate. (Alternatively, the zest can be dried for about 14 hours at room temperature.) The crystal lime zest can be stored for 1 week refrigerated; 3 months frozen.

SERVE THE PIE

8. Just before serving, wet a large dish towel with very hot water. Set it in the sink and shape it into a nest. Set the pie plate into the hot towel so that it surrounds the entire pie plate up to the rim, and allow it to sit for a minute before slicing and serving. Carefully slip a small metal spatula under the border to tcase it to release it from the rim. When adequately heated, the crust including the rim will detach easily from the pie plate. After removing the first piece, it helps to run the spatula under the bottom crust to be sure it releases. If necessary, return the pie plate to the hot towel. (To serve the pie *semi freddo*—semifrozen—set the cut slices in the freezer for 20 minutes, but not longer or the whipped cream will freeze.)

STORE WITHOUT THE WHIPPED CREAM, covered with plastic wrap that has been lightly coated with nonstick cooking spray: refrigerated, 3 days.
WITH THE WHIPPED CREAM: refrigerated, 2 days, or 3 days if covered with an inverted bowl.

(continued)

Making "Key Lime" Pie

Combine the crumb crust ingredients in the food processor.

Process into crumbs.

Use the bottom of a glass tumbler to press the crumbs evenly on the bottom of the pie plate.

Use plastic wrap to press the crumbs up the sides, pressing at the juncture where the sides meet the bottom and forming a border at the top.

Scrape the filling into the pie shell.

Top with whipped cream.

Make decorative swirls.

Sprinkle with crystal lime zest.

Chocolate Cream Pie

SERVES 8

REFRIGERATION TIME:
8 to 12 hours

BAKING EQUIPMENT:
One 9 inch standard pie plate

A 10 loop piano wire whisk (see Baking Pearls, page 240)

For the chocolate lover this is, hands down, the most glorious of American pies. The buttery, crisp, fragile chocolate crumb crust blends perfectly with the satiny dark chocolate filling and lofty whipped cream topping.

CHOCOLATE CRUMB CRUST FOR A 9 INCH PIE Makes about 250 grams/1½ cups

unsalted butter	100 grams	7 tablespoons (¾ stick plus 1 tablespoon)
Chocolate Wafers (page 63) or Nabisco Famous Chocolate Wafers	255 grams	2 cups crumbs, lightly packed
fine sea salt (omit if using purchased wafers)	.	2 pinches
pure vanilla extract	.	½ teaspoon (2.5 ml)

MAKE THE CRUST

1. In a 1 cup glass measure with a spout, in the microwave, or in a small saucepan over medium-low heat, melt the butter.

FOOD PROCESSOR METHOD

2. Process the cookies and salt, if using, into fine crumbs. Add the melted butter and vanilla and pulse a few times just until incorporated.

HAND METHOD

2. Place the cookies in a gallon-size reclosable freezer bag and use a rolling pin to crush them into fine crumbs. Transfer the crumbs to a medium bowl and mix in the salt, if using. With a fork, stir in the melted butter and vanilla and toss to incorporate.

BOTH METHODS

3. Use your fingers or the back of a spoon to press the crumb mixture into the pie plate and partway up the sides. If the crumbs stick to your fingers, place plastic wrap on top of the crumbs.

4. After the crumbs have been spread out, use a flat-bottomed, straight-sided measuring cup or glass tumbler to smooth them evenly over the bottom and all the way up the sides. Press the crumbs at the juncture where the bottom meets the sides, which always tends to be thicker.

5. As you press the crumbs against the sides they will rise above the rim. To create an attractive border, use your opposing index finger to press against them

(continued)

The ratio of white to yolk in an egg can vary to such a degree that you may need as few as 4 or as many as 6 eggs for this recipe. It is therefore advisable to weigh or measure the separated yolks and add or reduce if needed.

A fine-wire 10 loop piano wire whisk makes it easier to produce a smooth chocolate cream filling.

If you would like to add the whipped cream several hours to 1 day ahead, make the cornstarch-stabilized version on page 330.

from the other direction, which will form a little ridge. Chilling the crust for a few minutes firms the butter and makes this easier. Refrigerate the pie shell while making the filling. It needs to be cold and firm when covering the filled pie with plastic wrap.

CHOCOLATE CREAM FILLING

4 (to 6) large egg yolks (see Baking Pearls, left)	74 grams	¼ cup plus 2 teaspoons (69 ml)
milk	726 grams	3 cups (711 ml), *divided*
unsweetened cocoa, preferably alkalized	25 grams	⅓ cup (sifted before measuring)
cornstarch	27 grams	3 tablespoons
sugar	133 grams	⅔ cup
fine sea salt	.	a pinch
fine-quality dark chocolate, preferably 61% cacao	170 grams	6 ounces
unsalted butter	28 grams	2 tablespoons
pure vanilla extract	.	1 teaspoon (5 ml)

MISE EN PLACE

- Set a medium-mesh strainer over a large bowl and place it near the cooktop.

- Into a 2 cup measure with a spout, weigh or measure the egg yolks.

- Into a 4 cup measure with a spout, weigh or measure the milk.

- Grate or finely chop the chocolate.

MAKE THE CHOCOLATE CREAM FILLING

1. Add the cocoa, cornstarch, and 60 grams/¼ cup/59 ml of the milk to the egg yolks, and, with a small whisk, blend until smooth.

2. In a heavy medium saucepan, use the large piano wire whisk to combine the remaining 666 grams/2¾ cups/652 ml milk, the sugar, and salt. Bring the mixture to a full boil over medium heat, stirring often. Whisk about ¼ cup of this mixture into the egg yolk mixture. Then whisk the egg mixture back into the rest of the milk mixture.

3. Over low heat, continue cooking, whisking rapidly and making sure to reach into the bottom edge of the pan, until the mixture starts to bubble, thickens, and begins to pool a little when dropped back on the surface. Remove the pan from the heat and whisk in the chocolate and butter. Whisk until the chocolate and butter have melted and the mixture is smooth, and then whisk in the vanilla. Immediately use a silicone spatula to press the mixture through the strainer and scrape any mixture clinging to the underside into the bowl.

(continued)

4. Place a piece of plastic wrap that has been lightly coated with nonstick cooking spray directly on top of the chocolate filling to keep a skin from forming. Without stirring, allow the filling to cool just until room temperature or barely warm, about 1½ hours.

5. Without stirring, scrape the chocolate filling into the prepared pie shell. It will fill the shell up to the top. With a small offset spatula, smooth the surface to make it even. Lightly coat a new piece of plastic wrap with nonstick cooking spray and place it directly on top of the chocolate filling.

6. Refrigerate the pie for at least 8 hours to set thoroughly.

LIGHTLY SWEETENED WHIPPED CREAM Makes 244 grams/2 cups/474 ml

heavy cream	232 grams	1 cup (237 ml)
superfine sugar	13 grams	1 tablespoon
pure vanilla extract	.	1 teaspoon (5 ml)

1. At least 15 minutes before whipping, in a medium metal bowl, mix together the heavy cream, sugar, and vanilla. Cover and refrigerate with the handheld mixer beaters alongside.

2. Using a handheld mixer, whip the mixture, starting on low speed and gradually raising the speed to medium-high as it thickens, until it mounds softly when dropped from a spoon (or just until stiff peaks form when the beater is raised if planning to pipe it).

APPLY THE WHIPPED CREAM

7. Up to 1 hour before serving, remove the plastic wrap from the pie. Top the pie with the whipped cream and use the back of a spoon or an offset spatula to make opulent swirls. (Alternatively, spoon the whipped cream into a pastry bag fitted with a decorative pastry tube and pipe it over the top of the pie.) If desired, garnish the top with chocolate curls (see page 360).

SERVE THE PIE

8. Just before serving, wet a large dish towel with very hot water. Set it in the sink and shape it into a nest. Set the pie plate into the hot towel so that it surrounds the entire pie plate up to the rim, and allow it to sit for a minute before slicing and serving. When adequately heated, the crust including the rim will detach easily from the pie plate. After removing the first piece, it helps to run a small offset spatula under the bottom crust to be sure it releases. If necessary, return the pie plate to the hot towel.

STORE WITHOUT THE WHIPPED CREAM, filling covered with plastic wrap that has been lightly coated with nonstick cooking spray: refrigerated, 3 days.
IF USING A STABILIZED WHIPPED CREAM: refrigerated, 2 days, or 3 days if covered with an inverted bowl.

Making Chocolate Cream Pie

Add the cocoa mixture to the milk.

The cocoa mixture will begin to pool on itself when whisked.

Whisk in the chocolate and butter.

Press plastic wrap on the surface to prevent a skin from forming.

Scrape the mixture into the pie shell.

Smooth the surface.

Top with whipped cream.

Decorate with chocolate curls, if desired.

BlueRaspberry Crisp

SERVES 6 TO 8

OVEN TEMPERATURE:
400°F/200°C,
425°F/220°C if not
using a Pyrex dish

BAKING TIME: 30 to 40
minutes

BAKING EQUIPMENT:
One 8 by 2 inch square
baking dish, preferably
Pyrex, no preparation
needed

A fresh berry crisp is a delightfully easy and enjoyable dessert. It has the best texture when still warm from the oven, when the berries will be juicy and the topping crisp. The raspberries mostly collapse but the blueberries stay pleasingly plump, offering a nice contrast in texture as well as flavor.

CRUMB TOPPING Makes 123 grams/almost 1 cup

unsalted butter	28 grams	2 tablespoons
lemon zest, finely grated	4 grams	2 teaspoons, loosely packed
sugar	6 grams	½ tablespoon
rolled oats	25 grams	⅓ cup
fine sea salt	.	a pinch
bleached all-purpose flour	36 grams	¼ cup plus 2 teaspoons (lightly spooned into the cup and leveled off)
pure vanilla extract	.	¼ teaspoon (1.2 ml)

PREHEAT THE OVEN

▪ Thirty minutes or longer before baking, set an oven rack in the lower third of the oven. Set the oven at 400°F/200°C if using a Pyrex baking dish, at 425°F/220°C if using some other dish.

MISE EN PLACE

▪ Thirty minutes to 1 hour ahead, cut the butter into 4 pieces and set it on the counter at room temperature (65° to 75°F/19° to 24°C).

▪ With dish washing liquid, wash the lemons. Rinse, dry, and zest them for both the topping and filling (see page xxv).

MAKE THE CRUMB TOPPING

FOOD PROCESSOR METHOD

1. In a food processor, pulse together the lemon zest, sugar, rolled oats, and salt until well combined.

2. Add the flour, butter, and vanilla and pulse until the mixture is coarse and crumbly.

3. Empty the crumb topping into a small bowl and, with your fingertips, lightly work the mixture until it starts to clump together.

Make This Recipe Your Own

I like to serve this crisp with vanilla ice cream. Lemon and raspberry also go well with it.

HANDHELD MIXER METHOD

1. In a medium bowl, mix the butter, sugar, vanilla, and lemon zest on medium speed until smooth and creamy.

2. In a medium bowl, whisk together the flour, rolled oats, and salt.

3. Add the flour mixture to the butter mixture and mix on low speed just until incorporated.

4. Remove the bowl from the stand and, with your fingertips, lightly work the mixture until it starts to clump together.

BERRY FILLING

sugar	175 grams	¾ cup plus 2 tablespoons
cornstarch	36 grams	4 tablespoons
fine sea salt	.	a pinch
lemon zest, finely grated (about 2 lemons)	6 grams	1 tablespoon, loosely packed
raspberries	510 grams	4½ cups
blueberries	255 grams	1¾ cups
lemon juice, freshly squeezed and strained (about 2 lemons)	63 grams	¼ cup (59 ml)

MAKE THE BERRY FILLING

1. In a large bowl, stir together the sugar, cornstarch, salt, and lemon zest.

2. Add the raspberries and blueberries and toss to coat them. Sprinkle with the lemon juice and, with a silicone spatula, gently mix the berries until the sugar is moistened. Allow to sit for 10 to 15 minutes for the berries to exude some of their juices.

3. Transfer the berry mixture to the baking dish.

APPLY THE CRUMB TOPPING

4. Sprinkle the crumb topping evenly over the filling.

BAKE THE CRISP

5. Bake for 30 to 40 minutes, or until the topping is crisp and golden brown and the juices beneath are bubbling thickly.

COOL THE CRISP

6. Set the baking dish on a wire rack and let the crisp cool for at least 20 minutes. Serve the crisp warm or at room temperature, preferably with a scoop of ice cream slowly melting on top.

STORE: Best eaten soon after baking. If necessary, store uncovered, refrigerated, for 1 day.

(continued)

Making BlueRaspberry Crisp

Mix the crumb topping until it begins to clump together.

Coat the berries with the sugar mixture.

Transfer the berry mixture to the baking dish.

Sprinkle with the crumb topping.

Peaches and Cream Kuchen

SERVES 6

OVEN TEMPERATURE:
375°F/190°C

BAKING TIME: 40 to
45 minutes

BAKING EQUIPMENT:
One 8 by 2 inch square
baking dish, straight-
sided metal or Pyrex

This dreamy dessert combines sliced fresh peaches, a crisp and tender pastry crust, and a creamy vanilla and almond custard. It deserves waiting for the height of peach season.

KUCHEN PASTRY

unsalted butter	113 grams	8 tablespoons (1 stick)
bleached all-purpose flour	212 grams	1¾ cups (lightly spooned into the cup and leveled off)
baking powder, only an aluminum free variety	1.1 grams	¼ teaspoon
fine sea salt	.	⅛ teaspoon
sugar	25 grams	2 tablespoons

PREHEAT THE OVEN

■ Thirty minutes or longer before baking, set an oven rack at the middle level. Set the oven at 375°F/190°C.

MISE EN PLACE

■ About 1 hour ahead, set the butter on the counter at room temperature (65° to 75°F/19° to 24°C).

MAKE THE DOUGH

1. In a food processor, process the flour, baking powder, salt, and sugar for a few seconds to mix.

2. Add the butter in a few pieces and pulse just until coarse meal.

LINE THE PAN

3. Empty the dough into the pan and press it evenly into the bottom and about two-thirds of the way up the sides. If the dough softens, it helps to set a sheet of plastic wrap directly on top before continuing to press it. Press well into the corners and at the juncture where the bottom meets the sides. If making the crust several hours ahead, cover and refrigerate it. *(continued)*

Make This Recipe Your Own

Peaches are very juicy and will moisten the bottom crust. This is not noticeable if the kuchen is served chilled, but if you prefer to serve it at room temperature, it is best to waterproof the bottom crust with apricot preserves: First chill the crust for a minimum of 1 hour or freeze it for about 15 minutes (if not in a Pyrex pan). Heat 64 grams/ 3 tablespoons/45 ml apricot preserves until bubbling. Strain and add a little water if necessary to make them spreadable. Use the back of a spoon to spread them gently and evenly over the bottom crust before adding the peaches.

PEACH FILLING AND CUSTARD TOPPING

about 4 firm ripe peaches, 624 grams/1 pound 6 ounces	482 to 500 grams (sliced)	3 cups (peeled, pitted, and sliced ¼ inch thick)
sugar, preferably superfine	150 grams	¾ cup
ground cinnamon	2.2 grams	1 teaspoon
2 large egg yolks	37 grams	2 tablespoons plus 1 teaspoon (35 ml)
heavy cream	174 grams	¾ cup (177 ml)
full-fat sour cream	60 grams	¼ cup
pure almond extract	.	½ teaspoon (2.5 ml)
pure vanilla extract	.	¼ teaspoon (1.2 ml)

MISE EN PLACE

▪ Fill a medium bowl with ice and water. Slip the peaches into a pot of boiling water and cook for 1 to 2 minutes. With a slotted skimmer, transfer them to the ice water. Use a small sharp knife to begin peeling off the skins. They should slip off easily.

MAKE THE PEACH FILLING

1. Slice and pit the peaches and set them in a medium bowl.

2. In a small bowl, whisk together the sugar and cinnamon.

3. Arrange the peaches in the dough-lined pan in slightly overlapping rows, sprinkling with the sugar mixture on top of each layer.

4. Bake for 15 minutes. While the peaches are baking, make the custard topping.

MAKE THE CUSTARD TOPPING

5. Into a 2 cup measure with a spout, weigh or measure the egg yolks. Whisk in the heavy cream, sour cream, and almond and vanilla extracts. Pour this topping evenly on top of the peaches and continue baking for 25 to 30 minutes, or until the custard is golden brown and a knife inserted near the center comes out clean. An instant-read thermometer should read 180°F/82°C. When moved, the custard will jiggle slightly.

COOL THE KUCHEN

6. Set the pan on a wire rack and cool for at least 1½ hours, until room temperature or barely warm. Cover and refrigerate for 1 hour or longer.

7. Serve slightly chilled. Run a thin blade between the sides of the pan and the crust. Cut into squares and use a pancake turner to lift them onto serving plates.

STORE LIGHTLY COVERED: refrigerated, 2 days.

Making Peaches and Cream Kuchen

The dough should have the consistency of coarse meal.

Press the dough onto the bottom of the pan.

Use a dough scraper to press the dough up the sides of the pan.

Press the dough well into the corners of the pan.

Arrange the peaches in the pan.

Sprinkle with the sugar mixture.

Pour on the custard topping.

Bake until a knife comes out clean.

249

Peach Cobbler with Biscuits

SERVES 6 TO 9

OVEN TEMPERATURE:
400°F/200°C

BAKING TIME: 35 to 40 minutes

BAKING EQUIPMENT:
One 8 by 2 inch square baking dish, preferably Pyrex, no preparation needed

A cookie sheet, lined with aluminum foil

Baking the biscuits separately, splitting them, and then setting them cut side down on the peach filling near the end of baking ensures that the biscuits stay soft on the bottom without becoming soggy from the peach juices. Nine biscuit halves are needed, so you can opt for a checkerboard effect by alternating biscuit tops and bottoms, or use all biscuit tops.

BUTTER BISCUITS

Dough for Butter Biscuits, preferably with ginger (page 284)	620 grams	9 biscuits

1. Bake and cool the biscuits. Use a 3-tined fork to split 5 of them in half horizontally. You will need only 9 biscuit halves for the cobbler.

PEACH FILLING

unsalted butter	21 grams	1½ tablespoons
about 8 firm ripe peaches, 1247 grams/2¾ pounds	964 grams (sliced)	6 cups (peeled, pitted, and sliced ¼ inch thick)
lemon juice, freshly squeezed and strained (1 lemon)	16 grams	1 tablespoon (15 ml)
sugar	113 grams	½ cup plus 1 tablespoon
fine sea salt	.	a pinch
cornstarch	12 grams	1 tablespoon plus 1 teaspoon
ground cinnamon	.	½ teaspoon
pure almond extract	.	½ teaspoon (2.5 ml)
grated fresh ginger (optional)	15 grams	1 tablespoon, loosely packed

MISE EN PLACE

▪ Thirty minutes to 1 hour ahead, set the butter on the counter at room temperature (65° to 75°F/19° to 24°C).

▪ Fill a medium bowl with ice and water. Slip the peaches into a pot of boiling water and cook for 1 to 2 minutes. With a slotted skimmer, transfer them to the ice water. Use a small sharp knife to begin peeling off the skins. They should slip off easily.

Make This Recipe Your Own

Serve with dulce de leche or vanilla ice cream, or softly whipped cream (page 329).

MAKE THE FILLING

1. Into a large bowl, slice the peaches about ¼ inch thick. You should have about 964 grams. Add the lemon juice, sugar, and salt and toss gently to mix. Allow the peaches to macerate for a minimum of 30 minutes, or up to 1 hour, at room temperature. Transfer the peaches to a colander suspended over a bowl to capture the juices. The peaches will release close to 1 cup/237 ml juices.

2. In a small saucepan, preferably nonstick, over medium-high heat, boil down the juices with the butter until syrupy and lightly caramelized. Swirl, but do not stir. (Or coat a 4 cup glass measure with a spout with nonstick cooking spray, add the juices and butter, and boil it in the microwave for a few minutes, stirring every 30 seconds, until reduced to ¼ cup plus 2 tablespoons/90 ml. Watch carefully, as it goes really quickly toward the end.)

3. While the juices are reducing, transfer the peaches to a bowl and toss them with the cornstarch, cinnamon, almond extract, and the ginger, if using, until all traces of the cornstarch have disappeared.

4. Pour the hot syrup over the peaches, tossing gently. Don't be concerned if the syrup hardens on the peaches; it will dissolve during baking.

PREHEAT THE OVEN

- Thirty minutes or longer before baking, set an oven rack in the lower third of the oven. Set the oven at 400°F/200°C.

5. Empty the peaches into the baking dish. Cover it with aluminum foil and make a 1 inch slash in the middle.

BAKE THE COBBLER

6. Set the baking dish on the cookie sheet and bake the peaches for 30 minutes, or until the juices are bubbling and the peaches are almost tender but feel a little firm when pierced with a metal skewer. Remove the foil and top with the 9 biscuit halves, cut side down. Press them into the peaches. Cover loosely with the foil and continue baking for 5 to 10 minutes, or until the peaches feel tender and the juices are thickly bubbling.

COOL THE COBBLER

7. Set the baking dish on a wire rack and cool the cobbler for 20 to 30 minutes before serving.

8. Use a small pancake turner or large spoon to scoop out servings.

STORE AIRTIGHT: room temperature, 2 days; frozen, 3 months.

(continued)

Making Peach Cobbler with Biscuits

Collect the peach juices.

Add butter to the juices.

Reduce the juices to a syrup.

Pour the hot syrup over the peaches.

Transfer the peaches to the baking dish.

Arrange the biscuits on top.

Flaky Cranberry Scones

MAKES 8 SCONES

OVEN TEMPERATURE:
375°F/190°C

BAKING TIME: 20 to 25 minutes

BAKING EQUIPMENT:
Optional: one 9 by 2 inch round cake pan

A cookie sheet, preferably insulated, or a double layer of two cookie sheets, lined with parchment

There is no pastry more satisfying or easier to make than a scone, and this one is a felicitous balance of crunchy top and tender, soft, buttery interior, with the sweet, lilting punch of the dried cranberries and lemon zest. This is a great make-ahead treat, as the scones have the best shape when baked from frozen.

unsalted butter	142 grams	10 tablespoons (1 stick plus 2 tablespoons)
heavy cream	232 grams	1 cup (237 ml)
dried cranberries	100 grams	⅓ cup
lemon zest, finely grated (2 medium lemons)	6 grams	1 tablespoon, loosely packed
Gold Medal bread flour, or half other bread flour and half unbleached all-purpose flour	300 grams	2⅓ cups (lightly spooned into the cup and leveled off)
sugar	50 grams	¼ cup
baking powder, only an aluminum free variety	13.5 grams	3 teaspoons
fine sea salt	.	⅜ teaspoon
honey	28 grams	1 tablespoon plus 1 teaspoon (15 ml)

MISE EN PLACE

- Cut the butter into ½ to ¾ inch cubes. Return them to the refrigerator to chill for a minimum of 30 minutes.

- At least 15 minutes before whipping, into a medium metal bowl, place the heavy cream. Cover and refrigerate with the mixer beaters alongside.

- Whip the cream just until soft peaks form when the beaters are lifted. Place in the refrigerator.

- With small scissors, cut the cranberries in half.

- With dish washing liquid, wash the lemons. Rinse, dry, and zest them (page xxv).

MAKE THE DOUGH

1. In a large bowl, whisk together the flour, sugar, baking powder, salt, and lemon zest. Add the butter and, with a fork, toss to coat it with the flour. Press the butter cubes between your fingers to form very thin flakes. Stir in the cranberries. Make

(continued)

To make half-size scones, divide the dough into two equal pieces (250 grams each) and shape each into a 6 inch disc.

If using a cake pan to mold the discs, use a 6 inch pan. You can lift the first disc out of the pan right after you shape it, wrap it, and then reline the pan to shape the second disc.

In Step 5, after the first 10 minutes of baking, the remaining baking time will be only about 5 minutes more.

a well in the center. Pour the whipped cream and honey into the well and, with a silicone spatula, stir the flour mixture into the cream mixture until all of it is moistened.

2. Lightly knead the dough in the bowl just until it holds together. Turn it out onto a lightly floured counter. Gently knead it a few times until it is a little stretchy and can be shaped into a smooth disc.

3. Line the cake pan with plastic wrap and press the dough evenly into it, or shape the dough into a 9 by ¾ inch thick disc without using the pan. Press in any loose cranberries. Cover with plastic wrap and refrigerate for a minimum of 30 minutes, or up to overnight.

PREHEAT THE OVEN

■ Thirty minutes or longer before baking, set an oven rack at the middle level. Set the oven at 375°F/190°C.

SHAPE THE SCONES

4. Lift out the dough disc using the plastic wrap. Use a sharp knife to cut the disc into 8 even wedges. Place them, 2 inches apart, on the prepared cookie sheet. (Alternatively, wrap the wedges individually and freeze.)

BAKE THE SCONES

5. Bake for 10 minutes. For even baking, rotate the cookie sheet halfway around. Continue baking for 10 to 15 minutes or until golden brown. (An instant-read thermometer should read 212° to 215°F/100° to 102°C.) If baking frozen scones, bake first for 20 minutes, rotate the cookie sheet, cover loosely with foil, and continue baking for 10 minutes longer.

COOL THE SCONES

6. Set the cookie sheet on a wire rack. Use a pancake turner to transfer the scones to another wire rack to cool until warm or room temperature. The scones will be slightly moist. If you prefer a more traditional, drier scone, allow them to sit uncovered overnight.

STORE AIRTIGHT: room temperature, 2 days; frozen, 3 months.

Making Flaky Cranberry Scones

Press the butter cubes to form thin flakes.

Add the dried cranberries.

Stir in the whipped cream.

Lightly knead the dough in the bowl.

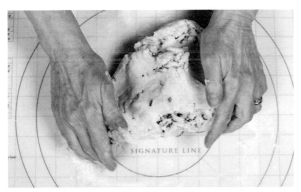

Knead the dough just until a little stretchy.

Shape the dough into a ball.

Press the dough evenly into a lined cake pan.

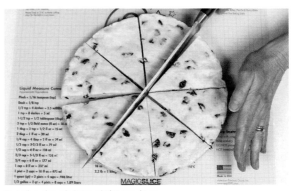

Cut the dough into eight wedges.

Lemon and Blueberry Tart

SERVES 6

OVEN TEMPERATURE:
300°F/150°C

BAKING TIME: 7 to 10 minutes

BAKING EQUIPMENT:
One 9½ by 1 inch high fluted tart pan with a removable bottom, coated with baking spray with flour if not nonstick

A cookie sheet

Tart and creamy lemon curd topped with a burst of fresh blueberries is one of the most delicious flavor combinations I know. The sweet cookie tart crust maintains its crunchy texture even after refrigeration, and provides an ideal balance to the brightness of the filling.

SWEET COOKIE TART OR PIE CRUST (PÂTE SUCRÉE)

Sweet Cookie Tart or Pie Crust (page 200) prebaked in a tart pan (page 208), still in the pan on the cookie sheet	321 grams	1 recipe

LEMON CURD FILLING

Lemon Curd (page 40)	330 grams	1¼ cups (296 ml)

PREHEAT THE OVEN

▪ Twenty minutes or longer before baking, set an oven rack at the middle level. Set the oven at 300°F/150°C.

MAKE THE TART

1. Spread the lemon curd smoothly into the prebaked tart shell.

BAKE THE TART

2. Bake for 7 to 10 minutes, or until the curd barely jiggles when the pan is moved gently from side to side. It should not begin to color.

COOL THE TART

3. Set the tart on a wire rack and cool completely before adding the blueberry topping.

BLUEBERRY TOPPING

blueberries	400 grams	about 3 cups
arrowroot or cornstarch	9 grams	1 tablespoon
sugar	67 grams	⅓ cup
water	118 grams	½ cup (118 ml)
lemon juice, freshly squeezed and strained	8 grams	1½ teaspoons (7.5 ml)

Baking Pearl

Arrowroot gives a lovely sparkle to the syrup. Unlike cornstarch, however, which has an indefinite shelf life if stored away from humidity, arrowroot will not thicken if it is much more than a year old.

Make This Recipe Your Own

Replace the lemon curd with Lime Curd (page 41) or Pastry Cream (page 357) and top with other fresh berries of your choice such as raspberries or strawberries, but do not glaze them in a sugar syrup as these berries are too fragile.

MISE EN PLACE

- Rinse the berries and dry them well with paper towels. Place them in a bowl.

- Have a strainer or colander suspended over a medium bowl.

MAKE THE BLUEBERRY TOPPING

1. In a medium saucepan, mix the arrowroot and sugar.

2. Gradually stir in the water and lemon juice.

3. Cook over medium heat, stirring constantly until clear and thickened. (If using cornstarch, it will need to come to a full boil.)

4. Immediately remove the mixture from the heat and quickly fold in the blueberries until completed coated with the syrup and dark blue in color.

5. Transfer the blueberry mixture to the strainer and drain any syrup not clinging to the berries. Reserve the syrup.

6. Spoon the blueberry topping onto the lemon curd. If there are any spots of blueberries that are not coated, brush them with the reserved syrup. Refrigerate the tart, uncovered, for a minimum of 1 hour, to set before serving.

UNMOLD THE TART

7. Place the tart pan on top of a canister that is smaller than the bottom opening of the tart pan's outer rim. Press down on both sides of the tart ring. The outer rim should slip away easily. If you have used white chocolate to seal any holes in the crust (as described on page 186), you will need to melt it to release the bottom of the pan. Simply set the tart on a hot towel or heated inverted cake pan for about a minute, or until you can easily slide the tart onto a serving plate. If necessary, slide a thin-bladed knife or long metal spatula under the crust to release it.

STORE UNCOVERED: refrigerated, 4 days.

(continued)

Making Lemon and Blueberry Tart

Spread the lemon curd in the baked tart shell.

Drain excess syrup from the blueberries.

Spoon the blueberries on top of the lemon curd.

Slide off the sides of the tart pan.

Slide the tart onto a serving platter.

Pecan Tart

SERVES 6 TO 8

OVEN TEMPERATURE:
350°F/175°C

BAKING TIME: 15 to
20 minutes

BAKING EQUIPMENT:
One 9½ by 1 inch high
fluted tart pan with
a removable bottom,
coated with baking
spray with flour if not
nonstick

A cookie sheet lined
with nonstick aluminum
foil or with regular foil
lightly coated with
nonstick cooking spray

A foil ring to protect the
edges of the crust

This pecan pie, baked as a tart, is less sweet than other versions due to the addition of heavy cream, the mellow butterscotch flavor from the golden syrup, and the lovely flavor notes from the Muscovado sugar. The filling has an appealing soft consistency with just a little flow. I like to serve it with vanilla ice cream or unsweetened lightly whipped cream. Pecan Pie ranks as one of the most beloved holiday pies and is even better still as a 9 inch tart. If you prefer, you can make it as a pie in a standard pie plate.

PERFECT FLAKY AND TENDER CREAM CHEESE PIE CRUST

Dough for a 9 inch tart shell (page 189), prebaked (page 208), still in the pan on the cookie sheet	321 grams	1 recipe

PECAN FILLING

unsalted butter	57 grams	4 tablespoons (½ stick)
5 (to 8) large egg yolks	93 grams	¼ cup plus 2 tablespoons (89 ml)
pecan halves	200 grams	2 cups
golden syrup, preferably Lyles, or corn syrup	113 grams	⅓ cup (79 ml)
light Muscovado or dark brown sugar	108 grams	½ cup, firmly packed
heavy cream	58 grams	¼ cup (59 ml)
fine sea salt	.	a pinch
pure vanilla extract	.	1 teaspoon (5 ml)

PREHEAT THE OVEN

■ Twenty minutes or longer before baking, set an oven rack at the middle level. Set the oven at 350°F/175°C.

MISE EN PLACE

■ Thirty minutes to 1 hour ahead, cut the butter into small pieces, and set it and the eggs on the counter at room temperature (65° to 75°F/19° to 24°C).

■ Have ready a medium-mesh strainer suspended over a 2 cup glass measure with a spout, lightly coated with nonstick cooking spray.

(continued)

Variations

FROZEN PECAN TART

If you use the Sweet Cookie Tart Crust (page 200) instead, you can cut and eat the tart right from the freezer.

CHOCOLATE PECAN TART

Add unsweetened alkalized cocoa powder to the egg yolk mixture: 9 grams/2 tablespoons for a more custardy texture and lighter flavor, or 27 grams/¼ cup plus 2 tablespoons for slightly fudgy texture and more intense flavor (sift the cocoa before measuring). Stir until smooth. Cook on low heat only until hot to the touch (115° to 120°F/46° to 49°C). Unless there are lumps, there is no need to strain. Baking time may be 5 minutes longer. For an all chocolate version, you can use the Sweet Chocolate Cookie Tart Crust (page 202). It also freezes well.

■ Shortly before making the filling, into a 1 cup measure with a spout, weigh or measure the egg yolks.

ARRANGE THE PECANS AND MAKE THE FILLING

1. Place the pecans, top sides up, on the bottom of the baked crust.

2. Place the egg yolks in a heavy medium saucepan. With a silicone spatula, stir the syrup, brown sugar, butter, cream, and salt into the egg yolks.

3. Cook the mixture over medium-low heat, stirring constantly, until it is uniform in color and just begins to thicken very slightly, about 7 minutes. Do not allow it to boil. An instant-read thermometer should read 150°F/66°C. Immediately pour the mixture into the strainer, press it through, and scrape any mixture clinging to the underside into the bowl. Stir in the vanilla.

4. With the glass measure's spout just above the pecans, slowly pour in the filling, lightly coating the nuts and moving from the center to the edge of the tart. Once the filling is completely poured the pecans will float. Gently shake the tart pan to distribute the nuts. Use your fingers to rearrange them.

BAKE THE TART

5. Place a foil ring on top to protect the edges from overbrowning. Set the cookie sheet with the assembled tart in the oven. Bake for 15 to 20 minutes, or until the filling is puffed and golden and just beginning to bubble around the edges. When the tart is moved gently, the filling will shimmy only very slightly. An instant-read thermometer, when inserted near the center, should read 190° to 200°F/88° to 93°C. Check early to prevent overbaking; otherwise the filling might end up too dry.

COOL THE TART

6. Set the tart, still on the cookie sheet, on a wire rack and cool until warm.

UNMOLD THE TART

7. Place the tart pan on top of a canister that is smaller than the bottom opening of the tart pan's outer rim. Press down on both sides of the tart ring. The outer rim should slip away easily. If you have used white chocolate to seal any holes in the crust (as described on page 186), you will need to melt it to release the bottom of the pan. Simply set the tart on a hot towel or heated inverted cake pan for about a minute or until you can easily slide the tart onto a serving plate. If the sticky filling has leaked through the crust, after warming the bottom slide a long metal spatula between the crust and the bottom of the pan, loosening it all around if necessary. Cool completely. Serve at room temperature.

STORE COVERED: room temperature, 1 week.

Making Pecan Tart

Combine the filling ingredients and cook until slightly thickened.

Press the cooked filling through a strainer.

Pour the filling over the pecans.

The baked tart.

Milk Chocolate Caramel Tart

SERVES 10 TO 12

REFRIGERATION TIME:
about 4 hours

BAKING EQUIPMENT:
One 9½ by 1 inch high fluted tart pan with a removable bottom, coated with baking spray with flour if not nonstick

A cookie sheet

An instant-read or candy thermometer

If ever there was a melt-in-the-mouth dessert, this is it! Chocolate and caramel tarts are high on the list of the most popular desserts. Because milk chocolate and caramel are rich and on the sweet side, the texture and flavor of this tart is at its best lightly chilled, but it is also delicious at room temperature. If you are a milk chocolate lover this is for you—but I urge you also to try the bittersweet chocolate variation that follows.

SWEET COOKIE TART OR PIE CRUST (PÂTE SUCRÉE)

Sweet Cookie Tart or Pie Crust (page 200), prebaked in a tart pan	321 grams	1 recipe

FILLING

Milk Chocolate Ganache (page 350)	273 grams	1 recipe

DÉCOR

fleur de sel or Maldon salt	.	⅛ teaspoon

THIN CARAMEL LAYER Makes 120 grams/¼ cup plus 2 tablespoons/89 ml

unsalted butter	28 grams	2 tablespoons
heavy cream	29 grams	2 tablespoons (30 ml)
sugar	67 grams	⅓ cup
light corn syrup	20 grams	1 tablespoon (15 ml)
cream of tartar	.	⅛ teaspoon
water	15 grams	1 tablespoon/15 ml

MISE EN PLACE

- About 30 minutes ahead, cut the butter into a few pieces and set it on the counter at room temperature (65° to 75°F/19° to 24°C).

- Into a 1 cup glass measure with a spout, weigh or measure the cream. Heat it for a few seconds in a microwave until hot to the touch, and then cover it.

- Place the baked tart shell near the cooktop. Have ready a small offset spatula lightly coated with nonstick cooking spray beside it.

(continued)

MAKE THE CARAMEL

1. In a heavy 4 cup saucepan, preferably nonstick, stir together the sugar, corn syrup, cream of tartar, and water until all the sugar is moistened.

2. Heat over medium heat, stirring constantly, until the sugar dissolves and the syrup is bubbling. Stop stirring completely and let it boil undisturbed until it turns a deep amber color and reaches 370°F/188°C on an instant-read thermometer, or a few degrees below, as the temperature will continue to rise. Remove the caramel from the heat as soon as it reaches temperature.

3. Slowly and carefully pour the hot cream into the caramel. It will bubble up furiously.

4. Add the butter and use a silicone spatula or wooden spoon to stir the mixture gently, scraping the thicker part that settles on the bottom. Return it to a very low heat, continuing to stir gently for 1 minute, until the mixture is uniform in color and the caramel is fully dissolved.

5. Immediately pour the caramel into the baked tart shell. Tilt the tart shell back and forth to spread the caramel evenly to cover the entire bottom of the tart shell. Set the tart pan on the cookie sheet and allow the caramel to cool until warm or room temperature. Then set it in the refrigerator or freezer for a few minutes before adding the chocolate.

COMPLETE THE TART

6. If you made the milk chocolate ganache ahead, you will need to reheat it to a pourable consistency. Microwave the ganache for about 20 seconds or heat it in a double boiler, just until lukewarm; an instant-read thermometer should read 96°to 100°F/36° to 38°C. Pour the ganache over the caramel. It will form a smooth layer. Any large bubbles that form can be pricked with a clean needle. Smaller bubbles will disappear almost completely after chilling.

CHILL THE TART

7. Refrigerate the tart, uncovered, for at least 4 hours, or until the ganache has set. Sprinkle with the fleur de sel.

UNMOLD THE TART

8. Place the tart pan on top of a canister that is smaller than the bottom opening of the tart pan's outer rim. Press down on both sides of the tart ring. The outer rim should slip away easily. If you have used white chocolate to seal any holes in the crust (as described on page 186), you will need to melt it to release the bottom of the pan. Simply set the tart on a hot towel or heated inverted cake pan for about a minute or until you can easily slide the tart onto a serving plate. If necessary, slide a thin bladed knife or long metal spatula under the crust to release it.

9. Allow the tart to sit at room temperature for 20 to 30 minutes before serving. Cut with a serrated knife. If desired, spoon unsweetened lightly whipped cream on the side of each slice.

STORE COVERED: refrigerated, 5 days. Do not freeze; freezing dulls the flavor.

(continued)

Making Milk Chocolate Caramel Tart

Heat the sugar syrup until boiling.

Continue to cook until deep amber and 370°F/188°C.

Add the hot cream to the caramel.

Add the butter.

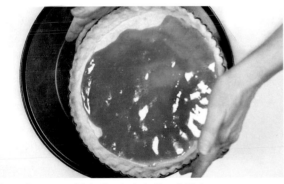

Pour the caramel into the tart shell and tilt to coat the bottom.

Top the caramel with the milk chocolate ganache.

Variation

DARK CHOCOLATE CARAMEL TART

Bittersweet chocolate tempers the sweetness of caramel, so a thicker layer of caramel is in perfect balance. The caramel has the texture of a thick sauce, and this thicker layer is best served cold.

Make a triple recipe of the thin caramel layer but using only 77 grams/⅓ cup/79 ml heavy cream. Refrigerate for 1 hour before pouring on the ganache.

Replace the milk chocolate ganache with a three-quarter recipe of Classic Ganache (page 345). If using liqueur, Kahlúa is a nice enhancement. Refrigerate the tart for 30 minutes. Sprinkle with the fleur de sel and cover the tart with a large bowl. (Dark chocolate ganache will become too firm if not covered.) Allow it to set for a minimum of 3 hours before serving. Cut with a serrated knife.

French Chocolate Tart

SERVES 10 TO 12

OVEN TEMPERATURE:
300°F/150°C

BAKING TIME:
20 minutes

BAKING EQUIPMENT:
One 9½ by 1 inch high
fluted tart pan with
a removable bottom,
coated with baking
spray with flour if not
nonstick

A cookie sheet

This is the creamiest of chocolate custards in an embrace of sweet almond cookie tart crust. It is very much like a pot de crème, but even more chocolaty.

CRUST

Sweet Almond Cookie Tart or Pie Crust (page 202), prebaked (page 208), still on the pan on the cookie sheet OR	312 grams	1 recipe
Sweet Chocolate Cookie Tart Crust (page 202), prebaked (page 208), still on the pan on the cookie sheet	455 grams	1 recipe

CHOCOLATE CUSTARD FILLING

2 large egg yolks	37 grams	2 tablespoons plus 1 teaspoon (35 ml)
dark chocolate, 60% to 62% cacao, chopped	200 grams	7 ounces
sugar	19 grams	1½ tablespoons
heavy cream	232 grams	1 cup (237 ml)
milk	81 grams	⅓ cup (79 ml)
unsweetened alkalized cocoa powder, for dusting	.	1 teaspoon

PREHEAT THE OVEN

■ Twenty minutes or longer before baking, set an oven rack at the middle level. Set the oven at 300°F/150°C.

MISE EN PLACE

■ Shortly before making the filling, into a 1 cup measure with a spout, weigh or measure the egg yolks.

■ Have ready a fine-mesh strainer suspended over a small glass bowl.

MAKE THE FILLING

1. In a food processor, process the chocolate and sugar until very fine.

2. In a 2 cup glass measure with a spout, in the microwave, scald the cream and milk: Heat them to the boiling point; small bubbles will form around the periphery. (Alternatively, scald them in a small saucepan over medium heat, stirring often.)

(continued)

Make This Recipe Your Own

Drizzle with Caramel Sauce (page 353) and/or serve with Lightly Sweetened Whipped Cream (page 329).

3. With the motor running, pour the cream and milk mixture through the feed tube in a steady stream into the chocolate mixture. Process for a few seconds until smooth, scraping the sides of the bowl as needed.

4. With the motor running, add the egg yolks and process for a few seconds.

5. Press the custard filling through the strainer and scrape any mixture clinging to the underside into the bowl. Then scrape it into the baked tart shell.

BAKE THE TART

6. Bake for 20 minutes, or until slightly puffy at the edges and set. When gently moved, the filling should jiggle all over like jello. If in doubt, the first time making it you may want to use an instant-read thermometer inserted near the center (although then you will have a hole in the surface). It should register 180°F/82°C.

COOL THE TART

7. Set the tart on a wire rack to cool to room temperature, about 1 hour. Then refrigerate it for a minimum of 2 hours to set.

DUST THE TART WITH COCOA

8. Place the cocoa in a fine-mesh strainer and dust the surface of the tart. Allow it to sit for a minimum of another hour before serving.

UNMOLD THE TART

9. Place the tart pan on top of a canister that is smaller than the bottom opening of the tart pan's outer rim. Press down on both sides of the tart ring. The outer rim should slip away easily. If you used white chocolate to seal any holes in the crust (as described on page 186), you will need to melt it. To release the bottom of the pan, set the tart on a hot towel or heated inverted cake pan for about a minute, and repeat if necessary, until you can easily slide the tart onto a serving plate. If necessary, slide a thin bladed knife or long metal spatula under the crust to release it.

SERVE

10. Cut with a thin sharp knife, run under hot water and wiped dry. Allow the slices to sit for 20 to 30 minutes at room temperature.

STORE UNCOVERED: room temperature, 1 day.
COVERED AND REFRIGERATED: 1 week. Do not freeze; freezing dulls the flavor.

Making French Chocolate Tart

Scrape the chocolate custard into a strainer.

Press the custard through the strainer into a bowl.

Pour and scrape the custard into the baked tart shell.

Dust the cooled tart with cocoa.

Cream Puffs, Profiteroles, and Éclairs

**MAKES TWENTY-FOUR
2 INCH CREAM PUFFS
OR EIGHT 4 INCH LONG
ÉCLAIRS**

OVEN TEMPERATURE:
425°F/220°C, then
350°F/175°C

BAKING TIME: 25 to 30
minutes for cream puffs
or 35 to 40 minutes
for éclairs, oven off and
ajar for 10 minutes,
then oven closed for
1½ hours

BAKING EQUIPMENT:
One 15 by 12 inch cookie
sheet or an inverted
17¼ by 12¼ by 1 inch
half-sheet pan, lined
with parchment or
coated with vegetable
shortening and floured

A pastry bag fitted with
½ inch (#6) plain round
pastry tube for the
puffs, or ¾ inch (#7) for
the éclairs

A wire rack set on a
cookie sheet

A disposable pastry
bag or a quart-size
reclosable freezer bag
for the filling

These crisp little pastry balloons or éclairs can be filled with whipped cream, pastry cream, or Chocolate Mousse Ganache. When filled with ice cream and drizzled with warm ganache, they are called "profiteroles." This dough is unique in that it is cooked on the stovetop before baking.

Makes 324 grams/1⅓ cups

unsalted butter	57 grams	4 tablespoons (½ stick)
bleached all-purpose flour	71 grams	½ cup (lightly spooned into the cup and leveled off) plus 1½ tablespoons
2½ large eggs	125 grams	½ cup (118 ml)
water	118 grams	½ cup (118 ml)
sugar	.	½ teaspoon
fine sea salt	.	a pinch

PREHEAT THE OVEN

▪ Thirty minutes or longer before baking, set an oven rack at the middle level. Set the oven at 425°F/220°C.

MISE EN PLACE

▪ About 30 minutes ahead, cut the butter into a few pieces and set it on the counter at room temperature (65° to 75°F/19° to 24°C).

▪ Sift the flour onto a piece of parchment.

▪ Into a 1 cup measure with a spout, weigh or measure the eggs and lightly beat them.

MAKE THE DOUGH

1. In a medium saucepan, preferably nonstick, mix together the water, butter, sugar, and salt and bring it to a full rolling boil. Immediately remove the saucepan from the heat and add the flour all at once.

2. Stir with a silicone spatula or wooden spoon until the mixture forms a rounded mass, leaves the sides of the pan, and clings slightly to the spatula.

3. Return the pan to low heat and cook, stirring and mashing continuously, for about 3 minutes to cook the flour.

(continued)

Make This Recipe Your Own

For 18 larger (2½ inch) cream puffs, pipe the dough 2 inches in diameter, about 18 grams each. They will need a scant tablespoon of filling each.

Variation

DELUXE PUFFS

For extra light and airy puffs, use bread flour or unbleached all-purpose flour, and in place of the 125 grams/½ cup/118 ml whole eggs, use 8 grams/1½ tablespoons/22 ml egg yolk and 90 grams/6 tablespoons/89 ml egg whites. Bread flour is heavier, so you will need only ½ cup, lightly spooned, plus ½ tablespoon for the same weight.

The pastry will stick to parchment, so instead, coat the pan with shortening and flour. (Do not use baking spray with flour because it will be more slippery when piping the puffs.)

4. Without scraping the pan, transfer the mixture to a food processor. With the feed tube open to allow steam to escape, process for 15 seconds. With the motor running, pour in the eggs all at once and continue processing for 30 seconds. If necessary, remove the blade and, using a silicone spatula, mix the pastry to a uniform consistency.

HAND METHOD

4. Without scraping the pan, empty the mixture into a bowl. Add the eggs in four parts, beating vigorously with a wooden spoon after each addition.

BOTH METHODS

5. The dough will be smooth and shiny, and should be too soft to hold peaks when lifted with a spoon. If it is too stiff, add a little extra water. The dough can be stored in an airtight container and refrigerated overnight or up to 2 days. Beat the mixture lightly with a wooden spoon before piping.

6. If using parchment, dab a small dot of the dough in each corner of the cookie sheet, under the parchment, and press it lightly to affix it. This will hold it in place while you pipe.

TO SHAPE PUFFS

7. Scrape the cream puff dough into the pastry bag. Pipe 24 puffs, about 1½ inches in diameter and ½ to ¾ inch high (13 grams each), about 1 inch apart. (Alternatively use a teaspoon, lightly coated with nonstick cooking spray, to scoop out the dough. With a fingertip, push the dough off the spoon and onto the cookie sheet.)

8. Dip a fingertip into water and smooth the tops. Spritz or brush the puffs lightly with water.

TO SHAPE ÉCLAIRS

7. Pipe eight 4 by 1 inch lengths, ½ to ¾ inch high (about 40 grams each), centered about 3 inches apart, onto the cookie sheet. (If you are using a spoon, use a metal spatula, dipped in water, to spread them into shape, making the ends slightly wider than the centers.)

8. Spritz or brush the éclairs lightly with water. If desired, run the tines of a fork down the length of the tops. This will help the éclairs crack evenly during baking but will result in a wider shape.

BOTH PUFFS AND ÉCLAIRS

9. If making several batches or if you are not ready to bake the pastries immediately, coat them lightly with nonstick cooking spray and cover lightly with plastic wrap. Refrigerate if not baking within 1 hour.

BAKE THE PUFFS OR ÉCLAIRS

10. Bake for 10 minutes. To prevent them from collapsing, do not open the oven door. Lower the heat to 350°F/175°C and continue baking for 15 to 20 minutes for puffs or 25 to 30 minutes for éclairs, or until golden brown. Turn off the oven.

11. **TO RELEASE THE STEAM FROM THE INSIDE OF THE PASTRIES:** Either make a small slit in the side of each one, or transfer the pastries to a wire rack set on a cookie sheet. Either way, return them to the turned-off oven. Use a wooden spoon covered with foil to prop open the oven door and let the pastries dry in the oven for 10 minutes.

12. Close the oven door and leave the pastries in the turned-off oven for 1½ hours to dry out completely (alternatively continue baking at 200°F/90°C for 45 minutes). Test a pastry by cutting it in half horizontally. The dough inside should not be soft to the touch. If it is still soft, let it dry for a little longer.

COOL THE PUFFS OR ÉCLAIRS

13. Let the pastries cool completely on a wire rack and then store them in a gallon-size reclosable freezer bag or airtight container until ready to fill.

FILL THE PUFFS OR ÉCLAIRS

14. Use a serrated knife to cut each pastry horizontally in half. If using whipped cream, fill shortly before serving. If using Cornstarch-Stabilized Whipped Cream, Chocolate Mousse Ganache, or Pastry Cream, the filled pastries can be refrigerated for up to 2 days.

15. For the cream puffs, use 2 teaspoons of Lightly Sweetened Whipped Cream (page 329), Pastry Cream (page 357), or Chocolate Mousse Ganache (page 351), or a small scoop of ice cream. For the éclairs, use 3 to 3½ tablespoons filling. If using pastry cream, make 1½ times the recipe for the original pastry cream. You will have enough if making the Chiboust cream variation with added whipped cream (page 358).

16. If desired, dust the pastries with powdered sugar, or drizzle with Ganache Drizzle Glaze (page 348) and/or Caramel Glaze (page 353). (You can also use a small metal spatula to spread the glaze on top of the éclairs.)

STORE UNFILLED AIRTIGHT: room temperature, 1 day; refrigerated, 1 week; frozen, 6 months.

FILLED, AIRTIGHT: room temperature, up to 3 hours; refrigerated, up to 2 days. For crisp pastry, fill shortly before serving. The pastries start to soften once filled but are still delicious.

(continued)

Making Cream Puffs or Éclairs

Cook the mixture until it forms a ball and cleans the sides of the pan.

Add the eggs.

The dough should be smooth, shiny, and soft.

Fill the pastry bag.

Use a dough scraper to push the dough toward the tip.

Twist the pastry bag to seal.

Pipe the cream puffs.

Smooth the tops of the puffs.

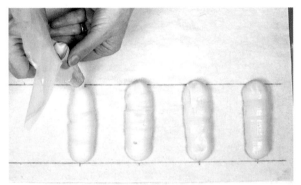

Pipe the éclairs

Cut open the baked puffs and éclairs, and fill.

Pavlova

SERVES 8 TO 10

OVEN TEMPERATURE:
225°F/105°C

BAKING TIME: 1 hour
plus 20 minutes, oven
off 30 minutes, then
oven ajar 30 minutes

BAKING EQUIPMENT:
One pizza pan or
cookie sheet topped
with a 12 inch round of
parchment

This dreamy pastry is actually very easy to make. The finished meringue has the finest smooth, crisp outer shell with a soft marshmallowy interior. The combination of crunchy sweet meringue, billowy creamy slightly tangy whipped cream, and fresh fruit is truly heavenly. For an even tangier whipped cream filling, try the Lemon Curd or Pink Pomegranate Whipped Cream (see Whipped Cream variations, page 331). The Pavlova is the national dessert of Australia and New Zealand.

MERINGUE

4 large egg whites	120 grams	½ cup (118 ml)
cream of tartar	.	½ teaspoon
superfine sugar	240 grams	1 cup plus 3 tablespoons

PREHEAT THE OVEN

▪ Twenty minutes or longer before baking, set an oven rack at the middle level. Set the oven at 225°F/105°C.

MISE EN PLACE

▪ Into the bowl of a stand mixer, weigh or measure the egg whites, cream of tartar, and sugar and whisk them together until blended. Cover and allow it to sit at room temperature for a minimum of 30 minutes, or up to 6 hours.

▪ Draw a 9 inch circle on the parchment and invert it onto the pan. With masking tape, secure the edges of the parchment to the pan in three or four places.

MAKE THE MERINGUE

1. Attach the whisk beater, and starting on low speed and gradually raising the speed to high, beat the egg white mixture for 12 minutes. The meringue will be very thick and glossy and form curved peaks when the whisk is raised.

2. With a large spoon, scoop the meringue onto the center of the parchment and use the back of the spoon to spread the meringue within the 9 inch circle. Form a deep depression in the middle to create a nest with a border that is about 1 inch wide by 1¼ to 1½ inches high. Remove the tape.

(continued)

Baking Pearls

Meringues work best in low humidity.

The mixer bowl and whisk must be free of any grease to enable the whites to beat to stiff peaks.

Many recipes call for vinegar and even cornstarch to maintain the desired soft interior and make the meringue stable, but using the proper amount of cream of tartar yields the best texture as well as flavor.

Do not use convection for baking the Pavlova, as it may cause cracking.

A higher temperature is required for this larger, thicker meringue than that used for flat or smaller meringues; this prevents bubbling at the base.

Make This Recipe Your Own

Drizzle the baked meringue with melted chocolate before adding the whipped cream.

Replace the sour cream with 66 grams/¼ cup lemon curd or 78 grams/¼ cup jam.

BAKE THE MERINGUE

3. Bake for 1 hour and 20 minutes without opening the oven door. Turn off the oven, and let the meringue site for 30 minutes. Then prop open the door, and let the meringue sit for 30 minutes longer. Remove it to a wire rack to cool.

UNMOLD THE MERINGUE

4. When the meringue is completely cool, lift it off the parchment and onto a serving plate or an airtight container. It will have expanded to 9½ inches by 1¾ to 2 inches high.

STORE AIRTIGHT: room temperature in low humidity, 5 days; frozen, 3 months.

MAKE THE TOPPING

■ Shortly before serving, prepare the topping.

PAVLOVA TOPPING

heavy cream	232 grams	1 cup (237 ml)
fresh berries or other fruit	about 340 grams	3 cups
full-fat sour cream	60 grams	¼ cup
pure vanilla extract	.	1 teaspoon (5 ml)

1. At least 15 minutes before whipping, into a medium metal bowl, pour the cream. Cover and refrigerate with the handheld mixer beaters alongside.

2. PREPARE THE BERRIES AND/OR FRUIT: Rinse the berries and dry them on paper towels. If using large berries, cut them in halves or quarters. Peaches should be pitted, sliced, and then cut into chunks.

3. Using a handheld mixer, whip the cream, starting on low speed and gradually raising the speed to medium high as it thickens, until softly whipped. Add the sour cream and vanilla and whip just until stiff peaks form when the beater is raised.

4. With a large spatula, scrape and spread the whipped cream into the Pavlova.

5. Arrange the berries or fruit decoratively on top.

(continued)

Making Pavlova

Combine the egg whites, sugar, and cream of tartar.

Beat the meringue until thick and glossy.

The meringue should hold thick, droopy peaks.

Use the back of a spoon to spread the meringue.

Form a depression with a 1 inch border.

Bake the Pavlova.

Variation

EIGHT MINI PAVLOVAS

These little Pavlovas, 4 inches by ⅞ inch high, can be filled with the same ingredients as the large Pavlova, but are also terrific filled with ice cream and frozen until shortly before serving, then topped with the topping of your choice, such as fresh berries or other fruit, or Ganache Drizzle Glaze (page 348).

To achieve the same texture and appearance for these small Pavlovas, position the oven racks in the upper and lower thirds of the oven and set the oven at 200°F/90°C. If baked at a higher temperature they will rise to 1 inch in height and form little bubbles around the base.

Line two 15 by 12 inch cookie sheets with parchment. Draw four 4 inch circles on each parchment sheet and invert them onto the cookie sheets. With masking tape, secure the edges of the parchment to the cookie sheets in two or three places.

With a tablespoon, spread the meringue within the 4 inch circles. With the back of the spoon, form a 2 inch hollow in the middle of each to create a 1 inch border that is about ¾ inch high. Remove the tape.

Bake for 1 hour and 35 to 45 minutes without opening the oven door until about 10 minutes before the end of baking, at which point it's fine to check the interior of one of the Pavlovas. With the tip of a small sharp knife, dig out a little of the meringue from the inside border. It should be a little soft and sticky. If not planning to serve the same day, remove the meringues when softer inside, as they will dry faster than the large meringue. Remove the Pavlovas from the oven and set the cookie sheets on wire racks to cool to room temperature.

Of all baking, it is bread that grounds me the most and gives me the greatest joy. From mixing the dough, to watching it rise, to smelling it baking, homemade bread gives deep satisfaction to all the senses. Here I share eight of the most popular breads, including the famed "no-knead bread," multigrain sandwich bread, whole wheat sandwich bread, butter biscuits, and beer bread made in a food processor. You will also learn my secrets for making better-than-pizza-parlor pizza.

BREAD

SOLUTIONS FOR POSSIBLE PROBLEMS

The dough does not rise fast enough.

SOLUTIONS: Create a warm humid environment. Most dough rises well and develops good flavor at 80°F/27°C; above 85°F/29°C, the bread will develop off flavors. Rising at a lower temperature will develop even more flavor but will take longer. See opposite for suggested rising environments.

If you are using active dry yeast, and not instant yeast, it will not rise as quickly unless you use one-and-a-quarter times the amount by either volume or weight. It is advisable to proof it in warm water with a pinch of sugar, unlike instant yeast which is added directly to the flour. Use water from the total amount listed in the recipe and add the proofed yeast mixture when adding the rest of the water to the dough.

The bread does not rise enough.

SOLUTIONS: Use newer yeast (check the expiration date). Do not let the dough rise too much; if the dough rises too much before baking, it will not rise well in the oven. The yeast must be mixed into the flour before the salt, because direct contact with salt will kill it. Use a baking stone and preheat the oven for a minimum of 45 minutes before baking; the blast of high heat when the bread is put in the oven causes it to rise at the beginning of baking. This is called "oven spring."

The bread bursts and cracks during baking.

SOLUTION: The dough was underproofed, which means it needed to rise more before baking. Let dough rise until the indentation fills in slowly when pressed gently with a fingertip.

The bread collapses during baking.

SOLUTIONS: The dough was overproofed, which means it rose too much before baking. Do not let the dough rise too much; if it rises too much before baking it will weaken the structure. Use a higher protein flour or add vital wheat gluten, 1 to 4 percent of the weight of the flour or ½ to 2 teaspoons per cup flour.

The bread has too tight a crumb.

SOLUTIONS: Use more liquid, and/or avoid adding too much flour when handling the dough. (Dough sticks less to wet hands.) Using the bench scraper as an extension of your hand will help you to lift and move dough that is softer and wetter.

The bread is underbaked and pasty.

SOLUTION: Allow it to cool completely, which will complete the baking process, before slicing it.

SUGGESTED RISING ENVIRONMENTS

The rising time indicated in these bread recipes is for a temperature of 80° to 85°F/27° to 29°C. A lower temperature will develop even more flavor, but it will increase the rising time.

Create a warm, humid environment. Because warm air in a room rises, the space above the refrigerator can be a good temperature. You can also set a cup of very hot tap water in an enclosed container, such as a large plastic box, a Styrofoam cooler, or the microwave oven, to create a warm and humid environment for the dough. There is no need to cover the dough if moisture is provided. Reheat the water every 30 to 45 minutes to maintain the temperature.

An electric proofer, such as the one by Brød & Taylor, works perfectly for rising dough and also for melting chocolate, making yogurt, and many other uses.

Tips for Shaping the Dough

FOR A LOAF

For the best shape, first dimple the dough to get rid of small air bubbles and let it rest 15 minutes.

Flatten with a rolling pin to get rid of any more bubbles that may have formed.

If the dough is very stretchy, fold the top halfway down and bring the bottom up to meet it.

Starting from the top, tightly roll the dough, pushing it back with your thumbs to tighten it and pushing in the sides so that it is no larger than the bottom of the loaf pan.

Pinch the seam at the end and roll over the dough so that the seam is at the bottom.

FOR A BOULE

Bring up the edges and pinch them together.

Turn over the dough so that the pinched ends are at the bottom.

Cup your hands around the side of the dough farthest from you and, without lifting the dough from the counter, bring it toward you.

Rotate the dough a quarter turn and repeat 3 to 5 times to achieve a round firm ball.

Butter Biscuits

MAKES NINE 2½ INCH BY 1½ INCH HIGH BISCUITS

OVEN TEMPERATURE:
375°F/190°C, then 400°F/200°C, then 375°F/190°C

BAKING TIME: 15 to 20 minutes

BAKING EQUIPMENT:
One 15 by 12 inch cookie sheet, preferably insulated, or a double layer of two cookie sheets lined with parchment

A 2½ inch scalloped cookie or biscuit cutter

These biscuits are exceptionally soft, tender, and velvety. The secret ingredient is from James Beard, with whom I studied fifty years ago: hard cooked egg yolk. These are the biscuits I choose when I make strawberry shortcake or cobblers (page 250). They are also wonderful for breakfast, especially sandwiched with sausage patties. They are great to have on hand in the freezer, unbaked, because they can be ready for breakfast in under a half hour.

3 large eggs, hard cooked, yolks only	37 grams	¼ cup plus 2 tablespoons, lightly packed
unsalted butter	85 grams	6 tablespoons (¾ stick)
bleached all-purpose flour (see Baking Pearls, page 285)	182 grams	1½ cups (lightly spooned into the cup and leveled off)
bleached cake flour (see Baking Pearls, page 285)	86 grams	¾ cup (lightly spooned into the cup and leveled off)
baking powder, only an aluminum free variety	13.5 grams	3 teaspoons
fine sea salt	6 grams	1 teaspoon
sugar	50 grams	¼ cup
heavy cream OR buttermilk OR a combination of the two	174 grams OR 181 grams	¾ cup (177 ml)
Topping (optional): melted butter, cooled sugar for sprinkling	14 grams	1 tablespoon/15 ml about 1 teaspoon

MISE EN PLACE

- Into a small bowl, press the egg yolks through a medium-mesh strainer and cover.

- Cut the butter into ½ inch cubes and refrigerate for at least 30 minutes or freeze for 10 minutes.

PREHEAT THE OVEN

- Thirty minutes or longer before baking, set an oven rack at the middle level. Set the oven at 375°F/190°C.

MAKE THE DOUGH

1. In a large bowl, whisk together the all-purpose and cake flours, baking powder, salt, and sugar. Add the butter and, with your fingertips, press the cubes into small pieces until the mixture resembles coarse meal. (Alternatively, use a stand mixer, fitted with the flat beater, on low speed to blend the butter into the flour mixture, and then proceed by hand.)

2. Add the sieved egg yolks and whisk them in to distribute evenly.

3. Stir in the cream just until the flour is moistened, the dough starts to come together, and you can form a ball with your hands.

4. Empty the dough onto a lightly floured counter and knead it a few times until it develops a little elasticity and feels smooth. Dust the dough lightly with flour if it feels a little sticky. Pat or roll the dough into a ¾ inch high rectangle.

SHAPE THE DOUGH

■ Have ready a small dish of flour for dipping the cutter.

5. Dip the cutter into flour before each cut. Cut cleanly through the dough, lifting out the cutter without twisting it so that the edges will be free for the maximum rise; twisting the cutter compresses the edges, which keeps the biscuits from rising as high. Use up the remaining dough by rekneading it only briefly, so it won't become tough, and cut out more biscuits.

6. For soft sides, place the biscuits almost touching (about ¼ inch apart) on the cookie sheet. For crisp sides, place the biscuits 1 inch apart. Brush off any excess flour and, if an extra crisp top is desired, brush with the melted butter and sprinkle lightly with the sugar.

BAKE THE BISCUITS

7. Place the biscuits in the oven and raise the temperature to 400°F/200°C for 5 minutes. Lower the temperature to 375°F/190°C and continue baking for 10 to 15 minutes, or until golden. An instant-read thermometer inserted into the center of a biscuit should read 200°F/93°C. If baking frozen biscuits, bake them at 375°F/190°C for the entire time for a total of 20 to 25 minutes.

COOL THE BISCUITS

8. Remove the biscuits from the oven and transfer them to a wire rack to cool until just warm, top side up.

SERVE THE BISCUITS

9. Split the biscuits in half, preferably using a 3-tined fork.

STORE: Biscuits are at their best when baked shortly before eating. They can be stored, tightly covered, for up to 1 day. To reheat, it works well to cover them with a lightly moistened paper towel and heat for a few seconds in the microwave. The unbaked biscuits can be frozen, well wrapped, for up to 3 months. Bake them without thawing.

(continued)

Making Butter Biscuits

Press the butter cubes.

Add the sieved egg yolks.

Add the cream.

Mix the dough just until it comes together.

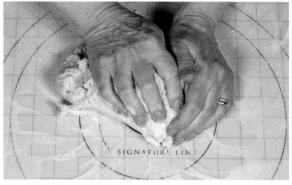

Knead the dough lightly.

Cut out the biscuits.

Basic Hearth Bread

MAKES ONE 7½ BY
4 INCH HIGH FREE
FORM LOAF

OVEN TEMPERATURE:
475°F/250°C, then
425°F/220°C

BAKING TIME: 30 to 40
minutes

BAKING EQUIPMENT:
One cookie sheet, lined
with parchment

A baking stone

A cast-iron skillet lined
with aluminum foil (to
prevent rusting) or a
cake pan

All bakers value having a basic hearth bread recipe. This free form loaf is an excellent bread for beginning bread bakers. The small amount of whole wheat flour adds greatly to the flavor, but can be replaced with an equal weight or volume of bread flour. For still more flavor you can make the dough ahead and refrigerate it overnight. You can also bake the dough in a loaf pan for sandwich bread, and if you want to have a softer crust and crumb, add the optional oil.

Makes 830 grams dough (884 grams with oil)

water	325 grams	about 1⅓ cups (325 ml)
bread flour	454 grams	3½ cups (lightly spooned into the cup and leveled off)
whole wheat flour	36 grams	¼ cup (lightly spooned into the cup and leveled off) plus ½ tablespoon
instant yeast	3.2 grams	1 teaspoon
fine sea salt	9 grams	1½ teaspoons
honey, pasteurized (see Baking Pearls, page 288)	7 grams	1 teaspoon (5 ml)
oil of your choice (optional)	54 grams	¼ cup (59 ml)

MISE EN PLACE

- Thirty minutes to 1 hour ahead, weigh or measure the water and cover it.

MAKE THE DOUGH

1. In the bowl of a stand mixer (or large bowl if mixing by hand), whisk together the bread and whole wheat flours and yeast. Then whisk in the salt.

2. With a wooden spoon, make a well and stir in the water, honey, and the oil, if using. Cover the bowl and allow the dough to rest for 20 minutes.

3. Attach the dough hook and knead the dough on low speed for 7 minutes, or until smooth and springy. (If kneading by hand, transfer the dough to a lightly floured counter and knead for 10 minutes, adding as little flour as possible.) The dough should be soft and just sticky enough to cling slightly to your fingers. If it is too stiff, spray it with a little water and knead it in.

LET THE DOUGH RISE

4. Into a 2 quart/2 liter or larger dough rising container or bowl, lightly coated with nonstick cooking spray, place the dough. Press it down and lightly coat the top of the dough with cooking spray.

(continued)

Be sure to use whole wheat flour that has been stored for no longer than 3 months at room temperature; if it has been stored in the freezer, longer is fine. Older whole wheat flour will taste bitter due to the oil in the germ, which becomes rancid on longer storage.

Unpasteurized natural honey has antibacterial enzymes that will kill the yeast. Most grocery store brands are pasteurized; natural honey from your farmers' market or health food store most likely isn't.

If you would like to add Biga (Dough Enhancer) for extra flavor and a firmer texture, see page 326.

Alternatively, in place of the biga, a ready addition is to moisten some leftover bread with water to the consistency of a soft dough. Add the water by the teaspoonful and knead it into the bread with your fingers. Use the same weight or volume as the biga, but do not increase the salt.

Make This Recipe Your Own

For a standard loaf, use a 9 by 5 by 3 inch (7 cup) bread pan, coated with nonstick cooking spray. The shaped dough before rising will be ½ inch from the top of the pan. When it's ready to bake, the dough should be 1 inch above the sides of the pan at the highest center point. Make one long ½ inch deep slash lengthwise down the top.

5. Cover the container with a lid or plastic wrap. With a piece of tape, mark on the side of the container approximately where double the height would be. Allow the dough to rise, ideally at 80° to 85°F/27° to 29°C, until doubled, about 1½ hours. (See page 283 for suggested rising environments.) If in doubt, insert a fingertip about ½ inch into the center of the dough; it should hold the indentation. If the indentation fills in, you need to allow it to rise longer. If baking it the following day, press down the dough and set it in a gallon-size reclosable freezer bag, the inside first lightly coated with nonstick cooking spray. Leave a little bit open for the gas that forms to escape, and refrigerate it. (You can leave the dough in the bowl if you coat the top of the dough with nonstick cooking spray and cover the bowl tightly.) Remove it to room temperature 1 hour before shaping.

SHAPE THE DOUGH AND LET IT RISE

6. Turn the dough onto a lightly floured counter and press it down gently to flatten it into a disc. Dimple the dough with your fingertips to deflate any large air bubbles. Use only as much flour as necessary to shape it into a ball. Start by bringing up the edges of the dough. Pinch them together and turn the dough over so that the pinched ends are at the bottom. Move the dough to an unfloured area of the counter. Cup your hands around the side of the dough farthest from you, and without lifting the dough from the counter, pull it toward you. This tightens the dough. Rotate the dough a quarter turn and repeat three to five more times to achieve a round, firm ball.

7. Set the dough on the prepared cookie sheet. Cover it with a large container or plastic wrap that has been lightly coated with nonstick cooking spray.

8. Let the dough rise for about 1 hour, until it measures 8 inches in diameter and 3 inches high, and the indentation fills in very slowly when pressed gently with a fingertip.

PREHEAT THE OVEN

▪ Forty-five minutes or longer before baking, set an oven rack in the lower third of the oven and set the baking stone on it. Place the cast-iron skillet on the floor of the oven. Set the oven at 475°F/250°C.

SLASH AND BAKE THE BREAD

9. With a sharp knife or straight edged razor blade, make ½ inch deep slashes in the top of the dough.

10. Spritz the bread with water. Quickly but gently set the cookie sheet on the hot stone and toss about ½ cup of ice cubes into the pan beneath. Immediately shut the door.

11. Bake for 10 minutes. Lower the temperature to 425°F/220°C and continue baking for 10 minutes. For even baking, rotate the cookie sheet halfway around. Tent the bread loosely with aluminum foil and continue baking for 10 to 20 minutes, or until golden brown. A wooden skewer inserted into the center will come out clean, and an instant-read thermometer should read 195° to 205°F/90° to 96°C. For an extra crisp crust, transfer it directly to the stone, turn off the oven, and leave it in the oven for an extra 5 to 10 minutes with the door ajar.

12. Remove the bread from the oven and transfer it to a wire rack to cool completely, top side up.

STORE IN A PAPER BAG: room temperature, 2 days;
AIRTIGHT: frozen, 2 months.

Making Basic Hearth Bread

Mise en place for the ingredients.

Mix the dough.

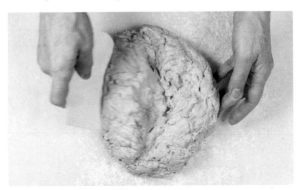

Use the dough scraper to gather the dough together.

Knead by pushing the dough away from you.

Lift up the sticky dough while kneading.

Mark the dough rising container where double the height will be.

(continued)

Making Basic Hearth Bread (cont'd)

Check to see if the dough holds an indentation.

Dimple the dough.

Bring up the edges of the dough to form a ball.

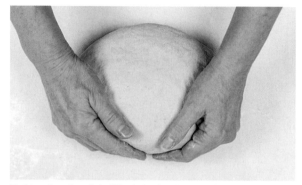

Tighten the dough ball by bringing it toward you without lifting it from the counter.

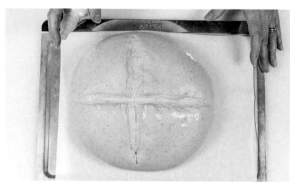

Spritz the slashed dough with water.

Add ice cubes to create steam.

Beer Bread

OVEN TEMPERATURE:
400°F/200°C, then
375°F/190°C

BAKING TIME: 30 to 40
minutes

PLAN AHEAD: If adding
the Biga (Dough
Enhancer), start it 3
days before baking the
bread.

BAKING EQUIPMENT:
One 8½ by 4½ by
2¾ inch (6 cup) loaf
pan, lightly coated with
nonstick cooking spray

A baking stone

A cast-iron skillet lined
with aluminum foil (to
prevent rusting) or a
cake pan

*This bread can be mixed in a food processor in less than 3 minutes. It
makes an excellent sandwich bread. You can substitute nonalcoholic
beer or even water if desired.*

Makes 775 grams dough

Biga (Dough Enhancer), page 326 (optional); see Baking Pearls, page 292	80 grams	⅓ cup
porter or Guinness stout, cold	255 grams	1 cup plus 2 tablespoons (267 ml)
canola or safflower oil	40 grams	3 tablespoons (45 ml)
Gold Medal bread flour, or half other brand bread flour and half unbleached all-purpose flour	371 grams	2¾ cups (lightly spooned into the cup and leveled off) plus 2 tablespoons
whole wheat flour	30 grams	3 tablespoons plus 1 teaspoon
non-diastatic malt powder OR barley malt syrup (see Baking Pearls, page 292)	9.3 grams OR 21 grams	1 tablespoon
instant yeast	6.4 grams	2 teaspoons
fine sea salt (see page xxi)	9 grams	1½ teaspoons

MISE EN PLACE

▪ Shortly before mixing the dough, remove the biga, if using, from the refrigerator.

▪ Into a 2 cup glass measure with a spout, weigh or measure the beer. (If measuring it by volume, allow it to sit after opening until the fizz disappears.) Keep it chilled.

▪ Add the oil to the beer.

MAKE THE DOUGH

1. In a food processor, process the bread and whole wheat flours, malt, and yeast for 30 seconds. Pulse in the salt.

2. Add the biga, if using, and process for 15 seconds until combined.

3. With the motor running, pour in the beer mixture. After the dough comes together, process for 45 seconds.

4. If the dough doesn't clean the bowl, add a little more flour and process for a few seconds to incorporate it. The dough should be tacky.

(continued)

Malt powder or syrup is sometimes added to bread as a flavor enhancer. It is available in health food stores. You can substitute it with an equal volume of sugar but avoid using honey for this bread because the beer darkens the crust; honey would make it too brown and have a tendency to burn.

If the sides are pale, bake the bread for an additional 5 minutes directly on the stone.

If not using the biga, decrease the salt by ⅛ teaspoon; use a total of 8.2 grams/1⅜ teaspoons. The bread will be shorter in height.

Alternatively, in place of the biga, a ready addition is to moisten some leftover bread with water to the consistency of a soft dough. Add the water by the teaspoonful and knead it into the bread with your fingers. Use the same weight or volume as the biga, but reduce the salt by ⅛ teaspoon as above.

Make This Recipe Your Own

Choose your favorite beer.

LET THE DOUGH RISE

5. Into a 2 quart/2 liter dough rising container or bowl, lightly coated with non-stick cooking spray, place the dough. Press it down and lightly spray the top of the dough with cooking spray.

6. Cover the container with a lid or plastic wrap. With a piece of tape, mark on the side of the container approximately where double the height would be. Let the dough rise, ideally at 80° to 85°F/27° to 29°C, until doubled, for 1 to 1½ hours. (See page 283 for suggested rising environments.) If in doubt, insert a fingertip about ½ inch into the center of the dough to see if it will hold the indentation. If the indentation fills in, you need to allow it to rise longer.

SHAPE THE DOUGH AND LET IT RISE

7. Turn the dough onto a lightly floured counter and press it down gently to flatten it into a rectangle. Dimple the dough with your fingertips to deflate any large air bubbles. It will still be a little sticky, but use only as much flour as absolutely necessary to keep it from sticking. Allow the dough to rest, covered, for 20 minutes.

8. Shape the dough into a loaf (see page 283) and set it, seam side down, in the prepared loaf pan. When pressed down, it will be ½ inch from the top of the pan. Cover it with a large container or plastic wrap that has been lightly coated with nonstick cooking spray.

9. Let the dough rise for 1 to 1½ hours; when pressed gently with a fingertip, the indentation should fill in very slowly. The dough should be about 1 inch above the sides of the pan at the highest center point.

PREHEAT THE OVEN

▪ Forty-five minutes or longer before baking, set an oven rack in the lower third of the oven and set the baking stone on it. Place the cast-iron skillet on the floor of the oven. Set the oven at 400°F/200°C.

BAKE THE BREAD

10. Spritz the top of the bread with water. Quickly but gently set the loaf pan on the hot stone and toss about ½ cup of ice cubes into the pan beneath. Immediately shut the door.

11. Bake for 15 minutes. Lower the temperature to 375°F/190°C. For even baking, rotate the loaf pan halfway around. Continue baking for 15 to 25 minutes, or until the bread is golden brown. A wooden skewer inserted into the center will come out clean, and an instant-read thermometer should read about 200°F/93°C.

COOL THE BREAD

12. Remove the bread from the oven, unmold it from the pan, and transfer it to a wire rack to cool completely, top side up.

STORE IN A PAPER BAG: room temperature, 2 days;
AIRTIGHT: frozen, 2 months.

(continued)

Making Beer Bread

Add the biga, if using, to the flour mixture.

Add the beer and oil with the motor running.

The dough should be stretchy and tacky.

Transfer the dough to a dough rising container.

Let rise until doubled in volume.

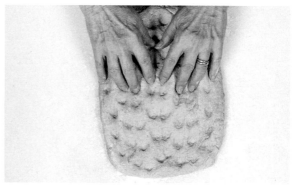

Dimple the dough.

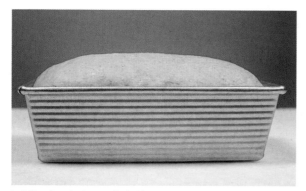

Let the dough rise again in the pan.

Bake until golden brown; a thermometer will read 200°F/90°C.

No-Knead Bread

MAKES ONE 9 INCH
DIAMETER BY 3 TO
3¾ INCH HIGH LOAF

OVEN TEMPERATURE:
450°F/230°C

BAKING TIME: 45 to 50
minutes

PLAN AHEAD: The bread
needs to ferment for
18 hours before shaping,
and then another
2 hours before baking.

BAKING EQUIPMENT:
One 5 quart/4¾ liter
Dutch oven with a lid
An insulated 15 by
12 inch cookie sheet or
a double layer of two
cookie sheets

The bread that baker Jim Leahy made famous is so virtually effortless that even beginning bread bakers are eager to try it. His original recipe called for about 400 grams/about 1⅔ cups/400 ml water, which resulted in a very sticky dough. I have decreased the water a little, which makes it more manageable for beginners and makes the holes in the finished bread a little less large. This bread is baked in a preheated Dutch oven, which maintains the shape of the soft dough that would otherwise have a tendency to spread.

One of the characteristics of no-knead bread is that it has a crumb that is wonderfully spongy, but sometimes to the point of being pasty. To remedy this, all you have to do is slice the bread, set it on a large rack, and let it sit for a few hours.

Makes 830 grams dough

water	355 grams	1½ cups (355 ml)
bread flour, preferably Gold Medal	468 grams	3½ cups (lightly spooned into the cup and leveled off) plus 1½ tablespoons
instant yeast	0.8 gram	¼ teaspoon
fine sea salt	9 grams	1½ teaspoons

MISE EN PLACE

- Thirty minutes to 1 hour ahead, weigh or measure the water and cover it.

MAKE THE DOUGH

1. In a 2 quart/2 liter or larger bowl, whisk together the flour and yeast. Then whisk in the salt.

2. Add the water and stir with a silicone spatula or your fingers just until there is no loose flour.

LET THE DOUGH RISE

3. Cover the bowl tightly with plastic wrap and let it sit at cool room temperature (65° to 70°F/19° to 21°C) for 18 hours. It will increase greatly in volume to about 8 cups, be filled with bubbles, and will just begin dropping at the edges. This long, slow rise is to develop flavor.

(continued)

If you are using a nonenameled cast-iron Dutch oven for the first time, be sure it is well seasoned so that the baked loaf releases easily.

Rising at cooler temperatures is fine but it will take longer, the crumb will be less open, and the loaf will be shorter.

Make This Recipe Your Own

For larger holes in the crumb, you can use up to 400 grams/about 1⅔ cups/400 ml water. The larger amount of water will give you a higher loaf.

For extra flavor but a slightly tighter crumb, you can use 433 grams/3⅓ cups bread flour and add 35 grams/¼ cup plus 1 teaspoon whole wheat flour. If measuring by volume, be sure to spoon the flour lightly into the cup and level it off. In this case, I also add 1 tablespoon/15 ml more water.

STRETCH AND FOLD THE DOUGH

4. Scrape the sticky dough onto a well-floured dough mat or floured counter. Dust it lightly with flour and dimple the dough with your fingertips to deflate it and create larger air bubbles. Do two business letter folds (fold the dough in thirds), rotating the dough 90 degrees between folds.

5. If there are sticky bits of dough on the dough mat, discard them and wipe off the surface. Add more flour to the mat. (If you don't have a dough mat, lightly flour a cookie sheet.) Gather up and pinch the dough together at the bottom to form a taut rounded shape. Set it back on the mat or cookie sheet. Cover it with a large container or plastic wrap that has been lightly coated with nonstick cooking spray.

6. At 80°F/27°C, the dough will take about 2 hours to rise to about 9 inches in diameter by 2 inches high; when pressed lightly with a wet fingertip, the indentation should fill in slowly. (See page 283 for suggested rising environments.) After the first hour, preheat the oven.

PREHEAT THE OVEN

■ Forty-five minutes or longer before baking, set an oven rack in the lower third of the oven and place the covered Dutch oven on it. Set the oven at 450°F/230°C.

7. If using a dough mat, brush off any excess flour, invert it over the hot pot, and allow the dough to fall into the pot. If the dough sticks to the mat, scrape it off, including any little bits that may have stuck, which will form an attractive design on the baked bread. (If using a cookie sheet, push the dough off the sheet into the pot.)

8. Dip sharp scissors in water to prevent sticking and cut a deep cross into the top of the dough. Set the hot lid back on top of the pot.

BAKE THE BREAD

9. Bake for 20 minutes. Remove the lid and continue baking for another 10 minutes.

10. Remove the pot from the oven and invert the loaf onto the insulated cookie sheet. Reinvert the loaf so that it is top side up and bake for 10 minutes longer. Check after 7 minutes and if it is very brown, tent loosely with a sheet of heavy-duty aluminum foil.

11. Use a heat-proof implement such as metal tongs to keep the oven door a few inches ajar and let the loaf sit for 5 minutes. Then turn off the oven, open the door completely, and let the loaf sit for another 5 minutes.

COOL THE BREAD

12. Transfer the loaf to a wire rack to cool completely, top side up. If desired, for a soft but not pasty crumb, slice the loaf and set the slices on wire racks for a few hours before storing.

STORE AS A LOAF, IN A PAPER BAG: room temperature, 3 days; frozen, 3 months.
AS SLICES, TIGHTLY COVERED: room temperature, 2 days; frozen, 3 months.

Making No-Knead Bread

The risen dough starting to recede.

Scrape the dough onto a well-floured surface.

Dimple the dough.

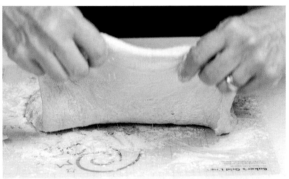

Start the first fold.

Finish folding the dough in thirds.

Rotate the dough 90 degrees for the second fold.

Gather up the edges and pinch them together.

Form a smooth ball.

(continued)

Making No-Knead Bread (cont'd)

Slide the dough into the hot pot.

Cut a deep cross in the top of the dough.

Whole Wheat Sandwich Bread

MAKES ONE 9 BY 6 BY 4½ INCH HIGH LOAF

OVEN TEMPERATURE: 450°F/230°C, then 400°F/200°C

BAKING TIME: 30 to 40 minutes

PLAN AHEAD: If adding the Biga (Dough Enhancer), start it 3 days before baking the bread.

BAKING EQUIPMENT: One 9 by 5 by 2¾ inch (7 cup) loaf pan, lightly coated with nonstick cooking spray
A baking stone
A cast-iron skillet lined with aluminum foil (to prevent rusting) or a cake pan

This loaf uses one-quarter as much whole wheat flour as bread flour, which is my preference for a pleasant wheaty flavor and firm but airy texture. If you prefer to use 50 percent whole wheat flour, see Make This Recipe Your Own (page 301). The loaf will be slightly stronger in flavor, and denser.

Makes 990 grams dough

Biga (Dough Enhancer), page 326 (optional); see Baking Pearls, page 301	80 grams	⅓ cup
water, at room temperature (65° to 75°F/19° to 24°C)	326 grams	1¼ cups plus 2 tablespoons (326 ml)
honey, pasteurized (see Baking Pearls, page 288)	21 grams	1 tablespoon (15 ml)
Gold Medal bread flour, or half other brand bread flour and half unbleached all-purpose flour	400 grams	3 cups (lightly spooned into the cup and leveled off) plus 1 tablespoon
whole wheat flour	100 grams	¾ cup (lightly spooned into the cup and leveled off) plus 1 teaspoon
nonfat dry milk, preferably King Arthur Baker's Special	30 grams	3 tablespoons (6 tablespoons if another brand)
instant yeast	3.6 grams	1⅛ teaspoons, *divided*
canola or safflower oil	27 grams	2 tablespoons (30 ml)
fine sea salt (see page xxi)	9.7 grams	1½ teaspoons plus ⅛ teaspoon

MISE EN PLACE

- If using the biga, 30 minutes to 1 hour before mixing the dough, cut it into small pieces into the bowl of a stand mixer with small sharp scissors.

- Add the water and honey to the biga and allow it to sit until softened, about 30 minutes. (If not using the biga, combine the water and honey in the bowl of the stand mixer.)

- In a medium bowl, whisk together the bread and whole wheat flours, dry milk, and yeast.

(continued)

MAKE THE DOUGH

1. Add 300 grams/about 2 cups of the flour mixture to the biga mixture or water-honey mixture and whisk until smooth, with a consistency of thick pancake batter.

2. Add the rest of the flour mixture. Attach the dough hook and mix on low speed for about 1 minute to moisten the flour and form a rough dough.

3. Scrape down the sides of the bowl. Cover it with plastic wrap and allow the dough to rest for 20 minutes.

4. Add the oil. Continuing on low speed, knead the dough with the dough hook for 7 minutes. As soon as the oil is mixed in, evenly sprinkle in the salt. The dough should be sticky enough to cling to your fingers. If it is not at all sticky, spray it with a little water and knead it in.

LET THE DOUGH RISE

5. Into a 3 quart/3 liter or larger dough rising container or bowl, lightly coated with nonstick cooking spray, place the dough. Press it down and lightly spray the top of the dough.

6. Cover the container with a lid or plastic wrap. With a piece of tape, mark on the side of the container approximately where double the height would be. Let the dough rise, ideally at 80° to 85°F/27° to 29°C, until doubled, 1 to 1½ hours. (See page 283 for suggested rising environments.) If in doubt, insert a fingertip about ½ inch into the center of the dough to see if it will hold the indentation. If the indentation fills in, you need to allow it to rise longer. For extra flavor development, you can refrigerate the dough overnight after an hour.

SHAPE THE DOUGH AND LET IT RISE

7. Turn the dough onto a lightly floured counter. Press it down gently to flatten it into a rectangle and dimple it with your fingertips to deflate any large air bubbles. Let it relax, covered, for 15 minutes. If it was refrigerated, let it rest for 1 hour.

8. Shape the dough into a loaf (see page 283 and photos on page 307) and set it in the prepared loaf pan. When pressed down, it will be ¾ inch from the top of the pan. Cover it with a large container or plastic wrap that has been lightly coated with nonstick cooking spray.

9. Let the dough rise for 45 minutes to 1 hour; when pressed gently with a fingertip, the indentation should fill in very slowly. It should be 1 to 1½ inches above the sides of the pan at the highest center point.

PREHEAT THE OVEN

▪ Forty-five minutes or longer before baking, set an oven rack in the lower third of the oven and set the baking stone on it. Place the cast-iron skillet on the floor of the oven. Set the oven at 450°F/230°C.

Baking Pearls

If not using the biga, decrease the salt by ⅛ teaspoon; use a total of 9 grams/1½ teaspoons. Use an 8½ by 4½ by 2¾ inch (6 cup) loaf pan.

Alternatively, in place of the biga, a ready addition is to moisten some leftover bread with water to the consistency of a soft dough. Add the water by the teaspoonful and knead it into the bread with your fingers. Use the same weight or volume as the biga, but reduce the salt by ⅛ teaspoon as above.

Be sure to use whole wheat flour that has been stored no longer than 3 months at room temperature; if it has been stored in the freezer, longer is fine. Older whole wheat flour will taste bitter due to the oil in the germ, which becomes rancid on longer storage.

Do not use organic honey, as the antibacterial enzymes will kill the yeast.

Make This Recipe Your Own

To make a 50 percent whole wheat loaf, use 342 grams/ 1½ cups minus 1 tablespoon/ 342 ml water, 42 grams/ 2 tablespoons/30 ml honey, and 247 grams/2 cups minus 4 teaspoons whole wheat flour and an equal weight or volume of bread flour.

BAKE THE BREAD

10. Spritz the top of the bread with water. Quickly but gently set the loaf pan on the hot stone and toss about ½ cup of ice cubes into the pan beneath. Immediately shut the door and lower the temperature to 400°F/200°C.

11. Bake for 20 minutes. For even baking, rotate the pan halfway around. Tent it loosely with aluminum foil and continue baking for 10 to 20 minutes, or until the bread is golden brown. A wooden skewer inserted into the center should come out clean and an instant-read thermometer should read 195° to 205°F/90° to 96°C.

COOL THE BREAD

12. Remove the bread from the oven, unmold it from the pan, and transfer it to a wire rack to cool completely, top side up.

STORE IN A PAPER BAG: room temperature, 2 days;
AIRTIGHT: frozen, 2 months.

Multigrain Bread

MAKES ONE 8 BY 4 BY 4¾ INCH HIGH LOAF

OVEN TEMPERATURE:
425°F/220°C, then
400°F/200°C

BAKING TIME: 35 to 45 minutes

PLAN AHEAD: If adding the Biga (Dough Enhancer), start it 3 days before baking the bread. Soak the grains for a minimum of 8 hours, or up to 24 hours, before mixing the bread.

BAKING EQUIPMENT:
One 8½ by 4½ by 2¾ inch (6 cup) loaf pan, lightly coated with nonstick cooking spray

A baking stone

A cast-iron skillet lined with aluminum foil (to prevent rusting) or a cake pan

This bread is my top favorite. It gets its wonderful crunchy texture and multidimensional flavor from a mixture of grains and seeds. It's fine to use a multigrain cereal mix, but the seeds and grains are more apparent when you mix your own as suggested in Make This Recipe Your Own, page 305. The dough will be very soft and sticky in order to incorporate the large amount of the grain mixture.

Makes 840 grams dough

10 grain cereal mix (such as Bob's Red Mill brand)	100 grams	½ cup plus 2 tablespoons
water	100 grams	½ cup minus 1 tablespoon (100 ml)
Biga (Dough Enhancer), page 326 (optional); see Baking Pearls, page 304	80 grams	⅓ cup
water	177 grams	¾ cup (177 ml)
non-diastatic malt powder OR barley malt syrup (see Baking Pearls, page 292)	9.3 grams OR 21 grams	1 tablespoon
bread flour, preferably King Arthur (see Baking Pearls, page 304)	324 grams	2½ cups (lightly spooned into the cup and leveled off), *divided*
instant yeast	3.2 grams	1 teaspoon
canola or safflower oil	54 grams	¼ cup (59 ml), *divided*
fine sea salt (see page xxi)	9 grams	1½ teaspoons

MISE EN PLACE

■ **SOAK THE GRAINS:** In a medium bowl, place the cereal mix. Weigh or measure the 100 grams/½ cup minus 1 tablespoon/100 ml water and heat it until hot. Stir it into the cereal mix until thoroughly combined. Cool to room temperature, cover, and refrigerate for a minimum of 8 hours.

■ If using the biga, 30 minutes to 1 hour before mixing the dough, cut it into small pieces into the bowl of a stand mixer with small sharp scissors.

■ Add the 177 grams/¾ cup/177 ml water and the malt to the biga and allow it to sit until soft, 30 minutes to 1 hour. (If not using the biga, combine the water and malt in the mixer bowl.)

■ Into another medium bowl, weigh or measure the flour.

(continued)

Baking Pearls

If using Gold Medal bread flour, which has a lower protein than King Arthur bread flour, add vital wheat gluten (12 grams/ 4 teaspoons) to the initial flour and biga mixture. (You can buy vital wheat gluten at most grocery stores or order it online.) It strengthens the protein network of the dough enough to support the large amount of grains. Otherwise, when using a lower-protein flour, the grains tend to cut through the gluten strands and thus result in an unpleasantly dense bread.

If not using the biga, decrease the salt by ⅛ teaspoon; use a total of 8.2 grams/ 1⅜ teaspoons. The bread will be shorter in height.

Alternatively, in place of the biga, a ready addition is to moisten some leftover bread with water to the consistency of a soft dough. Add the water by the teaspoonful and knead it into the bread with your fingers. Use the same weight or volume as the biga, but reduce the salt by ⅛ teaspoon as above.

MAKE THE DOUGH

1. Add all but 24 grams/3 tablespoons of the bread flour to the mixture in the mixer bowl.

2. Sprinkle the yeast on top of the flour in the mixer bowl.

3. Attach the dough hook and mix on low speed for 1 minute, or until the flour is moistened and the dough is in dry, shaggy pieces.

4. Cover the bowl and allow it to rest for 20 minutes.

5. On medium-low speed, add half of the oil, and knead with the dough hook for 7 minutes. The dough will become soft and smooth and form a firm ball around the dough hook.

6. With the mixer off, add the cereal mixture, and then the remaining oil. Knead for another 3 minutes, or until evenly incorporated. The dough will be very sticky.

7. With the mixer on, evenly sprinkle in the salt and knead for another 2 minutes.

8. Remove the bowl from the stand and dust the dough with a little of the reserved flour. Use your hand to knead the very sticky dough in the bowl, adding the rest of the flour as needed, until the dough is only slightly sticky. (If you weighed the ingredients, you will be adding most of the flour.)

LET THE DOUGH RISE

9. Into a 2 to 4 quart/2 to 4 liter dough rising container or bowl, lightly coated with nonstick cooking spray, place the dough. Press it down and lightly spray the top of the dough with cooking spray.

10. Cover the container with a lid or plastic wrap. With a piece of tape, mark on the side of the container approximately where double the height would be. Let the dough rise, ideally at 80° to 85°F/27° to 29°C, for 1 to 1½ hours or until doubled. (See page 283 for suggested rising environments.)

11. Remove the dough to the floured counter, flour the dough, and press down on it gently to form a rectangle. Give it two stretches, folding it in thirds after each one. Round the corners by folding them under, and set it back in the dough rising container. Again, spray the top of the dough, cover, and let it rise for 30 minutes to 1 hour, until doubled. If in doubt, insert a fingertip about ½ inch into the center of the dough to see if it will hold the indentation. If the indentation fills in, you need to allow it to rise longer.

SHAPE THE DOUGH AND LET IT RISE

12. Turn the dough onto a lightly floured counter. Roll it into a 14 by 8 inch rectangle. Shape it by rolling it tightly into a loaf and set it, seam side down, in the prepared loaf pan. When pressed down, it will be ½ inch to 1 inch from the top of the pan. Cover it with a large container or plastic wrap that has been lightly coated with nonstick cooking spray.

Make This Recipe Your Own

To make your own ten grain/seed cereal, mix together 1 tablespoon of each of the following, or choose grains and seeds of your preference. Before soaking, toast buckwheat, sunflower seeds, and pumpkin seeds: In a preheated 325°F/160°C oven, on a cookie sheet, toast the sunflower seeds and buckwheat, stirring once or twice, for 3 minutes. Add the pumpkin seeds and continue toasting for 2 to 3 minutes, just until they begin to brown lightly.

coarse buckwheat
sunflower seeds
pumpkin seeds
polenta
poppy seeds
barley flakes
flax seeds
millet
steel cut oats
cracked wheat or bulgur

13. Let the dough rise for 45 minutes to 1 hour; when pressed gently with a fingertip, the indentation should fill in very slowly. It should be about 1½ inches above the sides of the pan at the highest center point.

PREHEAT THE OVEN

■ Forty-five minutes or longer before baking, set an oven rack in the lower third of the oven and set the baking stone on it. Place the cast-iron skillet on the floor of the oven. Set the oven at 425°F/220°C.

BAKE THE BREAD

14. Spritz the top of the bread with water. Quickly but gently set the loaf pan on the hot stone and toss ½ cup of ice cubes into the pan beneath. Immediately shut the door.

15. Bake for 15 minutes. Lower the temperature to 400°F/200°C. For even baking, rotate the pan halfway around. Continue baking 20 to 30 minutes, or until the bread is golden brown. A wooden skewer inserted into the center will come out clean and an instant-read thermometer should read 205° to 208°F/96° to 98°C.

COOL THE BREAD

16. Remove the bread from the oven, unmold it from the pan, and transfer it to a wire rack to cool completely, top side up.

STORE IN A PAPER BAG: room temperature, 2 days;
AIRTIGHT: frozen, 2 months.

(continued)

Making Multigrain Bread

Cut the biga, if using, into small pieces.

Mix until the dough is in shaggy pieces.

Add the grains.

Mix until the grains are evenly incorporated.

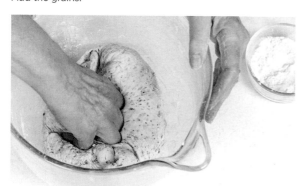

Knead in the reserved flour.

Press down the dough in the dough rising container.

Stretch the dough.

Fold the dough one third of the way.

Finish folding the dough in thirds.

Round the dough.

Let rise until doubled in volume.

Roll the dough into a 14 by 8 inch rectangle.

Shape the dough into a loaf.

Push in the ends to fit in the pan.

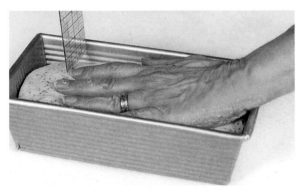

The dough will be ½ inch to 1 inch from the top of the pan.

After rising, the dough will be 1½ inches above the sides of the pan.

Japanese Milk Bread

MAKES ONE 8½ BY 4½ BY 4½ INCH HIGH LOAF

OVEN TEMPERATURE: 325°F/160°C

BAKING TIME: 30 to 40 minutes

BAKING EQUIPMENT: One 9 by 5 by 2¾ inch (7 cup) loaf pan, lightly coated with nonstick cooking spray

A baking stone

A cast-iron skillet lined with aluminum foil (to prevent rusting) or a cake pan

I discovered this exquisite loaf over thirty years ago on a visit to Japan. It is extraordinarily soft and light. I tried to recreate it, but was unsuccessful until I found a simple but perfect recipe and video on Vietnamese baker Linh Trang's blog, Rice 'n Flour. She adapted it from a blog called Angie's Recipes and I have adapted it further to make it as one loaf.

This soft white bread is slightly chewy, but when toasted becomes amazingly light and less chewy. Its touch of sweetness is a lovely complement to the smokiness of ham, but my favorite way to enjoy it is as a grilled cheese sandwich. I fondly refer to it as "squishy bread" because of its readiness to compress, but it still maintains its light, delicate texture. I use a mix of bread flour and cake flour to achieve this texture, but I give an alternative in the Baking Pearl on page 310, depending on which brand of flour you may have on hand. This loaf flies in the face of artisanal breads, having the addition of sugar, a large amount of yeast, no whole grain, and no long rise. What I love most is that, more so than any other, it captures the exact flavor of one of civilization's most enticing aromas: baking bread.

Makes 590 grams dough

whole milk	125 grams	about ½ cup/122 ml
heavy cream	75 grams	⅓ cup/79 ml
½ large egg	25 grams	1½ tablespoons (23 ml)
bread flour, preferably King Arthur (see Baking Pearls, page 310)	238 grams	1¾ cups plus 1 tablespoon (lightly spooned into the cups and leveled off)
bleached cake flour	62 grams	½ cup (lightly spooned into the cup and leveled off) plus 2 teaspoons
sugar, preferably superfine	40 grams	3 tablespoons plus 1 teaspoon
nonfat dry milk, preferably King Arthur Baker's Special	17 grams	1½ tablespoons (3 tablespoons if other brands)
instant yeast	9 grams	2¾ teaspoons
fine sea salt	4.5 grams	¾ teaspoon

(continued)

Baking Pearl

You can use 100 percent unbleached all-purpose flour but the blend of bread and cake flours produces the best flavor and texture. If your bread flour has a lower protein content, such as Gold Medal, increase the bread flour to 270 grams/2 cups and decrease the cake flour to 30 grams/¼ cup.

MISE EN PLACE

■ Into a 1 cup measure with a spout, weigh or measure the milk, cream, and egg.

MAKE THE DOUGH

1. In the bowl of a stand mixer (or large bowl if mixing by hand), whisk together the bread and cake flours, sugar, dry milk, and yeast. Then whisk in the salt.

2. With a wooden spoon, make a well in the flour mixture and stir in the milk mixture until the flour is moistened and the dough is in shaggy pieces.

3. Cover the bowl and allow the dough to rest for 20 minutes.

4. Attach the dough hook and knead the dough on medium speed for 12 to 15 minutes, or until smooth and springy. (If kneading by hand, transfer the dough to a lightly floured countertop and knead for a minimum of 20 minutes, adding as little flour as necessary.) When gently stretching a small piece of the dough with your fingers, it should form a translucent "window" that does not tear. The dough should be soft and smooth.

LET THE DOUGH RISE

5. Into a 1 quart/1 liter or larger dough rising container or bowl, lightly coated with nonstick cooking spray, place the dough. Press it down and lightly spray the top of the dough.

6. Cover the container with a lid or plastic wrap. With a piece of tape, mark on the side of the container approximately where double the height would be. Let the dough rise, ideally at 80° to 85°F/27° to 29°C, until doubled, for 1 to 1½ hours. (See page 283 for suggested rising environments.) If in doubt, insert a fingertip about ½ inch into the center of the dough to see if it will hold the indentation. If the indentation fills in, you need to allow it to rise longer.

SHAPE THE DOUGH AND LET IT RISE

7. Turn the dough onto a lightly floured counter and press it down gently to flatten it into a rectangle. Allow the dough to rest, covered, for 20 minutes.

8. Flip the dough over so that the smooth side is down. Roll it with a rolling pin into a longer rectangle to eliminate any air bubbles.

9. Shape the dough into a loaf (see page 283 and photos on page 307) and set it, seam side down, in the prepared loaf pan. When pressed down, it will be about 1½ inches from the top of the pan. Cover it with a large container or plastic wrap that has been lightly coated with nonstick cooking spray.

10. Let the dough rise for 1 to 1½ hours; when pressed gently with a fingertip, the indentation should fill in very slowly. It should be about ½ inch above the sides of the pan at the highest center point.

PREHEAT THE OVEN

■ Forty-five minutes or longer before baking, set an oven rack in the lower third of the oven and place the baking stone on it. Place the cast-iron skillet on the floor of the oven. Set the oven at 325°F/160°C.

BAKE THE BREAD

11. Spritz the top of the bread with water. Quickly but gently set the loaf pan on the hot stone and toss about ½ cup of ice cubes into the pan beneath. Immediately shut the door.

12. Bake for 20 minutes. For even baking, rotate the loaf pan halfway around, and if the bread is golden brown, tent it loosely with aluminum foil. Continue baking for 10 to 20 minutes, or until a wooden skewer inserted into the center comes out clean. An instant-read thermometer should read 195° to 205°F/90° to 96°C.

COOL THE BREAD

13. Remove the bread from the oven, unmold it from the pan, and transfer it to a wire rack to cool completely, top side up. For a softer crust with what Trang calls a lovely "glow," as soon as you unmold the bread, brush it on the top and sides with about 1 tablespoon of heavy cream.

STORE IN A PAPER BAG: room temperature, 2 days;
AIRTIGHT: frozen, 2 months.

Making Japanese Milk Bread

Mix the milk mixture into the flour mixture.

The consistency of the dough on the dough hook.

Check the dough for a translucent window.

Let the dough rise to double its volume.

Babka Swirl Loaf

MAKES ONE 8½ BY 5 BY 4 INCH HIGH LOAF

OVEN TEMPERATURE: 350°F/175°C

BAKING TIME: 45 to 50 minutes

PLAN AHEAD This babka takes a minimum of 6½ hours from start to finish, plus 1½ hours to cool before slicing. It can be refrigerated overnight at different stages, so you won't need to be home for 6½ hours straight.

Plan to make the starter a minimum of 1 hour, or up to 4 hours, ahead of mixing the dough.

BAKING EQUIPMENT: One 9 by 5 by 2¾ inch (7 cup) loaf pan, lightly coated with nonstick cooking spray, lined width-wise with a strip of parchment overhanging the long edges by a few inches, and coated again with nonstick cooking spray (preferably a nonstick pan, as the sugar caramelizes on the pan bottom and sides)

A cast-iron skillet lined with aluminum foil (to prevent rusting) or a cake pan

Everyone loves babka, an egg- and butter-rich dough spiraled with a cinnamon sugar filling that is a cross between a pastry and a bread. The supple, silky dough is a pleasure to work with.

DOUGH STARTER (SPONGE)

water	89 grams	¼ cup plus 2 tablespoons (89 ml)
Gold Medal bread flour, or half other bread flour and half unbleached all-purpose flour	49 grams	¼ cup plus 2 tablespoons (lightly spooned into the cup and leveled off)
nonfat dry milk, preferably King Arthur Baker's Special	17 grams	1½ tablespoons (3 tablespoons if other brands)
instant yeast	3.6 grams	1⅛ teaspoons

MISE EN PLACE

▪ A minimum of 1 hour ahead, set the butter for the dough on the counter at room temperature (65° to 75°F/19° to 24°C).

▪ Into two separate small bowls, weigh or measure the water for the starter and for the dough and cover them.

▪ Into a 1 cup measure with a spout, weigh or measure the eggs. Whisk lightly and pour 25 grams/1½ tablespoons/22.5 ml through a strainer into another cup to reserve for the filling on page 315. Cover both cups and refrigerate.

MAKE THE DOUGH STARTER (SPONGE)

1. In the bowl of a stand mixer, place the water, flour, dry milk, and yeast. Whisk by hand for about 2 minutes, until very smooth, to incorporate air. The sponge will be the consistency of a thick batter.

2. Scrape down the sides of the bowl. Cover with plastic wrap and set the sponge aside while you make the flour mixture.

(continued)

DOUGH Makes 680 grams

unsalted butter, must be very soft	85 grams	6 tablespoons (¾ stick)
2 large eggs	100 grams	⅓ cup plus 1 tablespoon (94 ml)
Gold Medal bread flour (or half other bread flour and half all-purpose flour)	267 grams	2 cups (lightly spooned into the cup and leveled off) plus 1 tablespoon
sugar	56 grams	¼ cup plus ½ tablespoon
instant yeast	3.6 grams	1⅛ teaspoons
fine sea salt	4.5 grams	¾ teaspoon
water, at room temperature	45 grams	3 tablespoons (45 ml)
pure vanilla extract	.	1 teaspoon (5 ml)

COMBINE THE FLOUR MIXTURE FOR THE DOUGH

3. In a medium bowl, whisk together the flour, sugar, and yeast. Then whisk in the salt. Sprinkle the flour mixture over the sponge, forming a blanket of flour, and cover it tightly with plastic wrap. Let it ferment for 1 to 4 hours at room temperature, or 1 hour at room temperature and up to 24 hours refrigerated. During this time, the sponge will bubble through the flour blanket in places.

MAKE THE DOUGH

4. Attach the dough hook to the stand mixer. Add the butter, eggs, water, and vanilla to the flour-covered sponge and beat on low speed for about 1 minute, or until the flour is moistened. Raise the speed to medium and knead for about 7 minutes, or until the dough is shiny and very elastic. It will not clean the sides of the bowl, but will be very stretchy when pulled with your fingers. It will be very sticky.

LET THE DOUGH RISE

5. Using a spatula or dough scraper that has been lightly coated with nonstick cooking spray, scrape the dough into a 2 quart/2 liter dough rising container or bowl that has been lightly coated with nonstick cooking spray. It will be very soft and elastic and will stick to your fingers. Do not be tempted to add more flour at this point; the dough will firm up considerably after rising and chilling. Push down the dough and lightly coat the surface with nonstick cooking spray. Cover the container with a lid or plastic wrap. With a piece of tape, mark the side of the container at approximately where double the height of the dough should be after rising. Let the dough rise in a warm place, ideally at 75° to 85°F/24° to 29°C, until it reaches the mark, 1 to 1½ hours.

DEFLATE AND CHILL THE DOUGH

6. Lightly flour the counter and your hands, because the dough will still be a little sticky. Using a spatula or dough scraper that has been lightly coated with cooking spray, remove the dough to the counter. Deflate it gently with your fingertips. Round the dough by gently stretching it out and folding it in to the center on all four sides. The dough will be very soft.

7. Set the dough back in the container. Lightly coat the surface with nonstick cooking spray, cover, and refrigerate it for a minimum of 1 hour, or up to overnight. (If overnight, deflate it gently after the first hour or two of refrigeration. Let it sit at room temperature for 30 minutes before shaping.)

CINNAMON SUGAR FILLING

granulated sugar	50 grams	¼ cup
light Muscovado or dark brown sugar	108 grams	½ cup, firmly packed
ground cinnamon	2.2 grams	1 teaspoon
½ large egg, beaten and strained (reserved from page 313)	25 grams	1½ tablespoons (22.5 ml)

MAKE THE CINNAMON SUGAR FILLING

8. Using a medium-mesh strainer, sift the granulated and brown sugars and cinnamon into a medium bowl. Whisk to combine them evenly. Into a small bowl, spoon 28 grams/2 tablespoons of the cinnamon sugar mixture; reserve it.

SHAPE THE DOUGH, FILL, AND LET IT RISE

9. Turn the dough onto a well-floured counter and press down on it with floured hands to form a rectangle. Roll the dough into a 16 by 14 inch rectangle, flouring the counter and the rolling pin, if necessary, to keep the dough from sticking. It will be a little under ¼ inch thick. Brush off any excess flour from the top.

10. Brush the entire surface of the dough with the beaten egg, using as little as possible to create an even coating; too much egg wash will dissolve the sugar, making the dough more difficult to shape. Sift the larger portion of the cinnamon sugar mixture onto the dough and use your fingers to smooth it as evenly as possible over the dough.

11. Starting from the top, use your fingers and a long plastic ruler to roll up the dough, using the ruler to help support the dough as you roll it. Slip the edge of the ruler slightly under the dough and use it to lift up and roll/push the dough toward you. With each roll, dust any flour from the surface of the dough. Press firmly, squeezing gently with your fingers, all along the dough roll to keep it from separating, easing the dough gently toward the ends. Work carefully without rushing. When you reach the bottom edge of the dough, pinch it against the outside of the dough to make a tight seam. Set the dough roll seam side up. Pinch the ends of the dough together firmly. To prevent it from becoming thinner at the ends, with one hand hold down the dough near an end and with your other hand, push in the end. Repeat with the other end. The roll should be no longer than 16 inches. Brush off any excess flour.

12. Brush the top of the roll with the remaining beaten egg, sprinkle with the reserved sugar and cinnamon mixture, and fold the roll over itself. Gently twist the dough twice and set it into the prepared loaf pan. Press it down firmly into the pan. The highest point will be about 1 inch from the top of the pan.

(continued)

13. Cover the pan loosely with plastic wrap, lightly coated with nonstick cooking spray. Let the dough rise, in a warm place (ideally at 75° to 85°F/24° to 29°C), for 45 minutes to 1½ hours, or until the highest point is about 1 inch above the top of the pan.

PREHEAT THE OVEN

▪ Forty-five minutes or longer before baking, set an oven rack in the lower third of the oven. Place the cast-iron skillet on the floor of the oven. Set the oven at 350°F/175°C.

BAKE THE BABKA

14. Quickly but gently set the loaf pan on the rack and toss about ½ cup of ice cubes into the pan on the oven floor. Immediately shut the door and bake for 20 minutes. For even baking, rotate the pan halfway around. Cover the top loosely with foil and continue baking for 25 to 35 minutes, or until golden brown. (An instant-read thermometer inserted into the center should read 200° to 205°F/93° to 96°C.)

CREAM GLAZE

heavy cream	29 grams	2 tablespoons (30 ml)

UNMOLD AND COOL THE BABKA

15. Lay a sheet of parchment on the counter and place a wire rack on top. Remove the babka from the oven, lift it out of the pan by grasping the two ends of the parchment, and set it onto the wire rack. If necessary, use a small metal spatula to dislodge the babka at the short ends of the pan not lined with the parchment. Slip out the parchment from under the babka and brush the cream onto the top and sides of the babka to soften it and give it extra shine. Cool completely, about 1½ hours.

STORE IN A PAPER BAG: room temperature, 2 days;
AIRTIGHT: frozen, 2 months.

Making Babka Swirl Loaf

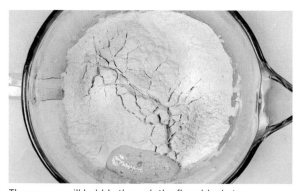

The sponge will bubble through the flour blanket.

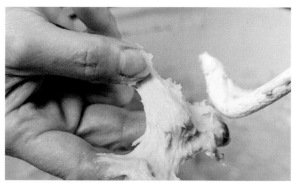

The dough will be stretchy and sticky.

Use a dough scraper to move the dough.

Mark the dough rising container where double the height will be.

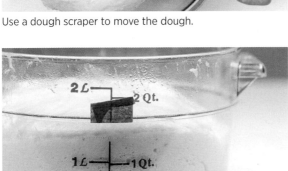

Let the dough rise until doubled.

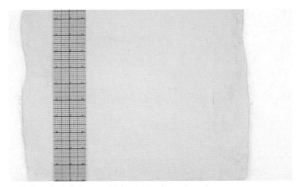

Roll the dough into a 16 by 14 inch rectangle.

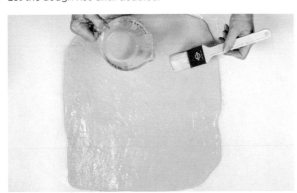

Brush the dough with beaten egg.

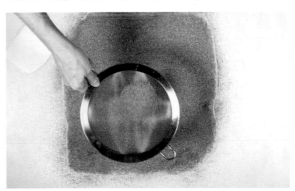

Coat the dough with the cinnamon sugar mixture.

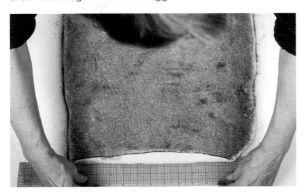

Use a ruler to help start rolling up the dough.

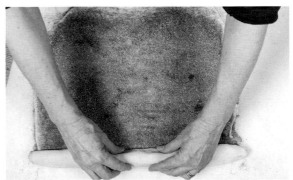

Squeeze the dough together as you roll.

(continued)

Making Babka Swirl Loaf (cont'd)

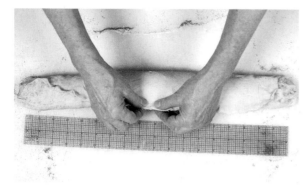

Pinch the seam together.

Coat with the reserved cinnamon sugar mixture.

Fold the dough in half over itself.

Twist the dough.

Twist the dough again.

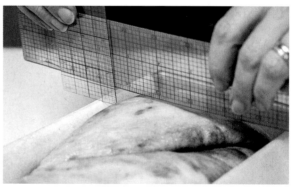

Let the dough rise until it comes to 1 inch above the sides of the pan.

Use the parchment to lift the loaf out of the pan.

Brush the baked babka with cream.

Pizza Rosa

MAKES ONE 12 INCH PIZZA; SERVES 2 OR 3

OVEN TEMPERATURE: 475°F/250°C; 500°F/260°C if using a baking stone

BAKING TIME: 8 to 12 minutes

PLAN AHEAD: Mix the dough a minimum of 24 hours, or up to 48 hours, before baking (or see Baking Pearls, page 320, for making and baking the dough the same day).

BAKING EQUIPMENT: A baking steel, cast-iron pizza pan, or baking stone

A sheet of parchment

A baking peel, or 15 by 12 inch cookie sheet

Pizza is everywhere, so if you're going to the effort of making it at home, it has to be worth it. This is the pizza dough that will spoil you forever in favor of homemade pizza. It sports a thin, crisp crust with a puffy, bubbly border that is soft inside. It is slightly chewy, crunchy, and flavorful. This pizza does not need to be eaten with a knife and fork like some Neapolitan-style pizzas, as the tip does not dip. The small amount of whole wheat flour or bran adds greatly to its flavor.

The dough takes just minutes to mix, but for the best texture and flavor make it 1 to 2 days before baking. The secrets to the crisp, light, bubbly crust are the long, slow rise and a fully preheated baking surface, ideally a baking steel or cast-iron pizza pan. To maintain maximum crispness, I bake the crust without the toppings for the first 5 minutes.

DOUGH Makes 332 grams (336 grams if using whole wheat flour)

water	133 grams	½ cup plus 1 tablespoon (133 ml)
unbleached all-purpose flour	182 grams	1½ cups (lightly spooned into the cup and leveled off)
wheat bran OR whole wheat flour	8 grams OR 14 grams	1½ tablespoons plus ¼ teaspoon OR 2 tablespoons
instant yeast	1.2 grams	⅜ teaspoon
fine sea salt	4.5 grams	¾ teaspoon
olive or vegetable oil, for shaping and coating	13 grams	1 tablespoon (15 ml), *divided*
fine cornmeal, for dusting	8 grams	1 tablespoon

MISE EN PLACE

- Thirty minutes to 1 hour ahead, weigh or measure the water and cover it.

MAKE THE DOUGH

1. In a medium bowl, whisk together the flour, wheat bran, and yeast. Then whisk in the salt.

(continued)

Baking Pearls

Whole wheat flour is high in oil and prone to rancidity and off flavors if not stored correctly. It should be stored at cool room temperature or refrigerated for no longer than 3 months, but will keep frozen for a few years.

There is no need to use your expensive extra virgin olive oil, as the high baking heat will completely destroy its flavor. The oil in this recipe serves two purposes: to keep the dough from sticking during shaping and to create a crisper crust. If desired, after baking, drizzle the pizza lightly with extra virgin olive oil.

For a slight crunch for the bottom of the crust, use finely ground polenta in place of the cornmeal.

To make and bake the dough the same day, after stretching and folding, allow the dough to double. At 80° to 85°F/27° to 29°C, it will take 4 to 5 hours. (At 70°F/21°C, it will take about twice as long. If your environment is cool, you may want to double the yeast, but the resulting crust will not be as airy.) Preshape and refrigerate it or allow it to relax at room temperature for 20 minutes before stretching.

To make the dough more than 48 hours ahead and freeze, use 10 to 25 percent more yeast (the larger amount if planning to freeze for 2 weeks or longer). After the dough has risen to about 2 cups/ 500 milliliters, 1 to 1½ hours, oil the dough, wrap it well, place it in a quart-size reclosable freezer bag, and freeze it. Remove it to the refrigerator the night before to thaw, and then proceed as for the regular method.

2. With a silicone spatula, make a well and stir in the water just until the flour mixture is moistened.

3. Cover and allow the dough to rest for 20 minutes.

4. Use your fingers to spread about 1 teaspoon/5 ml of the oil on the counter. Scrape the dough onto it. Shape the dough into a rough rectangle, stretch it to a longer rectangle, give it a business letter fold (fold it in thirds), and repeat. Round the corners by tucking them under and press the dough into a 1 quart/ 1 liter dough rising container or bowl that has been lightly coated with nonstick cooking spray.

5. Let the dough rest for 20 to 30 minutes, and then repeat the stretching and folding process.

LET THE DOUGH RISE

6. Return the dough to the dough rising container or bowl. Mark the side of the container where double the height would be. Cover the container tightly and set it in a warm place, preferably 80° to 85°F/27° to 29°C. (See page 283 for suggested rising environments.)

7. Let the dough rise to about 2 cups/500 milliliters, 1 to 1½ hours.

8. Set the container in the refrigerator until the next morning. Depending on the temperature of your refrigerator, by then it should have risen until doubled. If it has not, let it sit at warm room temperature.

9. Lightly oil the counter and preshape the dough: Stretch it from each of four sides (as shown in the photos on page 323). Bring up the sides to the center and pinch them together. Move the dough to an unoiled area of the counter. Place each hand against the side of the dough farthest away from you and press the dough toward you. Rotate the dough a quarter turn and repeat. Do this a total of four times to tighten it into a ball.

10. Set the ball of dough, pinched side down, on a cookie sheet that has been lightly coated with nonstick cooking spray. Spray the top of the dough, cover with plastic wrap, and refrigerate until 15 minutes before the final shaping. (Preshaping will make stretching the dough easier.) If freezing the dough for future use (see Baking Pearls, left), first coat it with nonstick cooking spray, wrap it with plastic wrap, and set it in a quart size reclosable freezer bag. Thaw it in the refrigerator for about 12 hours before the final shaping.

PREHEAT THE OVEN

▪ One hour or longer before baking, set an oven rack in the lower third of the oven and place the pizza pan on it. Set the oven at 475°F/250°C, or 500°F/260°C if using a baking stone.

Baking Pearls

A cast-iron pizza pan is just as effective as a baking steel and less expensive. A baking stone requires a higher temperature. If using a stone, increase the temperature to 500°F/260°C.

In summer, rather than heating up the kitchen I use my four burner gas grill. I set a cast-iron pizza pan on the grill and preheat it with all burners on high for 10 minutes, at which point it is over 500°F/260°C. Then I open the lid, turn all four burners to medium, and allow the grill to cool for about 5 minutes to bring the surface of the pan to about 475°F/250°C. I slide the pizza onto the pan (be sure first to trim any overhanging parchment), lower the lid, and bake for exactly 3 minutes without opening it. I then remove the pizza pan to a wire rack, turn off the center 2 burners, and after topping the dough, set the pizza, without the parchment, in the center, directly on top of the grill grates. It takes about 9 minutes to finish baking the pizza, which becomes exceptionally crunchy, with grill marks on the bottom. I also like to transfer the pizza to a cookie sheet and set it under a preheated broiler for about a minute to give the top crust extra browning.

SHAPE THE PIZZA

11. One hour before baking, roll the dough into a 7 inch disc. Tape down the parchment to the counter on all four corners, to prevent sliding. Sprinkle the parchment with the cornmeal and place the dough on top. Brush it with about 1 teaspoon/5 ml of the remaining oil. Then gently stretch and press the dough into a 12 inch circle, keeping the outer ½ inch border thicker than the center. Remove the tape.

12. Brush the surface of the dough all over with the final 1 teaspoon/5 ml oil and set it in a warm area, preferably 80° to 85°F/27° to 29°C, to start rising while the oven is preheating.

13. Prepare the toppings of your choice (see Make This Recipe Your Own, page 325).

BAKE THE PIZZA

14. Slip the peel under the parchment and slide the dough-topped parchment onto the hot pizza pan. Bake for 5 to 7 minutes, depending on the heat of your oven. The dough will puff up in the center and form large bubbles. After 3 minutes of baking, gently press it down.

15. Use the peel to remove the crust-topped parchment from the oven and slide it onto a cooktop or heat resistant counter. Slip the peel between the parchment and the crust and discard the parchment, leaving the pizza on the peel.

16. Top the crust evenly with the topping ingredients, scattering on garlic, if using, before the cheese to protect it from burning.

17. Slide the pizza back into the oven and bake for 3 to 5 minutes, or until the cheese is fully melted and the crust is browned.

18. Remove the pizza to a cutting board and cut into servings. A pizza wheel and sharp scissors work best.

STORE UNBAKED DOUGH, AIRTIGHT: refrigerated, 2 days; frozen, 2 months.
PREBAKED PIZZA CRUST (WITHOUT TOPPINGS), AIRTIGHT: frozen, 2 months.

(continued)

Making Pizza Rosa

Mise en place for the ingredients.

Mix until the flour mixture is moistened.

Shape the dough into a rough rectangle.

Stretch the dough for the folds.

Fold the dough into thirds.

Shape the dough into a ball.

Mark the rising container where double the height will be.

Let the dough rise until doubled.

Stretch one side of the dough.

Fold the stretched side to the center. Repeat with the remaining sides.

Pinch the dough together at the center.

Tighten the dough into a ball by bringing it toward you without lifting it from the counter.

Cover and refrigerate.

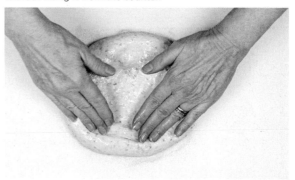

Press the dough on the cornmeal-sprinkled parchment.

Stretch the dough to enlarge it.

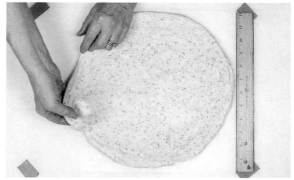

Stretch to form a ½ inch thick border.

(continued)

Making Pizza Rosa (cont'd)

Let the dough rise before baking.

Transfer the dough, still on the parchment, into the oven.

Add toppings to the baked dough.

Bake until the cheese is melted and the crust browned.

If you like a very brown crust, verging on blackened, it's fine to bake the pizza at 500°F/260°C or above.

Pizza is personal. Use toppings of your choice, but to keep the bottom crust from getting soggy, avoid overloading the pizza. I like to use 170 to 227 grams/ 6 to 8 ounces sliced or grated mozzarella; 1 sausage, crumbled and sautéed; 4 large mushrooms, sliced and sautéed; 2 large cloves garlic, chopped and lightly sautéed; and oven roasted cherry tomato halves. If using tomato sauce, I use a very thick one that is not too watery (my recipe at right), and spread a very thin layer (about 52 grams/⅓ cup/79 ml) onto the crust. I sometimes also add little dabs of sauce on top of the cheese. To remove excess fat from pepperoni, I slice it, set it on a half sheet pan or parchment-lined cookie sheet to absorb the fat, and cook it in the hot oven for about 2 minutes or just until it exudes excess fat. Then I set it on paper towels until ready to use. Fresh herbs are best added after baking.

My Favorite Pizza Tomato Sauce

I always have some on hand in the freezer.

Makes 270 grams/1 cup/237 ml

olive oil or vegetable oil	9 grams	2 teaspoons (10 ml)
fine sea salt	4.5 grams	¾ teaspoon
dried oregano	.	⅛ teaspoon
crushed red pepper flakes	.	⅛ teaspoon
one 14 ounce can whole peeled tomatoes, preferably San Marzano	400 grams	1¾ cups
1 medium clove garlic	.	.
red wine vinegar	.	½ teaspoon (2.5 ml)

1. In a food processor, add the olive oil, salt, oregano, red pepper flakes, and tomatoes. Pulse until only small pieces of tomato remain.

2. Scrape the mixture into a medium saucepan, preferably nonstick. Grate the garlic using a Microplane or finely chop it and add it to the pan. Simmer for 30 minutes to an hour, stirring often, until reduced to 270 grams/a little over 1 cup/237 ml. Stir in the vinegar.

Biga (Dough Enhancer)

**MAKES 80 GRAMS/
⅓ CUP**

PLAN AHEAD Make
the biga a minimum of
6 hours, preferably
3 days, before adding
it to the dough.

BAKING EQUIPMENT:
One small mixing bowl

This quick-to-make mixture of flour, yeast, and water requires only one thing extra—a few days of forethought. But the payoff is that when added to bread dough, it measurably increases flavor, texture, and keeping quality. This natural enhancer is called a biga in Italian. Unlike a sourdough starter, it does not add a sour flavor but rather a more dimensional one. I recommend it in the Beer Bread (page 291), Multigrain Bread (page 303), and Whole Wheat Sandwich Bread (page 299). If you would like to use it for other bread recipes, such as the Basic Hearth Bread (page 287), be sure to add an additional ⅛ teaspoon salt to balance the extra flour. Use the same flour as indicated in the bread dough recipe. Cut the biga into small pieces and allow it to soak in the water for about 1 hour before mixing the dough.

water	30 grams	2 tablespoons (30 ml)
bread flour	50 gram	¼ cup (lightly spooned into the cup and leveled off) plus 2 tablespoons
instant yeast	0.2 gram	1/16 teaspoon

MISE EN PLACE

- Thirty minutes ahead, weigh or measure the water and cover it.

MAKE THE BIGA

1. In a small bowl, whisk together the flour and yeast.

2. With a silicone spatula or wooden spoon, stir in the water. Continue stirring or kneading with your fingers for 3 to 5 minutes, or until very smooth and just barely tacky. If toward the end of mixing there are a few dry particles, add water by the drop.

LET THE BIGA RISE

3. Cover the bowl tightly with plastic wrap that has been lightly coated with non-stick cooking spray (or place it in a coated 1 cup/237 ml food storage container and cover it with a lid). Set it aside in a warm place, 80° to 85°F/27° to 29°C, until doubled in volume, almost ⅔ cup/150 ml. It will take 4 to 6 hours. If stored in a clear container, you'll see large bubbles on the sides. (See page 283 for suggested rising environments.)

4. With the back of your fingers, press down the biga to deflate it to its original size. Refrigerate the biga, preferably for 3 days before making the dough.

This chapter contains all the components for topping and filling cakes, pies, and pastry. Included are several basic buttercreams with flavor variations, mousseline (the ultimate buttercream), royal icing, whipped creams, pastry creams, and a wide variety of chocolate ganache. You will also learn how to make caramel sauce and glaze and meringue toppings for pies.

TOPPINGS AND FILLINGS

SOLUTIONS FOR POSSIBLE PROBLEMS

The sugar crystalizes when making a sugar syrup.

SOLUTIONS: If any sugar crystals land on the sides of the pan, use a wet brush to brush them down into the syrup. Avoid stirring the syrup after the sugar has completely dissolved and begins to boil.

Egg whites won't whip.

SOLUTIONS: Make sure the bowl, beater, and egg whites are entirely free of any oil or fat, including egg yolk. Avoid plastic bowls, which can retain residual oil. Use metal bowls. Glass is slippery and the whites don't beat as well.

Neoclassic Buttercream will not firm up after adding the butter.

SOLUTION: Make sure the mixture is completely cool to the touch before adding the butter.

Mousseline buttercream will not firm up and begins to separate after mixing the meringue into the butter.

SOLUTIONS: Use an instant-read thermometer to ensure that the temperature is between 65° to 70°F/19° to 21°C and adjust as needed. If not using a thermometer, try adjusting the temperature with just a small amount of the buttercream as described on page 343 in step 8. If all else fails, with your hands, squeeze out the liquid that has separated and pour it into a large measuring cup with a spout. On high speed, beat the remaining buttercream until it becomes smooth. Then gradually beat in the liquid. The resulting buttercream will be less airy but perfectly emulsified and silky smooth.

The buttercream has an off flavor.

SOLUTIONS: Butter readily absorbs other odors, so be sure to store butter and buttercream well wrapped. Buttercream frosted cakes, if refrigerated, should be stored in a container or covered with a cake dome or inverted bowl.

The ganache breaks and separates.

SOLUTIONS: Avoid stirring the ganache while it is cooling to room temperature. If you used heavy cream with a low percentage of butterfat, try reheating the ganache slightly and stirring in a little more heavy cream. An immersion blender works best for this because it does not to incorporate air.

The caramel is too dark even though the correct temperature guide was followed.

SOLUTIONS: Make sure your thermometer is accurate. Use a light colored silicone spatula to determine by eye the color of the caramel. It should be a deep amber. When the mixture approaches the desired finished temperature, be sure that the burner heat is no higher than medium-low, so that the temperature will not keep rising too much after the pan is removed from the heat. Remove the pan from the heat a little before it reaches the desired temperature or color, because the pan's residual heat will cause the temperature to rise.

Whipped Cream

Whipped cream is the loveliest of toppings for many types of pies and cakes. But when it needs to be held at room temperature or refrigerated for several hours, it can start to separate; stabilizing it with cornstarch or gelatin will help it keep longer. This is also useful if the cream in your area is lower in butterfat and difficult to whip.

Cornstarch is the lightest in texture and an excellent choice if the whipped cream will be refrigerated until shortly before serving. It will not hold up well at room temperature but it will keep for 2 days refrigerated.

Gelatin or lemon curd are the best choices if whipped cream has to stand at cool room temperature for several hours. The gelatin version will hold at a room temperature up to about 75°F/24°C for as long as 8 hours. The lemon curd variation will hold for as long as 6 hours.

MISE EN PLACE FOR ALL THREE VERSIONS

■ Cream whips best if it is as cold as possible, so it helps to refrigerate a medium metal bowl and the handheld mixer beaters alongside. If you are whipping 1½ cups/355 ml or less cream, a handheld mixer works better than a stand mixer.

LIGHTLY SWEETENED WHIPPED CREAM Makes 244 grams/2 cups

heavy cream	232 grams	1 cup (237 ml)
superfine sugar	13 grams	1 tablespoon
pure vanilla extract	.	1 teaspoon (5 ml)

1. At least 15 minutes before whipping, in a medium metal bowl, mix together the cream, sugar, and vanilla. Cover and refrigerate with the handheld mixer beaters alongside.

2. Using a handheld mixer, whip the mixture, starting on low speed and gradually raising the speed to medium-high as it thickens, until it mounds softly when dropped from a spoon (or just until stiff peaks form when the beater is raised if planning to pipe it).

(continued)

Heavy cream, also referred to as "heavy whipping cream," contains 56.6 percent water and 36 to 40 percent fat, averaging 36 percent. Whipping cream has only 30 percent fat. The higher the butterfat and the colder the cream, the easier it is to whip and the more stable the whipped cream. Do not use light cream.

Pasteurized cream, which is not heated to as high a temperature as ultrapasteurized, is more flavorful and more stable. Ultrapasteurized cream usually has additives to enable it to whip adequately. When non-ultrapasteurized cream is not available, my preference in ultrapasteurized is Organic Valley or Stonyfield, which are 40 percent butterfat.

Though heavy cream will not whip when it has been frozen and thawed, frozen heavy cream can be used for making ganache.

CORNSTARCH-STABILIZED WHIPPED CREAM Makes 244 grams/2 cups

heavy cream	232 grams	1 cup (237 ml), *divided*
pure vanilla extract	.	1 teaspoon (5 ml)
powdered sugar	14 grams	2 tablespoons
cornstarch	.	1 teaspoon

1. At least 15 minutes before whipping, into a medium metal bowl, pour 174 grams/¾ cup/177 ml of the cream and the vanilla. Cover and refrigerate with the handheld mixer beaters alongside.

2. In a small saucepan, whisk together the powdered sugar and cornstarch. Gradually whisk in the remaining cream.

3. Bring the mixture to a boil on low heat, stirring constantly with the whisk, just until thickened. It will not thicken until it comes to a full boil.

4. Immediately scrape the mixture into a small bowl or custard cup and allow it to cool just to room temperature. Cover until ready to whip the cream.

5. Using a handheld mixer, whip the reserved refrigerated cream just until traces of the beater marks begin to appear.

6. Continuing by hand with a whisk, add the cooled cream-cornstarch mixture in four additions, whisking lightly after each one. Whisk just until stiff peaks form when the whisk is lifted.

GELATIN-STABILIZED WHIPPED CREAM Makes 244 grams/2 cups

heavy cream	232 grams	1 cup (237 ml), *divided*
pure vanilla extract	.	1 teaspoon (5 ml)
powdered sugar	14 grams	2 tablespoons
powdered gelatin	.	1 teaspoon

1. At least 15 minutes before whipping, into a medium metal bowl, pour 174 grams/¾ cup/177 ml of the cream and the vanilla. Cover and refrigerate with the handheld mixer beaters alongside.

2. In a small saucepan, mix together the powdered sugar and gelatin. Gradually stir in the remaining 58 grams/¼ cup/59 ml cream.

3. Bring the mixture just to a boil on low heat, stirring constantly. It will thicken slightly.

4. Scrape the mixture into a small bowl or custard cup and allow it to cool just to room temperature or barely warm.

5. Using a handheld mixer, whip the reserved refrigerated cream just until traces of the beater marks begin to show. Add the cooled gelatin mixture in a steady stream, beating constantly. Whip just until stiff peaks form when the beater is raised.

Variations

LEMON CURD WHIPPED CREAM

Makes about 360 grams/2½ cups

Not only is this variation utterly delicious, but lemon curd also stabilizes the whipped cream, preventing it from becoming watery. It will keep for 2 days refrigerated.

Make the Lightly Sweetened Whipped Cream on page 329 but omit the sugar. When the beater marks begin to show distinctly, add 132 grams/½ cup Lemon Curd (page 40) and whip just until the mixture mounds softly when dropped from a spoon.

POMEGRANATE SYRUP

Makes about 300 grams/1 cup plus 1 tablespoon/222 ml

100% pure pomegranate juice, preferably POM Wonderful	382 grams	1½ cups (355 ml)
sugar, preferably superfine	175 grams	¾ cup plus 2 tablespoons
lemon juice, freshly squeezed and strained	.	1 teaspoon (5 ml)
heavy cream	174 grams	¾ cup (177 ml)

Have ready by the cooktop a 1 cup glass measure with a spout that has been lightly coated with nonstick cooking spray.

1. In a small saucepan, preferably nonstick, over medium-high heat, reduce the pomegranate juice to 127 grams/½ cup/118 ml. Remove from the heat and stir in the sugar until dissolved. Return to the heat and bring to a boil, stirring constantly to ensure that the sugar is dissolved completely.

2. Pour the pomegranate syrup into the prepared glass measure. Stir in the lemon juice. You should have about 300 grams/1 cup minus 1 tablespoon/222 ml. You will only need about two-thirds of it for the whipped cream, but can add more to taste or reserve the rest for garnishing the dessert or serving plate.

PINK POMEGRANATE WHIPPED CREAM

Makes about 366 grams/2¼ cups

Concentrating pomegranate juice to a glossy, thick, garnet colored syrup gives a lilting flavor to whipped cream and turns it a lovely pink color. The syrup also makes a stunning decoration when drizzled onto a dessert or serving plate. The whipped cream will keep for up to 2 days in the refrigerator but will need to be re-whisked lightly until soft peaks form when the whisk is lifted. The pomegranate syrup will keep for months in the refrigerator, although it will crystallize slightly after 3 weeks. It can be restored by reheating it.

3. Allow the syrup to cool, uncovered, to room temperature. Cover it and refrigerate for several hours until cold.

4. At least 15 minutes before whipping the cream, into a medium metal bowl pour the cream. Cover and refrigerate with the handheld mixer beaters alongside.

5. Whip the cream just until traces of the beater marks begin to show. Add about 211 grams/ ⅔ cup/158 ml of the cooled pomegranate syrup and continue whipping until stiff peaks form when the beater is lifted.

Neoclassic Buttercream

**MAKES 420 GRAMS/
2 CUPS BUTTERCREAM;
DOUBLE THE RECIPE
FOR A 9 INCH TWO-
LAYER CAKE OR 13 BY
9 INCH SHEET CAKE**

This is a silky smooth buttercream that can be flavored in many ways. Buttercream made with egg yolks not only has extra flavor, but because the yolks are also great emulsifiers they produce a silky texture. Classic buttercream, which is usually made with a sugar-water syrup, requires an accurate thermometer, but this version, which uses corn syrup, makes taking the temperature unnecessary. A handheld mixer works best for this amount, but if doubling the recipe a stand mixer is fine.

unsalted butter	227 grams	16 tablespoons (2 sticks)
3 (to 4) large egg yolks (see Baking Pearls, opposite)	56 grams	3½ tablespoons (52.5 ml)
superfine sugar	75 grams	¼ cup plus 2 tablespoons
corn syrup	82 grams	¼ cup (59 ml)
pure vanilla extract	.	1 teaspoon (5 ml)

MISE EN PLACE

▪ One hour ahead, set the butter on the counter at room temperature (70° to 75°F/21° to 23°C).

▪ Shortly before making the buttercream, into a medium bowl, weigh or measure the egg yolks.

▪ Have ready a 1 cup glass measure with a spout, lightly coated with nonstick cooking spray, near the cooktop.

MAKE THE BUTTERCREAM

1. With a handheld mixer on high speed, beat the egg yolks until light in color.

2. In a small saucepan, preferably nonstick, stir together the sugar and corn syrup until all the sugar is moistened.

3. Cook on medium heat, stirring constantly, until the sugar dissolves and the syrup is bubbling all over the surface with large bubbles. Immediately transfer the syrup to the glass measure to stop the cooking.

4. Add the syrup to the egg yolks, a little at a time, keeping it well away from the beaters to prevent it from spinning onto the sides of the bowl. (If using a stand mixer fitted with the whisk beater, begin by pouring in a small amount of syrup. Immediately beat on high speed for 5 seconds. Add the remaining syrup in three

If you are concerned about using raw egg yolks, use pasteurized eggs in the shell (see page xxiii).

The ratio of white to yolk in an egg can vary to such a degree that you may need 3 or 4 eggs for this recipe. It is therefore advisable to weigh or measure the separated yolks and add or reduce if needed.

When making the syrup for this neoclassic version, corn syrup replaces the water. The entire surface needs to be covered with bubbles to reach the proper temperature. When brought to a full boil, it reaches about 238°F/114°C, which is the same temperature as when making a classic buttercream.

Using a handheld mixer makes it easier to keep the syrup from spinning onto the sides of the bowl. You can add the syrup while a stand mixer is on; just take care not to drizzle the syrup onto the beaters.

The egg and syrup mixture must be completely cool to the touch before you add the butter.

parts, with the mixer off between additions.) For the last addition, use a silicone spatula to remove the syrup clinging to the glass measure and scrape it against the beater.

5. Continue beating on high speed for 5 minutes. Then allow the mixture to cool completely. To speed cooling, you can place the bowl in an ice water bath or in the refrigerator, stirring occasionally.

6. When the outside of the bowl feels cool to the touch, beat in the butter by the tablespoon on medium-high speed. The buttercream will not thicken completely until almost all of the butter has been added.

7. Beat in the vanilla on low speed until it is incorporated. If using a stand mixer, for a smoother, less airy consistency, switch to the flat beater and beat for an additional 2 minutes.

8. Place the buttercream in an airtight bowl. Use it at once or keep at room temperature for up to 4 hours. If keeping it longer, refrigerate the buttercream; before using, bring it to room temperature and beat it to restore the texture. To avoid curdling, do not beat when it is still cold.

STORE AIRTIGHT: room temperature, 6 hours; refrigerated, 1 week; frozen, 6 months.

(continued)

Make This Recipe Your Own

For a whole-egg recipe, replace the egg yolks with 1½ whole eggs (75 grams/4¾ tablespoons/70 ml). You will have 440 grams/2¼ cups buttercream. It will be slightly fluffier but also slightly less flavorful.

Golden syrup can be substituted in equal weight or measure for the corn syrup. It offers a lovely lilting butterscotch flavor. It will have a slight crunch until it stands for several hours.

Your favorite honey also can be substituted for the corn syrup. Use 112 grams/⅓ cup/79 ml.

Additions to the Completed Buttercream

CHOCOLATE BUTTERCREAM

Beat in 85 grams/3 ounces dark chocolate, 60% to 70% cacao, melted and cooled.

COFFEE BUTTERCREAM

Beat in 30 grams/2 tablespoons/30 ml coffee extract or 1 tablespoon/4 grams instant espresso powder, such as Medaglia d'Oro, dissolved in ½ teaspoon/2.5 ml water. This can also be added to the chocolate buttercream above for a mocha version.

LEMON OR ORANGE BUTTERCREAM

Beat in ¼ teaspoon/1.2 ml pure lemon or orange oil, preferably Boyajian; do not use extracts, which can have an off taste. (Alternatively, beat in 12 grams/2 tablespoons loosely packed finely grated zest.

STRAWBERRY BUTTERCREAM

Beat in 95 grams/⅓ cup strawberry butter, preferably American Spoon brand, or strained strawberry preserves. If using the preserves, add 1 teaspoon/5 ml freshly squeezed lemon juice.

Making Neoclassic Buttercream

Beat the yolks until light in color.

Cook the syrup until the entire surface is covered in bubbles.

Add the sugar syrup to the yolks in three parts.

Beat for 5 seconds between each addition.

Beat on high speed for 5 minutes.

Beat in the softened butter.

Chocolate Meringue Buttercream

**MAKES 500 GRAMS/
2¼ CUPS BUTTERCREAM**

This is a great chocolate buttercream to have in your repertoire, because it is silky smooth and airy, and has a great consistency for frosting. It is temperature sensitive but easy to make, and uses egg whites instead of yolks.

unsalted butter	227 grams	16 tablespoons (2 sticks)
2 large egg whites	60 grams	¼ cup (59 ml)
cream of tartar	.	¼ teaspoon
superfine sugar	100 grams	½ cup
dark chocolate, 60% to 62% cacao	142 grams	5 ounces

MISE EN PLACE

▪ About 1 hour ahead, set the butter on the counter at cool room temperature (65° to 70°F/19° to 21°C).

▪ Thirty minutes to 1 hour ahead, into a medium bowl, weigh or measure the egg whites, cream of tartar, and sugar. Stir until the sugar is moistened, and cover with plastic wrap.

▪ Coarsely chop the chocolate.

MAKE THE BUTTERCREAM

1. In a medium microwavable bowl, stirring with a silicone spatula every 15 seconds, heat the chocolate until almost completely melted. (Alternatively, melt the chocolate in the top of a double boiler over hot, not simmering, water—do not let the bottom of the container touch the water—stirring often with a silicone spatula.)

2. Remove the chocolate from the heat source and stir until it is fully melted. Let the chocolate cool until it is no longer warm to the touch but still fluid (80° to 85°F/27° to 29°C).

3. In the bowl of a stand mixer fitted with the flat beater, beat the butter on medium-high speed until creamy, about 1 minute. Set it aside in a cool place.

4. With a handheld mixer, beat the egg white mixture until foamy. Raise the speed to high and continue beating until glossy and curved peaks form when the beater is raised.

This buttercream is soft enough to accommodate almost double the amount of chocolate that can be added to the neoclassic egg yolk buttercream. It does not require a hot syrup, as it gets its stability from the chocolate.

If you prefer, it's fine to use pasteurized egg whites (see page xxiii).

5. Return the mixer bowl containing the butter to the stand and attach the whisk beater. Beat on medium-high speed for about 3 minutes or until it lightens in color but is no warmer than 70°F/21°C.

6. Scrape the meringue into the butter and beat on medium speed for about 2 minutes, until smooth and creamy, scraping down the sides of the bowl as needed. At first the mixture will look slightly curdled. If it starts to separate and become watery, check the temperature: It should feel cool, but be no lower than 65°F/19°C and no higher than 70°F/21°C. If too warm, set it in a bowl of ice water, stirring gently to chill it down before continuing to whisk. If too cool, suspend the bowl over a pan of simmering water (do not let the bottom of the bowl touch the water) and heat very briefly, stirring vigorously when the mixture just starts to melt slightly at the edges. Dip the bottom of the bowl in a larger bowl of ice water for a few seconds to cool it. Remove the bowl from the ice water and beat the buttercream by hand until smooth.

7. Whisk about 1 cup of the meringue mixture into the melted chocolate. Then scrape the chocolate mixture into the mixer bowl containing the rest of the meringue and beat on medium speed until evenly incorporated.

8. Place the buttercream in an airtight bowl. Use it at once, or keep at room temperature for up to 1 day. If keeping it longer, refrigerate the buttercream; before using, bring it to room temperature and beat to restore the texture. To avoid curdling, do not beat when it is still cold.

STORE AIRTIGHT: room temperature, 2 days; refrigerated, 10 days; frozen, 6 months.

White Chocolate Cream Cheese Frosting

**MAKES 822 GRAMS/
3½ CUPS FROSTING**

This delicious frosting is especially ideal for carrot and banana cakes and cupcakes. The white chocolate serves both as the sweetener and to emulsify the cream cheese and butter into a luxuriously creamy texture.

full-fat cream cheese	400 grams	1½ cups plus 1 tablespoon
unsalted butter	113 grams	8 tablespoons (1 stick)
white chocolate containing cocoa butter	300 grams	10.6 ounces
crème fraîche or full-fat sour cream	25 grams	1 tablespoon plus 2 teaspoons
pure vanilla extract	.	½ teaspoon (2.5 ml)

MISE EN PLACE

▪ Thirty minutes ahead, set the cream cheese and butter on the counter at cool room temperature (65° to 70°F/19° to 21°C). Cut the butter into 4 pieces.

▪ Coarsely chop the white chocolate.

MAKE THE FROSTING

1. In a medium microwavable bowl, stirring with a silicone spatula every 15 seconds, heat the white chocolate until almost completely melted. (Alternatively, melt the chocolate in the top of a double boiler over hot, not simmering, water—do not let the bottom of the container touch the water—stirring often with a silicone spatula.)

2. Remove the white chocolate from the heat source and stir until it is fully melted. Let the white chocolate cool until it is just slightly warm to the touch and still fluid (80° to 85°F/27° to 29°C).

3. In a food processor, process the cream cheese, butter, and crème fraîche for a few seconds until smooth and creamy. Scrape down the sides of the bowl.

4. Add the cooled melted white chocolate and pulse it in several times until it is smoothly incorporated.

5. Add the vanilla and pulse it in. For the smoothest silkiest texture, press the frosting through a medium-mesh strainer into a bowl.

STORE AIRTIGHT: cool room temperature, 2 hours; refrigerated, 1 week; frozen, 3 months.

Baking Pearl

The cream cheese and butter should be softened, but still cool (65° to 70°F/19° to 21°C).

Peanut Butter Cream Cheese Frosting

**MAKES 700 GRAMS/
3 CUPS FROSTING**

Peanut butter is a great addition to a cream cheese frosting, for both texture and flavor. It is also a delicious frosting for carrot and banana cakes and cupcakes. It takes only a few seconds to make.

smooth peanut butter, preferably Jif	266 grams	1 cup
full-fat cream cheese	224 grams	¾ cup plus 2 tablespoons
unsalted butter	113 grams	8 tablespoons (1 stick)
full-fat sour cream	20 grams	1 tablespoon plus 1 teaspoon
powdered sugar	100 grams	¾ cup (lightly spooned into the cup and leveled off) plus 2 tablespoons
pure vanilla extract	.	2 teaspoons (10 ml)

MISE EN PLACE

■ About 1 hour ahead, set the peanut butter, cream cheese, and butter on the counter at cool room temperature (65° to 70°F/19° to 21°C). Cut the butter into 4 pieces.

MAKE THE FROSTING

In a food processor, combine the peanut butter, cream cheese, butter, sour cream, powdered sugar, and vanilla. Process until smooth, creamy, and uniform in color, scraping down the sides of the bowl as needed.

STORE AIRTIGHT: cool room temperature, 2 hours; refrigerated, 1 week; frozen, 3 months.

Baking Pearl

The cream cheese and butter should be softened but still cool (65° to 70°F/19° to 21°C).

Light Italian Meringue Toppings for Pies

I love a fluffy meringue topping. Classic meringue usually has double the volume of sugar to egg whites, which helps to stabilize the meringue but also makes it, to my taste, too sweet. I have modified my meringue topping to use equal volume of sugar to egg white so that it's not too sweet. And to give it enough stability—so that it does not become watery on top of the pie—I make an Italian meringue. This means making a hot sugar syrup that is beaten into the egg whites. The syrup needs to be hot enough to stabilize the egg whites, but not too hot or it will break them down. An accurate thermometer will ensure that the syrup reaches the ideal temperature. If you do not have one, I also give a variation on the next page that is almost as stable without needing to take the temperature. I call it "neoclassic" because it was inspired by my Neoclassic Buttercream (page 332).

LIGHT ITALIAN MERINGUE Makes 225 grams/6½ cups

4 large egg whites	120 grams	½ cup (118 ml)
cream of tartar	.	½ teaspoon
sugar, preferably superfine	100 grams	½ cup
water	30 grams	2 tablespoons (30 ml)
pure vanilla extract	.	¼ teaspoon (1.2 ml)

MISE EN PLACE

■ Have ready a 1 cup glass measure with a spout (not coated with nonstick cooking spray) near the cooktop.

■ Into the bowl of a stand mixer, weigh or measure the egg whites and add the cream of tartar.

MAKE THE LIGHT ITALIAN MERINGUE

1. In a small heavy saucepan, preferably nonstick and with a spout, stir together the sugar and the water until the sugar is completely moistened. Cook on medium heat, stirring constantly, until the sugar dissolves and the syrup is bubbling. Stop stirring and turn down the heat to the lowest setting. (If using an electric cooktop remove it from the heat.)

It is best to avoid making meringue on humid days.

The mixer bowl and beater must be entirely free of any fat, which includes oil and egg yolk.

When making the syrup for the neoclassic version, corn syrup replaces the water. The entire surface needs to be covered with large bubbles to reach the proper temperature. When brought to a full boil it reaches about 230°F/110°C, which is not quite as high as the 236°F/113°C of the Italian meringue. It is not quite as stable but works well as a meringue topping for a pie. (Note: a classic Italian meringue reaches 248° to 250°F/120°C, but I use a lower temperature for a pie topping as it will continue to bake after topping the pie.)

If making a smaller amount of this recipe, using a handheld mixer instead of a stand mixer makes it easier to keep the syrup from spinning onto the sides of the bowl.

Light Italian Meringue and Neoclassic Italian Meringue are almost as light in texture as a Swiss meringue, in which the egg whites are heated with the sugar, but the temperature is not nearly as high as when a syrup is beaten into the egg whites. Therefore, Swiss meringue is not as stable and will water out more readily. All meringue shrinks slightly on standing but the Italian meringues hold up the best.

2. Attach the whisk beater and beat the egg whites and cream of tartar on medium-high speed until stiff peaks form when the beater is raised slowly.

3. Increase the heat on the cooktop and boil the syrup until an instant-read thermometer registers 236°F/113°C. Immediately pour the syrup into the glass measure to stop the cooking.

4. With the mixer off, pour a small amount of syrup over the whites. Immediately beat on high speed for 5 seconds. Stop the mixer and add one-third of the syrup. Beat on high speed for 5 seconds. Add the remaining syrup in two parts, with the mixer off between additions. For the last addition use a silicone scraper to remove the syrup clinging to the measure and scrape it against the beater.

5. Continue beating on medium speed for about 4 minutes or until the outside of the bowl is no longer hot to the touch. Beat in the vanilla.

NEOCLASSIC ITALIAN MERINGUE Makes 230 grams/7 cups

4 large egg whites	120 grams	½ cup (118 ml)
cream of tartar	.	½ teaspoon
sugar, preferably superfine	67 grams	⅓ cup
corn syrup	61 grams	3 tablespoons (45 ml)
pure vanilla extract	.	¼ teaspoon (1.2 ml)

MISE EN PLACE

■ Have ready a 1 cup glass measure with a spout (not coated with nonstick cooking spray) near the cooktop.

■ Into the bowl of a stand mixer, weigh or measure the egg whites and add the cream of tartar.

MAKE THE NEOCLASSIC ITALIAN MERINGUE

1. Attach the whisk beater and beat the egg whites and cream of tartar on medium-high speed until stiff peaks form when the beater is raised slowly.

2. In a small saucepan, preferably nonstick and with a spout, stir together the sugar and corn syrup until the sugar is completely moistened. Cook on medium heat, stirring constantly, until the sugar dissolves and the syrup is bubbling all over the surface with large bubbles. Immediately transfer the syrup to the glass measure to stop the cooking.

3. With the mixer off, pour a small amount of syrup over the whites. Immediately beat on high speed for 5 seconds. Stop the mixer and add one-third of the syrup. Beat on high speed for 5 seconds. Add the remaining syrup in two parts, with the mixer off between additions. For the last addition, use a silicone scraper to remove the syrup clinging to the measure and scrape it against the beater.

4. Continue beating on medium speed for about 4 minutes, or until the outside of the bowl is no longer hot to the touch. Beat in the vanilla.

STORE ITALIAN MERINGUES AIRTIGHT: room temperature, 2 hours; refrigerated, 2 days. You can rebeat to restore the texture but the volume will decrease by half.

Mousseline

MAKES 440 GRAMS/
2¼ CUPS MOUSSELINE;
DOUBLE THE RECIPE
FOR A 9 INCH TWO-
LAYER CAKE OR 13 BY
9 INCH SHEET CAKE

This is the queen of buttercreams. It has the lightest texture and holds up best at warmer temperatures, but it is difficult to make in hot and humid weather. The butter needs to be softened but cool, and high-fat butter works best. An accurate instant-read thermometer is imperative.

unsalted butter, preferably high-fat	227 grams	16 tablespoons (2 sticks)
2½ large egg whites	75 grams	¼ cup plus 1 tablespoon (74 ml)
cream of tartar	.	½ teaspoon
sugar, preferably superfine	100 grams	½ cup, *divided*
water	30 grams	2 tablespoons (30 ml)
pure vanilla extract	.	½ teaspoon (2.5 ml)
liqueur of your choice (optional)	42 to 90 grams	3 to 6 tablespoons (45 to 90 ml)

MISE EN PLACE

■ Thirty minutes to 1 hour ahead, set the butter on the counter at cool room temperature (65° to 70°F/19° to 21°C). The butter needs to be about 65°F/19°C.

■ Thirty minutes to 1 hour ahead, into a medium bowl, weigh or measure the egg whites and add the cream of tartar. Cover with plastic wrap.

■ Have ready a 1 cup glass measure with a spout (not coated with nonstick cooking spray) by the range.

MAKE THE MOUSSELINE

1. In the bowl of a stand mixer fitted with the flat beater, beat the butter on medium-high speed until creamy, about 1 minute. Set it aside in a cool place (no higher than 70°F/21°C).

2. In a small heavy saucepan, preferably nonstick and with a spout, stir together 75 grams/¼ cup plus 2 tablespoons of the sugar and the water until all of the sugar is moistened. Heat on medium, stirring constantly, until the sugar dissolves and the mixture is bubbling. Stop stirring and reduce the heat to low. (On an electric range remove the pan from the heat.)

3. With a handheld mixer, beat the egg whites on medium-low speed until foamy. Raise the speed to high and beat until soft peaks form when the beater is raised. Gradually beat in the remaining 25 grams/2 tablespoons sugar, until stiff peaks form when the beater is raised slowly.

Make This Recipe Your Own

See Additions to Neoclassic Buttercream (page 334). Use a liqueur that is compatible with your choice of additions.

It is best to avoid making meringue on humid days.

The mixer bowl and beater must be entirely free of any fat, which includes oil and egg yolk.

If doubling the recipe, it's still fine to use a stand mixer for the egg whites, but be sure to avoid letting the syrup hit the beaters so that it doesn't spin it onto the sides of the bowl.

The mousseline becomes spongy and fluffy on standing, which is lovely once on the cake. If you don't use it right away, whisk it lightly by hand to maintain a silky texture before applying it to the cake. Do not, however, rebeat chilled mousseline until it has reached 70°F/21°C; otherwise it may break down. If this happens, see Solutions for Possible Problems (page 328).

4. Increase the heat under the sugar syrup and continue to boil the syrup for a few minutes until an instant-read thermometer reads 248° to 250°F/120°C. Immediately pour the syrup into the glass measure to stop the cooking.

5. Beat the syrup into the egg whites in a steady stream. Don't allow the syrup to fall on the beaters or they will spin it onto the sides of the bowl. Use a silicone spatula to remove the syrup clinging to the measure.

6. Lower the speed to medium and continue beating for up to 2 minutes. Refrigerate the meringue for 5 to 10 minutes, until 70°F/21°C. Whisk it after the first 5 minutes to test and equalize the temperature.

7. Set the mixer bowl containing the butter on the stand and attach the whisk beater. Beat on medium-high speed for about 3 minutes or until it lightens in color and is no warmer than 70°F/21°C.

8. Scrape the meringue into the butter and beat on medium speed until smooth and creamy, about 2 minutes, scraping down the sides of the bowl as necessary. At first the mixture will look slightly curdled. If it starts to separate and become watery, check the temperature: It should feel cool, but be no lower than 68°F/20°C and no higher than 70°F/21°C. If too warm, set it in a bowl of ice water, stirring gently to chill it down before continuing to whisk. If too cool, suspend the bowl over a pan of simmering water (do not let the bottom of the bowl touch the water) and heat for just a few seconds, stirring vigorously when the mixture just starts to melt slightly at the edges. Dip the bottom of the bowl in a larger bowl of ice water for a few seconds to cool it. Remove the bowl from the ice water and beat the buttercream by hand until smooth. If the mixture breaks down and will not come together, it can still be rescued. See Solutions for Possible Problems, page 328.

9. Gradually beat in the vanilla and the liqueur, if using.

STORE AIRTIGHT: room temperature, 1 day; refrigerated, 3 days; frozen, 2 months.

Making Mousseline

Cook the sugar syrup until bubbling.

Beat the meringue until stiff peaks form.

(continued)

Making Mousseline (cont'd.)

Pour in the sugar syrup.

Beat the butter until light in color.

The butter and meringue should be about the same temperature.

The buttercream will be slightly curdled at the beginning.

The finished buttercream will be smooth.

Classic Ganache

MAKES 466 GRAMS/
1¾ CUPS GANACHE;
MAKE 1½ TIMES THE
RECIPE FOR A 9 INCH
TWO-LAYER CAKE OR
13 BY 9 INCH SHEET
CAKE

PLAN AHEAD: Make the ganache several hours before using.

Ganache is arguably the most perfect way to experience the full flavor of dark chocolate. This simple mixture of dark chocolate and heavy cream is the basis of chocolate truffles, and makes a smooth, creamy, and intensely chocolate frosting. The flavor is entirely dependent on the quality of chocolate you choose.

heavy cream	232 grams	1 cup (237 ml)
dark chocolate, 60% to 62% cacao	227 grams	8 ounces
pure vanilla extract	.	2 teaspoons (10 ml)
liqueur of your choice, or additional heavy cream	28 grams	2 tablespoons (30 ml)

MISE EN PLACE

- Into a food processor, break the chocolate into pieces.

- Into a 2 cup glass measure with a spout or into a small saucepan, weigh or measure the cream.

- Have a fine-mesh strainer suspended over a medium glass bowl.

MAKE THE GANACHE

1. Process the chocolate until very fine.

2. In the glass measure, in the microwave, scald the cream: Heat it to the boiling point; small bubbles will form around the periphery. (Alternatively, scald it in a saucepan over medium heat, stirring often.)

3. With the motor running, pour the cream through the feed tube into the chocolate in a steady stream. Process for a few seconds until smooth, scraping the sides of the bowl as needed. Pulse in the vanilla and liqueur or extra cream.

4. Press the ganache through the strainer into a bowl and scrape any mixture clinging to the underside of the strainer. Let it sit for 1 hour.

5. Cover it with plastic wrap and let it sit for several hours, until the mixture reaches a soft frosting consistency (70° to 75°F/21° to 24°C).

STORE AIRTIGHT: cool room temperature, 3 days; refrigerated, 2 weeks; frozen, 3 months.

(continued)

Baking Pearls

Ganache has the best frosting consistency at around 80°F/27°C. To restore it to frosting consistency if frozen, it is best to thaw it overnight in the refrigerator and then allow it to sit at room temperature until spreadable. If necessary, soften it in a microwave with 3 second bursts, stirring gently to ensure that it does not overheat or incorporate any air, or in a double boiler set over hot, not simmering, water. (Alternatively, set a glass of hot water in a microwave or an insulated food container with the ganache and allow the ganache to sit for about 30 minutes.)

For a spreadable consistency that does not separate from a cake layer, it is important to use the specified chocolate percentage. If using a higher percentage chocolate use the following guidelines, based on 227 grams/8 ounces of dark chocolate:

For 63% to 64% cacao chocolate, use 283 grams cream (1¼ cups/288 ml).

For 66% cacao chocolate, use 312 grams cream (about 1⅓ cups/318 ml).

For 70% cacao chocolate, use 340 grams cream (about 1½ cups/347 ml).

If using the 2 tablespoons liqueur you will need to subtract the 28 grams (2 tablespoons/30 ml) from the cream.

Ganache makes an excellent crumb coating for a cake. After it has thickened but before it has set completely, pour some of the ganache on top of the cake and use a long metal spatula to spread it in a thin layer over the surface. By the time the rest of the ganache has thickened enough to spread and create swirls or a smooth finish, the crumb coating will have set, sealing in any crumbs.

Make This Recipe Your Own

For a lighter and airy ganache you can add softened unsalted butter, preferably high-fat. Use about one-sixth the weight of the chocolate in butter (4.7 grams/1 teaspoon butter per 28 grams/1 ounce chocolate). Stir it into the ganache immediately after straining it.

A touch of cayenne or chipotle powder (⅜ to 1 teaspoon) will give the ganache a long finish similar to that of a fine red wine. I call it "Wicked Good Ganache" because it sings in the mouth!

To enrich the flavor and produce an incredibly smooth texture and glossier appearance, replace the liqueur or extra cream with the following:

GANACHE ENRICHMENT
Makes about 110 grams/6 tablespoons/89 ml

corn syrup	82 grams	¼ cup (59 ml)
unsweetened chocolate, chopped	32 grams	1.25 ounces

In a small bowl or custard cup, heat the corn syrup in the microwave in 3 second bursts, until almost boiling. Stir in the chocolate until fully incorporated. Pulse it into the ganache right after adding the cream, or wait until the ganache has cooled to room temperature and stir it in. (Ganache can be stirred when just made and still hot, but should not be stirred as it cools if it is above 86°F/30°C or it will break.)

Making Classic Ganache

Place the coarsely chopped chocolate in a food processor.

Process the chocolate until fine.

Pour the hot cream into the chocolate with the motor running.

Press the ganache through a strainer into a bowl.

Ganache Drizzle Glaze

**MAKES 212 GRAMS/
A FULL ¾ CUP**

This consistency of ganache is ideal for plating and for drizzling, for example on cream puffs and éclairs. It is best made shortly before using but can be reheated in 3 second bursts in the microwave, or in a double boiler.

dark chocolate, 60% to 62% cacao	113 grams	4 ounces
heavy cream, hot	113 grams	½ cup minus ¾ teaspoon (115 ml)

1. Finely chop the chocolate.

2. In a small microwavable bowl, stirring with a silicone spatula every 15 seconds, heat the chocolate until almost completely melted. (Alternatively, melt the chocolate in the top of a double boiler over hot, not simmering water—do not let the bottom of the container touch the water—stirring often with a silicone spatula.) Remove the chocolate from the heat source and stir until fully melted.

3. Pour the hot cream on top of the chocolate and stir gently until completely smooth. The mixture should drop thickly when dropped from the spatula. If it is too thin, let it cool for a few minutes before drizzling or piping.

4. Pour the glaze into a disposable pastry bag or a quart-size reclosable freezer bag. Cut a very small semicircle from the tip or one corner and drizzle the glaze.

Dark Chocolate Malt Ganache

MAKES 630 GRAMS/ 2½ CUPS GANACHE, ENOUGH FOR A 9 INCH TWO-LAYER CAKE OR 13 BY 9 INCH SHEET CAKE

PLAN AHEAD: Make the ganache several hours before using.

Malt adds a delicious flavor accent to chocolate, making it more mellow and full flavored.

dark chocolate 60% to 62% cacao	227 grams	8 ounces
heavy cream	290 grams	1¼ cups (296 ml)
malt powder	84 grams	¾ cup
light corn syrup	41 grams	2 tablespoons (30 ml)

Baking Pearls

Ganache has the best frosting consistency at around 80°F/ 27°C. To restore it to frosting consistency if frozen, it is best to thaw it overnight in the refrigerator and then allow it to sit at room temperature until spreadable. If necessary, soften it in a microwave with 3 second bursts, stirring gently to ensure that it does not overheat or incorporate any air, or in a double boiler set over hot, not simmering, water. (Alternatively, set a glass of hot water in a microwave or in an insulated food container with the ganache and allow the ganache to sit for about 30 minutes.)

For a spreadable consistency that doesn't separate from a cake layer, it is important to use the specified chocolate percentage.

MISE EN PLACE

- Into a food processor, break the chocolate into pieces.

- Into a 4 cup glass measure with a spout or a small saucepan, weigh or measure the cream. Whisk in the malt powder and corn syrup until the malt is dissolved.

- Have a fine-mesh strainer suspended over a medium glass bowl.

MAKE THE GANACHE

1. Process the chocolate until very fine.

2. In the glass measure, in the microwave, scald the cream mixture: Heat it to the boiling point; small bubbles will form around the periphery. (Alternatively, scald it in a saucepan over medium heat, stirring often.)

3. With the motor running, pour the cream mixture through the feed tube in a steady stream. Process for a few seconds until smooth, scraping the sides of the bowl as needed.

4. Press the ganache through the strainer and let it sit for 1 hour.

5. Cover the bowl with plastic wrap and let it sit for several hours, until the mixture reaches a soft frosting consistency (70° to 75°F/21° to 24°C).

STORE AIRTIGHT: cool room temperature, 3 days; refrigerated, 2 weeks; frozen, 3 months.

Milk Chocolate Ganache

**MAKES 673 GRAMS/5¼
CUPS FOR FILLING; 731
GRAMS/5½ CUPS FOR
FROSTING**

This ganache, reminiscent of a chocolate bar, is for the many milk chocolate lovers. It makes a luscious, creamy filling for the Milk Chocolate Caramel Tart (page 263) and is also excellent to use to frost a cake, but will require the larger amount of heavy cream for a spreadable consistency.

Baking Pearls

Ganache has the best frosting consistency at around 80°F/27°C. To restore it to frosting consistency if frozen, it is best to thaw it overnight in the refrigerator and then allow it to sit at room temperature until spreadable. If necessary, soften it in a microwave with 3 second bursts, stirring gently to ensure that it does not overheat or incorporate any air, or in a double boiler set over hot, not simmering, water. (Alternatively, set a glass of hot water in a microwave or in an insulated food container with the ganache and allow the ganache to sit for about 30 minutes.)

If using milk chocolate with lower than 40% cacao, the filling will be sweeter and less firm, so you will need to increase the cacao percentage by adding unsweetened chocolate. Calculate how much you need based on the difference in percentage: For each 1% below 40%, you will need 1 gram unsweetened chocolate per 100 grams milk chocolate. For example, if your milk chocolate is 35%, which is 5% lower than 40%, you will need 5 grams unsweetened chocolate for every 100 grams of milk chocolate, which equals 22.7 grams for 454 grams/1 pound.

milk chocolate, 40% cacao, chopped (see Baking Pearls, left), preferably Valrhona	454 grams	1 pound
heavy cream	232 grams for filling	1 cup (237 ml) for filling
	290 grams for frosting	1¼ cups (296 ml) for frosting
corn syrup	34 grams	1 tablespoon plus 2 teaspoons (25 ml)

MISE EN PLACE

- Into a food processor, break the chocolate into pieces.

- Into a 2 cup glass measure with a spout or into a small saucepan, weigh or measure the cream.

- Have a fine-mesh strainer suspended over a medium glass bowl.

MAKE THE GANACHE

1. Process the chocolate until very fine.

2. Pour the corn syrup over the chocolate.

3. In the glass measure, in the microwave, scald the cream: Heat it to the boiling point; small bubbles will form around the periphery. (Alternatively, scald it in a small saucepan over medium heat, stirring often.)

4. With the motor running, pour the cream through the feed tube in a steady stream. Process for a few seconds until smooth, scraping the sides of the bowl as needed. If the cream was not hot enough and the chocolate is not melted completely, scrape the ganache into a bowl and heat it as described in the Baking Pearls.

5. Press the ganache through the strainer. If using for a filling, reheat it if necessary to a pourable consistency. If using as a frosting, let it sit for 1 hour.

6. Cover the bowl with plastic wrap and let it sit for several hours, until the mixture reaches a soft frosting consistency (70° to 75°F/21° to 24°C).

STORE AIRTIGHT: cool room temperature, 2 days; refrigerated, 2 weeks; frozen, 3 months.

Chocolate Mousse Ganache

**MAKES 330 GRAMS/
2 CUPS GANACHE;
DOUBLE THE RECIPE
FOR A 9 INCH TWO-
LAYER CAKE OR 13 BY
9 INCH SHEET CAKE**

This light whipped ganache could easily stand alone as a chocolate mousse dessert. Proportionally, it uses twice as much cream as the classic ganache, and can be whipped to a much lighter consistency.

dark chocolate, 53% to 62% cacao	113 grams	4 ounces
heavy cream	232 grams	1 cup (237 ml)
pure vanilla extract	.	1 teaspoon (5 ml)

MISE EN PLACE

- Into a food processor, break the chocolate into pieces.

- Into a 2 cup glass measure with a spout or into a small saucepan, weigh or measure the cream.

MAKE THE GANACHE

1. Process the chocolate until very fine.

2. In the glass measure, in the microwave, scald the cream: Heat it to the boiling point; small bubbles will form around the periphery. (Alternatively, scald it in a small saucepan over medium heat, stirring often.)

3. With the motor running, pour the cream through the feed tube in a steady stream and continue processing for a few seconds until smooth.

4. Pour the mixture into the bowl of a stand mixer and refrigerate until cold, 40 minutes to an hour, stirring after the first 30 minutes. (You can speed chilling by setting the bowl in an ice water bath and stirring frequently.) Do not allow the mixture to get too cold or it will be too stiff to incorporate air. The ideal temperature is 65° to 68°F/20°C.

5. Add the vanilla, and with the whisk beater, beat on low speed for about 30 seconds, or just until the mixture forms very soft floppy peaks when the beater is raised. It will continue to thicken after a few minutes at room temperature. The safest way to prevent overbeating is to use the stand mixer until the ganache starts to thicken and then continue with a whisk.

STORE AIRTIGHT: cool room temperature, 1 day; refrigerated, 1 week; frozen, 3 months.

Baking Pearl

If the mixture becomes over-beaten and grainy, you can restore it by melting, chilling, and rebeating it.

Caramel Sauce and Glaze

**MAKES 300 GRAMS/
1 CUP/237 ML GLAZE**

Satiny and pleasingly sticky, caramel is one of the most delicious additions to cakes and pastries. The longer the caramel cooks, the darker and less sweet it becomes. You can judge the color by eye or with an accurate instant-read thermometer. Cream of tartar and corn syrup both help prevent crystallization in the finished caramel sauce.

unsalted butter	28 grams	2 tablespoons
heavy cream	87 grams	¼ cup plus 2 tablespoons (89 ml)
sugar, preferably superfine	200 grams	1 cup
corn syrup	41 grams	2 tablespoons (30 ml)
cream of tartar (optional)	.	⅜ teaspoon
water	59 grams	¼ cup (59 ml)
pure vanilla extract	.	2 teaspoons (10 ml)

MISE EN PLACE

▪ About 30 minutes ahead, cut the butter into a few pieces and set it on the counter at room temperature (65° to 75°F/19° to 24°C).

▪ Into a 1 cup glass measure with a spout, weigh or measure the cream. Heat in the microwave until hot, then cover it.

▪ Have ready a 2 cup glass measure with a spout, lightly coated with nonstick cooking spray, near the cooktop.

MAKE THE SAUCE

1. In a heavy 6 cup saucepan, preferably nonstick, stir together the sugar, corn syrup, cream of tartar, if using, and water until all the sugar is moistened.

2. Heat, stirring constantly with a silicone spatula, until the sugar dissolves and the syrup is bubbling. Stop stirring and let it boil undisturbed until it turns a deep amber and the temperature reaches 370°F/188°C or a few degrees below, as the temperature will continue to rise. Remove it from the heat as soon as it reaches temperature.

3. Slowly and carefully pour the hot cream into the caramel. It will bubble up furiously.

(continued)

4. Use a silicone spatula or wooden spoon to stir the mixture gently, scraping the thicker part that settles on the bottom. Return it to a very low heat, continuing to stir gently for 1 minute, until the mixture is uniform in color and the caramel is fully dissolved.

5. Remove the caramel from the heat and gently stir in the butter until incorporated. The mixture will be a little streaky but will become uniform once cooled and stirred.

6. Pour the caramel into the prepared glass measure and let it cool for 3 minutes. Gently stir in the vanilla and let it to cool until room temperature and thickened, stirring it gently once or twice.

STORE AIRTIGHT: room temperature, 3 days; refrigerated, 1 month.

Making Caramel Sauce and Glaze

Cook the caramel until almost 370°F/188°C.

Stir in the hot cream.

Stir in the butter.

Scrape the caramel into a glass measuring cup.

Royal Icing

MAKES 530 GRAMS/2¼ CUPS ICING

Royal icing is both decorative and useful as an edible "glue" to attach other elements such as candies, edible glitter, and sparkling colored sugar, especially for Holiday Cookies (page 50) and Gingerbread Folks (page 53). Royal icing is easy to make but also can be purchased at cake decorating supply stores.

powdered sugar	460 grams	4 cups (lightly spooned into the cup and leveled off)
3 large egg whites	90 grams	¼ cup plus 2 tablespoons (89 ml)

MISE EN PLACE

- Into the bowl of a stand mixer, weigh or measure the powdered sugar.

- Into a 1 cup glass measure with a spout, weigh or measure the egg whites.

MAKE THE ROYAL ICING

1. Pour the egg whites into the sugar.

2. Attach the whisk beater to the stand mixer and beat on low speed until the sugar is moistened.

3. Gradually raise the speed to high and beat until the icing is very glossy, with stiff peaks that curve slightly when the beater is raised slowly (about 6 minutes). If necessary, scrape down the sides of the bowl. If the icing is too thin, beat in more powdered sugar.

4. Use a silicone spatula to scrape the mixture into a small bowl. Keep the bowl covered with a damp towel.

STORE AIRTIGHT in a glass container (plastic is petroleum based and can break down the icing): refrigerated, 3 days. Rebeat lightly before using.

(continued)

Baking Pearls

It is best to avoid making royal icing on humid days.

The mixer bowl, beater, spatula, small bowl, pastry bag, and decorating tips must be entirely free of any fat, which includes oil and egg yolk.

When piping decorations, be sure to keep the pastry tip covered with a damp cloth when not in use, so that the icing doesn't harden in the tip.

½ teaspoon/2.5 ml edible glycerine, available in cake decorating supply stores, will keep the royal icing soft longer.

Make This Recipe Your Own

It's fine to use pasteurized egg whites. Also, meringue powder, available in cake decorating supply stores, can be substituted for the egg white. Replace the 3 egg whites with 30 grams/ 3 tablespoons meringue powder and 89 grams/ 6 tablespoons/89 ml warm water. It will keep for up to 2 weeks and does not require refrigeration.

If you want to add food color to royal icing, use only a variety that is free of fat, such as liquid or powdered food color.

For a light chocolate royal icing, add 7 grams/ 1½ tablespoons sifted unsweetened cocoa powder to the powdered sugar.

If you would like to use the royal icing to paint a thin coat onto cookies (as for Holiday Cookies, page 50), thin it with water, a few drops at a time, until when lifted with a spoon it disappears completely back into the surface. Use a fine artist's brush reserved for this purpose to brush it evenly onto the cookie. Immediately sprinkle with sparkling sugar or edible glitter and attach any other decorative elements. Work quickly, as royal icing dries and hardens very quickly.

Pastry Cream

**MAKES 334 GRAMS/
1⅓ CUPS**

BAKING EQUIPMENT:
One small piano wire
whisk, preferably with
10 loops

Pastry cream is the classic filling for cream puffs and éclairs. I also give a variation with whipped cream folded in, called Chiboust cream, which is richer and lighter in texture. This recipe will enable you to make either version, which can be flavored with chocolate, coffee, or your favorite liqueur.

sugar	50 grams	¼ cup
vanilla bean, split lengthwise OR vanilla bean paste or pure vanilla extract	.	1 inch piece OR ½ teaspoon (2.5 ml)
1 large egg	50 grams	3 tablespoons plus ½ teaspoon (47.5 ml)
cornstarch	14 grams	1½ tablespoons
half-and-half or milk	242 grams	1 cup (237 ml), *divided*
fine sea salt	.	a pinch
unsalted butter	10 grams	2 teaspoons

MISE EN PLACE

▪ Have ready a medium-mesh strainer suspended over a 1 cup glass measure with a spout or a small bowl.

▪ In a small saucepan, preferably nonstick, place the sugar and vanilla bean, if using. Use your fingers to rub the seeds into the sugar.

▪ Into a small bowl, weigh or measure the egg.

MAKE THE PASTRY CREAM

1. Whisk the cornstarch into the egg. Gradually add 60 grams/¼ cup/59 ml of the half-and-half, whisking until the mixture is smooth and the cornstarch is dissolved.

2. Into the sugar mixture in the saucepan, stir in the remaining half-and-half and the salt. Over medium heat, bring the mixture to a full boil, stirring constantly.

3. Whisk 2 tablespoons of the hot half-and-half mixture into the egg mixture. Pass the egg mixture through the strainer into the 1 cup glass measure.

4. Remove the vanilla bean from the half-and-half mixture and bring the mixture back to a boil over medium heat.

(continued)

Baking Pearls

For a velvety smooth pastry cream, it is helpful to use a piano wire whisk.

Once thickened, do not whisk the pastry cream vigorously; otherwise the cornstarch can break down and the pastry cream thin.

The used vanilla bean pod can be rinsed and dried and added to the sugar bin or a bottle of vanilla extract.

Make This Recipe Your Own

You can make the following additions to the pastry cream:

Stir 42 grams/1.5 ounces grated dark chocolate, preferably 60% to 62% cacao, into the hot pastry cream until evenly incorporated.

In step 2, to the sugar mixture add 2 teaspoons instant espresso powder, such as Medaglio d'Oro, or powdered instant coffee. If desired, stir 1 tablespoon/15 ml Kahlúa into the hot pastry cream.

Gently whisk up to 1 tablespoon/ 15 ml liqueur into the hot or cooled pastry cream.

Variation

CHIBOUST CREAM
Makes 450 grams/2⅓ cups

This cream was named for the pastry chef who created Le Gâteau St. Honoré, an elaborate confection of puff pastry, caramel-topped cream puffs, and Grand Marnier imbued Chiboust cream.

Up to 1 hour before filling the pastry, whip 116 grams/½ cup/ 118 ml heavy cream just until soft peaks form when the beater is raised. Use a whisk to fold it into the chilled pastry cream.

5. Quickly add all of the egg mixture, whisking rapidly. Continue whisking rapidly for 20 to 30 seconds, being sure to go into the bottom edge of the pan. The pastry cream will start to bubble and become very thick.

6. Remove the pan from the heat and gently whisk in the butter. If using, whisk in the vanilla bean paste or extract.

7. Immediately pour the mixture into a bowl and place a piece of plastic wrap lightly coated with nonstick cooking spray directly on top of the cream to keep a skin from forming.

COOL THE PASTRY CREAM

8. Let the pastry cream cool to room temperature, about 45 minutes, then refrigerate until cold.

STORE AIRTIGHT: refrigerated, 3 days. Do not freeze, as the pastry cream will thin on thawing.

Making Pastry Cream

Rub the vanilla bean seeds into the sugar.

Temper the egg mixture with a little hot half-and-half.

Strain the tempered egg mixture.

Bring the half-and-half mixture back to a boil.

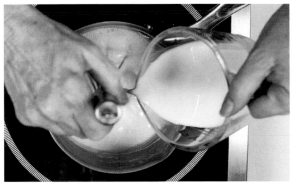

Whisk the strained egg mixture into the half-and-half.

Whisk until thickened.

Transfer the pastry cream to a bowl.

Press plastic wrap on the surface of the pastry cream to prevent a skin from forming.

Chocolate Curls

This lovely garnish for cakes, pies, or tarts can be made with dark, milk, or white chocolate.

1. Set a block of chocolate in a warm place, under a lamp, or warm it with 3 second bursts in a microwave, turning it over several times. It should remain solid but just softened enough so that you can scrape off malleable curls.

2. Use a paper towel to hold the chocolate and a sharp vegetable peeler to form the curls. Start at the upper edge and bring the peeler toward you. Firmer pressure will form thicker curls.

3. Use a wooden skewer to lift the curls gently and set them on top of the dessert as a garnish. (Alternatively, you can use a melon baller to scrape the chocolate into flakes, allowing them to fall directly onto the top of the dessert.)

Making Chocolate Curls

Use a vegetable peeler to shave off curls.

ACKNOWLEDGMENTS

This is my eleventh cookbook, and I have been blessed with a production team of talented professionals. Thank you to the production crew: **Woody Wolston** of team "RoseWood," who is an equal partner in every aspect of this book and who was the stylist for all the step-by-step photos; **Stephanie Fletcher**, editor, who gave me the idea for this, my dream book, of step-by-step photos and, with full support and extraordinarily detailed attention, expertly shepherded it to completion. **Matthew Septimus**, gifted photographer and generous dear friend, who joyfully made the long trip from Brooklyn so many times to capture all the exceptional step-by-step photos here on a mountaintop in Hope, New Jersey (and his daughter, **Nora**, who took the photo of our production group on page 362); **Marina Padakis Lowry**, dedicated managing editor and baker, and **Jamie Selzer**, production editor; **Alison Lew** of Vertigo Design NYC, who after three books has become a valued friend, and who created the book's inspired design and layout; **Suzanne Fass**, copyeditor par excellence. **Deri Reed**, proofreader, and **Zach Townsend**, a second set of eyes and delightful friend with whom I've shared many an adventure here and in France; **Erin Jeanne McDowell**, amazing food stylist for the beauty shots and even more amazing friend; Erin's assistant, **Katie (Kaitlin Wayne)**, who came from Toronto, Canada, to assist with the beauty shots; **Joan Shapiro**, indexer; **Jessica Gilo**, marketing director, and **Sari Kamin**, publicity manager, whose creativity and enthusiasm made the most of our book promotion.

Special Mentions: **Dan O'Malley** of American Products Group, who launched Rose's Signature Series and has become a valued friend; my longtime friends **Robert and Nicole Laub** of Harold Import Co., who help me produce and market my Rose Levy Beranbaum bakeware line of specialty baking equipment, especially Rose's Perfect Pie Plate. **Organic Valley**, who supplied me with vast quantities of the best butter and dairy for all the recipe testing; **Nita Livvix** of Clabber Girl, who supplied the best Rumford baking powder and cornstarch; **Gretchen Goehrend** of India Tree, who unearthed and supplied the most delicious sugars. **Valrhona** and **Guittard**, who supplied their fabulous chocolates; **Mary Rodgers** and **Rachel Litner** of Cuisinart and **Beth Robinson** of KitchenAid, whose mixers and food processors make us all better bakers; **Mike Quinlan** of Nordic Ware, whose excellent pans create beautifully shaped cakes.

Brad Pile of USA Pan, whose cake and loaf pans are without equal; **Michael Taylor** of Brød & Taylor, whose bread proofer is a great asset for bread baking; **Mark Kelly** of Lodge, whose cast-iron pizza pan makes the best pizza and crisp bottom crusts for pies and tarts; **James Baldwin** of Stretch-Tite, for his miles/kilometers of the best plastic wrap; the wonderful **Giovannucci/Esposito family** of Fante's and the lovely **Lisa Mansour** of NY Cake, all of whom make it possible for the home baker to have access to high-quality commercial equipment and imported specialty pans.

This book has been enriched by the inspiration of longtime friends and colleagues.

I am deeply grateful to our international community of bloggers, both professional and home bakers, for their continuous encouragement through their appreciation and feedback. **Lisa Yockelson**, esteemed colleague and dearest friend, who generously contributed her chocolate biscotti recipe. **Sally Longo**, who contributed one of her special family recipes—the fabulous

Date Nut Roll Cookies; **Lindsay Stewart**, pastry chef at Natirar, who inspired the Milk Chocolate Caramel Tart; **Hector Wong**, who remains a great springboard for creative ideas; our neighbors **the Meneguses**, for their truly free-range eggs and true friendship.

Love to my parents, **Lillian Wager Levy** and **Robert Maxwell Levy**, who are always with me in spirit and from whom I derived my love of profession and work ethic. I especially thank them for giving me **Michael Levy**, the best brother in the world.

Unending and infinite appreciation always goes to my husband, **Elliott**, who continues to give me 100 percent enablement and invaluable wisdom.

Me with the fantastic photography team: food stylist assistant Katie Wayne, Woody, food stylist Erin McDowell, and photographer Matthew Septimus

APPENDIX

Ingredient Equivalences and Substitutions

FOR	SUBSTITUTE
1 cup/217 grams light brown sugar	1 cup/200 grams granulated sugar plus 1 tablespoon/15 ml/20 grams light molasses
1 cup/239 grams dark brown sugar	1 cup/200 grams granulated sugar plus 2 tablespoons/30 ml/40 grams light molasses
1 pound unsalted butter	1 pound lightly salted butter. Remove 1 teaspoon/6 grams salt from the recipe.
1 cup/237 ml whole milk	1 cup minus 1 tablespoon/222 ml half-and-half. Remove 1 tablespoon/14 grams butter from the recipe and add 2 tablespoons/30 ml water.
1 cup/237 ml half-and-half	¾ cup/177 ml whole milk plus ¼ cup/59 ml heavy cream or ½ cup/118 ml whole milk plus ½ cup/118 ml light cream
1 cup/100 grams sifted bleached cake flour	¾ cup/85 grams sifted bleached all-purpose flour plus 2 tablespoons/20 grams potato starch or cornstarch
1 cup/114 grams sifted bleached all-purpose flour	1 cup plus 2 tablespoons/114 grams sifted bleached cake flour or ¾ cup plus 1½ tablespoons/114 grams Wondra flour
1 cup/114 grams lightly spooned pastry flour	⅔ cup/76 grams lightly spooned bleached all-purpose flour plus ⅓ cup/38 grams lightly spooned bleached cake flour
1 teaspoon instant yeast	1¼ teaspoons active dry yeast or 1½ teaspoons packed fresh (cake) yeast
1 packed tablespoon fresh (cake) yeast	2 teaspoons/6.4 grams instant yeast or 2½ teaspoons/8 grams active dry yeast

Recipes Using Only Egg Whites

1 WHITE EQUALS 30 GRAMS/2 TABLESPOONS/30 ML

1½ large whites/45 grams/3 tablespoons (45 ml)
Basic White Cupcakes, page 95
Chocolate Wafers, page 63

2 large whites/60 grams/¼ cup (59 ml)
Chocolate Spangled Meringue Kisses, page 26
Chocolate Meringue Buttercream, page 336
Cocoa Meringues Variation, page 27
Fudgy Praline Pecan Meringue Ice Cream
    Sandwiches, page 29

2½ large whites/75 grams/¼ cup plus 1 tablespoon (74 ml)
Mousseline, page 342

4 large whites/120 grams/½ cup (118 ml)
Light Italian Meringue, page 340
Neoclassic Italian Meringue, page 341
Pavlova, page 277

6 large whites/180 grams/¾ cup (177 ml)
Basic White Layer Cake, page 92

16 large whites/480 grams/2 cups (474 ml)
Chocolate Spangled Angel Food Cake, page 149

Recipes Using Only Egg Yolks

1 YOLK EQUALS 18.7 GRAMS/1 TABLESPOON PLUS ½ TEASPOON/17.2 ML

3 to 4 yolks/56 grams/3½ tablespoons (52 ml)
Cream Cheese Crunch Pound Cake, page 105
Neoclassic Buttercream, page 332

4 to 6 yolks/74 grams/¼ cup plus 2 teaspoons (69 ml)
Chocolate Cream Pie, page 239
"Key Lime" Pie, page 234

5 to 8 yolks/93 grams/¼ cup plus 2 tablespoons (89 ml)
Lemon Curd, page 40
Pecan Pie, page 259

6 to 9 yolks/112 grams/¼ cup plus 3 tablespoons (103 ml)
Marble Cake, page 102

7 to 11 yolks/130 grams/½ cup (118 ml)
Triple Lemon Velvet Bundt Cake, page 109

8 to 12 yolks/149 grams/½ cup plus 4 teaspoons (138 ml)
Lemon Meringue Pie, page 229

INDEX